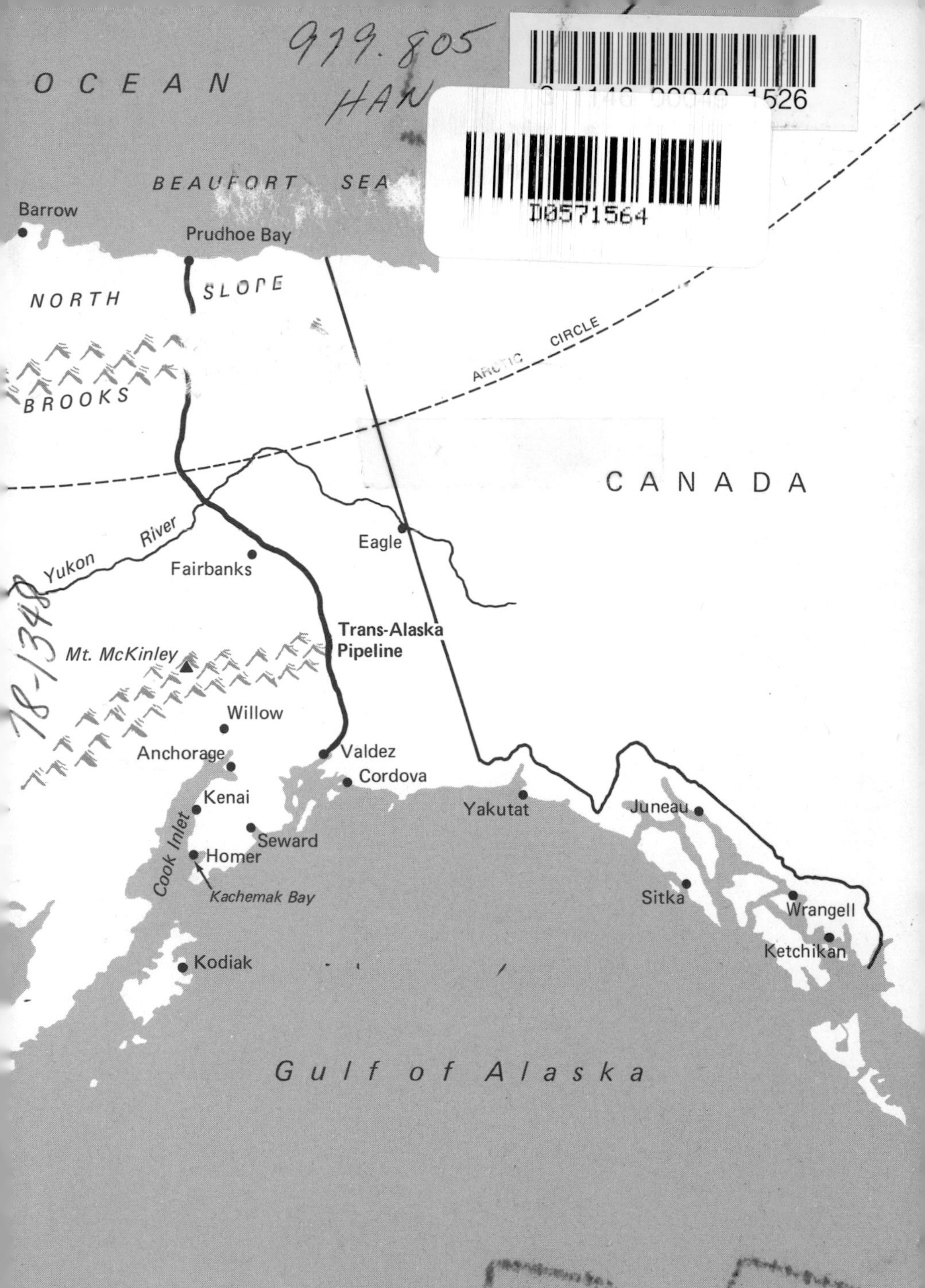
OCEAN
BEAUFORT SEA
Barrow
Prudhoe Bay
NORTH SLOPE
BROOKS
ARCTIC CIRCLE
CANADA
Yukon River
Fairbanks
Eagle
Trans-Alaska
Pipeline
Mt. McKinley
Willow
Anchorage
Valdez
Cordova
Kenai
Yakutat
Juneau
Seward
Homer
Cook Inlet
Kachemak Bay
Sitka
Wrangell
Ketchikan
Kodiak
Gulf of Alaska
OCEAN

Lost Frontier: The Marketing of Alaska

John Hanrahan

Peter Gruenstein

Lost Frontier: The Marketing of Alaska

Introduction by Ralph Nader

W · W · NORTON & COMPANY · INC · NEW YORK

Library of Congress Cataloging in Publication Data

Hanrahan, John, 1938–
Lost frontier.

Includes bibliographical references and index.
1. Alaska—Economic conditions. I. Gruenstein, Peter, joint author. II. Title.
HC107.A45H35 1977 330.9'798'05 77-10957
ISBN 0 393 08804 9

2 3 4 5 6 7 8 9 0

For Deborah Hanrahan
and
Jacqueline Zoberman
and
the peoples
of Alaska

Contents

Maps and Illustrations

Acknowledgments

WE WISH to express our special gratitude to Mildred Stearman for her near-flawless typing and unfailing good humor, to David Bollier for his fine editing and sage advice, and to Jamie Love for his incisive critique of an early draft of the manuscript.

We also wish to thank Tim Williams, Jon Rowe, John and Alda Grammes, Ron and Molly Crenshaw, and Terry Berman for their help and friendship.

Introduction

A CONSTELLATION of crucial decisions now confronts the residents of Alaska, and the decisions made will determine the future of America's giant state. As the authors, John Hanrahan and Peter Gruenstein, show, the problems and dilemmas Alaska faces are not the parochial concerns of a distant, frigid state but matters of urgent importance to the entire nation.

In what other state, the authors ask,

. . . is there so much mineral wealth?

. . . is the fishing industry so vital or in such jeopardy?

. . . is the agricultural potential so unrealized?

. . . is the fate of a land mass the size of California—the so-called "national interest" lands—very much in doubt?

. . . have the huge multinational corporations been so active in recent years, in such numbers, and with such single-mindedness?

. . . does one foreign country—Japan—have such an economic interest?

. . . is the potential for disaster from the offshore oil program so great?

. . . are such distinctive ways of life so threatened?

Lost Frontier: The Marketing of Alaska, is a book about Alaska, but, almost equally, it is a book about our country. Will it be a future that includes pristine wilderness? Will it be a future where life-determining decisions are made by absentee corporations, where a quad of energy is more valued than a native people's culture? Will ours be an economy increasingly dependent on the ever more disruptive, costly production of non-renewable resources? Or will it be based on renewable, life-sustaining and life-enriching activities—agriculture and fishing, for instance? Will our wealth be used wisely or will it be monopolized, squandered, or worse, used destructively?

If the call of the wild becomes a rasping cough what is the prospect for the rest of us?

"Quality of life" issues are showing up more prominently each year on the scale of citizen preferences, as reported by national public opinion surveys. The nation's cities provide ample explanation. Air pollution indices regularly announce the silent assault on the health and property of millions. Filth, debris, noise, and congestion take their psychic toll; a serious aesthetic deprivation is also evident. Neighborhood groups struggle to defend the remaining open spaces—from less than an acre to a few acres—in the suburban as well as urban centers. Urban foresters search for the types of trees hardy enough to withstand urban chemistry and provide some greenery among the asphalt and concrete roadways between the canyons of buildings. Poor children, if they are fortunate enough, are sent to two weeks of summer camp where they feel clean breezes, sink their feet into soil, and generally introduce themselves to the earth. It can be traumatic: one New York City child recoiled at seeing vegetables growing "in all that dirt." Another saw her first horizon in utter astonishment.

These are slices of human experience which make up the larger matter of healthful and accessible environment. The bridges are largely built; it is the polluted water that awaits attention. The buildings are in place; it is the contaminated air around them that afflicts. Massive organizations and runaway technology have generated political, economic, and social discontents which transcend differing ideologies and go to the basic condition of humanity. A society whose major problems increasingly arise from its self-created successes is in need of considerable civic introspection. Our production prowess has led to a prowess in soiling our own nests. This is only one facet of an industrialized culture whose benefits may no longer be keeping up with its negative impacts. A mass dependency has grown far beyond the advantages of interdependency. Fewer social functions are now performed by families, neighborhoods, communities, and other historically small, self-reliant networks. They are being assumed directly or derivatively by giant corporate and governmental structures enmeshed with one another to concentrate and bureaucratize decision making. Complexity and waste become acceptable methods of confusion, ways of shielding illegitimate power and keeping the economic machine expanding. Ours has become a merchant society—few areas of our culture are considered off limits to mercantile values or invasions.

Now comes Alaska into our consciousness with the discovery of oil. Not many nations as developed as ours have the opportunity to contemplate one-fifth of their territory anew. One-fifth! Alaska is replete with vast renewable and non-renewable mineral and natural resources. The diversity and scope of its wealth extend well beyond its public image in the Lower-48. Having lost its frontier sheen, it is entering a stage where determined economic interests savor the oil, gas, timber, uranium, fisheries, coal, and a score of other minerals which vulnerable political interests can make available to them.

Traditionally, the frontier in American history was changed through migrations of people, often with ties back in settled regions. The options that Americans had—to leave the settled areas for the frontiers, for the homestead or the mining stake—had profound impacts on the places they left as well as the places they founded. Alaska—the last frontier—was a part of this American horizon. But the Alaskan frontier of today is not. Its penetration is not fundamentally from the movements of people but from the movements of corporations, especially multi-national corporations. The second discovery of Alaska is quite different from the gold rush; it is planned and persistent. Unlike transient people willing to risk much to find riches, the corporations plan for the avoidance of uncertainty.

Their quest is extraction, not settlement; their driving force is riches, not quality of life. And in pursuit of this ambition, the corporations must make Alaska and Alaskans over in their own image. They come often as consortiums or joint ventures in a closed, cost-plus enterprise system. Their roots in the outposts are solely economic; as corporations they *do* live by bread alone, and limited by the rules of Mammon, leave behind debris and scars for future generations.

A broader vision is needed for a just and productive society. Many Alaskans are thinking about this vision. The present governor, some state legislators and judges, many Natives, newcomers and old hands are looking down the road ahead and saying there isn't much time. In the past, nature and distance gave Alaska an isolation which modern technology has erased. And once the tracks are greased for the corporate system, the chance for contemplation of alternative futures will dissolve into last ditch struggles over residuals. The greasing process is already advanced. The emergence of a coalition of powerful structures to service and bolster the corporate vanguard is becoming clear. Already the economic government is comprised of large companies, especially oil and gas, a large Teamster union, a large newspaper, and, most remarkably, some of the Native corporations created by the unprecedented Alaska Native Land Claims Act of 1971.

History has taught us that economic governments usually prevail over political governments where the former are unified. The erosion of the moderately populist executive and legislative branches of government has begun in Alaska. The debate has been suitably polarized into two camps—the "growthers" and the "no-growthers." There are, to be sure, a powerful bloc of "growthers" commanding the pinnacles of most of Alaska's power elites. They want almost any kind of growth that is profitable, subsidizable, or possessed of speculative effects on other assets. They are well named and need no qualifying adjectives.

The "no-growthers," on the other hand, are victims of a semantic stereotype mercilessly advanced by the Anchorage *Times*, the state's dominant newspaper. What these misnamed Alaskans are searching for is a way to avoid turning one-fifth of America into a self-destructing mineral haven for the worst appetites of our industrialized system. Plunder on the tundra is more than a euphonic phrase; with the land's fragility, it could become a reality. We need only guess what the state of the American West would have been if the settlers had not been around to temper the ravages of fast-buck exploiters. Indeed, the populist-progressive movement was possible because there were settlers—farmers and ranchers—who had a right to participate in a decentralized economy which such laws as the Homestead Act permitted. Who are the comparable stakeholders—the counterforce—in Alaska as the extractive industries make their entry? Alaskans and all other Americans. Both their stakes are intertwined.

For Alaskans, Alaska is a homeland, not a frontier. Within this small population of less than a half-million people are conflicting preferences and objectives in alliance with outside interests. Thus, the Boomers talk of building pipelines while the environmentalists talk of saving the land, the productive fisheries, the beauty, and the native people's culture. The former speak of minerals and business and jobs and larger populations; the latter speak of America's last great breathing space—a heritage of unspoiled Arctic and sub-Arctic nature as glorious as it is vulnerable to the advance of the industrial juggernaut.

The Native peoples are divided themselves between the old life of self-sufficiency and the new life oscillating between wage employment and welfare, between the corporatists running the Native corporations for maximum profit and the traditionalists who plumb the meaning of life with their culture, their traditions, and their relationship with the land. It is a culture built on a renewable resource base of hunting and fishing that has much to say to the dependency-creating industrial system that thrives on non-renewable resources.

This is not to say that hunting and fishing and the simple life are the message. It is much deeper, much less simple than that. The word "development" in Alaska is generally defined as it is in the Lower-48—by the *Fortune* 500 and supporting cast. Yet Alaska has a wondrous wealth of opportunity to define it differently and to permit the best of the new and old to prosper.

Consider the contemporary Alaskan crossroads. One road can lead to a contaminating uranium industry,* denuded and eroded forests, oil-polluted fishery grounds, and a state criss-crossed by the scars of extractive industries run riot. Another road can emphasize the development—profitably—of renewable resources to meet people's more basic needs. It is not generally recognized that Alaskan waters harbor one of the world's greatest fishing grounds, that some 16 million acres of land (the size of five Connecticuts) are suitable for agriculture such as barley and wheat. Or that the state has scarcely tapped its tourist potential. In a word, oil means Exxon; fisheries *might* mean small business. Agriculture means numerous farmholders; minerals mean a few multi-national corporations.

The choices of economic development are choices of the kind of society that will evolve. This is why, for example, a pipeline decision is more than just a pipeline decision. Its effects radiate broadly and deeply throughout the entire fabric of Alaskan society and its fragile environment. A pipeline to Valdez means oil in tankers negotiating treacherous waters, which translates into the perils of oil spills and their effects on valuable fishing grounds. Pipelines have impacts on the wilderness and the cities, on alcoholism and welfare,

* Several years ago Westinghouse quietly proposed construction of a uranium enrichment plant in Alaska. The plan was withdrawn after Alaskan Senator Mike Gravel strongly objected. It is doubtful, however, that the irony of building such a technological monstrosity in the last wilderness ever dawned on the fertile corporate minds who thought of it.

on corruption and inflation, as any boom-to-bust project would produce.

These impacts may mean little to skilled workers who are temporarily in the state until the construction is finished. But they are far from temporary for the Native peoples, who are becoming better-organized political and economic powers in Alaska and, as far as the Arctic peoples are concerned, beginning to connect with their counterparts across the North Country into Canada and Greenland. The Canadian jurist Thomas R. Berger took acute notice of the impact on the northern peoples that a proposed MacKenzie Valley pipeline would have in Canada's vast Northwest Territories. In his sensitive and learned report, he wrote of what he found after exhaustive field hearings in 1975 and 1976:

"The fact is that large-scale projects based on non-renewable resources have rarely provided permanent employment for any significant number of native people. . . . The pipeline contractors and unions have made it plain that native northerners are not qualified to hold down skilled positions in pipeline construction, and that they will be employed largely in unskilled and semi-skilled jobs. Once the pipeline is built, only about 250 people will be needed to operate it. Most of these jobs are of a technical nature and will have to be filled by qualified personnel from the south . . .

"The real economic problems in the north will be solved only when we accept the view the native people themselves expressed so often to the Inquiry: that is, the strengthening of the native economy. We must look at forms of economic development that really do accord with native values and preferences."

These thoughts have profound meaning for Alaska's Native economy. It is rare that a dominant culture can satisfy its moral obligation to respect an economically weaker culture and, while exercising that respect, itself learn an important lesson about the need to protect the vast renewable resource potential of the state. In his book, *Technology and Empire*, George Grant lends us an appropriate philosophical perspective:

> In this era when the homogenising power of technology is almost unlimited, I do regret the disappearance of indigenous traditions, including my own. It is true that no particularism can adequately incarnate the good. But is it not also true that only through some particular roots, however partial, can human beings first grasp what is good and it is the juice of such roots which for most men sustain their partaking in a more universal good?

Indeed, as more Americans ask the fundamental questions about what is best for the people, more visibility is given to fundamental values which societies are neglecting. Should we emphasize solar energy (renewable) or atomic fission (non-renewable)? Should we prefer natural fibers (cotton) or synthetic fibers (polyester)? Should we replace chemical pesticides in agriculture with environmentally safe methods of crop protection? Should prevention be the primary ethic against pollution or man-made cancer, or should resources be heavily directed toward finding treatments to industrial diseases?

There is much truth in Justice Berger's observation on the proposed Canadian pipeline: "Once construction begins, the concentration on the non-renewable resource sector and the movement away from the renewable resource sector will become inexorable." If Alaska is to become a giant quarry for the world, pockmarked by mines, pipelines, and a vast uranium mining and milling industry as corporate interests desire, it is not difficult to see the crowding out of other, more tolerant forms of economic activity. Already conflicts are arising between commercial fishermen and the oil industry's drive to initiate extensive offshore drilling.

All this is not to suggest rigid conclusions about future Alaskan development. It is to plead for sensitive distinctions between different kinds of economic development and the consequences that these alternatives render for the quality of life, choice, and democracy in the North Country. Alaska is fortunate in having the natural abundance that permits the luxury of such choices. It would be tragic not to have our largest state benefit from the full lessons of human experience only to find itself plunging into the vortex of corporate determinism. Few Americans would escape the consequences of such determinism wherever they reside. Such is the measure of what Alaska will mean to our country.

RALPH NADER

August 1977

Call of the Semi-Wild

An Alaskan is someone who wants to be able to "urinate off his front porch and yell for an hour without anyone answering." That earthy definition by former state Representative Edward F. Naughton of Kodiak speaks volumes about Alaskans' attitudes and the kinds of lives they have traditionally led in the vast wilderness of the Far North.

Call it the spirit of the pioneer, romance, rugged individualism, or the desire to find a little "elbow room," the fact is that Alaska has exerted a powerful pull on the imagination of the adventurous for decades, drawing them to its natural beauty, its abundance of wildlife, its unmatched wilderness. For every person who has picked up and gone to Alaska, there undoubtedly have been thousands of others who have heard tales of the Alaskan and Canadian Yukon gold rushes, read the stories of Jack London, and were tempted to make the journey north themselves.

To those who did make the trip and who were tough enough to endure the discomforts of Alaska's climate, the state has a special meaning. For these people, Alaska truly is the last frontier—a place to live a life-style different from anywhere else in the United States.

Much of Alaska's appeal is its wide open spaces where neighbors are hard to come by, even with the North Slope oil boom. Covering a land area of 586,412 square miles, more than twice the size of Texas and one-fifth the entire Lower-48 states, Alaska has a population of 400,000—less than one person per square mile (0.7, to be exact).[1] The state's largest glacier, Malaspina, spanning 2,937 square miles, is larger than Delaware and more than twice the size of Rhode

[1] The only state with fewer people is Wyoming, with an estimated 1975 population of 374,000.

Island. Its coastline of 6,640 miles is 900 miles longer than the entire coastline of the rest of the United States. From east to west, Alaska measures 2,400 miles and stretches over four time zones—as many as there are in the entire Lower-48 states. Superimposed on a map of the Lower-48, portions of Alaska extend from the Atlantic to the Pacific Coast, and from the Canadian border as far south as Texas.

Much of what Alaskans do is controlled by geography and the climate, which ranges from comparatively mild in southeastern Alaska to almost uninhabitable in the Arctic regions. Precipitation can vary from an average of 152 inches a year in Ketchikan in southeastern Alaska to desertlike conditions in the Far North. Barrow, Alaska's northernmost point, holds the state record for the least precipitation in a year (1.61 inches in 1935) and least snowfall in a winter season (3 inches in 1935–36). In Fairbanks, in the interior of the state, temperatures range from the 80s in the summer to minus 60 in the winter, an incredible annual variation of nearly 150 degrees. And, of course, Alaska is also the land of the midnight sun and the noon moon, depending upon the season.

Alaska's terrain is as diverse and as spectacular as its scope. It is a land of awesome glaciers, untamed rivers, crystal lakes, dramatic mountains, vast tundra, unlikely sand dunes, and lush forests. From the splendor of the Brooks Range in the North, to Mt. Mckinley and other towering mountains of the interior and the coast, to the magnificent fjords, islands, and rain forests in the southeast, the state is an unexcelled display of nature's handiwork. In wild places scarcely touched by man, millions of creatures roam, fly, and swim. Caribou, moose, wolves, black and brown bears, dall sheep, trumpeter swans, eagles, ducks, geese, gyrfalcons, peregrines, salmon, shrimp, crab, whales, seals, sea lions, sea otters, albatross, bison, musk ox, polar bears, lynx, marmot, deer—all live in a delicate balance with nature.

But while this gigantic state is mother to abundant animal life, it is also the womb to other natural treasures. Cradling hundreds of billions of dollars worth of oil, natural gas, timber, coal, gold, silver, gemstones, uranium, copper, molybdenum, nickel, lead, zinc, tin, tungsten, fluorite, iron, mercury, antimony, platinum-group metals, barite, zeolite and chromite, among others, Alaska probably exceeds the rest of the nation in the potential value of its resources. Its natural wealth is, in fact, so vast that the second least populous state will probably have more impact on the lives of Americans over at least the next half century than any of the other forty-nine states.

About 60 percent of the state's 400,000 people live in the Anchorage and Fairbanks areas; 160,000 others are scattered throughout the state in more than 340 communities and Bush areas. And Alaska's population is a young one—in fact, the youngest in the United States, with a median age of just 22.9 in 1970, according to the U.S. Census Bureau. (Utah was next with 23.1 years). Although Alaska is forty-ninth among the states in population, its number of residents has almost doubled since 1960. Since 1970, the population has increased by about 100,000. Much of this influx of people can be traced directly to the emergence of Alaska as an oil state.

* * *

With the major strike of oil on Alaska's North Slope at Prudhoe Bay in 1968, and the subsequent construction of the trans-Alaska pipeline, Alaska suddenly found itself in a period of tumultuous transition. So-called civilization, which had always been kept at arm's length by Alaskans, began encroaching heavily on their way of life. Many Alaskans, especially the pre-pipeline residents, began to feel that things would never be the same.

That discovery, and development of oil at Prudhoe Bay, set in motion an extraordinary drama, which has pitted those who prefer the more traditional Alaskan way of life against those who favor full-scale development of the state's resources—with most Alaskans falling somewhere in between. Actors in the drama include the conservationists, who are firm in their opposition to any new development project that will intrude upon Alaska's spectacular wilderness and plentiful fish and wildlife; those Natives who fear development will mean an end to their subsistence way of life; old-time Boomers (sometimes called "colonialists")—those longtime residents of Alaska, generally business people originally attracted to the state by its moneymaking potential, who have always advocated rapid development of the state's resources; the new Boomers—those recently attracted by Alaska's oil and other wealth, who have only a narrow interest in the state; modern-day frontiersmen—mostly young, but also many middle-aged—searching for a hassle-free life in the Far North; commercial fishermen—many of whom fear offshore oil development could ruin their livelihood; the sportsmen—who regard Alaska as a fishing and hunting paradise; and the state's omnipresent landlord—the federal government.

Since the Prudhoe Bay discoveries, this cast of Alaskans has been wrangling over how Alaska should use or not use its newfound wealth. Lanie Fleischer, a leading Anchorage activist and a member of the governor's Investment Advisory Committee on state oil royalties, explained the competing forces:

> Right now, we're moving in two, if not four, directions, and that makes it very difficult to steer a middle ground. Some people obviously came to Alaska to get rich, and those people are in direct opposition to the ones who came here because Alaska is the last wilderness. Others came because of the hunting and fishing and they are in direct opposition to the people who depend on wildlife for subsistence. Others, who work for large corporations and the military, are here because they were sent here and not because they want to be here.

Mike Bradner, a former speaker of the Alaska House of Representatives, told us, "There's a real conflict going on in most Alaskans' minds. The individual Alaskan goes in cycles. The booster mentality is continuous [though]." For Alaskans, the pipeline has become a symbol of development with implications that reach far beyond itself. Ron Rau, a free-lance writer and pipeline worker, described the hidden forces the pipeline represents:

> In many ways the pipeline is like an iceberg. What you see with your eyes is only a fraction of what is really there. The real threat to the Alaskan wilderness and life-style is the part of the pipeline you cannot see: the money, the people, and most of all, the boom-town mentality that has permeated Alaskan society—a warm, modern house, a steady job, and two snowmobiles in every garage. It is an attitude completely alien to the old Alaska, concerned with a more traditional mode of survival. Pre-oil Alaska was a land of dreams and dreamers, and those of us who remain from those days are preparing for a search that will take us away from the pipeline corridor. It will be a quest for the genuine Alaska we knew and loved, where comfort was a small log cabin, catch-as-catch-can and a dog team for the trap line. . . . Since oil, the frontier-civilization balance in Fairbanks has swung toward civilization. And I'm afraid it's no longer a pendulum balance. The weight of civilization is too heavy. . . .

That weight of civilization on the state's frontier style and pace of life could be quite painful for the non-Natives who make up 85 percent of the state's population (about 82 percent white, 3 percent black). But for the Natives—Eskimos, Indians, and Aleuts who comprise 15 percent of Alaska's population—nothing less than entire cultures are at stake. Although most Natives have some contact with Western culture and use many of its modern devices (snowmobiles, for example, have replaced dogsleds), the majority of the state's Natives today still pursue a subsistence way of life similar to that of their ancestors. About 60 percent of them continue to hunt, fish, trap, and pick berries to provide much of the food for their families.[2]

But in recent years, a new social and economic class of college-educated, business-oriented Natives, sometimes referred to as "Brooks Brothers Natives" by both their admirers and detractors, has emerged. This new group became especially influential in the Native community with the passage of the Alaska Native Claims Settlement Act (ANCSA) in 1971. Granted by the U.S. Congress to settle the Natives' aboriginal land claims, the act created 12 for-profit Native regional corporations and 220 village corporations to administer the 44 million acres and $1 billion awarded under the act. It is through these new corporations that many of these "Brooks Brothers Natives" have found a new identity, one essentially estranged from the traditional Native way of life. Many of the new Native corporations have made it clear that they want rapid development of oil, natural gas, and other resources sitting under and on top of their lands. Several corporations also expressed willingness to provide onshore support facilities for offshore oil development; still others had contracts related to construction of the trans-Alaska oil pipeline. Since the corporations were formed, many of the Native state legislators have also rallied to the interests of the new corporations and have recently been voting quite conservatively in the state legislature on measures designed to regulate or tax business.

Because events are moving so fast in Alaska, most non-Native leaders, and even some Native leaders, have shown little concern for the survival of the Natives' cultures. Many of the newly formed Native corporations are oriented more toward maximizing profits than toward the old life-style of cooperation. Already, some Native corporation stockholders concerned with maintaining their traditional way of life have clashed with leaders of some of the Native corporations over the question of profits at the expense of the culture. Many stockholders who want to preserve their culture and pursue the traditional subsistence way of life fear that Native corporation devel-

[2] Natives aren't the only ones to rely on the subsistence way of life. Many whites living in the Bush also hunt and fish for their food. Even some white city-dwellers live a partial subsistence life. One Alaskan we encountered, for example, was regularly unemployed, occasionally earning some money by flying other people on his airplane. In the summer he fished, and in the fall he killed a moose and swapped it for deer and caribou meat. His goal was different from that of the white sportsman who wants a moose's head as a trophy: to him, hunting and fishing provided a good portion of the food supply for himself, his wife, and his young son.

opment plans are disrupting the hunting and fishing they depend upon, just as the government and the white man have done in the past.

The debate in the Native community over development—and at what cost to their way of life—is not a parochial, isolated concern. Indeed, as the staggering wealth of Alaska's natural resources is confirmed, this debate has become a central political issue, if not *the* issue, for the state government and residents. The recurring questions are whether to control or encourage development, to what degree, and under what stipulations.

* * *

The trans-Alaska pipeline was the state's first real encounter with these knotty questions. Although welcomed by an apparently large majority of Alaskans a few years ago, the pipeline has produced mixed feelings in recent years. Alaskans show a real schizophrenia toward the pipeline and other development issues. On the one hand, they want to keep the "old Alaska." On the other hand, they like the bigger paychecks that boom times bring, even with the concomitant increases in prices and strain on public and private services. The best evidence of this dichotomy may be that most Alaskans enthusiastically supported pipeline construction and later, in 1974, elected as governor Jay Hammond, a Republican who had publicly expressed deep reservations about the pipeline.

In many ways, Jay Hammond has tried, usually unsuccessfully, to bridge the deep-seated antagonisms many Alaskans feel toward others who have different aspirations for their state. Hammond represents a middle ground between environmentalists, who would prefer to see sharply limited development of the state, and supergrowthers. The governor generally supports only that development which has little environmental impact and which pays its own way, a position which he sees as both prudent policy and good politics.

It's risky to generalize about such a diverse group of people as Alaskans, but the state's unusual history and geography, as well as its isolation from the Lower-48, have forged a people of unmistakable character. Their pride is often a state chauvinism of such proportions that, by comparison, Texans seem modest. Their peculiar circumstances have fostered a parochial world view, a strong streak of libertarianism, and an unpretentiousness in demeanor and dress.

To Outsiders,[3] Alaska seems much like a foreign country where

[3] The "Outside," to Alaskans, is any place that is not in Alaska.

most of the inhabitants just happen to speak English. Indeed, in our travels around the state, we occasionally encountered people who felt that Alaska would be better off as a separate country, especially given its newly discovered wealth. A couple of years ago one Fairbanks man felt so strongly about separatism that he went around town painting "Alaska for Alaskans, Yankee Go Home" on out-of-state cars. He was arrested but was let off without punishment, the judge merely instructing him to henceforth use only bumper stickers (which he then went out and purchased.)

Many Natives have also voiced similar sentiments for ethnic reasons. In 1970, for example, Native leaders were growing more disturbed and angry over Congress's failure to pass a just land claims settlement for them. Emil Notti, president of the Alaska Federation of Natives and a political moderate, warned that if the Natives were not dealt with fairly, he would:

> . . . recommend a course of action to our statewide board of directors that we petition Congress and the United States to set up a separate Indian nation in the western half of Alaska. That area is ninety percent Native anyway, and will not get any non-Native settlers until there is something discovered that can be exploited.

Notti's comment echoes a widely held belief among Alaskans that many Outsiders are not lured to Alaska for its intrinsic charms but for its riches. And, in recent years, more and more "Cheechakos"[4] have been coming to Alaska, drawn primarily by the big money to be made in connection with construction of the trans-Alaska pipeline. Since its purchase in 1867, Alaska's history has been dominated by Outsiders and Cheechakos, with representatives of the federal government being the most persistent and intrusive ones. Longtime residents—sourdoughs—who remember the days before statehood still tend to see the state as somehow just a colony of the United States. Often during our visit we heard people refer to something happening "down in the United States," as if Alaska were somehow not part of the U.S. In many ways, this view is understandable. Before statehood, Alaska was entirely the ward of the Department of the Interior and the U.S. government. Ernest Gruening, a territorial governor from 1939 to 1953 and later a U.S. senator, likened the federal government in those days to "an occupying power" that imposed its will on the territory's citizens. During this same period,

[4] "Cheechakos"—a derivative of "Chicago"—means newcomer, and is not a term of endearment.

Outside corporations, such as mining interests and the Seattle fish processing industry, were exploiting Alaska resources and giving little in return to the territory.

Even since statehood, many Alaskans are still convinced that their state is still being victimized by the federal government and Outsiders generally, and that too many key decisions affecting its future are made in Washington, D.C. One example is the outer continental shelf (OCS) exploration program proposed for Alaskan waters by the Nixon and Ford administrations. Such development could be destructive of the state's fishing industry and coast communities. Yet Alaska was not consulted in the decision to push ahead with a crash OCS program for the state. (The same, of course, was true for other oil-bearing coastal states.)

Alaskans bridle at other forms of less obvious Outside intrusion and discrimination. Long-distance telephone rates were an example. "Alaska and Hawaii have been treated like foreign countries under the rate structure," noted Dr. Edwin B. Parker, professor of communications at Stanford University and consultant to the state on the use of communication satellites to provide health care to remote villages. Parker explained that in the Lower-48 states, the Federal Communications Commission had applied the principle of rate averaging for all rural and urban areas in setting rates. But because Alaska was not included in this rate averaging, calls made between those two states and the other forty-eight states cost considerably more for comparable distances—as well as for shorter distances. Thus, a call from Washington, D.C., to Seattle, Washington, 2,329 air miles away, cost less than a call from Anchorage to Seattle, some 1,500 air miles apart.[5]

This disparity over telephone rates is seen by Alaskans, understandably, as yet another example of how their state is treated discriminatorily by federal agencies and corporations from the Lower-48. The state government filed a complaint with the FCC seeking to have Alaska included in the rate integration structure so that its phone rates would be on the same footing as those for the Lower-48 states. In early 1977, the FCC finally granted Alaskans relief, approving a settlement reducing by one third the cost of long-distance calls between the state and the Lower-48. Shortly thereafter, RCA

[5] In Alaska, RCA Alaska Communications, Inc., rather than AT&T, is the phone company for long-distance communications. Parker said that he and others familiar with the situation view the reason behind the discriminatory rate structure for Alaska and Hawaii as being "really a battle between AT&T and RCA."

Alaska Communications, Inc., the state's phone company, said it planned to file for rate increases averaging about 100 percent on long-distance calls within the state.

Alaskans are sensitive to another type of victimization by Outsiders—misunderstanding fostered through news media hype. A November 18, 1975 article in the *Los Angeles Times* was headlined, "Alaska Today—Runaway Crime and Union Violence." The hyped lead read:

> ANCHORAGE—Widespread lawlessness, a helpless government and the stranglehold of a single Teamsters Union chief severely threaten a state crucial to the nation's future energy independence.
>
> Police officials admit they are staggering under a runaway crime wave that has left vast areas of this country's largest state virtually unprotected.

In a state with only seven daily newspapers, limited local television and radio news coverage, and limited network news, Alaska is not saturated with the news as the Lower-48 states are. (Just recently, the state agreed to provide grants to Alaska television stations to allow them to bring more live news and sports programs to the state via communications satellites.) Thus, an "Outside" story hits the state with considerably more impact than would, say, a *Los Angeles Times* story critical of Maryland. And the *LA Times* story hit like a thunderbolt. Governor Hammond and other top state officials, Teamster boss Jesse L. Carr, the *Anchorage Times*, and the *Anchorage Daily News* attacked the article as sensationalized and uninformed. Other politicians, environmentalists, super-growthers and no-growthers told us in milder tones that, unfortunately, the article was overblown, and that some of its legitimate criticisms of Alaskan life were lost amid its exaggerations of "lawlessness." The *Anchorage Times* even ran a page one banner headline for a story on Carr's response to the *Los Angeles Times*. "Carr Blasts 'Hatchet Job,' " screamed the banner in the December 6, 1975, edition.

Alaskans had a right to be angry. In our own investigation, we found that although the state has experienced a substantial increase in crime since the advent of the pipeline, there certainly was little evidence of "widespread lawlessness" or "a runaway crime wave." The point, though, is that many Alaskans feel so strongly about their state that they respond angrily to news stories that might in other states provoke a "so what?" shrug from most residents. Time and again during our visits to the state, we were reminded by Alaskans that the *Los Angeles Times* article was "typical of the kind of nonsense that Outsiders always write" and were put on notice that we, as Outsiders, should make sure we had the right perspective before we put word one on paper.

Because Alaskans have been frequent victims at the hands of Outsiders and the federal government, they often resent *any* "meddling" by Outsiders. Many Alaskans, particularly super-growthers, told us that they resented Outsiders such as the Sierra Club coming in and trying to tell them how to preserve their state. In the bitter fight over construction of the trans-Alaska pipeline, many Alaskans pasted "Sierra Go Home" bumper stickers on their cars as an unambiguous message to the California-based club. These Alaskans told us they didn't interfere in the environment-development controversies in other states, so why should people from other states meddle in their affairs?

The answer to that is that Alaska—despite the protests of some residents—is a part of America. Not only is it linked to the other forty-nine states as part of a political union, but—even after generous land grants to the state and the Natives—60 percent of its 375 million acres are owned by 215 million Americans. And that land is a national asset of inestimable value.

In the same vein, super-growthers complain that the federal government is continuing its exploitation of Alaska through its plan to retain ownership of 60 percent of the state's land. But this is not unusual; the federal government owns one third of the nation's land—which means that Alaska isn't the only state with substantial federal ownership. In fact, eleven western states have between 29 and 86 percent of their land owned by the federal government.[6] Three states (topped by Nevada with 86.6 percent) will have a greater proportion of their land owned by the federal government than Alaska will have when the land grants to the state and the Natives are completed. Put another way, the amount of land awarded Alaska after statehood is the size of California, the nation's third largest state. And just as all Americans have an interest in preserving the natural beauty and the environment of federal lands in the Lower-48, they likewise have an interest in safeguarding the only huge, unspoiled wilderness left in this country—and that just happens to be in Alaska.

The pride most Alaskans have for their state extends to a pride

[6] Besides Nevada, the others are: Utah, 66.1 percent; Idaho, 63.7; Oregon, 52.6; Wyoming, 47.8; California, 45.2; Arizona, 42.8; Colorado, 36.1; New Mexico, 33.6; Montana, 29.7; Washington, 29.5.

in their region or town—a local chauvinism. To the residents of Anchorage and Fairbanks, who are more centrally located in the state, the distant and isolated capital of Juneau in southeastern Alaska somehow isn't part of the state. A similar putdown goes on between residents of Anchorage and Fairbanks. Anchorage, for example, is considered by Fairbanksans and many other Alaskans to be highly urbanized and, therefore, not really Alaska. Frequently, one hears from Fairbanksans: "Anchorage is a nice place. It's only an hour's drive from Alaska," or "Anchorage is an American city. But that's OK. It's close to Alaska."

Nowhere has this competition between Anchorage and Fairbanks shown up more clearly than in the extraordinary, long-running battle over moving the capital from Juneau to a more central location in the state. Previous efforts had always faltered because of suspicions by many Alaskans that Anchorage or Fairbanks was trying to grab off the capital for itself. After two earlier ballot measures to move the capital were defeated, voters in 1974 authorized relocating the capital. One reason for the success of the 1974 initiative was the influx of newcomers who felt that a capital should be located nearer the centers of population of Anchorage and Fairbanks. A more decisive factor, though, was a provision in the ballot measure which stipulated that the new capital could not be located within thirty miles of either Anchorage or Fairbanks—thereby averting suspicions that the move was a power grab by either. In 1976, the site nearest Anchorage—Willow, 35 miles north of the city—was selected from a choice including two other alternatives.

Despite bickering among themselves and reservations about present and future development, Alaskans from Chamber of Commerce super-growthers to ardent environmentalists are quick to tell visitors that Alaska is *the* finest place to live in the United States. At a time when many Americans are cynical about their ability to control institutions which affect them, many Alaskans believe their individual actions can make a difference. Even those who don't like the changes brought about by the pipeline will proudly tell visitors that Alaska is a place where the individual can have a large voice in state affairs. "It's exciting, but it's changing," one Anchorage resident, Liz Johnson, told us. "We came up in 1970, really the last prepipeline years. Now it freaks us out to see the shopping centers, the paved roads, the houses that weren't here before. But, still, this is the first place I've ever been where I felt that I could have a voice in what was going on. Here, you can work to get people you know personally to become judges or to get elected to office. They're people, you know—neighbors, even." Another Anchorage resident, who often lets his hair grow until it streams to his waist, came to Alaska from Washington, D.C., a few years ago. Alaska, he told us, "is the most un-uptight place I've ever lived in. People aren't always passing judgment on other people and aren't striving for status all the time. Even most of the elected officials here are unpretentious, and not impressed with themselves. I can't think of many other places where that's true—certainly not Washington, D.C."

One other characteristic evident in many Alaskans is a frontier-style equality. It matters little what you did in the Lower-48 before you came to Alaska. Whether you were a "success" or a "failure" in your life there, or even whether you had been involved in some criminal act, seems genuinely not to matter to most Alaskans. Alaska indeed does seem to be a place where everyone (at least non-Natives) begins on an equal footing.

Many Alaskans draw a real distinction between those Cheechakos who want the kind of life-style Alaska offers and those who came to make a fast buck. The latter kind can rub Alaskans the wrong way—like the pipeline worker who told an interviewer in 1976, "You can talk to me all you want about the last frontier. To me, it's just plain Fat City." Still, some who come for the quick buck end up being won over by the state's grandeur. As another pipeline worker, a truck driver, said: "I came up here from Washington State just to get the big paycheck. But hell, this is great country. Darned if I'm not tempted to stay . . ."

In recent years, most of those seeking a new life in the North have come mainly to Anchorage. Although Anchorage today still seems like a typical mid-sized city to visitors, to many of the longer-term residents there who have witnessed its recent growth, it seems like a typical American metropolis bursting at the seams with Cheechakos.

"It's just getting too crowded," said Nat Goodhue, a state of Alaska park planner who lives in Anchorage. When we talked to Goodhue in late 1976, he and his wife Gail, in true Alaska style, were building their own house several miles outside of Anchorage. Even though the one dirt road near their property probably would be snowed in most of the winter, which would render their car useless, the Goodhues didn't regard this as a drawback. Instead, they said they and their two young children could walk, jog, or ski—to work, to school, to shops, to wherever they needed to go. In exchange for this seeming inconvenience, they have a breathtaking view of the mountains, a small lake, a lovely woods to hike in, and wild animals in abundance. The Goodhues, although living close to Anchorage, fit in nicely with the Alaskan homesteading tradition. Over the years, thousands of non-Natives have come to Alaska and homesteaded on Federally owned land.[7]

Although the federal homesteading program and a similar state-run open-to-entry program have ended, it is clear that the kind of pioneer living afforded by such programs continues to exert a strong appeal to Alaskans' imagination.[8] In the 1976 state legislature, for example, there was much support for what was termed the "Hippie Homestead Bill," which would have provided two and a half acres of land to anyone living on the property for seven months of the year for three consecutive years. Although Hammond, himself a homesteader, opposed that measure as not well thought out, he was in early 1977 drawing up his own limited homesite program for introduction to the legislature. As Guy Martin, then state natural resources commissioner,[9] told us in late 1976, some homesteading legislation is needed "to meet the increasing call for more public land to be put into private hands."

The common homesteading impulse in Alaska is part of a quite extraordinary streak of individualism and libertarianism that cuts across traditional political designations. Alaska, for instance, was among the first states to pass a liberal abortion law. And in 1975, within days after the state legislature decriminalized the use of marijuana, the state supreme court ruled that Alaskans have a constitutional right to use the weed in the privacy of their own home. The court thus went one full step farther than even the handful of other states which have decriminalized the use of marijuana. Most revealing of this Alaskan libertarianism was the fact that, in almost any other state, such a development would have provoked a firestorm of

[7] However, the system under which a person could gain title to land by living on it and farming it had been overromanticized. In the 76 years of the program, which was terminated in 1974, some 5,000 people gained title to more than 500,000 acres in Alaska. Yet thousands more failed in homesteading attempts—some because of the climate, some because the land on which they settled was inadequate for agriculture.

[8] Although there is some privately held land available, particularly in the Matanuska-Susitna Valley, prices for it are beyond the range of most Alaskans. In the last five years, prices for this land have soared almost 500 percent, according to state studies.

[9] Martin was nominated by President Carter in early 1977 to become assistant interior secretary for land and water resources.

protest. But in Alaska by 1976 the marijuana law and court ruling were hardly an issue. An effort to put an antimarijuana measure on the 1976 ballot did not even succeed in gathering the required 10,000 signatures. And it wasn't just freaks and hippies who were taking advantage of the new law. Various state legislators estimated to us in 1976 that well over half of the then current forty-member state house of representatives, and about one third of the twenty-member state senate, smoked marijuana. One top state official even used cocaine on occasion. All of this dope usage is well-known in political circles, yet no one tried to make an issue out of it during the 1976 election campaign, not even *Anchorage Times* publisher and supergrowther Robert B. Atwood, who privately abhors the use of grass, and is one of the severest critics of the state legislature.

Governor Hammond, who signed the marijuana bill into law, is a self-confessed puritan—a rarity in the state—who neither smokes (tobacco or marijuana) nor drinks. He signed the bill with great reluctance. "I would rather have seen illegalization of alcohol . . . than legalizing marijuana," he told us. According to Hammond's attorney general, Avrum Gross, the governor decided that Alaska traditionally has been so individualistic and tolerant of people's private vices that there was no reason marijuana should be singled out. During our visits to Alaska, we personally witnessed many legislators and state officials smoking marijuana, oftentimes in the presence of constituents and campaign workers. Older persons and non-marijuana smokers on these occasions gave no indication—overtly, at least—that they didn't approve. Simply put, marijuana smoking in Alaska is almost as socially acceptable among all age groups as social drinking is in the Lower-48.

The concept of personal freedom, which is evident in people's private lives, also carries over into Alaskans' attitude toward politics. About half of Alaska's registered voters have filed as independents, compared to about one third as Domocrats and one fifth as Republicans. Such a state of affairs makes party organization and discipline even more difficult than in other states. And it also makes for a lot of ticket splitting, with emphasis on the candidate rather than the party label. This is certainly true when it comes to Alaska's three members of the U.S. Congress. In fact, so independent are Alaska voters that in 1972 they reelected a dead man to the state's lone seat in the U.S. House of Representatives. This happened when a plane in which Representative Nick Begich (Democrat, Alaska) and Representative Hale Boggs (Democrat, Louisiana) were passengers disappeared and presumably crashed in Alaska just prior to the 1972 general election. Despite the virtual certainty that Begich, a liberal, was dead, he outpolled Republican Don Young in the general election. Young, a conservative, won the seat a few months later in a special election. The other members of the Alaska congressional delegation are Senator Mike Gravel, a liberal Democrat, and Senator Ted Stevens, a conservative Republican.

The Alaskan voter's independence also carries over into elections on the state level. In gubernatorial elections since statehood, the Democrats have won three of five times.[10] The state legislature has generally been Democratic-controlled, but has fluctuated between conservative and liberal leadership. In the early 1970s, a group of young, liberal politicians, calling themselves the Ad Hoc Democrats, began making inroads into the Democratic party. After winning a few state legislative seats in 1972, the Young Turks, riding the crest of the nationwide Democratic tide following the Watergate scandal, won control of the House in 1974. Over the next two years, they established a record of support for public interest and environmental legislation.

Unlike those of other states, Alaska's legislature is not lawyer-dominated. The 1976 legislature contained just three attorneys in the forty-member House and four in the twenty-member Senate. Said Chancy Croft,[11] then-Senate president and himself a lawyer: "Frankly, I think the balance is a good one."

In the 1976 legislative elections, conservative Democrats and Republicans made gains, which gave the pro-business and pro-development forces greater influence. The leading spokesman for these development forces and the quintessential old Boomer is Bob Atwood, editor and publisher of the *Anchorage Times.* Atwood is the state's number one cheerleader for more oil and natural gas exploration onshore and offshore; more mineral development; more roads; less regulation of the timber industry; the moving of the state capital from Juneau to a more centrally located site; and the opening of the North Slope Haul Road (used to service the trans-Alaska pipeline) to general tourist traffic.

Although Atwood is number one, there are plenty of other old-

[10] William A. Egan was the successful Democrat each time. Hammond, in 1974, and Walter J. Hickel, in 1966, were the successful Republicans.

[11] Croft, considered a possible gubernatorial candidate in 1978, was not up for reelection in 1976, but he lost the senate presidency during reorganization for the 1977 legislative session.

time Boomers around. Best-known to most Americans is Walter J. Hickel, the former U.S. secretary of the interior and former Alaskan governor. Others include the Chambers of Commerce, the Alaska Miners Association, and such influential figures as Anchorage banker Elmer Rasmuson (Atwood's brother-in-law), and hotel magnate William Sheffield. While Hickel often expresses concern for protection of the environment, he also makes speeches that laud the oil and natural gas industry and even call for mineral development on other planets. Typical was Hickel's October 21, 1976, speech to a fund-raising dinner in Los Angeles for the City of Hope, a medical center located in Duarte, California. He was characteristically expansive about future energy prospects:

> There are untold resources awaiting man in the Arctic, to say nothing of the oceans, the Antarctic and the great jungles of the Southern Hemisphere . . . It is the energy industry that more than any other factor in modern civilization has freed man from slavery, poverty, and ignorance. . . . In terms of future centuries, I might be worried if this was the only planet we could see, the only star in the sky. We'll soon discover that the planets out there are made up of copper, iron ore, phosphorus, and so on—they will all be available for humans to use. Yes, we'll be mining in space. I see no limits on man. The only limits are those we place on ourselves.

A phalanx of newer super-growthers see Alaska in similar terms. The most prominent ones are the major oil companies; other large corporations from outside Alaska which are interested in mineral development; the Alaska Teamsters Local 959; and many of the leaders of the new Native regional corporations.

As noted earlier, the Native corporations are not unanimously in favor of development. Torn between traditional and Western values, they are in a period of transition and uncertainty. No such split exists in the hierarchy of the Alaskan Teamsters. The Teamsters' boss, Secretary-Treasurer Jesse L. Carr, is unabashed in his support for rapid development. Through his union's 25,000 members, and its bloated pension funds, Carr exerts enormous economic power in the state and holds a potential, largely unrealized to date, for concomitant political power.

Other than his militancy at the collective bargaining table and over working conditions, Carr's economic views are indistinguishable from those of the other super-growthers. For example, the Teamsters worked in 1976 to unseat a number of state legislators whose voting records on many issues were in line with positions of national unions. Despite their pro-labor voting records, those legislators were opposed by the Teamsters because of their support for consumer protection measures and higher oil taxes, which Carr sees as harmful to the state's development. In fact, Jess Carr is so well regarded by Boomers that the *Anchorage Times*, a staunch opponent of organized labor, even suggested in early 1976 that he would make a good governor.

Carr denies claims made by Governor Hammond, the *Anchorage Daily News*, and some Lower-48 media that the Teamsters have a stranglehold on key industries in the state. As he told us in an August 16, 1976, interview:

> I have to answer to myself when I look in the mirror every morning. What good does it do to shut people down? What good does it to do to destroy the state? We're trying to build the state. . . . That's my argument with this governor of ours. We've got a hell of an argument between us on the growth of this state. We can't go back fifty to seventy-five years, you know, like his no-growth administration is. Nobody's going to hold Alaska back. . . . Alaska can become the richest state in the union, handled properly.

The oil companies, although omnipresent in Alaska, keep a much lower profile. While other Boomers like Atwood and Carr are constantly sounding off against no-growthers, the petroleum firms—which must play to a national audience and not just to Alaska—are more self-conscious, subdued, and subtle in plying their influence. Where the Atwoods and the Carrs openly assail the environmentalists, the oil companies—including the Alyeska Pipeline Service Company, which built the pipeline—publish brochures and advertisements, and issue press releases stressing their record of environmental concern. And they involve themselves in civic affairs totally unrelated to oil development as a means of winning the goodwill of the community.

Often, the oil firms flex their political muscles indirectly through conservative but nonpartisan groups such as Common Sense for Alaska and Individuals for Alaska (IFA). Common Sense is a front group bankrolled in 1976 mainly by the oil companies and banking interests to help defeat certain incumbents in the legislative elections. Those politicians targeted for opposition were those who had supported legislation to curb questionable business practices and had favored additional oil taxes. Common Sense's effectiveness was neutralized to some extent after the primary election when a group of liberal activists paid the small membership fee and produced enough votes to elect three of their own people to the organization's board. By contrast, Individuals for Alaska, another front group, heavily financed by real estate and other business interests, was quite successful. Twelve of the seventeen Anchorage-area candidates it endorsed won their elections. In addition to its endorsements, IFA attacked other candidates as "anti-business." In the general election, IFA's efforts were directed primarily to a series of negative campaign advertisements that slashed at some pro-consumer, liberal incumbents with frequently misleading charges. In spending about $60,000 in the primary and general elections, IFA was widely believed to have played a major role in the defeat of some incumbents.

Still another pro-business group, the Jeffersonian Democratic Committee, formed about two weeks before the general election. The group attacked six incumbents—three of them connected with Ad Hoc Democrats—in concert with attacks by IFA and the *Anchorage Times*. Jeffersonian Democrats was chiefly a Teamster front group. Its major contributor, the *Anchorage Times* reported on November 1, 1976, was the political arm of the Alaska Teamsters. Of $2,400 collected by the Jeffersonians up to that point, $1,000 had come from Teamsters-ALIVE (Alaska Labor Independent Voter Education). The six candidates opposed by the Jeffersonians also were the same six who had failed to win Teamster endorsements.

But in areas where influence matters most in Alaska—the state legislature—the oil industry makes its presence felt more directly. In the 1976 session alone, seventeen oil and natural gas firms deployed thirty-two lobbyists at Juneau. In all, the oil lobby paid out $382,902 in fees, expenses, and other lobbying expenditures. This was more than 40 percent of the total of $935,348 spent by all state lobbyists—and is the equivalent of almost one dollar for every person in Alaska. The heavy lobbying and the proliferation of political front groups no doubt presage a major effort by the business and development interests to capture the governor's office in 1978.

James Love, director of the consumer-oriented Alaska Public Interest Research Group (AkPIRG), is among the Alaskans who viewed the formation of front groups as an effort to bolster pro-business sentiment and stifle the voices of critics. As Love told us:

> It's becoming like a company town. . . . You have allegiance by the Chamber of Commerce to the oil companies; the banks, they feel obligated to the oil companies; and then you have the oil companies themselves and

Bob Atwood, the Teamsters, and many of the Native corporations all saying the same things on these various development issues. It's hard for any other voices to get through. And, if you want to be a "success" here, the clear message is that "to get along, you've got to go along."

While the oil interests are still some distance from controlling the state's politics, they are wielding increasing amounts of influence. And their impact on the state's economy—even before one drop of oil had begun flowing through the Prudhoe Bay–Valdez pipeline—was even more profound. By 1976 more than 60 percent of the state government's budget was supported by oil revenues. U.S. Bureau of Mines figures for 1975 showed Alaska already ranked seventh among the states in oil production—again, even before the Prudhoe Bay oil had begun to flow.[12]

* * *

The pro-growth forces have an additional and unusually helpful ally: the state constitution, which has a clearly conservative, pro-development bent. The influence of the growth advocates on the constitution can clearly be seen in Article VIII, Sections 1 and 2, which state:

> It is the policy of the State to encourage the settlement of the land and the development of its resources by making them available for maximum use consistent with the public interest.
>
> The legislature shall provide for the utilization, development, and conservation of all natural resources belonging to the State, including land and waters, for the maximum benefit of its people.

To the super-growthers of today, this is a clear mandate for rapid development. Publisher Atwood made no bones about it to us: "The purpose of statehood is development. That's in the state constitution." But if the state constitution is pro-development, it is also a modern one—having been written in 1955–56. It contains many progressive provisions and includes the concept of a strong governor. U.S. District Court Judge James Fitzgerald of Anchorage, who served as special state legal counsel after statehood, said that the "strong governor" concept evolved in a reaction to the system of a

[12] Once the trans-Alaska pipeline is operating at its full two-million-barrel-a-day capacity, Alaska will be the number two oil-producing state, behind Texas, according to the Bureau of Mines. As production declines in other states, it's only a matter of time before Alaska, with increasing production, is number one, since the known reserves of Prudhoe Bay are the largest of any in the nation.

presidentially appointed, limited-power governor during Alaska's years as a territory.

"If you go back to the time of territorial status, the mind of man would have difficulty thinking up a government that was more inept," Fitzgerald told us. "The territorial governor was appointed by the president, but it was really with the approval of the Department of the Interior. . . . As a territory, there were no local prosecutions. All this was handled by the U.S. attorney. All the other federal agencies could operate pretty much as they saw fit. . . . Those departments, such as fish and wildlife, were not in any way responsible to the governor. Municipalities at the time had power to sell bonds and build roads, but the territorial governor couldn't sell bonds and build roads. So, coming from that sort of disorganized government, there came a real call for a strong centralized government with a strong governor."

The state's judicial system also received much praise from lawyers and judges we talked to, as well as from social activists. One activist termed the state's supreme court "one of the most progressive in the country," especially on personal freedom questions. Judge Fitzgerald, himself a former state supreme court justice, said that the state constitution's article on the judiciary was "once described by U.S. Supreme Court Justice [Tom] Clark as being the outstanding one among all the states." Fitzgerald noted that Alaska was the first state to implement statewide the "Missouri plan"[13] of appointing judges, which is designed to take the partisan politics out of judicial selections. Also, the court system is entirely state-operated; there are no municipal courts. A constitutional amendment also provides procedures under which judges can be removed from office.

Local government in Alaska is a somewhat confusing array of boroughs, municipalities, and cities of varying power. Boroughs are much like counties in other states. By mid-1976, there were just eleven boroughs, with many sparsely populated areas of the state not included in any borough.[14]

[13] A system whereby a joint lawyer–lay person judicial council supplies multiname lists to the governor who must fill vacant judgeships from the list. The person selected later must have his or her appointment ratified by the voters.

[14] There are three classes of boroughs, with first- and second-class boroughs having the most powers. Such powers include assessing, levying and collecting real estate and personal property taxes; electing borough assemblies and school boards; education; and land-use planning.

Incorporated cities generally provide more services than boroughs. There are two classes. First-class cities (those with over 400 residents) have broader taxing au-

Though construction on the trans-Alaskan pipeline involved as many as 20,000 employees in one year, the state's biggest employer continued to be government—federal, state, and local. Well over one fourth of Alaska's work force of more than 160,000 were government employees, according to mid-1976 figures. Even at the height of pipeline construction, the pipeline itself employed only about 12 to 13 percent of the state's work force.

The value of basic industries in Alaska in 1974, according to state figures, listed petroleum at an estimated $438.5 million, wood products at $222.8 million, fisheries at $254.4 million, tourism at $80 million, and agriculture at $7.8 million. Beyond this, Alaska has enormous untapped potential for oil, natural gas, and minerals, as well as for such renewable resources as timber and, surprisingly, agriculture.

But plans to extract that wealth often conflict with other interests. One traditional economic kingpin that feels threatened by various kinds of development is the fishing industry. Many commercial fishermen have been worried, and angry, ever since the Nixon and Ford administrations announced a program of accelerated outer continental shelf oil leasing in Alaska's waters. While the state's fisheries are among the world's most important, the Nixon and Ford administrations insisted on a crash OCS program despite the dangers of oil spills, and destruction and disruption of Alaskan fishing grounds that OCS could bring. Alaskan fishermen traditionally are tough, hardy individualists, and many we talked to said they would never permit any offshore development which posed a threat to their livelihood. Tom Casey, manager of the United Fishermen's Marketing Association (which represents 450 salmon and king-crab fishermen on Kodiak Island), told us in late 1976:

> One thing you can count on is that the fishermen of Alaska will not go peaceably to their destruction. You can be sure there will be widespread violence. Fishermen, in addition to being independent, don't like to encounter others in the ocean . . . and will combat another force, such as oil. They will not tolerate wholesale destruction of their livelihoods. . . . The United

---

thority and other powers, and are governed by a six-member council and a mayor. First-class cities may also adopt home-rule charters and, within limits, change their ordinances without state approval. A borough and cities within it may join together to form what is called a unified municipality, as happened in Anchorage. At the end of 1975, there were 150 incorporated units of local government, which broke down this way: 3 unified home-rule municipalities, 7 second-class boroughs, one third-class borough, 12 home-rule cities, 22 first-class cities, and 105 second-class cities.

States of America can count on a lot of trouble from us, if the United States of America doesn't cooperate. If they think the Kodiak bear is a ferocious beast, let them harass a lot of Kodiak and Bering Sea fishermen.

* * *

The vast mineral supplies of Alaska have remained untapped primarily because of the problem in transporting them to market from isolated, inaccessible areas of the state. Indeed, transportation of any kind is a difficult proposition in a state as vast and wild as Alaska. The road and rail systems are quite limited, so most travel within the state is by plane, sometimes by ferryboat. The state capital at Juneau is accessible from most parts of the state only by air, and not at all by auto. Although the number of scheduled airline flights between various points in Alaska has increased considerably in recent years, many small villages can be reached only by chartering a flight or flying one's own plane. And a large number of Alaskans own their own planes, and earn their livings as bush pilots.[15]

Travel by plane, of course, is expensive anywhere in the country. And although the disparity has decreased somewhat in recent years, it is more expensive in Alaska. The 600-mile air flight from Anchorage to Juneau, for example, cost about $77 in late 1976; interstate flights of the same distance were about 10 percent less.

The vastness of the state also has presented communications problems of various kinds, none probably more serious than that relating to health care. Until 1971, many remote villages of Alaska could be reached by two-way radio only one day out of seven, on the average. Since that time, an experimental communications satellite has provided daily radio contact between a Public Health Service doctor and Native health aides in fourteen remote villages. The aides, who receive sixteen weeks of training, provide much of the health care in the villages after consulting with the doctor via satellite. The state hopes to be able to have the system permanently expanded to cover all villages.

[15] Lyle K. Brown, Alaska regional director for the Federal Aviation Administration, said in October 1976 that according to accident statistics, Alaskan pilots were among the most reckless in the nation. With five percent of the nation's air taxis, Alaska managed to have 49 percent of all air taxi accidents in the U.S. through the first nine months of 1976. In these nine months, there were 252 air accidents, 62 air taxi accidents, 27 fatal accidents, and 74 airplane passengers killed in Alaska. The number killed represented 8 percent of all U.S. airplane deaths for that period. While the great majority of Alaskan pilots are quite skilled, we were told by some pilots that there are many people who fly airplanes in the state without licenses, believing that they are an unnecessary infringement on their freedom.

Improvements in health care in remote villages will be just one of the more benign changes Alaska will experience in the years to come. With various plans to develop the state's onshore and offshore oil and natural gas potential and to tap the state's mineral wealth, Alaska's current boom times could continue for some decades to come, forever changing the Alaskan way of life. While the present grab for the state's vast mineral wealth may permanently transform the character of Alaska, its history is replete with similar attempts to exploit the riches of this harsh and awesome land.

Call of the Wild

There's a land where the mountains are nameless,
and the rivers all run God knows where;
There are lives that are erring and aimless,
and deaths that just hang by a hair;
There are hardships that nobody reckons;
there are valleys unpeopled and still;
There's a land—oh, it beckons and beckons,
and I want to go back—and I will. . . .

—Robert W. Service, "The Spell of the Yukon"

A vast silence reigned over the land. The land itself was a desolation, lifeless, without movement, so lone and cold that the spirit of it was not even that of sadness. There was a hint in it of laughter, but of a laughter more terrible than any sadness—a laughter that was as mirthless as the smile of the Sphinx, a laughter cold as the frost and partaking of the grimness of infallibility. It was the masterful and incommunicable wisdom of eternity laughing at the futility of life and the effort of life. It was the Wild, the savage, frozen-hearted Northland Wild.

—Jack London, *White Fang*

ALASKA'S HISTORY since the arrival of the Russians two centuries ago shows that it has been mainly treasure, rather than the land's splendor, that has drawn Outsiders to the Far North country. For most of the last 200 years, Alaska has been exploited—first by the Russians, then by the Americans—and has been treated as a second-rate colony without any real voice in its own affairs. Even after the advent of statehood in 1959, Alaskans still found that major decisions affecting their land and their life-styles often have been made outside the state's boundaries—by federal bureaucrats in Washington, D.C., or by executives in the boardrooms of giant corporations. It has often been treated more like a Third World country than like the forty-ninth state.

To the Russians, furs were the prize. Later, under United States control, gold was the initial lure. Those early raids on Alaska's riches left the region largely unspoiled. But today, the scramble for the state's oil, natural gas, and minerals threatens to make Alaska's gold rush of three quarters of a century ago look like a scavenger hunt. At stake in this latest rush to the North is the nation's last great wilderness and Alaska's abundance of fish and wildlife. But even more, a way of life is threatened. Most of the 60,000 Natives[1] in Alaska still hunt, fish, trap, and pick berries in carrying on their traditional subsistence way of life; pell-mell development of the state's resources could upset the delicate balance of nature and drive away or kill the fish and wildlife most Natives depend upon. For the state's 340,000 non-Natives, helter-skelter, unchecked development would mean an end to a unique, individualistic life-style and would turn Alaska into the kind of polluted, scarred state that many of them came North to get away from.

Seen in the perspective of history, the recent construction of the trans-Alaska oil pipeline and its accompanying rapid growth have marred but not yet ravaged Alaska. But if corporate enterprise and, in some cases, the federal government have their way, the amount of development in Alaska over just the next decade would far surpass all previous growth over the 200 years since white men first came to the area. And the damage would be irreversible.

Until the Russians arrived in the mid-eighteenth century, Alaska had been inhabited solely by Native groups—Eskimos, Indians, Aleuts. It is generally believed that the Alaska Natives, and the other first inhabitants of the northern part of the Western Hemisphere, came from Asia, perhaps as long ago as 25,000 to 40,000 years. During that period, Asia and North America were joined by a tundra plain stretching across what is now the Bering Sea. This Bering land bridge apparently was first formed more than 40,000 years ago. After perhaps as many as 15,000 years had passed, the area became flooded. At some point several thousand years later, the land bridge again was formed and then was flooded again some 10,000 years ago.

[1] About one quarter of the 80,000 Alaska Natives now live outside the state.

So it is not known exactly when Alaska had its first inhabitants. But it is believed that inhabitation of the Copper River Valley, in south central Alaska, goes back 5,000 years. Also, archeological finds in the Canadian Yukon, just to the east of the boundary with Alaska, indicate human beings were present there as long ago as 25,000 to 30,000 years. But crude tools discovered thus far in Alaska date back only 11,000 years, compared to 35,000 years in the southwest area of the United States.

Regardless of when settlement first occurred, eighteenth century Alaska was populated by a number of distinct Native groups. The Eskimos inhabited western and northern Alaska, the Aleuts lived primarily in the Aleutian Islands, the Tlingit and Haida Indians in southeastern Alaska, and the Athabascan Indians mainly in the interior. In addition, there were other peoples, such as the Koniags of Kodiak Island, who came to regard themselves as Aleuts in the twentieth century. (While their life-style was similar to that of the Aleuts, the Koniags' language and physical characteristics bear a close resemblance to those of Eskimos.)

By the mid-1700s, there were some 74,000 Natives in Alaska, considerably more than today's figure of 60,000, which also includes people with as little as one quarter Native blood. The Natives in those earlier days usually respected each other's general boundaries and some groups even traded with one another, but there was little friendly contact or cooperation among the groups. And there were even occasional clashes. For example, according to various Alaska historians, if one Aleut village trespassed on another village's sea hunting area, the offense could mean war. But, for the most part, the various Native groups were preoccupied with simple survival in the rugged, freezing Alaskan climate.

The first white men known to set foot in Alaska came in 1741 in two Russian ships commanded by Danish-born Vitus Bering, an officer in the Imperial Russian Navy. Bering's discovery also marked the final filling in of the map on the North American continent. Until his voyage, it was not known whether Asia and North America formed one continuous land mass, or were separated by water. The land became known to the newcomers as "Alaska," a variation of the Aleut word *Alaxaxaq.*[2] Although Bering and thirty

[2] Anthropologist J. Ellis Ransom said the word referred to the mainland, and translated as "the object toward which the action of the sea is directed." Some Alaskan histories say the name derived from the Aleut word *Al-a-aska*, meaning "the great

other crewmen died during the expedition, the voyage was a success both from a scientific and an economic standpoint.

The economic motivation for the voyage had been Russia's desire to expand its fur trade. This same incentive had led the czars in the seventeenth century to conquer the semi-nomadic peoples of Siberia for that land's wealth in ermine, fur, and sable. However, by the eighteenth century the Siberian stock of fur-bearing animals had been largely depleted and new hunting grounds were needed.

Bering's crew brought back with it to Russia some skins of sea otters and information about the fur seal—both types of marine mammals which had been unknown to the rest of the Western world until that time. The discovery of these mammals set off a great binge of Russian fur-hunting in Alaska in the decades to follow.

The first great fur rush scoured the Aleutian Islands. The Russians conquered the Aleuts and thousands of them were either murdered[3] or died from diseases—measles, influenza, smallpox—brought about by their contacts with the outsiders. The Aleuts, with their primitive spears and bows and arrows, were no match for the heavily armed Russians, who plundered their sea-otter skins, killed those Natives who resisted, and enslaved thousands of others to aid their hunting of the sea otter. The Aleuts complained to the czar about the horror of the Russian occupation in a message sent to him in 1799:

> We receive them in friendly fashion, but they act like barbarians with us. They seize our wives and children as hostages, they send us early in the spring, against our will, five hundred versts [about 330 miles] away to hunt otters, and they keep us there until fall, and at home they leave the lame, the sick, the blind, and these, too, they force to process fish for the Company[4] and to do other Company work without receiving any pay. . . . The remain-

---

land." It has also been variously spelled "Aliaska," "Aliaksa," "Alakshak" and "Aliaksha."

[3] Some Aleuts were murdered because they resisted Russian efforts to steal their furs; others because they refused to be enslaved. Sometimes, the Russians killed them for "sport." As journalist Lael Mortan noted in her book *And the Land Provides:* "One Russian commander wondered how many men a musket ball could pass through, lined up twelve Aleuts, and reported later . . . that the shot stopped at the ninth man. In another village, by their own written account, hunters killed all the men and old women, sparing the young 'to serve them.' Then they kidnapped the women for their homeward voyage, dropping them overboard when they sighted the Russian mainland."

[4] The "Company" refers to the Russian-owned Russian-American Company, which was granted monopoly control over Alaska's commerce by the czar in 1799.

ing women are sent out on Company labor and are beaten to death. They are removed by force to desert islands, and the children are taken away from those who walk with crutches, and there is no one to feed them.

—*The Russian-American Company*, by S. B. Okun

At the time the first Russians arrived in Alaska, there were an estimated 15,000 to 20,000 Aleuts. By 1910, the Aleuts, by then the victims of mass slaughters, diseases, and the extermination of the sea and land creatures they depended upon for food and clothing, numbered only 1,500—including persons with mixed blood.

As the much prized sea otters and seals were depleted in the Aleutians, the Russian traders moved eastward into other areas of Alaska—Sitka Sound, Prince William Sound, Yakutat Bay, and Cook Inlet. By the 1820s, as the sea mammal population declined further, the traders migrated into the mainland along the Yukon, Nushagak, and Kuskokwim rivers. Because the Russians were involved solely in fur trading, they established few permanent settlements other than trading posts, and did not lay claim to tracts of lands. But as they moved eastward and inland, the fur hunters continued to slaughter Natives.

The Russians' policy generally was to steal from, rather than trade with, the Natives they encountered. Still, there were some Natives whom the Russians could not subjugate. The Tlingit Indians of southeastern Alaska had obtained guns through trades with other foreigners and had achieved a reputation for toughness. While most other Alaskan Natives with primitive weapons were no match for the gun-toting Russians, the Tlingits were able to resist the foreigners, sometimes through actual battle. As a result, the Tlingits traded with the Russians but were never conquered by them.

Although initially the fur trade in Alaska was conducted by independent hunters and a number of Russian companies, by the 1790s there were only a few firms still engaged in it. Then, in 1799, after the Czar granted it monopoly control over Alaska's commerce, the Russian-owned Russian-American Company became the sole governing and commercial power in Alaska until the territory was sold to the United States in 1867.

By the 1860s, both the Russian-American Company and the Russian government increasingly saw Alaska as an economic and political liability. Russia had seen its treasury depleted through its war with Britain in the Crimea (1854–56), and feared that if it again went to war with England Alaska would be a likely target for seizure by the British. Also, for much of the previous four decades, the powerful British trading company, the Hudson's Bay Company, had been pushing its way from its major trading area of Canada into Alaska despite an 1825 agreement between Russia and Great Britain which set the boundaries between British-ruled Canada and Alaska. Besides infringing on Russian commercial activities, British expansion into Alaska would put the enemy right on their doorstep across the Bering Straits. After just three weeks of negotiations, a treaty ceding Alaska to the United States was signed on March 30, 1867. The United States paid $7 million to the Russian government, plus another $200,000 to buy out the financially failing Russian-American Company's interests.

In the 1868 congressional debates on the appropriation for the acquisition, a vocal minority of members denounced the deal with a range of epithets, referring to Alaska as "Walrussia," "Icebergia," "Polaria," and "Seward's Icebox" (for Secretary of State William H. Seward, who had negotiated the Treaty of Cession for the United States). Much of the press already had attacked and ridiculed the purchase as "Seward's Folly." In an editorial view shared by many at the time, the *New York World* commented that "Russia has sold us a sucked orange." And, in what must be one of the worst prophecies in American history, a minority report by the House Committee on Foreign Relations stated:

> The possession of the country is of no value . . . to the United States . . . it will be a source of weakness instead of power, and a constant annual expense for which there will be no adequate return. . . . [it has] no capacity as an agricultural country . . . no value as a mineral country . . . its timber . . . [is] generally of a poor quality and growing upon inaccessible mountains . . . the fisheries [are] of doubtful value . . .

Even twenty years before Alaska's purchase by the United States, Americans had been engaged in commercial whaling in western Alaska waters and later along the coast of the Arctic Ocean. The whales were valuable for their oil, and used for lighting and for "baleen" (whalebone), found in the mouths of bowhead whales and used for women's corset stays. Although the Americans did not engage in mass slaughter of Natives and generally treated the Natives better than the Russians had, their commercial activities still had a severe, oftentimes fatal, impact on Native life. By 1915, most of Alaska's whales had been wiped out and Arctic Eskimos who depended on them for subsistence had to find other food sources or starve. When steamships replaced sailboats in the 1880s as the main means of tracking the whales, the commercial white whalers were able to roam over a much wider area and make many more kills. When kerosene replaced whale oil for lighting purposes, the whale hunters then took only the baleen and wastefully threw away the rest of the whale carcass. The hunters also tracked down walrus for their ivory tusks only and also threw away their carcasses. The effect on the Eskimo was devastating. As Ernest Gruening, the late Alaskan United States senator and territorial governor, wrote in his definitive history, *The State of Alaska:*

> These wasteful activities gravely imperiled the Eskimo's way of life, since he depended on the whale for both food and fuel, and on the walrus for food—both for man and sled dog—for some articles of clothing, for the hide to cover his *oomiak* or skin boat, and for the ivory for a variety of uses, including carvings, which provided his only cash income. . . . Starvation menaced the Eskimo coastal villages.

For about thirty years after its purchase, Alaska was largely ignored by the U.S. government and the American people. There were white men who were busily taking advantage of the state's wealth in natural resources for the two decades following the purchase, but few of these non-Natives made Alaska their home. In fact, in 1880 there were less than 300 white people living permanently in Alaska and all but about 30 of them resided in Sitka. In the 1880s and 1890s the California-based Alaska Commerical Company was awarded a twenty-year franchise on the seal rookeries in the Pribilof Islands in western Alaska. The salmon-canning industry, today still a mainstay of the Alaskan economy, began operating in 1878 in southeastern Alaska. Copper production, centered in the Kennecott mines in the Copper River Valley beginning in the 1880s, proved a profitable enterprise.

But it was the discovery of large strikes of gold in the late 1890s that gave Alaska its biggest economic boom—a boom that was not to be surpassed until the discovery of oil on Alaska's North Slope some seven decades later. The first big gold strike occurred in Canada's Yukon Territory in 1896 along a creek that flowed into the Klondike River, a tributary of the Yukon River which Alaska shares with Canada. And gold in the Canadian Yukon meant that there was almost certainly gold in Alaska, too. Some 60,000 fortune hunters swept northward from the United States to Alaska and Canada. Within three years, gold discoveries at Nome, on the Seward Peninsula in western Alaska just below the Arctic Circle, and in the Tanana Valley in central Alaska, sent prospectors scurrying all over the territory in their quest for gold. Gruening's history of Alaska recounted the impact the gold strikes had on American entrepreneurs. With just a few words changed, it could serve to describe the lure of Alaska's wealth today:

. . . kindled by the gold fever, a great new optimism about Alaska's riches surged through the land. Gold, of course—in abundance. Only the merest surface had been scratched! But also silver, copper, platinum, coal, furs, timber—a land of infinite potentialities! But how to reach these inland treasures? Docks, roads, railways would have to built to get the pioneers inland, to supply them and get their stuff out. Back in the states Alaska was a stock promoters' paradise. It attracted the great capitalists as well as the fly-by-night. It brought Alaska for the first time to the ken of millions of Americans. . . .

This was not, however, the first discovery of gold in Alaska. Some small strikes had been made in the 1870s, followed by an important discovery of gold in 1880 in the area of what was to become the city of Juneau. For the next sixty years, Juneau was to be the center of hard-rock gold mining in the state. Still, it was the gold strikes of the late 1890s that stirred the nation's imagination and sent men swarming to Alaska and the Candian Yukon. Even today, to many Americans and Canadians, the names Klondike, Yukon, Dawson, Juneau, Nome, conjure up visions of boom towns, "gold in the streets," and sourdoughs setting off into the rugged, unconquerable wilderness.

The turn-of-the-century gold rush is part of the American legend. But the romantic aura of the gold rush to Outsiders obscures its reality for Alaska's Native people. Even though individual Natives found many of the rich gold areas near Juneau and Nome, they could not legally stake claims because they were not "citizens." Traditional Native areas around Juneau and Nome were overrun by prospectors. The fortune seekers hunted caribou, moose, and small game for food for themselves, sharply reducing the supply available for Natives. Gold mining often silted up streams, killing salmon which the Natives also depended upon for food. And, as so many times before, the white man brought with him disease and drink, which resulted in death and additional hardship to many Natives.

After reaching a peak in 1906, gold production in Alaska began to drop off. Costs of transportation and the inaccessibility of most of the gold and other mineral fields discouraged further prospecting and much of Alaska's subsurface riches remained untapped. Restrictive federal policies also prevented Alaska's potentially lucrative coal deposits from being extensively mined.

The federal government took other steps that barred intensive development in Alaska. In 1907, for example, under President Theodore Roosevelt's conservationist-oriented administration, the government set aside more than 4.5 million acres in south central Alaska, around Prince William Sound, for the Chugach National Forest, and more than 16 million acres in southeastern Alaska for the Tongass National Forest. Additional federal land withdrawals followed. The Mount McKinley National Park, named for the nation's highest mountain peak, was established in 1916, followed soon after by the creation of the Katmai National Monument.[5] Today, the Park and Monument total about 1.9 million and 2.8 million acres, respectively. (The states of Delaware and Rhode Island together total about 2 million acres.) In 1925, a Glacier Bay National Monument of about 1.2 million acres, later expanded to more than 2.8 million acres, was established. In 1923, some 23 million acres on Alaska's North Slope, which were potentially rich in oil and minerals, were set aside as Naval Petroleum Reserve No. 4.

Also retarding development was the small amount of land in Alaska that was privately owned. Until statehood was achieved in 1959, almost all of the state's 375 million acres—an area more than twice the size of Texas—were owned by the federal government. With the passage of the Statehood Act and the 1971 Alaska Native Claims Settlement Act (ANCSA), the federal government relinquished almost 40 percent of its holdings in Alaska. The two acts, when fully implemented sometime in the 1980s, will leave just over 226 million acres in federal hands; 104.5 million acres in possession of the state; 44 million acres owned by the Native corporations established under terms of the Native Claims Act; and a relatively small amount of about one million acres held by private landowners other than the Native corporations.

Thus, until statehood, almost all development that did occur in Alaska was solely at the discretion of the federal government. Alaskans had little voice in their own affairs even after 1906, when a nonvoting delegate was allowed to represent Alaska in Congress, or after the approval of formal territorial status in 1912. The territorial legis-

[5] National monuments basically are the same as national parks.

lature established under the 1912 act lacked authority over development issues, and the territorial governor was appointed by the president.

A major factor that has worked against development in Alaska has been the absence of roads, rendering many of the natural resources inaccessible to exploration. Even by 1975, there were fewer than 11,000 miles of roads in Alaska, of which less than one fourth were surfaced.[6] The state's best-known road, the Alaska Highway (familiarly known as the Alcan Highway—for "Alaska-Canada"), joins Alaska with the Lower-48 states through Canada. It was not built until 1942, and only then because of the threat the Japanese posed to Alaska in World War II. The Japanese, in fact, occupied Alaska's Attu and Kiska Islands in 1942–43, and also bombed Dutch Harbor. The 1,520-mile-long Alcan Highway, of which 299 miles are in Alaska, was built to give overland access to Alaska so that the territory could be kept equipped with needed wartime equipment and materiel.

Another factor deterring development has been the state's climate, which is especially inhospitable to Outsiders, particularly in the northern Arctic and the central interior regions. Much of Alaska's land is covered with permafrost, permanently frozen subsoil that goes to depths of as much as 2,000 feet. Permafrost severely limits all types of development, because construction on it causes thawing which, in turn, leads to buckling of the melted ground. While present chiefly in Alaska's Arctic region, permafrost is also found in much of the interior and some of the south central portion of the state.

Potential military threats to Alaska during World War II and the Cold War hastened much of the development that occurred in Alaska between the gold rush and the 1968 discovery of oil on the North Slope. In 1940, the U.S. military buildup in Alaska began with the establishment of Fort Richardson and Elmendorf Air Force Base near Achorage. This was followed by considerable other defense-related construction and expenditures. Historian Claus-M. Naske, in his book, *An Interpretative History of Alaskan Statehood*, wrote that the federal government spent at estimated $3 billion in Alaska during World War II—none of which was taxed by the territory. Naske suggested that, "A small levy on the profits of the con-

[6] Every state in the union—even those with less than one percent of the land area of Alaska—has more miles of paved roads than Alaska. Texas, the second largest state in land area, has more than 170,000 miles of paved roads.

tractors and a modest income tax on the salaries of defense workers would have produced a great deal of revenue" for the fiscally hard-pressed territory. Other federal activities during World War II included construction of the 190-mile Glenn Highway, which connected Anchorage with Fairbanks to the north and Valdez to the east; stepped-up mapping and charting by the U.S. Geological Survey and Coast and Geodetic Survey; construction of housing; provision of matching funds for water and sewer works; and new school buildings for communities affected by the sudden influx of military personnel. During the war, some 300,000 army, navy, and air force personnel were stationed in Alaska.

World War II also pointed up the inadequacy of the Alaska Railroad. Linking Seward, Anchorage, and Fairbanks, the line was completed in 1923—even though it had been first authorized almost a decade earlier. Its construction had been preceded by many years of studies and congressional debate. Its biggest boost came when President Woodrow Wilson, in his first State of the Union message in 1913 to the Democratic-controlled Congress, called for government construction of a system of railways in the state. Wilson, sounding a theme that super-growth advocates in the state today can appreciate, said that the nation needed Alaska's coal and, "We must use the resources of the country, not lock them up." The way to do this, Wilson said, was to construct an Alaskan railroad system. But no "system" was built by the government—only one line, from Seward on the Gulf of Alaska, through Anchorage to Fairbanks. And from the start that line was plagued by poor construction. Territorial Governor George A. Parks wrote in 1925 that "The road as it is now constructed requires constant repairing to keep it in safe condition."

But insufficient federal appropriations stymied any efforts to upgrade the railroad. The railroad's inadequacy became a cause for concern during World War II, when the military virtually abandoned the Aleutian Islands and other areas on Alaska's periphery to concentrate on defending the territory's heartland. That included installations from Kodiak Island north through Anchorage and Fairbanks, and the railroad was vital to such an alignment. Because the rail line proved invaluable in the war, top military officials following the war pressured Congress to rehabilitate the railroad in the interest of national defense. Gradually, over a period of years, it was improved.

Ironically, the railroad never fulfilled its original purpose—to open up Alaska's treasure house of coal to development. Although coal mining did occur along the route, the nation had less need for Alaskan coal by the time the long-delayed railroad was completed. Oil was used more than coal, both by the navy and other domestic users, and the West Coast could obtain eastern coal more easily after completion of the Panama Canal in 1914—nine years before completion of the Alaska Railroad.

Following World War II, additional defense-related expenditures contributed to further growth in Alaska. Among the major projects was the joint U.S.–Canadian effort to construct the 3,000-mile-long defensive radar system, the Distant Early Warning System (DEW Line), throughout the Arctic region from Alaska to Iceland. A look at some statistics shows the impact the military has had on Alaska during and after World War II. In 1940, of a population of about 75,000, there were 1,000 members of the military in Alaska. By 1943, there were 152,000 military personnel in Alaska out of a total population of 233,000. In 1946, after the war had ended, the territory's population fell back to 99,000. But continued high defense expenditures in Alaska during the early Cold War years were in large part responsible for boosting the state's population to 138,000 by 1950. This influx of new people from the Outside—people who were accustomed to the benefits of statehood in the Lower-48—helped develop momentum for the statehood fight of the 1950s.

That fight was inextricably linked to the state's most potent industry: fishing. Commercial salmon operations in Alaska began with the establishment of canneries at Klawock and Old Sitka in 1878, and soon spread to Prince William Sound, Kodiak Island, Cook Inlet, the Alaska Peninsula, and Bristol Bay. As the industry grew, so did its political and economic power. Over the years leading to statehood, taxes levied against the industry were minuscule, thanks to the industry's allies in federal government and to the timidity of the territorial legislature. When Governor Ernest Gruening in 1941 urged the territorial legislature to revamp the state's makeshift tax structure and impose a moderate income and profits tax and a small levy on property outside of incorporated towns, the legislature refused. Gruening's proposal would have enabled the territory to extract an additional small amount of tax from the canning and mining industries, both of which lobbied heavily to defeat the bill. Historian Naske, commenting on the legislature's resounding rejection of Gruening's proposal, wrote:

The legislature, and indirectly the people, were not yet ready to bite the hand that seemed to feed them. The exploitative resource industries still held the threat of total withdrawal of livelihood over many Alaskans.

The salmon processing industry, as its power developed, came to symbolize the Outside oppression felt by many Alaskans. Throughout its history, the industry has been noted for its control by Outside interests—first, those based in Seattle, and, in more recent years, by the Japanese. Reflecting on this Outside domination, Anthony J. Dimond, Alaska's delegate to Congress, stated on April 11, 1934:

> Alaska has been cursed . . . with what in some of the old countries they called "absentee landlordism," where people who hold and control the resources of the country do not reside in the country and have no interest in it except to make as much money out of it as they can.

Using highly efficient fish traps, the Outside salmon interests overfished and drastically depleted the stocks, endangering both the future of the Alaskan fisheries and the Natives' subsistence life-style. The highly controversial traps were used almost entirely by non-Alaskans. Shortly after World War II, of the 434 fish trap licenses that had been issued by the Interior Department, only 38 belonged to Alaskans. Some 245 were held by eight major canning companies—all of them non-Alaskan. The traps became such a symbol of Outside oppression that one of the first acts of William Egan, the first governor after statehood, was to ban their use.

The economic benefits the salmon canneries brought to Alaska were small in those pre-statehood days. Because of the industry's and the Seattle-based unions' hiring practices, many Alaskans were denied work in the territory's canneries. In one typical year, 1946, almost 11,000 Alaskans were hired and paid some $3.7 million in wages for the seasonal work in the territory's canneries. By contrast, almost 12,500 cannery workers were transported from the Lower-48 and paid more than $7.2 million in wages for work in Alaska's canneries. The wages for the Outsiders (which averaged $577 for the season, compared to $340 for Alaskans) were not paid the workers until the end of the season when they went back to Seattle and other points of hire in the Lower-48. Thus, the territory was denied any economic benefits from those Outsiders' wages. That same year, the industry paid state taxes of just $630,000 on packed salmon valued at almost $56.6 million. This amounted to a tax of about 24 cents on a case of salmon, which contained 48 one-pound cans. The salmon interests further benefited from a lack of enforcement by the federal Bureau of Fisheries of what fishing laws did exist; the territory had no authority over the Alaskan fisheries—either to make regulations or enforce them. For all these reasons, the salmon industry was hated and feared by many Alaska residents. Fearful of losing its privileged position, the industry became a leading opponent of statehood. As a result of the industry's exploitative practices, Alaska's salmon fisheries today remain in serious condition and are in need of revitalization.

Statehood was the key to Alaskans' gaining a significant measure of control over their own destiny and development. The Organic Act of 1912, which gave Alaska full territorial status and created a territorial legislature, still left Alaska far from the goal of self-government. Even efforts to make the territorial legislature more democratic—such as a proposal in 1942 to create proportional representation in the misapportioned body—were rebuffed by congressional committees. The measures were rejected, according to Dimond, Alaska's nonvoting delegate to Congress, through the effective lobbying of Alaska's "absentee landlord" interests and of many Alaska Chambers of Commerce beholden to Outside interests.

In 1943, Dimond introduced a bill to grant statehood to Alaska. (The first such bill had been introduced by Alaska's congressional delegate, James Wickersham, in 1915.) Dimond figured that since reasonable, gradual steps toward full home rule for Alaska had failed, it would be no more difficult to fight for statehood than for partial measures. His bill marked the beginning of the successful sixteen-year push for statehood. In 1945, the territorial legislature for the first time passed a resolution requesting Alaska's admission to the union as the forty-ninth state. The legislature then enacted a bill providing for a referendum in 1946 to assess Alaska citizens' sentiment on the statehood issue.

The voters approved the referendum measure, 9,630 to 6,822. Much of the opposition came from Outside economic interests, particularly the mining and canned-salmon industries, which feared a loss of their privileged status under statehood. Also, several of the state's newspapers opposed statehood, including ones in Juneau (*Alaska Daily Empire*), Ketchikan (*Fishing News*), Fairbanks (*News-Miner*), and Anchorage (*Anchorage News*).

Boosted by the territorial referendum, the advocates of statehood pushed on, aided by a key advocate, President Harry S Truman. Eight months before Alaska's referendum, Truman stated that both Hawaii and Alaska should be granted statehood if their residents desired it. Following the referendum, Truman continued to speak out for statehood for Alaska and Hawaii—the first president ever to do so.

Leaders in the statehood fight were Governor Gruening and Edward L. (Bob) Bartlett who, by the time of the territorial referendum, was Alaska's delegate in Congress. In the years after statehood was achieved, Gruening and Bartlett served together in the U.S. Senate. Bartlett attributed much of the opposition to the statehood referendum to the sourdoughs who disliked "all the change and commotion that came about in 1940 when the army started to arm Alaska. . . . They would rather go back to . . . the good old days." Although there were Natives in the territorial legislature, most other Natives at the time lacked interest in political life and were indifferent to the idea of statehood. Statehood was seen by its supporters as the attainment of the democratic ideal of self-government and the throwing off of the shackles of federal government and Outside industry control.

The most formidable statehood opponent was Winton C. Arnold, nicknamed "Judge." Arnold, who had lived in Alaska for a time, in 1933 became the chief lobbyist for the Alaska Salmon Industry, Inc., and then moved to Seattle. Commuting back and forth, Arnold built up a reputation as the most powerful man in Alaska because of his ability to get the territorial legislature to do his bidding. His lobbying was instrumental in killing basic tax reforms affecting the salmon industry from 1939 until 1949, when the territorial legislature finally enacted a property and income tax.

Arnold repeatedly contended at statehood hearings that Alaska wouldn't be able to afford statehood. He also argued that federal lands conveyed to the new state would conflict with the Natives' aboriginal land claims. This was somewhat ironic, for in later years Arnold was to write a series of articles in the *Anchorage Times* against the Natives' demands for a meaningful land claims settlement.

In 1947, Alaska statehood bills were introduced in Congress by Bartlett and Representative Homer D. Angell (Republican, Oregon), who described Alaska as "a striking example of taxation without representation." When hearings were held that year in Washington, D.C., and Alaska, the first witness, U.S. Interior Secretary Julius A. Krug, stated succinctly why a majority of Alaskans favored statehood:

Alaska has suffered for many years under what is virtually a colonial system that has encouraged absentee exploitation of its natural resources without leaving enough social and economic benefits for the territory. If Alaska is granted statehood, its people will have more to say about their economic as well as their political destiny. Absentee interests, working for their special ends, will find it more difficult to dominate the economy of the area. This type of financial control will continue just as long as the Alaskan people find it necessary to travel six thousand miles to Washington in order to obtain the legislative action which they need to deal with their problems.

Predictably, mining and canning interests testified against the bill, as did representatives of a number of other Outside interests. One lobbyist, Al Anderson, executive secretary of the Alaska Miners Association, asserted that "the talk of Alaska's vast resources" was "greatly exaggerated, so that the resources to run the new state are limited indeed. . . ."

Alaskan statehood was not to be achieved for another twelve years. In the intervening years, statehood for both Alaska and Hawaii was regularly blocked by a coalition of southern Democrats and conservative Republicans. Some of the opposition to statehood for both territories was racist in nature. Some southern senators said the statehood drive was an effort by liberals to bring four more liberal members into the Senate and thereby increase chances of passage of civil rights legislation. One senator, John L. McClellan (Democrat, Arkansas), even trotted out the threat of communism as the rationale for rejecting statehood. McClellan said he opposed statehood for Hawaii and Alaska because of "Communist influence"[7] on Harry Bridges, head of the International Longshoremen and Warehousemen's Union. McClellan, during 1950 Senate debate, said that Bridges's union controlled Hawaii and now has "his men working in all the fishery towns in Alaska, trying to put under his thumb every union in Alaska. . . ."

Senator John C. Stennis (Democrat, Mississippi), during Senate debate in 1950, came up with a number of other arguments against Alaskan statehood. Because Alaska was not adjacent to the Lower-48, Stennis warned, this could mean that the U.S. was embarking on a whole new philosophy that could lead to statehood for

[7] Bridges, born in Australia, was one of the favorite targets of Red-baiters of the 1950s. Despite repeated efforts by the federal government to deport Bridges as a "subversive," no convincing evidence ever was presented that he belonged to the Communist party.

other far-flung or noncontiguous territories, such as Hawaii, the Virgin Islands, Puerto Rico, Guam, and Okinawa.

One novel argument used by Stennis involved Alaska's climate. Quoting from a newspaper article, the senator said: "The lack of development of Alaska does not arise because of any lack of law and order, but the explanation is to be found in that short sentence which I have read . . . 'Brief exposure can mean death.' " And Senator Clyde R. Hoey (Democrat, North Carolina) chimed in: "When we come to think about . . . the resources of Alaska, we find that they have not been developed because people do not want to stay there in the extremes of climates which are found there."

A statehood bill for Alaska did pass the House of Representatives in 1950. But Senate opponents blocked a floor vote. In addition to the congressional roadblocks, the election of Dwight Eisenhower as president in 1952 initially was a setback for the statehood drive. In his first State of the Union message, Eisenhower endorsed statehood for Hawaii but made no mention of Alaska. At subsequent press conferences, he said he felt Alaska was not yet ready for entry into the Union.

As the years passed, pro-statehood Alaskans stepped up their efforts. In 1955 the territorial legislature passed a bill to set up a constitutional convention. Delegates were elected and by early 1956 the convention had adopted—and the voters later endorsed—a constitution for the future state. Finally, in 1958 Congress voted statehood for Alaska. In the 1958 elections, Alaskans overwhelmingly voted "yes" on the question of whether Alaska should be admitted to the Union. President Eisenhower signed the statehood proclamation on January 3, 1959.

Although histories of the statehood fight do not list oil as a major factor in the battle, there are pro-oil people in Alaska today who will tell you that it figured importantly in convincing Congress that Alaska could support itself. One such believer is Robert B. Atwood, editor and publisher of the *Anchorage Times*, who was chairman of the Alaska Statehood Committee. Atwood claimed to us that the discovery of oil on the Kenai Peninsula's Swanson River Field in 1957 by the Richfield Company (now Arco) came at a most opportune time during the statehood battle, and showed that the speculation about Alaska's potential wealth in natural resources was not idle.

Even if oil discoveries did not add momentum to the statehood effort, the Kenai Peninsula oil find foreshadowed the Prudhoe Bay oil boom which set Alaska on the road to becoming an oil state. The 1957 strike was followed in 1960 by the discovery of more oil at Soldatna, south of Richfield's original well. Soon after came the discovery offshore of oil and natural gas in nearby Cook Inlet. In the decade following the Swanson River strike, Alaska stepped up its oil production and became the seventh leading oil-producing state. With the announcement on July 18, 1968, that there were 9.6 billion barrels of oil at Prudhoe Bay on the North Slope (a conservative oil company estimate), the state's latest—and biggest—boom was set off.

The oil industry soon launched a campaign to build a pipeline to carry the oil from Prudhoe Bay to the Alaskan port of Valdez, and from there to West Coast destinations. But there were two potential roadblocks to pipeline construction: the negative environmental impact of such a project, and a growing chorus of Alaska Natives demanding a just settlement of their aboriginal land claims. One obstacle was overcome in 1971 when the Alaska Native Claims Settlement Act, granting the Natives 44 million acres and $962.5 million, was enacted into law. Two years later, Congress passed legislation authorizing construction of the pipeline, despite predictions of environmental havoc. The passage of these two significant acts set in motion economic forces that are rapidly shaping the future of Alaska.

Citizen Atwood

FRONTIER JOURNALISM is alive and highly profitable in Alaska. As editor and publisher of the *Anchorage Times*, the state's most widely read newspaper, Robert B. Atwood, the Boomer extraordinaire, daily preaches the gospel of unlimited growth to the people of the last frontier. For nearly four decades the *Times* has dominated the other news media in the state. And for those four decades, the *Times* has helped mold state policy and orchestrate public opinion on major development issues. As a leader and spokesman for the super-growth forces in the state, Atwood, through his newspaper, is probably the most powerful person in Alaska today.

With a newsman's humility, Atwood rejects such notions. The *Times* "is not powerful at all," he curtly told us. But almost without pause the publisher broke into a smile, and told story after story which demonstrated that the *Times* has the clout to steer the state and Anchorage in directions they didn't realize they wanted to go.

In many ways, Bob Atwood invites comparison with William Loeb, the acerbic, autocratic, and powerful publisher of the *Manchester* (New Hampshire) *Union-Leader*. Both men control their state's dominant news medium, support conservative causes, and have close ties to the Teamsters. But while Loeb's influence in New Hampshire is tempered somewhat by the Boston newspapers which circulate heavily in his area, Atwood has no such worries about Outside competition. Seattle newspapers (the nearest Lower-48 major papers) are 1,500 air miles away, have small circulation in Alaska, and include little state news.[1] And since television and radio

[1] The Sunday *New York Times* has been available in Anchorage on Mondays—at $2.95 a copy.

stations in Alaska are small and have limited news resources, the *Times* has, in fact, a greater hold on news coverage than does the *Union-Leader* in New Hampshire.

The *Times*'s dominance of the state media has disturbing implications because the newspaper is no disinterested, neutral observer; Atwood and his newspaper are partisans that themselves help create much of the news occurring in Alaska. And the major news in Alaska is nearly always related to development.

Atwood's political clout in state affairs is apparent in the *Times*'s coverage of the construction of the trans-Alaska oil pipeline, the single most important issue in Alaska over the past decade. At no point during the years of debate over the pipeline did the *Times* in its editorial or news columns cast a critical eye on the project or explore the environmental risks it posed to the state. Instead, as former *Times* reporters recalled to us, the newspaper often ran press releases from Alyeska Pipeline Service Company, the pipeline builder, verbatim or nearly so.[2] In fact, the *Times* introduced a weekly puff section, "Oil and the Pipeline," distinguished by the sort of shallow reporting found in the real estate and travel sections of many United States newspapers. The weekly supplement combined Alyeska press releases and fluffy features that ballyhooed the benefits of oil to the state. Some typical headlines from the 1976 issues give the flavor of the "Oil and the Pipeline" section:

"Union Chief Says Welds Are Best"
"This Is Where the Oil Comes Out"
"Another 38 Miles to Go for Pipe Installation"
"Welders Finish Thompson Pass"
"Pipeline Will Leave Canyons Nearly Unmarred"[3]

[2] The *Times* was not alone in its strong support for the proposed trans-Alaska pipeline. The *Fairbanks Daily News-Miner*, as well as most of the state's news media, were ardent boosters of the pipeline and development in general. But by early 1976, the *News-Miner's* ardor had cooled. In an editorial it said: "As we sit back and look at the current status of Fairbanks, interior Alaska, and our state in general, we feel that conditions which prompted publication of our annual progress edition twenty-six years ago no longer exist. At present we can see no pressing need to attract more economic development and more people to Alaska. We do not need more 'progress' at the moment. Rather, priorities must now be directed toward identifying and solving problems incident to our hectic growth in recent months."

[3] This headline appeared at a time when the problem of inadequate welds and falsified X rays was receiving nationwide attention through the press and congressional investigations.

John Greely, a former Associated Press reporter who once used office space in the *Times* newsroom, recalled an especially blatant *Times* defense of Big Oil. In 1972, AP in Washington, D.C., moved a major story on its wire that a pipeline route through Canada to the Midwest was environmentally superior to the trans-Alaska line, according to the just-released Interior Department environmental impact statement on Prudhoe Bay. It was a big national story. But the banner headline in that afternoon's *Times* was: "U.S. Hears Wrong Story on Route for Pipeline." The banner for the following day's paper was: "State Hurt by AP Story." Greely recalled that the story under the second day's banner consisted of "an interview with a local stock analyst who laid the blame on [AP] for sending some Alaska-related stock dipping, fanning the flames of anti–oil development, and all but torching the Chamber of Commerce."[4]

The *Times* has even embarrassed its friends on occasion by being too zealous in their defense. One banner headline in 1977, for example, screamed: "Line Security Guaranteed, Sabotage Defense Assured." This prompted the editors of the weekly *Alaska Advocate* to send two reporters out to "blow up" the pipeline. Without a plan and armed only with a harmless smoke bomb, the saboteurs easily accomplished their mission, without detection, two miles north of Sourdough. In its June 2 story on the simulated terrorist attack on the pipeline, the *Advocate* quoted numerous Alyeska, state, and federal officials who freely acknowledged the pipeline was quite vulnerable to sabotage. "They could blow that thing up every thirty minutes and we couldn't do anything about it," one state official said. The *Times*'s story, the *Advocate* noted, was simply fallacious.

But oil and the pipeline are only one of the *Times*'s crusades. An older—and even dearer—one is the relocation of the state capital. A beaming Atwood boasted to us about the issue: "I created it." And indeed he did. As soon as statehood was achieved in 1959, he launched an editorial campaign to have the capital moved from isolated Juneau in southeastern Alaska to a site nearer the geographical and population centers of the state.

Over the years, news accounts in the *Times* of the capital move proposals highlighted the positive aspects (by Atwood's reckoning) of such a move and neglected the negative arguments—such as the potentially astronomical costs. Twice in the early 1960s, the capital move proposal was placed on the ballot by the initiative process, thanks largely to the *Times*'s advocacy of the issue; twice it was

[4] Greely's recollections were in the January 6, 1977, issue of *Alaska Advocate*.

soundly rejected by Alaska's voters. But Atwood kept plugging away and, in 1974, voters approved an initiative providing for the capital to be moved. Then in 1976, given the choice of three sites, voters selected Willow, 35 miles north of Anchorage, as the location for the new capital.

In "creating" issues like the capital move, the *Times* reveals its true power: to set the parameters of discussion on any issue and to mold public opinion through its news coverage. To these ends, liberal, conservationist, and consumer viewpoints get short shrift in the *Times*, while the interests of the Alaska Teamsters, the Chambers of Commerce, the oil industry, and other development forces regularly receive glowing press-release coverage, and are rarely subjected to intensive or objective scrutiny. As one small-business owner in Anchorage told us:

> The dangerous thing about Atwood is that he determines what are the boundaries of legitimate discussion. Those who fall outside the boundaries in their views, even slightly, are labeled crazies or radicals or "no-growthers." And it affects people who have liberal or progressive views. Atwood makes most of the liberal politicians behave a lot more cautiously, because they know what he can do to them if he turns his fire on them. Atwood's paper just totally distorts the discussion of issues in this state.

Indeed, public debate on major state issues is often misinformed or one-sided because the *Times* disseminates its version of events—with special interest news bias, and shrill, dogmatic editorials—to the largest readership in the state.

With a daily circulation approaching 50,000, in a metropolitan area with almost half of Alaska's population, the *Times* in early 1977 had more readers than the state's six other daily newspapers combined—and it had had that advantage for years. Its circulation was more than twice that of the next most widely read Alaskan daily, the *Fairbanks Daily News-Miner*. In the whole state there were fewer than three dozen weekly newsgathering operations—newspapers of uneven quality,[5] low circulation, limited budgets, and few journalistic resources.

[5] There are a handful of good newsgathering operations in the state. Among radio stations, KFQD in Anchorage has an aggressive news staff and does a lot of original reporting. *Alaska Advocate*, a new weekly newspaper, is outstanding. The *Tundra Times*, founded in 1962 and edited for many years by Howard Rock until his death in 1976, provides invaluable news coverage of Native communities and Native issues, written from a Native perspective. During the land claims fight, the *Tundra Times* under Rock gave Alaska's Natives for the first time a common voice and a recognized forum.

Original news reporting is virtually nonexistent among most of the state's radio and television stations;[6] those outlets' rip-and-read news broadcasts rely almost entirely on the Associated Press or the daily newspapers. The state's only top-quality daily newspaper, the morning *Anchorage Daily News*, a Pulitzer Prize winner in 1976, has a circulation only about one third that of the evening *Times*—and was on the verge of financial collapse in early 1977. Thus the *Times* for four decades has been in a strategic position to push its Manifest Destiny development philosophy for Alaska, drowning out competing voices in the process.

Although Atwood's political philosophy most easily slides into the category of conservative, he takes anything but a classical conservative approach to government's role vis-à-vis private development. He frequently rails against federal and state government overregulation, yet is among the first to call for government incentives, tax breaks, bailouts, loan guarantees—call them what you will—when development in his state is at stake. He is, in short, a very good representative of that special breed of Alaskan conservative—the Boomer—whose frontier philosophy places development as its overriding concern. One searches back issues of the *Times* in vain for an editorial opposing any Alaskan development scheme, no matter how farfetched or potentially damaging to the environment or the frontier way of life.

In talking to us about the state constitution, Atwood did not cite its high ideals, but rather its provisions emphasizing development as the goal of the state. In discussing the *Anchorage Times*, he talked not of lofty First Amendment principles or of rooting out the truth but about its role in building Anchorage and Alaska. With a fortune estimated at more than $25 million, thanks mainly to his newspaper and his oil interests on the Kenai Peninsula, Atwood's world view combines the sentiments of George Babbitt and Charles Foster Kane (in the movie *Citizen Kane*).

* * *

At age seventy, Bob Atwood can look back upon a rich career in which he helped build Anchorage into a city, win statehood for Alaska, and lead the fight for development of the state's natural

[6] Network news is available nightly at 11 P.M. in Anchorage but, of course, it seldom contains any news about Alaska. Also, it has been estimated that some 200 communities in Alaska are without any news coverage or news outlet at all. In the entire state, the press corps has been estimated to consist of about 100 members, and about 40 of them work for the *Anchorage Times*.

resources. Atwood came to Alaska with his wife, Evangeline, a social worker in Springfield, Illinois, after a stint as a reporter for the *Illinois State Journal* in Springfield. He borrowed money from his wealthy, influential father-in-law, Anchorage banker Edwin A. Rasmuson, to buy the *Times*, which had been started in 1925 by Rasmuson and a group of businessmen. Atwood's philosophy fit right in with that of the business-booster newspaper he took over in 1935. Since then, Anchorage has grown from a sleepy little town with unpaved streets and a population of 2,500 to a thriving city of more than 175,000, and the *Times* has mushroomed from a paper with 5 employees and a circulation of 650 to about 200 employees and almost 50,000 circulation.

Atwood helped to hasten the growth of both the newspaper and the city, and Anchorage has unquestionably benefited from some of his editorial efforts. He told us, for example, of how he had advocated and won passage of a building code to regulate the haphazard construction patterns in Anchorage; how he won adoption of the city manager form of government for Anchorage; and how he fought to have Fourth Avenue, one of the city's main streets, paved (and convinced other merchants to pave the streets on their blocks). But easily his proudest roles in state development have been in winning statehood for Alaska and in pushing the capital relocation issue.

As chairman of the Alaska Statehood Committee, Atwood was a key lobbyist in both Alaska and in Washington. It wasn't easy, Atwood recalled. Once, for example, he picked up a vote for statehood by keeping someone a congressman didn't want to see out of the lawmaker's office. This type of congressional indifference that he encountered in his lobbying, seen in the context of Alaskan history under U.S. ownership, helped convince Atwood that Congress and the federal bureaucracy didn't have the best interests of Alaska's development at heart.

If it were up to the folks in the nation's capital, Atwood told us, Alaska would have been locked up forever. Instead, he said, only somewhat tongue in cheek, it has been "friends in strange places" who have spurred Alaska's growth to date. He noted that the Japanese threat in World War II, followed by the Cold War, served to emphasize the military and strategic importance of Alaska. As a result, the federal government poured in hundreds of millions of dollars every year for military installations, which meant more roads, more services, more development, and a boost to the local economy. Finally, according to the Atwood capsule history of

Alaska's development, the Middle East oil producers' embargo of the United States in 1973–74 insured Alaska's future as an oil state by helping to force settlement of legal challenges to construction of the trans-Alaska pipeline. "If it hadn't been for the Arabs, we'd have no pipeline today, and the other plans for oil in the state would be stymied. So that's what I mean when I say we've had friends in strange places. Tojo, Stalin, the Arabs. They all caused the federal government to see how important Alaska is. Thanks to them, and no thanks to the people in Washington, D.C., we've had some development in Alaska."

These days Atwood looks back on the drive for statehood less as an effort to obtain rightful democratic sovereignty than as a way of displacing Outside economic interests in order to put more development-minded Alaskans in charge. Yet, at the time of the statehood battle, he was considered something of a liberal. Though a Republican, Atwood became friends with liberal Democrat Ernest Gruening, the territorial governor from 1939 to 1953, and later a U.S. Senator.[7] In 1949, the *Times* supported Gruening's successful proposal to increase taxes on the Outside interests—primarily the salmon industry. (By contrast, Atwood today opposes increased taxes for another Outside interest, the multinational oil companies.) At that time, Atwood was president of the Anchorage Chamber of Commerce, and had become concerned over state finances when in 1948 Alaska had been unable to meet all its bills because of its low taxation rate on key industries. Tax reform, he realized, was needed. As William A. Egan, then a state legislator and later a three-term governor of Alaska, told an interviewer in early 1977:

> Sure, Bob Atwood was a liberal. You can be a liberal without being a damn fool about spending money. Bob was a strong advocate for getting needed public services through a reasonable tax program.

Atwood's wife, Evangeline, also held a similar view of her husband in those prestatehood days. Her 1957 book, *Anchorage: All-American City*, was dedicated to her husband, "whose liberal newspaper editorials have kept Anchorage in the vanguard of American cities."

If Atwood worked against the Outside economic interests in prestatehood days, his tone changed abruptly once statehood appeared imminent. A turning point for both himself and the state

[7] Atwood later was to fall out with Gruening in the 1960s over the Vietnam War. Gruening was one of the most outspoken early critics of the war in the U.S. Senate, while Atwood strongly supported it.

came in 1957 when a rich strike of oil was made southwest of Anchorage in the Swanson River area of the Kenai Peninsula, adjacent to the Cook Inlet, where Atwood and some of his business friends owned leases.

There is much scuttlebutt in Alaska that Atwood cashed in on inside information provided by Fred A. Seaton, then interior secretary (interestingly, Ted Stevens, now senator, was then a top aide to Seaton). Indeed, Atwood acknowledged to us that it was more than just a hunch that prompted him and friends to buy leases in the Swanson River. But he insisted that his investment was made not for personal gain but to aid the statehood drive—an oil discovery would help convince Congress that Alaska was a land of riches and could make its won way economically. Atwood recalled how oil company geologists had been coming to the state since the 1930s, looking for oil. He said he and his associates befriended the geologists and were told where the promising oil fields were located on the Kenai Peninsula. Then Atwood and thirteen other businessmen bought several 60,000-acre packages of leases at bargain prices and sent one of their group off to sell the leases. In those days, Atwood said, "for two bits an acre you could get a three-year lease." According to Atwood, the group offered the leases to the then small Richfield Oil Company (now Arco) at no charge. Richfield, though, insisted on paying something, Atwood said, "and we got half our money back" on the group's investment in the leases. Richfield then bought some other leases and drilled on those, but with no luck. Finally, Richfield turned to the Atwood group leases, drilled on those and struck oil. Realizing the strike was a rich one, Atwood and his friends then bought more leases.

"We started leasing all over the Kenai Peninsula to other companies after that," Atwood said. "We went in deep then. The law limited us to 100,000 acres each and we all had the maximum level. We made money selling leases, but we didn't hold up the oil companies. So, my royalties all come from Kenai. I have no financial interest in oil anywhere else."

While declining to put a dollar figure on Atwood's oil wealth, the *Times*'s associate editor and general manager William J. Tobin told us it was "substantial." Other business sources have placed Atwood's earnings from oil at $1.5 million by 1977. His annual royalties from the Kenai oil fields were still running between $75,000 and $100,000 by 1977. It is not surprising that many critics believe Atwood's oil interests are at least partly responsible for the strong pro-oil news and editorial bias of the *Times*. Both Atwood and Tobin, who write most *Times* editorials, deny this. Says Tobin:

> We're accused of being in the pocket of big old dirty oil. Maybe that's a fair assessment somebody makes when they look at it from the Outside. We don't think we're in the pocket of big oil. We're interested in oil because the oil companies have contributed a very great deal to this state, and not just in money.

Says Atwood:

> They [the critics] are right to say I made some money from oil, but they're wrong to say that's the reason I support oil development in the state. I support oil because it's good for Alaska. I have nothing to gain from oil, except as a citizen of Alaska.

Be that as it may, the *Times* does go out of its way to defend its oil industry friends when they need help. In May 1976, for example, the oil drilling rig *George Ferris* got stuck in the mud of Kachemak Bay, causing great worry among fishing interests and environmentalists. They feared that the mired rig could cause a major oil spill which would kill marine life in the fish-rich and ecologically important bay. (Eventually the rig was blasted free with explosive charges.) In its May 12, 1976, editorial, "Oil Versus Fish," published before the problem was resolved, the *Times* pooh-poohed the environmental dangers, then went on to say how an oil spill could be something of a blessing in disguise:

> Monday what was described as a minimum amount of oil apparently oozed overboard. Its sheen spread from the rig in an obvious slick several miles long. Assuming that the oil slick does not represent a calamitous event, it might be regarded as beneficial in a sense.
>
> No oil, of course, would be ideal. But some oil, such as this, might give scientists an opportunity to come up with data that would show whether there really is cause for alarm. Maybe the marine life of Kachemak Bay can survive and flourish despite the inroads of industrial development. Maybe it can't.
>
> Maybe the *George Ferris* will provide the proof one way or the other.

Despite considerable evidence that oil spills can cause both short-term and long-term effects to marine life (see Chapter XII), the *Times*'s editorials accentuate the positive. Thus, the same editorial noted approvingly that oil company geologists "contend that oil and fish make very good neighbors and that there is no way oil and gas production activities can or will cause any substantial harm to shellfish or other marine life. Even in the event of a major calamity, the oilmen say, marine life will not be endangered."

Since oil tankers will carry the Prudhoe Bay oil to markets, most Alaskans are sensitive to oil spill dangers. Yet when the *Argo Merchant* ran aground off Nantucket Island, Massachusetts, on December 15, 1976, spilling 7.6 million gallons of oil and causing the largest Atlantic Coast oil spill ever, the *Times* weighed in with an editorial dismissing the spill as insignificant. It concluded that the "disaster was no such thing at all. And the sky didn't fall either." The list of editorials promoting and defending oil interests is a long one. A May 24, 1976, editorial typically entitled, "Don't Blame Big Oil," declared that those people who expressed concern over oil spills really were opposed to any kind of offshore or onshore oil development.

When it comes to Big Oil, the *Times* reminds one of a line from *Bambi:* "If you can't say nothin' nice, don't say nothin' at all." Not only does the *Times* abstain from any editorial criticism of the oil companies, it also protects the industry's pocketbooks from what it views as socialistic schemes to increase oil taxes. Virtually all of the presently known oil fields in Alaska are on federal or state lands, and are therefore the property of either the people of the United States or the people of Alaska. Yet instead of calling for the people to get a bigger share of the oil profits, the *Times* has repeatedly resisted such a temptation. In an early 1976 editorial, "Road to Socialism," the newspaper termed a variety of state legislative proposals for new oil taxes "astonishing." In ominous tones, the *Times* warned that the legislators making the proposals needed "a refresher course in the capitalistic system" because their taxation measures would mean that Alaska "is going to be the first to embrace socialism as a public policy." Suggestions that the oil companies could afford higher taxes, said the editorial, were "poppycock."[8]

The newspaper also permits its reporters and editors to take trips at the expense of the oil companies.[9] Managing Editor Clinton

[8] Michael Tanzer, a nationally known oil consultant hired by the state legislature, had just strongly suggested that state oil taxes could be increased by several hundred percent and still leave the oil companies with healthy profits.

[9] The ties between oil interests and the press in Alaska are fairly close and common. Alyeska, the pipeline consortium, oil companies, gas companies, and other development interests have former Alaska newspaper reporters working for them, and the Anchorage Press Club even has had as president a public relations official for Arctic Gas.

T. Andrews, Jr., told an interviewer in early 1977 that he had no qualms about sending a reporter, or going himself, on free trips at oil company expense. Such excursions, he said, "give us an opportunity to know them better." One of those who had benefited from a free trip—to New Orleans, courtesy of Shell Oil—was Andrews's wife, Susan Andrews, a *Times* reporter who often writes on oil topics.

While the *Times* instinctively supports the oil industry and a constellation of other development-oriented groups, it has entered into another, more puzzling editorial alliance. At first glance, the *Times*'s support for Teamsters Local 959 and its tough-minded chief, Jesse L. Carr, seems to contradict the *Times*'s conservative sympathies. Atwood has a businessman's hostility to organized labor, and his newspaper regularly opposes increases in workmen's compensation and tougher safety laws—two issues which are important to the Alaska Teamsters and the state's AFL-CIO-affiliated unions. But such differences are secondary to a more important concern shared by Jess Carr and his Teamsters, and by Bob Atwood and other Boomers in the state: the rapid, large-scale development of the state's oil, natural gas, mineral, and timber resources. Carr often sounds like the Chamber of Commerce, especially in his opposition to additional taxes on the oil industry. Whatever their differences on some traditional labor issues, Atwood and Carr agree that there are few, if any, limits to growth in Alaska.

Besides their philosophical similarities, Atwood has a more practical reason for currying favor with Carr. The *Times* fears that the hard-charging Teamsters will come in and organize workers at the newspaper.[10] In fact, the Teamsters made just such an effort in early 1976. According to the March 27, 1976, *Anchorage Daily News*, the Teamsters filed a petition with the National Labor Relations Board seeking a union representation election for drivers and mail wrappers at the *Times*. Curiously, five days later, in its April 1 edition, the *Times* endorsed Carr for governor even though the paper had never mentioned him for any political office before. The editor-

[10] The *Times*'s pressmen are unionized, though other employees were not. But in late 1976, the International Brotherhood of Electrical Workers filed a petition with the National Labor Relations Board seeking to represent most *Times* employees, including those in the newsroom. The employees rejected the IBEW in a close vote, but union organizers filed a list of complaints alleging harassment and other improper behavior by *Times* management. The issue was unresolved in early 1977, but a new representation election seemed likely, according to an NLRB spokesman quoted in the *Daily News*.

ial praised Carr for being a "tough, decisive . . . get-up-and-go guy" who would make a good governor. Five days later, on April 6, the Teamsters withdrew the petition that had been filed with the NLRB, sparking a lot of comment among *Times*-Teamsters critics over such an extraordinary coincidence.

Associate Editor General Manager Bill Tobin's cozy relationship with Carr also has something to do with the *Times*-Teamsters alliance. Tobin has always been a welcome guest at Teamster affairs. When Teamster International President Frank E. Fitzsimmons visited Alaska for the first time, in August 1976, in what was *the* major state Teamster event in recent years, Tobin served as master of ceremonies for the Teamster dinner in Anchorage honoring Fitzsimmons.[11] When we first interviewed Atwood shortly after that dinner, he said he saw no conflict of interest in Tobin's acting as master of ceremonies for an affair sponsored by one of the most controversial and newsworthy organizations in the state. In fact, Atwood said, it was logical for his general manager to preside at such an event, "because Bill is the best MC in town."

In an October 1976 interview, Tobin smiled when we asked him about the editorial he wrote endorsing Carr for governor.

> I said Jess Carr would be a good governor. My boss was kind of astonished when I said that, but what's a governor? He's an executive. He's got to be tough. I think he's got to be a doer, a guy of action, somebody who leads, particularly in Alaska with this constitution we've got that demands the leadership of a single individual. . . . The point was that whether you agree with him or disagree with him, he's a dynamic, action-type guy. And an awful lot of our friends, our social-type, business, Chamber of Commerce friends, said "good heavens, what are you doing writing an editorial that says maybe Jess Carr ought to be governor of Alaska?" But I did it more for fun than anything else, and the reaction was astonishing. I admire Jess Carr as an individual and regard him as a friend, because whatever else anybody might think of him, he's a man of his word.

Tobin also said: "I don't want the Teamsters coming in and organizing our plant." But he insisted that the *Times*'s endorsement of Carr was unrelated to Teamster organizing attempts at the paper. Whatever the case, it is unlikely that the *Times* will criticize Teamster

[11] The guests included the former Teamster president, Dave Beck, who served a prison sentence for union corruption; the former interior secretary and former governor, Walter J. Hickel; U.S. Senator Ted Stevens (Republican, Alaska); former governor William Egan; and members of the Teamster International executive board.

activities in its editorials or news columns as long as Tobin is general manager and associate editor.

In recent years, the *Times* has begun to forge another unlikely alliance with a traditional foe, this time with development-minded leaders of the Native corporations. The new cordiality marked a complete turnabout for Atwood, who in the late 1960s and early 1970s had been embroiled in a bitter fight with Eskimos, Indians, and Aleuts over their aboriginal land claims. But soon after passage of the landmark Alaska Native Claims Settlement Act in 1971, Atwood and the *Times* began to change their tune. The Act might just be a blessing in disguise, he reasoned, since it required the Native corporations to make a profit—a mandate which would enlist the Natives in the development cause. Atwood was right there to encourage their conversion to capitalism. A May 11, 1975, editorial, "Rich Natives: They Will Run Alaska," happily concluded:

> It is safe to predict that a major part of the future development in Alaska will be on the lands that are owned by the Natives. All these political and economic factors point to a brilliant opportunity for the Natives of Alaska. The future virtually belongs to them.

Similar editorials (such as the July 2, 1976, offering, "Native Groups Are Doers") approvingly noted the likelihood of widespread development of Native lands.

But pre–Claims Act editorials warned of imminent disaster for the state. Among other things, the *Times* declared, a generous Native settlement would "cripple the development of Alaska for all its citizens" and would have the effect of "sealing off" 97 percent of the state. One typical editorial, "AFN Asking Too Much" (December 5, 1969), exemplifies the *Times*'s technique of grossly overstating its opponents' position:

> The Natives are asking for everything—land, money, and resources—on a tax-free basis. The State and non-Natives would have only the marginal property and resources with which to build a tax base that would support the entire population—including the Natives.
>
> All the oil revenues from the North Slope would go to the Natives. All the royalties from the State [would be] turned over to the Natives.
>
> And when the process was completed, the Natives would own all the land that had economic value. They would have the lion's share of the revenues pouring into their treasury. They would control the development of the timber, oil, and fisheries.

They would have all this wealth tax-free. Their organization within the state would be more self-sufficient than the State itself. The State would be financially decrepit and helpless in meeting its responsibilities.

The State would have inadequate resources to provide the school, health, sanitation, law enforcement, and other programs that the law requires.

In addition to the editorials, the *Times* published a series of news articles by self-described land claims expert W. C. Arnold[12] that carried such typical headlines as "Goldberg Bill Would Tie Up the Best Land," "AFN Bill Called Peril to Forests," "Writer Sees State Loss of Fisheries," and "Writer Says Native Claims Bill Would Stifle Mining in Alaska." According to Mary Clay Berry in her incisive book, *The Alaska Pipeline*, Arnold's articles were "a startling mishmash of misinformation and innuendo."

Because the *Times* was the paper most Alaskans read, many non-Native state residents had gross misconceptions not only about the land claims issue, but about the Natives themselves. The *Times*'s almost-daily outbursts against the Native claims sparked a deluge of letters to members of Congress protesting the "giveaway" to the Natives. Summing up Atwood's role in fighting the Native Claims Act, Berry wrote:

The *Times* articulated the views of a powerful clique in Alaska represented by the Chambers of Commerce throughout the state. Atwood gave these views respectability by putting them into print. He was, one Native leader remarked bitterly, appealing to the "dark side of human nature." His editorials opened the floodgates, and many non-Natives, from bankers to homesteaders, began to say publicly what they may previously have thought or said only privately.

Despite his recent friendly overtures to some Native leaders, many Natives still aren't ready to think of Bob Atwood as their friend and ally. One such leader is Roy Huhndorf, president of Cook Inlet Region, Inc., the Native regional corporation in the Anchorage area. Huhndorf told us in an October 1976 interview that he believed that the *Times*'s editorial policy continues to be racist when Native interests conflict with other powerful interests:

When it comes to a clash between racism and economic interests, the *Times* often has difficulty making up its mind. It has gotten to the point, though,

[12] As previously noted, Arnold at one time during pre-statehood days had been the chief lobbyist for the canned salmon interests and had argued then that statehood could not be granted until the Native land claims were settled.

where the *Times* and other business interests often will let their economic interests win out over their racism.

As the Natives continue to evolve into one of the state's most powerful groups, it is a good bet that the *Times* will step up its late-blooming support for Native corporations. For there is nothing in the recent record of the *Times* to show that it would criticize the state's business and social establishment in any significant way; those weaker minorities who challenge the leading circle—the environmentalists, and the Natives before the land claims settlement—can expect less hospitable treatment. In a twist on an old social justice credo, Atwood carries out a philosophy of comforting the comfortable and afflicting the afflicted.

In one of our two interviews with him, for example, Atwood volunteered that his newspaper has a go-easy policy toward Alaska's more prominent citizens. He called it "a certain hometown policy we hang onto" from the days when the *Times* was a small-town newspaper. "We don't report arrests of professional people," Atwood said. "If they come to trial, we will report that. But accountants, doctors, professional people—we give them soft treatment because their reputations could really be hurt if they're arrested, even if the charges are dropped later." The publisher defended this double standard by maintaining he personally knows of cases in which policemen have arrested certain professional people simply because they held a grudge against them. No such policy of withholding publication exists, however, regarding arrests of non-professionals.

Friends of the *Times* also get front-page coverage for events that most newspapers would put in the society pages or would bury deep in the paper. M. R. (Muktuk) Marston, for example, had organized some 4,500 Alaska Natives in remote areas of the state as a protective force during World War II and, after the war, built this nucleus into a state National Guard. He also was a delegate to the state's constitutional convention in 1955–56 and a housing developer in the Anchorage area. Although Marston had many achievements, his is hardly a household name in the state. Yet the *Times*, in its October 25, 1976, edition, informed its readers in a front-page story and picture that Marston had been married the day before in Honolulu to Elsie Harvey, an employee in the *Times* advertising department for eleven years before retiring in 1974.

This reward-your-friends, punish-your-enemies approach to

news and editorial coverage is the hallmark of the *Times* philosophy. Few know it better than Bill Parker, an ebullient Anchorage Democrat who served two terms in the state House of Representatives until he ran afoul of the *Times* and other growth interests over the Atwood-created capital move issue.[13] Parker, whose voting record was strongly pro-consumer, questioned the cost of the capital move in 1975 and 1976—just before he was up for reelection. He argued that the state had more pressing priorities than the relocation of the capital at a potential cost of $2 billion. Parker's criticisms did not square too well with the *Times*'s regular capital move news and feature stories, which cited low potential costs and which downplayed and criticized high estimates. During the months preceding the election, the *Times* ran a series of buzz-saw editorials and news articles that regularly reminded people that "Bill Parker of *Juneau*" (as the *Times* once sarcastically referred to him) was a foe of the capital move. Nor did the *Times* let up. Twice—two and three days before the 1976 general election—the newspaper ran repetitive capital-move editorials reminding voters that Parker was the bad guy on the issue. The steady drumbeat of anti-Parker editorials, along with anti-Parker ads bought by front groups for business interests and the Teamsters, had their desired effects. He was defeated decisively in the November 1976 election.

The editorials against Parker seem almost mild compared to the *Times*'s regular, scathing attacks on Governor Jay Hammond. Although both Atwood and Hammond are Republicans, their views on development are quite at odds. Unlike most previous Alaska governors, Hammond takes a generally cautious approach: development must pay its own way through taxes, royalties, and jobs; develop-

[13] The *Times* was continuing its news and editorial campaign for the capital move in 1977; it feared that some legislators, who were concerned with the potential multi-billion-dollar cost, were trying to kill the proposal. On March 7, 1977, an editorial entitled "Incredible" attacked opponents of the capital move, saying: "There is reason to believe that opponents of relocation are conjuring up phony figures for the purpose of frightening rather than enlightening Alaskans. Their sincerity is questionable. . . ."

Until late 1976, the *Times* had never had a full-time Juneau correspondent. Then, the *Times* selected one and gave him a primary responsibility of riding herd on the capital move issue. It should be noted that, if the *Times* continues to have a Juneau bureau, only it and the Associated Press will be providing daily year-round coverage of the state capital, besides the small-circulation *Southeast Alaska Empire*, the capital's lone daily, which has little circulation outside its own area. Most other dailies do provide Juneau coverage during the legislative sessions.

ment must not be subsidized; it must be controlled and planned; and it must do minimum damage to the environment and to Alaskans' way of life. For this, Hammond has been repeatedly denounced as a no-growther in *Times* editorials that appeared both before and after the 1974 gubernatorial election. (See Chapter IV.) A few random anti-Hammond editorial headlines include: "The No-Growth Syndrome" (January 5, 1976); "Lock the Door" (January 19, 1976); "No Growth at Berners Bay" (March 16, 1976); and "Planning for No-Growth" (mid-May, 1976). The editorials are mostly variations on the same theme: Hammond is stifling the economic growth of Alaska. Atwood and Tobin made it quite clear to us that a major priority for the *Times* is to prevent Hammond from winning a second term, and to get a super-growther into the governor's office in 1978.[14]

Besides praising friends and attacking perceived enemies of growth, Atwood also has used his newspaper to respond to personal criticism. In the 1976 state legislative primary election campaign, Anchorage Democratic candidate Bill Weimar criticized a senior citizens' property tax exemption law which saved Atwood $5,000 a year. In Weimar's slick, very effective sixty-second television spots, the camera lingered over two luxurious houses belonging to Atwood and his brother-in-law, Anchorage banker Elmer Rasmuson—two of the wealthiest citizens in the state. Without mentioning the two men's names, Weimar asked voters if it was fair to grant property tax exemptions to homeowners of such obvious wealth.[15] "The basic thing to keep in mind," Weimar said, "is that those two men applied

[14] In Atwood's lone bid for public office in 1956 against later three-term Governor William A. Egan, he apparently did not unduly use the influence of his newspaper to promote his own candidacy. "As I remember it, he did not use his newspaper in any unusual way," Egan recalled in early 1977.

That election was an outgrowth of the 1955–56 state constitutional convention which adopted the so-called "Alaska-Tennessee Plan." This plan was based on the statehood strategies used by several former territories, including Tennessee. The territories would hold a constitutional convention, then elect two "senators," and send them to the nation's capital to present the case for statehood. In all, seven territories achieved statehood in this manner, but the plan got lost in the mists of the nineteenth century until Alaska tried to revive it. So, in 1956, Atwood, a Republican, was nominated for one of the "Senate" seats against the Democrat, Egan. Egan and Ernest Gruening won the Senate seat elections, and Ralph Rivers won the House seat, making it a clean sweep for the Democrats. When they went to Washington, D.C., however, the three were barred from floor privileges, and Alaska later attained statehood in 1959 after a vote of Congress, rather than through the Tennessee Plan.

[15] Atwood lives in a white, pillared mansion in the exclusive Turnagain area of Cook Inlet in Anchorage. His mansion is reputedly the biggest house in the state.

for the exemption; it wasn't automatic. They knew what they were doing. It seems obvious to me that when your net worth is in the multimillions you can afford to pay all your taxes."

Weimar's television ads brought a quick response from the *Times*; so quick, in fact, that the *Times* published an editorial on the subject even before the ad first appeared—indicating that someone had tipped off Atwood. Instead of confining its response to the editorial page, the newspaper ran a series of news articles lamenting the plight of elderly, property-owning citizens. The clear impression given was that those who wanted to tax the wealthy elderly were trying to hurt all senior citizens. Yet Weimar was not criticizing the property tax exemption for senior citizens on limited income but for millionaires and other wealthy citizens who had no legitimate need for the tax break.

The *Times*'s first editorial on the subject on July 30, 1976 pointed out that Atwood had "given the money saved from his tax bills to a foundation for use in some public project." But it failed to explain why he had bothered to file for the exemption in the first place. In its further defense of the tax exemption, the editorial argued that though the 1971 law originally had covered only senior citizens with annual incomes of less than $10,000, state legislators had removed that provision in 1972 because they "thought it unfair for an Alaskan to be 'penalized for being a success' and that the state should encourage all Alaskans to stay here."

Four days later, the *Times* discovered that the law had been further amended in the 1976 session to reduce or eliminate in 1977 the tax exemption for those senior citizens whose property fell into the highest 25 percent of assessed properties statewide. Atwood and Rasmuson would thus receive no exemption. Instead of preparing a news article on wealthy taxpayers who had been receiving big tax breaks over the last few years, the *Times* managed to find perhaps the only elderly couple in the Anchorage area who would be seriously hurt by the amended law. In the same issue (August 13), the *Times* ran an editorial, "The Shotgun Approach," which contended that the amended law was nothing more than an effort by state Senator Bill Ray of Juneau to "get" Bob Atwood.

* * *

The newspaper readers of Anchorage are fortunate in at least one respect. Their city is one of a relative handful in the country where genuine newspaper competition still exists, if only by a thin financial thread, and it would be difficult to find two more contrasting papers in any city. Where the *Times* is stridently right-wing and hard-hitting, the *Anchorage Daily News* is thoughtful and low-key in its generally liberal editorials. Where the *Times* gives scant news coverage to organizations concerned with social justice, the environment, and consumer affairs, the *Daily News* gives such groups reasonable and fair exposure. Where the *Times* supports all growth as good per se, the *Daily News* questions and analyzes proposals on their merits. The *Daily News* is also the only daily newspaper in the state with any claims to investigative news reporting. It won the 1976 Gold Medal Pulitzer Prize for public service for its articles analyzing the growing economic and political influence of the Alaska Teamsters, and it has won a half dozen other major national journalism awards in recent years. But, in ironic counterpoint, the *Times* is a thick and prosperous-looking newspaper while the *Daily News* manages a look of beleaguered but resolute quality at less than half the size of the *Times*, and with considerably less advertising.

Where the *Times* does not hesitate to use its editorial page to further the self-interests of its publisher, the *Daily News* runs a more democratic news and editorial operation. When a financial disclosure law for all state government commission and committee members took effect in 1974, publisher Kay Fanning was among 200 persons who resigned their state commission posts in protest. She had been a member of the Alaska Broadcasting Commission. Departing from Atwood's standard procedure, Fanning did not attempt to use her newspaper's editorial or news columns to register her personal protest, according to present and former *Daily News* staffers. In fact, the *Daily News* offered strong support for the financial disclosure law, despite Fanning's obvious disagreement.

Nowhere was the journalistic contrast between the *Times* and the *Daily News* more evident than in the way the two newspapers cover controversial issues and powerful economic interests: the *Daily News* won a Pulitzer Prize for its Teamster articles; the *Times* cozied up to the union. The *Daily News* regularly conducted in-depth reports of the Prudhoe Bay oil and the pipeline—before and during construction. In 1969, for example the *Daily News* ran a thirty-one-part series exploring various issues surrounding the Prudhoe Bay oil and the then-proposed construction of the pipeline. The scope of the series, as outlined in the first article, covered themes that the *Times* scarcely touched in the years to come:

> Alaska is facing its first environmental crisis. Two of its most valuable resources—oil and wilderness—are in conflict. . . .

Is it technically possible to remove the oil without ruining the North Slope's wilderness values? If not, how much damage can be considered acceptable?

If the tundra is damaged now, can it be repaired? What effect will oil development have on the wild fowl, the grizzlies, the caribou and the wolves on land, the fish in the streams, and the seals, walruses, whales, and polar bears offshore?

Perhaps most important, what is the oil industry's responsibility in developing the North Slope oil discovery? What is government's responsibility? What is the public responsibility? . . .

A 1975 *Daily News* series at the height of pipeline construction analyzed the potential oil surplus on the West Coast once the pipeline oil began to flow in 1977, the problems and dangers involved in transporting the oil from the pipeline terminal port at Valdez to West Coast ports, the impact Alaskan oil would have on the world oil market, and other complex issues. A fourteen-part series in 1976 investigated poor management on the pipeline project, the project's cost overruns, environmental problems, the controversy over inadequate welds, and the intricate financial relationships among the major oil companies owning the pipeline and Prudhoe Bay oil. It was fine reporting, not just by Alaskan standards, but by the standards of major metropolitan newspapers.

It is one of the real ironies of Alaska that one of the nation's best small papers was one of the most financially precarious as of early 1977. Although the *Daily News* had been financially ailing for years, many people believed that the beginning of the end came in December 1974 when the *Times* and the *Daily News* entered into a joint operating agreement. Under the pact, the *Daily News* retained its editorial independence and news staff but relinquished control of its business operations—printing, circulation, advertising, and other functions—to the *Times*. The *Daily News* was left with only a newsroom operation. Such agreements between newspaper competitors, authorized by the Newspaper Preservation Act of 1970 to sustain ailing newspapers, have worked reasonably well in many other cities of the Lower-48. But such last resort agreements rarely have included the major concessions that the *Daily News* made.

The most damaging concession made by the *Daily News* was agreeing to give up the keystone of its operation—its fat Sunday paper. Not only was it the only Sunday paper in the state, but the edition produced about half of the *Daily News*'s revenue—and was clearly the prize Atwood most coveted. The *Times*, formerly a six-day operation, thus began publishing seven days a week by 1975, and the *News* was never able to recover the revenue lost by giving up its 25,405 circulation Sunday paper. Worse, the *News*'s daily circulation immediately began to fall after the agreement took effect—plummeting from 15,404 to 13,700 by mid-1976. Worse still, home delivery fell from 11,600 a day to about 7,600 in the same period.

The joint agreement obligated the *Times* to promote the *Daily News* equally with the *Times* in terms of advertising and circulation. But given the opposition voice the *News* offered on development issues, turning these responsibilities over to Atwood was a little like giving General Motors control over American Motors's advertising campaign. Indeed, one of the *Daily News*'s most serious problems became promotion. On such a simple matter as answering the phones, the *Times* refused to alter its policy of answering "*Anchorage Times*," instead of "Anchorage Newspapers" or "*Anchorage Times* and *Daily News*." Supporters of the *Daily News* told us that the *Times* also failed to push advertising and circulation for the *Daily News;* used only the name "*Times*" on advertising billings, subscription forms, and delivery trucks; and failed to inform advertisers of the low discount rates given ads appearing in both papers.

Finally, on February 9, 1977, the *Daily News* filed a $16.5 million suit against the *Times* in U.S. District Court in Anchorage. The suit alleged antitrust violations, breach of contract and fraudulent inducement to contract, among other things. Basically, the suit contended that the *Times* failed to live up to the agreement by allegedly failing to promote the *Daily News* with the diligence required under the agreement.

To explain how the *Daily News* got into its financial difficulties requires a little background and history. The paper was founded in 1946 as a weekly by Norman C. Brown, a former *Times* employee. It soon blossomed into a seven-day-a-week operation, and served as an anti-statehood counterbalance to Atwood's *Times*. In 1967 Brown sold the paper for $450,000 to Katherine and Larry Fanning. Kay Fanning, the daughter of a wealthy Joliet, Illinois, banker, is the former wife of one of the nation's richest men, Chicago businessman and newspaper magnate, Marshall Field, IV.[16] After her divorce from Field, she moved to Alaska in 1965 with her three children and took a job as a librarian with the *Daily News*. She worked her way into reporting and after about a year she returned to Chicago to

[16] The Field family controls the *Chicago Sun-Times*, the *Chicago Daily News*, and World Book Encyclopedia, in addition to owning retail stores and real estate.

marry Larry Fanning, an executive editor of the *Chicago Sun-Times*. When the couple returned to Alaska for the ostensible purpose of moving Kay and her children out, Larry Fanning was immediately taken with the state—just as Kay said she knew he would be. They decided to stay and, after a year of negotiations, purchased the paper from Brown. Larry Fanning viewed the paper as a laboratory for both training young reporters and providing in-depth, quality coverage of major Alaskan issues that was lacking in the state's other news media. After her husband died in 1971, Kay Fanning decided to continue to run the paper—even though the *News* was losing money and its antiquated plant and decrepit equipment were inadequate to build up the newspaper.

For many years, the paper was able to absorb its huge deficits through family members' underwriting them. (Deficits grew to $625,034 the year before the operating agreement was signed and reached a peak of $942,782 in 1975.) Most of this money came from the trust fund of Frederick Field, Kay Fanning's son. But by 1974, her twenty-three-year-old son grew less willing to continue to subsidize the sinking paper. So, Fanning told us, the *Daily News* went into the joint operating agreement with the *Times* in December 1974 in an effort "to reduce and eventually eliminate the deficit." However, by October 1976, the deficit was "just as bad as when we went into the agreement" and her family's ability to keep absorbing the deficit had "vanished."

The *Daily News*'s financial plight became public knowledge in late 1976 when the paper was forced to eliminate nine job slots in the newsroom. This left the paper with just five reporters, one photographer, a features editor, and three desk people, two of whom were the paper's top editors. It also left the *News* without a librarian or copy aides to answer telephones, tear off wire copy, and take news releases over the phone. Hardly the way for a daily newspaper to survive in a city of 175,000.

The word quickly got around the community: the *Daily News* was in deep trouble. In a highly unusual outburst of public spiritedness, a group of business people, environmentalists, lawyers, and social activists banded together to help save the *Daily News* by drumming up more advertising and subscribers. Big-money investment in the paper was solicited and some persons even volunteered to fill on a part-time basis some of the newsroom jobs eliminated earlier. In November 1976 the Bristol Bay Native Corporation provided a $70,000 loan that could be converted into a minority equity interest.[17] At the time of that loan, Robert C. Bacon, general manager of the Native firm, said that other Native corporations also were studying the possibility of aid to the faltering newspaper.

Despite these extraordinary efforts, the *News*'s financial outlook continued bleak. The subscription drive had boosted circulation to almost 15,700 by February 1977 but that was still a far cry from the 25,000 Fanning told us was necessary for the *News* to survive. By the spring of 1977, the paper was struggling along on a week-to-week basis with the help of small loans and contributions. Then, in early May, following a fund-raising tour Outside, Fanning announced she had secured $500,000 in pledges, enough to keep the *Daily News* afloat for one year. While she wouldn't identify the sources of the paper's temporary solvency, we learned that a substantial portion of the new funding had come from the Natives. Nonetheless, Fanning said, the key to long-term success lay in winning the lawsuit.[18]

In addition to the *News*, the best hope for quality and fairness in the state's news media is a new weekly statewide newspaper that began publication in early 1977. Called the *Alaska Advocate*, the new newspaper was started by three former *Daily News* employees and two former Alaska-based Associated Press reporters. Among the paper's founders is Howard Weaver, one of the three *Daily News* reporters who wrote the Pulitzer Prize–winning Teamsters series for the *News*. In an October 1976 interview, Weaver said the *Advocate* founders hoped to follow the tradition of the muckraking *Texas Observer*. He said the paper will provide in-depth coverage of issues which simply aren't being covered by most of the state's news media—issues such as development proposals which vitally affect

[17] The Native firm's loan had one unfortunate immediate consequence: the *Daily News* killed a story written by one of its reporters concerning the profitability of Native corporations. The story would have reported that the Bristol Bay firm experienced a $390,000 loss in 1975. *News* editors said the story was killed because the report on which it was based was too vague.

[18] One of the more peculiar suggestions for financial assistance for the *Daily News* came from Benjamin C. Bradlee, the executive editor of the *Washington Post*. Bradlee suggested to Fanning that she seek funds from Atlantic Richfield, the oil giant which in late 1976 purchased the *London Observer*. That move prompted concern among many journalists and consumer advocates, such as Ralph Nader, who feared it presaged a disturbing trend of huge corporations buying up newspapers in order to spread their message. Bradlee's suggestion also ignored the fact that Arco is one of the major owners of Prudhoe Bay oil, and that for the *Daily News* to become indebted to it would severely compromise the newspaper's ability to cover pipeline and other oil-related news.

the future of the state. "We will have a definite point of view," Weaver said, "but we're not going to be an organ of the New Left or anything like that. Our appeal will be more to conservationists than to developers, but we'll also be a paper that developers will feel they'll have to read."

Judging by its first six months of issues in 1977, the *Advocate* may be the best thing to happen to Alaska journalism since Fanning purchased the *Daily News.* If the *Advocate* is able to survive, its viewpoint obviously would provide a welcome contrast to that of the *Times.* And, with bureaus in Anchorage, Fairbanks, Juneau, and even Washington, D.C., the *Advocate* is providing the closest thing to true year-round statewide coverage that Alaska has yet seen. Still, a small, underfunded weekly cannot begin to counterbalance the impact of perhaps the most powerful daily—in terms of influence over its local community—in the U.S. With the demise of the *Daily News,* that influence could only grow.

Eat your heart out, Bill Loeb.

IV

The Bush-Rat Governor

Now there are those who covet our largesse and view Alaska as a resource bank from which they would withdraw. And make no mistake, withdraw they will, for already they have passbooks and hold seats upon the board. But withdrawals from a bank are made in many ways: funds tolled out by tellers in sound commerce, or blasted from the vaults by brigands in the night. What choices that be ours must quickly be decided, guards posted and the interest rates established, lest we find a run made on the bank which leaves us naught but shambles of a future which may still be ours.

—Alaska Governor Jay S. Hammond, in his inaugural address, January 18, 1975

JAY HAMMOND is not your common garden-variety politician. He is an unusual political creature—a highly articulate former bush pilot, a bearded Republican who has been trying to put some reins on the threat of runaway development in the state, a pro-environmental fiscal conservative. And, before he became governor, a fairly obscure mayor and state legislator.

"Why did a relatively unknown like Hammond get elected governor in 1974?" Bob Bradley, an Anchorage area Democratic state legislator, asked us rhetorically. "It's because Hammond *is* Alaska. Have you seen or heard the guy? He's tall but not that tall. Yet the way he's built, the way he stands up so straight, he looks like a towering figure, like a goddamn Alaskan mountain. And that voice. He sounds like a goddamn untamed, rushing Alaskan river. And he was a homesteader. That's all part of the Alaskan mystique. And that beard. Beards aren't as common in Alaska as you might think. So that beard shows people he's independent. If someone asked me to construct someone who symbolized Alaska, I'd have him look and sound just like Jay Hammond."

But even if Hammond is Alaska, it does not mean he is uncontroversial. In his two years in office, Hammond has provided little comfort to the "brigands" who represent the forces for super-growth in Alaska. In fact, he might well borrow a line from a popular comedian in the 1960s and ask the state's powerful pro-development interests: Is there any group here I haven't offended?

By 1977, with his term half completed, Hammond was under regular attack as a "no-growther" by the *Ancorage Times.* Alaska Teamster boss Carr was denouncing him as a foe of development who opposed the creation of more jobs, and more Teamsters, in the state. Chamber of Commerce and business leaders were depicting the governor as a man who was strangling the state economically and denying Alaska's treasures to the rest of the U.S. The oil companies were gearing up to fight expected Hammond administration proposals to increase the state's share of oil production wealth, and were unhappy with Hammond's efforts to slow down the timetable for exploration of the federally-owned offshore lands on Alaska's outer continental shelf. And some of the more growth-minded Native leaders were distressed over Hammond's go-slow approach on road construction and mineral and oil development, which they saw as delaying the money-making potential of the Native regional corporations created under the 1971 Alaska Native Claims Settlement Act.

Then, too, some people who could be considered generally friendly to Hammond were unhappy as his term reached the halfway point. Some environmentalists felt that while the governor's heart was in the right place, he was too quick to compromise with the "brigands" rather than oppose them to the last barricade. Many culturally-oriented Natives criticized Hammond for being insufficiently concerned about maintaining the Natives' subsistence way of life. And some state legislators who basically shared his controlled development philosophy accused the governor of indecision in implementing his policies and of failure to work with them on such weighty matters as additional oil taxation. Worse, Hammond's own Republican party leaders viewed him as some sort of closet socialist who had betrayed the state GOP's guiding principle that business must be free to work its will on Alaska.

Although Hammond insisted that the criticism from the various prodevelopment forces showed that he must be doing something right and was not pandering to any special interests, he was nonetheless bothered by the criticism. So much so, in fact, that he often trimmed either his positions, or tone, or both, to try to show he really wasn't that much at variance with the super-growthers. In a number of speeches in 1976 and early 1977, in a defensive response to "no-growth" charges, he emphasized the development schemes he had supported. In his January 11, 1977, State of the State speech to the legislature, he laid out a whole string of actions he said he had taken to promote growth in Alaska:

> Our opposition to unnecessary Environmental Protection Agency restraints imposed on Ketchikan Pulp Company [cited for water pollution]; our support of an [oil] reserves tax credit; our veto of an extremely costly workman's compensation bill; our establishment of state budget limits through exercise of more vetoes than all other governors together; and our support of a trans-Alaska gas pipeline must confuse those who have been told this administration was determined to suppress even healthy enterprise. The truth is that we will no more stifle healthy growth than we will subsidize that which is unhealthy. . . . Despite those intent upon garbling that message, it seems slowly to be seeping out. I have little doubt that before this legislature adjourns . . . most of the electorate will recognize that the cost of doing business in Alaska, not phony charges of intent to do in Alaskan business, will determine the rate and health of our development.

At other times, however, Hammond charges ahead like a wounded Kodiak bear to tangle with those favoring rapid growth. A Lincoln Day speech on February 12, 1976, to Republicans in Fairbanks was one such occasion. The governor assailed his own party "as a special interest group of economic elitists who ever place spiritual, social, moral and environmental concerns second to economic considerations." And, he warned that the party must shed its "image of a wealthy, fat-cat, antiintellectual who, within his narrow, purse-string soul has no coin of compassion for the problems of the 'little man.' " Otherwise, he said, the party would die, deservedly so. Hardly the stuff of party unity. Then, Hammond really got divisive, telling the Republicans he didn't care if his limited-growth approach offended any "special interest" group, including the Republican party:

> It's my belief this state had gotten far off track simply because too many in political office succumb to special interest pressures in order to secure re-election. . . . Yet, according to some political observers more competent than I to assess such matters, Republicans may be the last to get the mes-

sage. Several public pulse takers have told me they believe that if a general election were held right now, I'd be unbeatable, yet most believe I could not make it through the primary. I suspect they're right.

Hammond may be, as some of his critics contend, an accidental governor who will fail because he breaks so many political rules. Or it could be that he is today one of the shrewdest politicians in the United States and has hit on a unique formula for winning reelection. A look at the political arithmetic tells Hammond that most people in the state are not oil company officials or Teamster leaders or Republicans or Chamber of Commerce activists. Hammond made it clear in late 1976 that he believed he had the support of most Natives, environmentalists, small business people, rank-and-file union members, liberal Democrats, independents and those Republicans who are concerned with the "Alaska way of life"—the rank and file of Alaska. And he realized that party labels are not of overwhelming importance in a state where in 1976 over half the registered voters (54 percent) were independents and only 15 percent Republicans.

As befits a man who presents himself to the voters as a maverick and non-politician, Hammond, until well into his thirties, stayed out of elective politics. Still, his early years do offer an abundance of clues that politics was something that came naturally to him.

Born July 21, 1922, in Troy, New York, the son of a Methodist minister, Jay Hammond was graduated from Scotia (New York) High School in 1940. His school's 1940 yearbook shows Hammond as the all-American boy—and a successful politician. As a sophomore, he was home room treasurer; as a junior, he was homeroom president and a member of the student senate; by his final year, he was president of both the senior class and the student senate. He was also a member of the National Honor Society in his senior year, played on the varsity basketball and football teams in his junior and senior years, and was tabbed by the yearbook editors as "most popular boy."

After finishing high school, Hammond studied petroleum engineering for two years at Penn State before enlisting in the navy. He served as a marine fighter pilot during World War II and was discharged with the rank of captain in 1946. Influenced by stories of Alaska he had heard as a child, and by his love of camping and the outdoors, Hammond bought a 1929-vintage Loening Keystone amphibious airplane after the war to make a trip to Alaska. While test-flying it, he crashed in Onondaga Lake near Syracuse, New York, in July 1946. Unhurt, he repaired the plane and set off for Anchorage. "When I crossed that border, it was like coming home for the first time," Hammond recalled. "Miles and miles of open land without any evidence of man."

Until the plane crashed again in October 1946, Hammond used it to fly a trap line for beaver, otter, mink, wolverine, and marten. He then worked as a trapper and apprentice guide until he reinjured his back, which he had initially hurt during one of the two serious crashes in which he was involved during the war. While recuperating, he decided to go back to college and received a B.S. degree in biological sciences from the University of Alaska in 1948. He then worked as a pilot-agent for the U.S. Fish and Wildlife Service until 1956. During that period, in another brush with death, he broke both of his legs in a freak airplane accident on King Cove.

He married Bella Gardiner of Dillingham, Alaska, in 1952. After he left federal employ, the Hammonds began homesteading at Lake Clark, in south central Alaska, in 1956. Hammond also built a house in Naknek on the Alaska Peninsula, fished commercially for salmon, and served as a master guide and air taxi operator. In 1959, after being persuaded by friends to run, he was elected to the Alaska House of Representatives as an independent. He switched to the Republican party two years later because, he said, "it became impossible to stay in the middle." During six years in the House, he attained the posts of minority whip and majority whip. In 1965 he became mayor of Bristol Bay Borough. In 1966 he was elected to the state Senate, where he served over the next six years as majority whip, majority leader, chairman of the Rules and Resources committees, and Senate president. He did not seek reelection in 1972 after his district was drastically reapportioned, but ran and was once again elected mayor of Bristol Bay Borough, serving in that job until he was elected governor in 1974.

In that 1974 election, the smart money most definitely was not on Hammond. Although not a complete political unknown due to his past legislative service, Hammond faced the formidable task of having to defeat two former governors—Walter J. Hickel and Keith H. Miller—in the Republican primary, and then an incumbent Democratic governor, William A. Egan, in the general election. Hickel, the former U.S. secretary of the interior, was the heavy favorite in the GOP primary because of his name and his substantial financial support from development forces. However, Hickel underestimated Hammond and saved his money for an anticipated tough battle with Egan. Hammond won the primary with almost 29,000 votes to Hickel's 21,000, and then, despite almost daily attacks on him as a "no-growther" by the *Anchorage Times*, squeaked past Egan by 287 votes.

During the 1974 campaign, Hammond did not shy away from his environmentalist views. "I've been accused of being a conservationist," he would say. "To that I plead guilty." Being a conservationist was supposed to be a political liability in Alaska, according to the prevailing wisdom of 1974. This was due mainly to the fact that the term had come to mean Outside interests, largely because most of the key environmental lobbying efforts and lawsuits affecting the state originated with organizations based in Washington, D.C., or California. Also, the constant pounding on environmentalists by the *Anchorage Times* and other development forces made even Alaskan conservationists somewhat wary of the terms. In addition, many people in the state were still seething over the environmental organizations' efforts to block construction of the trans-Alaska oil pipeline. And Hammond was especially vulnerable on this issue because he had gone on record early as opposing issuance of the federal permit for the pipeline until adequate consideration was given to proposed alternative routes (favored by environmentalists) that would have run partly through Canada. "At the time," Hammond said of his early pipeline position, "it was like shrieking an obscenity in church."

But despite these formidable obstacles, Jay Hammond, the self-described "bush rat who's more at home with his gum boots in bilge water," became governor of Alaska. What did it mean? Some Hammond supporters said it showed there was a silent but substantial environmentalist bloc in the state. Many development-oriented people said that Hammond's victory proved nothing of the sort. They said Hickel was pompous and unlovable, and Egan just ran a poor campaign and never tried to win over disaffected liberal elements in his own party. To others, Hammond's win was due to the "fresh-face" theory—he was the only nongovernor or non–former governor running and was also picturing himself as a non-politician. People were tired of the Hickels, the Egans, the Millers, and they just wanted someone not tied to the past.

What won the election for Hammond, according to Attorney General Avrum M. Gross, was a basic mistake by Egan which helped Hammond build a winning coalition of liberal Democrats, traditional Republicans and independent environmentalists. Gross, one of the many Democrats appointed to key posts in the Hammond administration, said that Egan's mistake came in 1970 after the Democratic gubernatorial primary in which he defeated Larry Carr, who was supported by most of the Democratic party's liberal wing. Although Carr was badly beaten, Gross said the primary showed "that a substantial segment of the Democratic party—nearly two fifths of it—was dissatisfied with the prospect of an Egan governorship. . . . [But] instead of trying to bring the Carr people back into the party, they in essence slammed the door on them." The miscalculation, Gross said, was that the liberals would have no choice in 1974 but to support Egan, since the Republicans were virtually certain of putting up a more conservative candidate for governor.

In 1972 the Carr supporters worked actively for the presidential candidacy of Senator George McGovern (Democrat, South Dakota) and joined with a new group of young Democratic activists in an organization which came to be known as the Ad Hoc Democrats. The new organization succeeded in electing a majority of McGovern delegates from Alaska to the Democratic National Convention. "But in the long run," Gross said, "the most significant aspect of Ad Hoc, as I see it, was that it kept alive and injected new blood into the coalition which opposed the established power base within the Democratic party. It was in essence a movement in search of a leader, and in 1974 the leader appeared . . . not within the Democratic party but within the Republican party and he appeared at exactly the right time. In the era of Watergate, Jay Hammond was a real political phenomenon—an expert politician who had never gained the image of being a politician . . . [who] had friends that stretched across the state and across the political spectrum. . . ."

According to Gross, Hammond's unlikely coalition "came from people discouraged with the course of government, both on a national and state level, people looking for a change, be it in style or government personnel. . . . There were several common threads which ran through all of these groups, but perhaps the basic issue was that of development."

Beyond the campaign issues, simple personal charm went a long way in holding together Hammond's coalition. Anchorage Democrat Bill Parker, no great fan of Hammond's, called him "a terrible governor. His attorney general [Gross] really runs the state through the legal advice he gives the governor," Parker asserted. But, he added, no more charismatic figure than Hammond has ever appeared on the Alaska political scene. It was this charisma, as much as anything, that was conveyed to the voters in 1974. Parker, a former state legislator, said, "He's a good-looking son of a bitch. He wears a fifty-inch jacket and he's got this thirty-two-inch waist. He ran these TV commercials in the '74 campaign that were the best goddamn thing ever to hit this state. The commercials were full of circle logic and epigrams, like the Sermon on the Mount. One of the spots was something like, 'You can tell a lot about a man by the way he builds his house.' And it showed him flying in to his cabin on Lake Clark, even splitting logs and everything, and with his kids and wife. Those commercials told you he was a bush pilot, a prophet, a builder, an outdoorsman, a loving father and husband. The other candidates never knew what hit them."

Hammond continued to project that image after becoming governor. In a state admirably disdainful of stuffed shirts, Hammond fits in well. He seems unimpressed with the trappings of power and has not isolated himself from the public with layers of aides. A number of Alaskans, ranging from environmentalists to lobbyists for commercial interests, told us Hammond was remarkably accessible, as were other top members of his administration. An incident witnessed by one of the authors gives an insight into Hammond's apparent lack of pretension. Like all previous governors, Hammond has no private plane—despite the fact that Alaska is a state in which most communities are accessible only by air. On a late 1976 flight, Hammond and an aide arrived at the airport counter too late to get adjacent seats in tourist class. So, the governor and his aide sat apart during the flight.

Another characteristic of Hammond that cheers his supporters and infuriates his opponents in his style of attacking his political foes. For example, Teamster boss Carr, in late 1975, was the target of this barbed reply from Hammond after he had assailed the governor for allegedly stifling state growth:

> My concern is not with the rank and file Teamster. Rather, my concern is with their leadership potential for strangling the state economically and the admitted practice of strong-arming elected officials who, for the most part, seem pathetically pliant when confronted with Teamster muscle. . . . In my view, federal trust-busting and anti-monopolistic constraints imposed on big business should be imposed on big labor. . . . Was I affronted when Carr called me an SOB? No. Just surprised. I knew he and I were both in the Marine Corps, but didn't think we had anything else in common. What do I think of him personally? Actually, though it may lose him sleep to learn it, aside from what he says and does, I kind of like the guy. Though, I don't think my mother would.

Hammond has also regularly used this technique of ridicule against the *Anchorage Times*'s Bob Atwood. He often has referred to Atwood as "my backward cousin Bob," and has chided him in doggerel verse:

In spite of what you all may think, I owe Bob an *awful* lot
So the most that I can do *to* him I fear is really not
Sufficient to repay him, so all that I can say
Is, No one has done half as much as Bob
To make me what you *think* I am today.

Despite his doggerel, Hammond's speeches often do have a poetic ring to them. Other times, his language is stilted and flowery, filled with figures of speech and sentence structures that sound like something out of the Old Testament. Hammond's prose even earned him a dubious spot in the *New Yorker* magazine (January 24, 1977) under the heading, "Sentences We Hated to Come to the End Of":

> Those who protest that the ship of state is swamping in a rising flood of deficit expenditures and yet fail to demand that such means of funding be provided for to meet new costs attending the new services they want simply open up to seacocks yet another tidal bore of red ink into which they and all of us hypocritical, malfunctioning, self-priming, bilge-pumping politicians who ignore such truths should be made to walk the plank.

In addition to his colorful use of the language, which distinguishes him from past governors, Hammond also differs from his predecessors on more substantive matters. Where most previous administrations, both Republican and Democratic, had sought to woo the development forces, Hammond both in his campaign and to at least some extent as governor, propounded a take-it-or-leave-it proposition to them. Developers of our oil, our natural gas, our minerals will accept our terms, not we theirs, Hammond said. There would be no subsidies or "incentives" to big corporations which lusted after Alaska's wealth. Development would have to pay its own way. The state must get a big share of the resources' wealth through taxes, royalties, lease arrangements, and other fiscal devices. And even when projects were fiscally sound, the state would oppose them if they were not environmentally, culturally and spiritually sound.[1]

[1] Hammond has not always followed his own guidelines. His support for the all-Alaska route for a natural gas pipeline from Prudhoe Bay marks an obvious accommodation with the state's super-growth forces. Environmentalists favor a gas pipeline route that goes through both Alaska and Canada. More on this in Chapter VIII.

The Natives' subsistence life-style of hunting and fishing for much of their own food must be protected. The fishing industry must not be wiped out by rampant, reckless offshore oil development. The state's economic future should be based on renewable resources—agriculture, the fishing industry, timber—not on such nonrenewable resources as oil, gas, and minerals. The environment must be safeguarded. The Alaskans' way of life must be preserved. Population increases must not be excessive.

In his first two years in office, Hammond determined not to make ad hoc decisions on individual projects but to consider development issues in their totality. Thus, his administration called for a slowdown in the timetable for the oil exploration on federally-owned submerged lands on Alaska's outer continental shelf (OCS); continued to limit, on a permit basis, the use of the North Slope Haul Road to specific pipeline-related activities; pushed legislation to buy back state-owned offshore oil leases in the ecologically important Kachemak Bay, in the Lower Cook Inlet;[2] and was studying a number of proposals that would enable the state government to get a larger share of the state's oil wealth.

As Hammond told us in late 1976 interviews, those advocating rapid-fire development of the state's nonrenewable resources "are not so concerned with the long term. While the state's oil and natural gas could be gone in a few decades, the state will have to live with the consequences." And if the environment is destroyed, and with it such mainstays of the Alaskan economy as the fishing industry, there's no going back to the way it is today. But he said his real message was not one of "zero growth," as his opponents charge. Indeed, some growth in Alaska is inevitable. But we must

> . . . convey clearly to the public distinctions between healthy growth and what I term unhealthy and malignant growth. . . . We've got to set up development criteria and make sure [industry] meets[s] those objectives. If they can meet them, fine; if they can't, I think we should discourage it [development]. . . . Of course, those who feel threatened, those who would really support any type of growth, super-growth, are queasy about this and immediately try to pin the label of growth on whomever suggests that some types of growth are inappropriate. . . . I'm convinced that we're on course with the majority viewpoint in Alaska if it is correctly perceived what we are intent on doing.

Despite such assurances that he is not anti-growth, the supporters of rapid development don't believe it. "No matter what he

[2] See Chapter XII for more on the Kachemak Bay leases.

calls his policy, it still translates into no-growth," the *Times*'s Bill Tobin told us. And Tobin's comment is a typical, if somewhat mild, example of the super-growthers' criticisms of Hammond. The *Times* constantly accused Hammond of pushing policies that hurt the state's economy and were antibusiness.

In addition to his go-slow policy on growth, Hammond also emphasizes fiscal conservatism, which he said goes hand in hand with his development philosophy. He has stressed fiscal caution despite the fortune in oil money the state will receive as its royalty share from the Prudhoe Bay oil. It is estimated that the state will get upwards of $1 billion a year annually by the mid-1980s from Prudhoe Bay oil alone—an amount substantially greater than the state's 1976–77 budget of about $700 million. At a time when state and local governments throughout the nation are beset by fiscal woes, Alaska stands in the unique position of trying to figure out what it will do with *surplus* money.

Why the caution by Hammond if the state soon will be rolling in dough? Hammond told us his fear is that the public will get used to the notion that the oil revenues are endless—"the idea that to pay for, say, a couple of more ferryboats to operate in southeast Alaska, all you have to do is sell another lease in the Lower Cook Inlet." His philosophy, that of a true conservative, is that a growth in government, a growth in bureaucracy, should be painful to the taxpayer. "There ought to be some method of having what I term tying a string from the public pocket to that booming bureaucracy, compelling us in public office to twitch that string every time you want the services and say, 'OK, Buster, this is what it'll cost you,' " Hammond said.

As for the wealth from Prudhoe Bay oil and the state's other nonrenewable resources, Hammond has come up with an imaginative, if flawed, proposal which calls for funneling some of that money back into taxpayers' pockets. His plan ties in to a constitutional amendment approved by voters in November 1976 which authorized creation of a state "permanent fund." The fund would be the repository for at least 25 percent of all mineral lease rentals, royalties, royalty sale proceeds, federal mineral revenue sharing payments, and bonuses received by the state for its nonrenewable resources (oil, natural gas, minerals). The principal of the fund could be used for income-producing investments only. Hammond has proposed that some of the income produced from those investments go into something to be called the "Alaska Investment Corporation," or

"Alaska, Inc." In January 1977, Hammond announced in his State of the State message that he would propose legislation during that session to create Alaska, Inc., but did not immediately offer specific details. As he outlined it to us, under the Alaska, Inc., concept, each Alaskan would be a stockholder and would receive one share of stock for each year's residency. The stockholder would not be eligible to receive any benefits until he or she had accumulated eighteen shares of stock. In other words, rather than paying dividends each year to every stockholder, the program would instead provide supplemental income only for long-term residents of the state.

If each stockholder were paid a dividend each year without regard to length of time in the state, Hammond said, this would just encourage more people to come to Alaska to share in the program. Making payments available only to those with at least eighteen shares would, of course, substantially reduce the number of persons eligible for payments. Also, Hammond figured in a "need" factor in his proposal, so that unemployed or financially needy persons with at least eighteen shares would receive payments of up to $6,400 annually, while other stockholders would receive $400 per share by 1985. Hammond saw his proposal as putting more money into people's pockets and thereby keeping welfare-related and other governmental programs from expanding. And, in his fiscally conservative manner, he emphasized that Alaska, Inc., would not involve redistribution of income. "It would not take money from the 'haves' and give it to the 'have-nots,' " he said. "Rather, it would take money earned from resources the people already own and use it in such a way as to provide direct and tangible benefits rather than simply expanding governmental services. It would not only give all Alaskans a sense of owning a piece of the action but would provide a means of securing higher education to those who desire it, shove up the economic base of many destitute Alaskans, reduce welfare burdens and administrative costs, and provide aid and comfort to the aged, as well as those who hope one day to qualify."

Besides a creative approach to the issues, Hammond showed imagination in his selection of cabinet members and other top administration aides. His cabinet choices ran the gamut from the probusiness Langhorne A. (Tony) Motley,[3] Commissioner of Commerce and Economic Development, and banker Sterling Gallagher,

[3] Motley left his state post in early 1977. Martin was nominated to be U.S. assistant secretary of the interior in March 1977.

Commissioner of Revenue, to liberal Attorney General Gross and Natural Resources Commissioner Guy R. Martin, both of whom are Democrats who strongly favored Hammond's go-slow development approach. As Hammond himself put it: "I calculatedly chose a crew with different viewpoints rather than simply selecting persons whose thinking was in lockstep with my own. Some were recruited from the Chamber of Commerce, some from the Conservation Society. Some are liberals. Some are conservatives. Some are even Republicans."

But what Hammond sees as a strength, many other state political activists view as a serious shortcoming which produces indecisiveness and a failure to delineate clear policies and priorities. Even those who agree with the governor's development philosophy say that the Hammond cabinet has so many built-in contradictions that it is not always clear exactly where it stands on certain issues. "He encourages dissent within his cabinet, and that's a good thing—but sometimes the disparate voices never get resolved into one administration position," complained one lobbyist for liberal causes. "The problem is, when the governor says he will support you on a bill, I expect very minimal help. For example, he said he would support us on a certain bill in the 1976 session. Yet his commissioner of commerce, Tony Motley, was down at the legislature lobbying against it. It wasn't that Hammond was trying to sabotage us; it's just that there was no coordination between the governor's lobbyists and Tony."

State Senator Chancy Croft, an Anchorage Democrat and himself a potential gubernatorial candidate, also gave Hammond a generally unfavorable review. "I'd give Hammond pretty good marks for asking questions; pretty low marks for carrying anything out. . . . It's not that there's too many voices coming from the administration; it's that Hammond doesn't provide a resolution coming from those voices. Hammond makes decisions in his administration by deciding who will decide. But he doesn't reconcile within his administration the competing statements that people make. So it's a common problem as far as the legislature is concerned to find the governor saying here's my position on one thing and to find out that people who are influencing the legislation for the administration are doing something else."

Attorney General Gross dismissed these charges as "an unfair and oversimplified analysis of the relationship" between the governor and the legislature. In a June 15, 1975 speech to an Associated

Press convention in Homer, Alaska, Gross explained that Hammond had a basic philosophy that a governor should not twist arms or threaten a legislature. Although Gross's view could be dismissed as self-serving, it is consistent with what both admirers and critics say about the governor and so bears quoting at some length:

> Hammond does have an unusual relationship with the legislature, a relationship which is different than any I have seen between a governor and a legislature. . . . If you really reflect on it, I think you will recognize that what some people tout as strong leadership for some political figures is nothing more than a sophisticated form of bribery. 'If you give me your vote on a bill, I'll give you an airfield or a judgeship.' Hammond has never done that as a governor and I hope he never does. . . . He honestly believes that the legislature will consider bills on their merits. If that seems a silly, naive way of looking at things, may I point out to you that this weak governor who did not twist arms or threaten legislators obtained nearly every major element of his administration's package, and the minor elements as well. . . .

Despite the complaints, according to the liberal lobbyist quoted above, Hammond "has injected a high standard for decency and fairness in state government." And, he noted, the pro-development forces in the state pack such a wallop that if there were also a super-growther as governor, there would be few persons of sufficient stature to offer alternative courses of development.

Besides antagonizing the growth forces, Hammond sometimes rankled the feelings of consumer and liberal activists, who felt he was not tough enough with the state's powerful economic interests. Representatives of environmental, consumer-oriented, and liberal groups told us they were miffed that Hammond refused to support additional taxes on the oil industry in the 1976 legislative session, despite the strong push given such legislation by Croft (then Senate president) and others. Hammond contended that additional taxes would be premature until the oil had begun to flow through the trans-Alaska pipeline, and that the entire matter needed further study. Even some Hammond admirers, however, viewed his lack of support for additional oil taxes in 1976 as a reaction to super-growthers' criticism of him.[4]

Hammond and other figures in his administration responded that such criticism from liberals and environmentalists (although

[4] Hammond, in the 1977 legislative session, did propose substantial increases in taxes on the oil companies. The legislature then approved increases less than what Hammond sought.

considerably milder than that from the super-growthers) missed the point. Said the governor: "As in anything, it's the art of the possible that we're aspiring to. I tell some of the conservation groups . . . that there would be nothing that would more clearly assure my being replaced by the most exploitative type imaginable if we were to stifle what is appropriately termed healthy growth."

Criticism of Hammond by some environmentalists, while heartfelt, is usually made with a clear understanding of what the alternatives to him are. As Jack Hession, who heads up the Sierra Club's Anchorage office, told us: "Hammond has done considerably well on environmental matters, but he has compromised more than we would like on some issues." But, added Hession, "I'd hate to think what would have happened if the last couple of administrations we had before Hammond had been in power since 1975 instead of Hammond. The place would be unlivable."

And despite antipathy from many of his fellow Republicans, Hammond had the respect of the state's other two major Republican political figures—Representatives Don Young and Senator Ted Stevens—even though he had had frequent clashes with them on development issues. Young described Hammond in February 1977 as a "close personal friend . . . a brilliant individual. . . . He can charm people." But Young, a leading growth advocate, cautioned that Hammond's "survival is dependent on broadening his appeal. I think the governor recognizes he's considered a zero-growth man. It's not correct to label him that, but that's how many people see him [and] he's slower than I'd like him to be." Stevens told us he felt Hammond was "misunderstood" on the growth issue. The senator said Hammond was not a no-growth advocate, but was genuinely concerned about "superheating the economy. He wants us to have more control. I don't have a great deal of fight with him. He's more cautious; I'm more development-oriented."

Some Democrats also gave high marks to Hammond's performance as governor. For example, the state's other U.S. senator, Mike Gravel, said that he supported Hammond's approach to development issues and felt that he was "doing a good job. He is not anti-growth, as some of his critics charge, but rather he is circumspect about the issue of growth."

Whatever label one applies to Hammond's position, his vision of a future Alaska contrasts sharply with that of quintessential Boomers, such as Bob Atwood. Atwood's dream is one of McDonald's, Standard Oil, and suburban sprawl, a continually growing, increasingly prosperous Alaska which attracts people not to its unique life-style or wilderness but to its opportunities to make money. Hammond's vision is of an Alaska that provides its people with adequate employment and income security but retains its extraordinary character—both physical and human.

The two visions are simply irreconcilable, and sporadic schizophrenic attempts by Hammond to make the two perspectives appear to be mere differences in tone or degree ill served both him and his constituents. Hammond is at his best when he tries to communicate to Alaskans his vision of future Alaska and the clear alternative it offers to the Boomers' dollar-sign dreams. Of course, it is never easy for one person to communicate a vision to a mass of people. But it is fortunate that a man of Hammond's scope has been governor at this stage of the state's life, for with the images of sugarplums dancing in many Alaskans' heads, some perspective—some vision—has been greatly needed. To the extent Hammond allows that vision to become muddled, to become confused with the Boomers' greed, as water with oil, he risks playing into the hands of the developers —and losing his own political identity in the process.

The Greening of the Natives

Until now, we, the Koniag people, never thought ourselves owners of the land. We were its guests, and we fed at the table of the sea. These were our hosts and we treated them with respect. Now we have won ownership of a portion of our ancestral lands. We accept them willingly, but not without a sense of awe and reverence.

—Koniag, Inc., 1974 Annual Report.

The land claims act taught the Natives three things: to wear button-down shirts, how to pack a suitcase, and how to spell VSOP [*an expensive brandy*].

—Tony Motley, Alaska state Commissioner of Commerce, 1976.

A UNIQUE EXPERIMENT in American capitalism is quietly taking place in this country's largest and second least populous state. In 1971, the federal government attempted to correct a century of injustice by resolving the aboriginal land claims of Alaska's Natives. Congress approved, and President Nixon signed into law, the Alaska Native Claims Settlement Act, which chartered 12 regional and 220 village corporations whose stockholders became some 80,000 Alaskan Indians, Aleuts, and Eskimos. The Act gave the Native corporations 44 million acres and $962.5 million, and directed them to emulate other for-profit corporations—by making money.

In most respects, the Native firms have patterned their operations and goals after those of IBM, General Motors, and U.S. Steel—with all that implies. There are boards of directors, annual corporate reports, proxy fights, and shareholders. (One hundred shares were given to all persons with at least one quarter Alaskan Native blood who were alive when the Act became law; they are the only eligible stockholders until 1992, when the stock may be freely traded—to non-Natives as well as Natives.) As with other U.S. corporations, investment and policy decisions are made by the board of directors and the corporate managers. Stockholders who disagree with corporate decisions can vote to unseat directors at the annual stockholders' meeting—in the accepted, but limited, method of accountability in other corporations. In fact, Native firms are generally subject to the same federal and state laws that apply to all other corporations—with a few exceptions. Native firms are exempt from certain reporting and disclosure requirements of the Securities and Exchange Commission until 1992 and, unlike the stockholders of other for-profit firms, all stockholders own an equal number of squares and thus have equal votes. Native corporations also have certain tax advantages: landholdings are exempt from property taxes until the stock goes public in 1992, unless they are developed or leased. Investment income is, of course, subject to state and federal income taxes.

The revolutionary land claims settlement, widely regarded as the fairest ever agreed to by the United States government in its history of dealing with Indians and other native peoples, emphasized the use of the corporate structure instead of outright land grants to individual Natives. The reason for this approach was that it would enable the Natives to continue their way of life. For most of them, this meant hunting, fishing, trapping, and berry picking as a means of survival, coupled with a centuries-old respect for the land as something held in common and not owned individually. A corporate structure would yield profits, and with that fiscal tonic, the Natives could surely improve their economic condition. What's more, the Natives could avoid having to sell off their land out of financial desperation. Their culture could remain intact and at the same time, with a little savvy, they could improve their financial security. So from the beginning, the settlement sanctioned a built-in contradiction: using the primary tool of capitalism—the corporation—to sustain and nourish a communal, prodominantly non-cash life-style.

Thus, the Native Claims Act is a unique experiment and an extremely important one. For what the Native corporations do with their considerable assets will determine, to a large degree, the cultural and economic future of their shareholders—as well as the rate of development of Alaska's massive resources and the future of the last great wilderness of the United States. Touching all these issues is the question of the adaptability of the American corporation—

whether the corporate structure can accommodate broader social purposes than the creation of profits.

* * *

The largest island in the United States lies in the Pacific Ocean, about two hundred miles south of Anchorage, facing the base of the Alaska Peninsula. It is Kodiak, a lush place of rolling hills and forests dominated by the Kodiak Wildlife Refuge. On the northeast part of the island sits the city of Kodiak, whose harbor is home to so many boats one can hardly see the water. Kodiak, the island and the city, has one major industry—fishing—and its catches of salmon, crab, and shrimp rank among the largest of any in the world.

So it is not surprising that many Kodiak fishermen we visited in 1976, both Native and non-Native, were upset with the federal government's plans to sell outer continental shelf (OCS) oil and gas leases in the Gulf of Alaska, east and south of Kodiak, in 1979.

The Kodiak shelf sale was one of nine scheduled or proposed OCS sales in Alaska's fish-rich, turbulent waters. The Kodiak sale worries Tom Casey, the burly, bearded, tough-talking manager of the United Fishermen's Marketing Association. He and the 450 Kodiak salmon and king crab fishermen he represents know that oil and fish don't mix. "If you blew a fart in one of those plants," he told us, waving a hand in the direction of the sixteen fish processing plants that dot the island, "the federal government would condemn the pack. Can you see the advertisement? 'Low-priced crab from the petroleum-contaminated waters of Alaska.' "

Surprisingly, the Native regional corporation, Koniag, Inc., is *not* particularly upset about the OCS sales. Even though most of its stockholders live on the island and are involved in commercial and subsistence fishing—3,300 Aleuts and Indians in all—Koniag from the beginning has steered clear of investments in fishing-related enterprises. It's not so much that the fishing industry is a bad investment but that there are more lucrative ones. Koniag has not even "adopted the posture of trying to create local jobs," complained Matt Jamin, a non-Native lawyer with Alaska Legal Services in Kodiak. "They see their mandate as making money and OCS as the way." Karl Armstrong, Koniag's secretary and spokesman, agreed. Armstrong, a broad-faced Aleut with a quick laugh, has a deep sense of the history of his people. But he is also a tough businessman—"slick," said one state official. Armstrong explained how he sees Koniag's role. "I think that corporations and people are contradictions; I don't think they go together," he declared, his lips curling

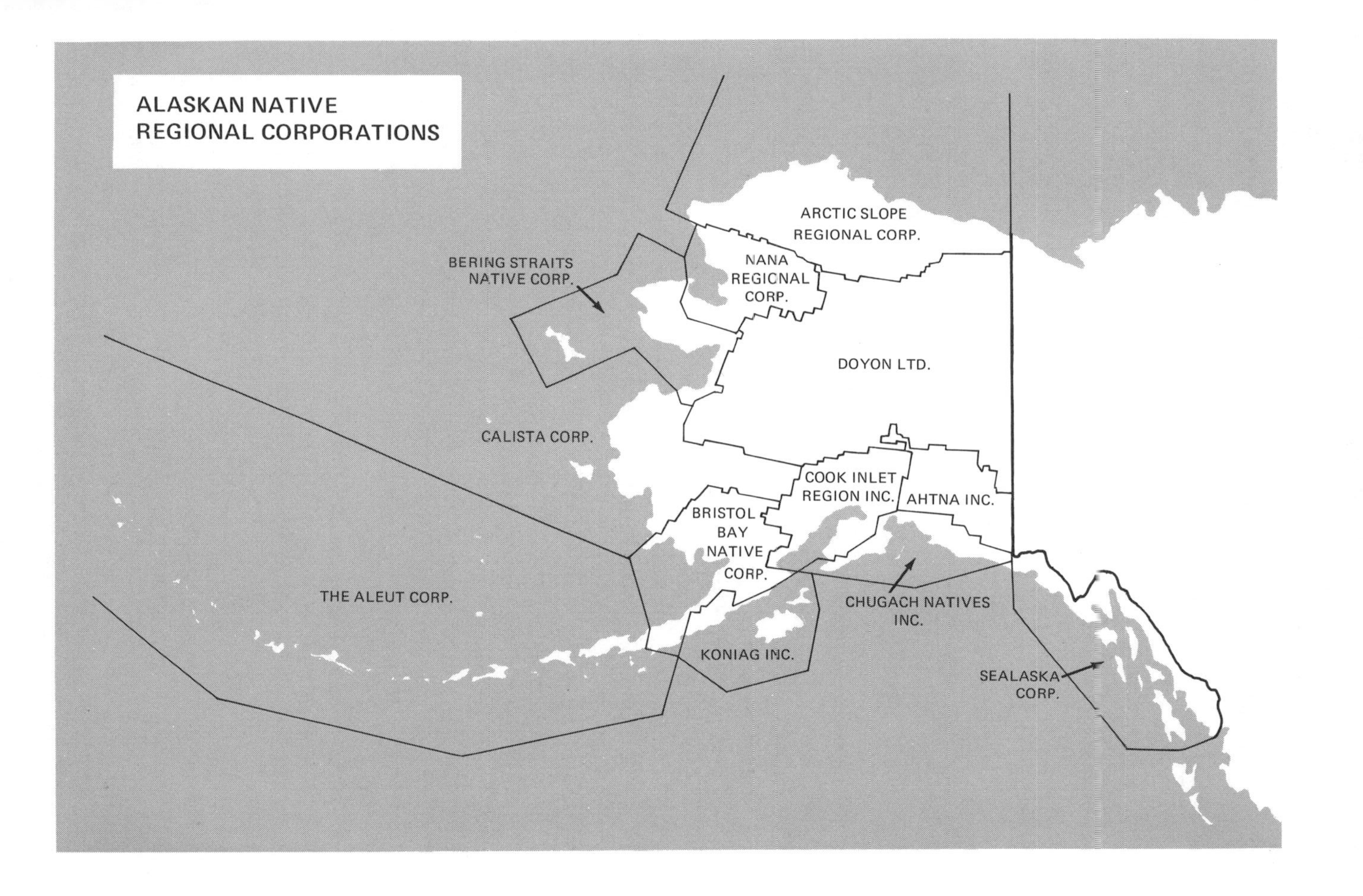

ALASKAN NATIVE
REGIONAL CORPORATIONS
ARCTIC SLOPE
REGIONAL CORP.
BERING STRAITS
NATIVE CORP.
NANA
REGIONAL
CORP.
DOYON LTD.
CALISTA CORP.
COOK INLET
REGION INC.
AHTNA INC.
BRISTOL
BAY
NATIVE
CORP.
THE ALEUT CORP.
CHUGACH NATIVES
INC.
KONIAG INC.
SEALASKA
CORP.

into a slight smile. "The decision was made early on by the board and management that Koniag could not afford for its businesses to be training schools. They are businesses and rather hard-nosed businesses. . . . There is this pro-development policy on the part of the corporate leaders, which is a necessity. They realize that they must make these corporations work. It will be the greatest disaster of all to the Native people if their corporations fail. They must succeed."[1]

To that end, Koniag by late 1976 had invested heavily in blue-chip stocks and real estate. The board of directors' largest investment had been a $1.5 million orange and gray apartment building in Kodiak, overlooking the harbor, where the Native firm's corporate offices were located. Even though the Outside construction firm that built it employed few Natives on the job, and even though few of Koniag's shareholders could afford its $400-per-month units, the building had been a good investment.

Much to the frustration of both the state and some of the corporation's own shareholders, Koniag had been actively negotiating with the oil companies to convert the former Cape Chiniak air force tracking station south of the city of Kodiak into an onshore supply port and storage base for OCS oil. In return for payments of royalties, Koniag hoped to lease the site to the oil companies.

Armstrong told us in late 1976 that negotiations had been inconclusive but amicable. "We tell the oil companies you're going to love [paying us royalties]. This is something you should want, and the people will love you." Koniag also told the oil executives, according to Armstrong, that oil companies "lack a great deal of credibility as far as a concern for the environment and for the people. A generous deal with the Natives would do much to enhance [their image]." Armstrong tells critics that OCS development is coming, and the best way to protect the environment—*and* reap economic rewards at

[1] Armstrong is a good example of a Native leader who shares many of the Boomer attitudes. For example, in 1970 when he was editor of the daily *Kodiak Mirror*, the U.S. government, in response to Japanese protests, was preparing to move its storehouse of nerve gas from Okinawa. Armstrong, amid the outraged protests of local residents, proposed that the deadly gas be brought to Kodiak Island as a means of boosting the local economy. In a May 22, 1970, article, the *Anchorage Daily News* reported that Armstrong and others had petitioned the U.S. Army for the storage rights on Kodiak. The article stated that Armstrong "said the resultant ammunition depot 'would bring in another $3 million to $4 million a year in payroll' and said the risk of being decimated by the nerve gas was worth it. According to sources, enough nerve gas is involved to kill every living thing in Alaska and part of Canada." Outraged residents prevailed and the plan was killed.

the same time—is for the Natives to sit down with the oil companies and talk turkey.

Harry Carter, the tough-talking vice-president of Koniag, sees the Natives' role in OCS development off Kodiak as partial payment for "over two hundred years of intrusions by the white man" who, throughout Alaska, "first took our whales, then our gold and now our oil." Rather than resist "the national and international cartels—the oil companies—who want to rip off our oil," Carter said, the Native corporations should try to get whatever financial benefits it can from OCS. Carter said he first became convinced that change was inevitable, and that Koniag should take advantage of it, when he and other Native leaders were called to the White House in 1974 and were told that the energy crisis demanded that oil be taken from Alaska's outer continental shelf. It was after this, he said, that Koniag's board "placed as our highest priority the development of OCS." Since then, Carter said that Koniag has attempted to reverse the historic roles "of who are the rapers and who are the rapees," a favorite catch phrase of some of the corporate Native leaders.

Carter, Armstrong, and Native corporation leaders in other areas of the state often cited the precedent of the Shetland Islanders in Scotland during the initial phase of North Sea oil exploration. The Scottish villagers had dictated to the oil companies what was going to be permitted off their shores and onshore, rather than the other way around. But Koniag's critics pointed out a crucial difference: that the Shetland Islanders had a fierce determination to protect their culture and environment; money was a secondary concern. Koniag, according to its critics, reversed this and, in the process, forfeited much of the leverage it had to dictate terms to the oil companies. And it is this approach that earned the corporation the suspicion of many Native and non-Native fishermen, who make their living and draw much of their own food from the sea.

Guy Martin, the state's commissioner of natural resources, said in August 1976 that he considered Koniag's approach naive, short-sighted, and dangerous. He too was convinced that the Shetland Islanders had taken the right approach:

> If villages or corporations assess themselves and their self-interest basically as protectors of the culture and life-style in the community, they tend to do better. If their leaders assess their basic self-interest as economic opportunity, they get fouled up right away. . . . You see it down at Kodiak; the Natives are off on that. They've got their land and they're trying to relate it to the federal OCS program. And the federal OCS guys love it and the in-

dustry loves it and the Native leaders love it, but the fishermen and the people of Kodiak aren't too hot for it.

Ed Naughton, a Koniag shareholder and a popular former state legislator[2] from Kodiak, is one of the firm's toughest critics. "Kodiak Natives," he told us in August 1976, "have been involved in fishing all their lives, at the bottom edge, and here was an opportunity to do something about that. But instead, they [Koniag] court the oil companies without understanding what OCS development means to our fishing industry. . . . The corporations must show that the Natives can win, that they can rewrite their life's script. What does it matter if a shareholder gets a dividend check from OCS development if it destroys his livelihood?"

Naughton thinks that Koniag should be investing its money in the marketing end of the fishing industry—"where we've been sucking hind tit all these years. The bind the Alaska fishermen are in is the same one the American farmers were in before they started farm co-ops." Jack Wick, the soft-spoken, thirty-one-year-old president of Koniag who has headed up the firm since 1971, succinctly explained the corporation's investment philosophy this way: "Fishing is high risk and the board set up criteria that are low risk."

In October 1976, there were some indications that the Koniag corporation was attempting to cooperate with fishermen and other concerned groups in the community. This reversal came when oil companies warned that they could go elsewhere for an onshore base for OCS development if the terms offered on Kodiak were too tough, according to Naughton. "So now suddenly Koniag is very anxious to join the borough and the local people," he said. "It's a very common thing for [Outside] people [such as oil company executives] to think that a profit-making corporation, the stockholders of which are Natives, is the spokesman for all the Natives. That's a very easy mistake to fall into, but it's not true. You'll find that a lot of Native people who are stockholders in the corporation do not agree with the directors and the officers. The oil companies have laid it on them [Koniag leaders], saying Chiniak is not vital to their operations and they can go somewhere else whenever they damn well please. Now suddenly the Koniag officers are wooing those other Kodiak people who in the past were saying, 'Slow down, let's figure out what the devil is happening here.' Now, they are saying, 'Let's all go out there and see to it that the fishermen are protected.' "

[2] Naughton did not seek reelection in 1976.

By mid-February 1977, Koniag's interest in OCS development off Kodiak took a new twist when the corporation confirmed reports that it might bid for the leases itself if it could arrange for the substantial backing needed for such a bid. The corporation disclosed that it had entered negotiations for financial backing with Saudi Arabia, which had given Koniag "some feedback that they are interested in resource development in this area," according to Koniag vice-president Carter.

The OCS development planned for Kodiak's waters presents risks to more than commercial fishing. It also threatens subsistence fishing and a way of life greatly dependent on that. Many Kodiak Natives fish commercially for part of the year, but must also allow time to catch their own families' supply for the winter. "Then, depending on what kind of a year he had, he may wind up coming into town trying to find a job to raise enough cash to get him and his family through the winter, and he'll probably wind up on food stamps," Naughton said. Even Koniag president Wick takes a couple of months off in the summer to go fishing. Naughton characterized this semi-subsistence, semicash economy life as both pleasant and hard, with "a lot of individual freedom involved." Naughton and many other Kodiak fishermen fear that OCS development will end the independent way of life for Natives and whites alike.

Subsistence, though the super-growth forces often pretend it doesn't exist, is still *the* way of life for the majority of Alaska's Natives. A 1974 federal study mandated by a provision in the Native Claims Settlement Act concluded that up to two-thirds of Alaska's 60,000 resident Natives still engage in a subsistence life-style to one degree or another. "Of roughly 150 Native villages of less than 300 people," the report said, "subsistence activity is estimated to provide at least half of the daily caloric intake." Hunting, fishing, trapping, whaling, berry picking, etc., are "supplemented with sugar, salt, flour, coffee, tea, sweets, and canned vegetables that must be purchased at the village store," the report noted.

The subsistence life-style is endangered, Naughton said, by oil companies which can pay extremely high wages, far more than normal pay levels of Native fishermen and processing plant employees. The salary opportunities are simply too attractive for both Natives and non-Natives to continue their traditional, less lucrative way of life. Naughton noted that two fish processing plants in Valdez, the port terminal for the trans-Alaska oil pipeline, "had to fold their tents" after Big Oil came in with its higher salaries "because even high school kids wouldn't work in those plants for less than ten dollars an hour."

The dilemma for these rural Natives is that the outside work gives them less time to devote to subsistence activities. In the case of the trans-Alaska pipeline, as with any major outdoor project, the best construction season is, of course, the warm summer—also the best time for gathering and stockpiling many subsistence foods for the winter.

To most Americans caught up in the cash economy, the loss of the Alaskan Natives' way of life may seem of little consequence, or even beneficial. But the Natives' culture—involving subsistence, art, music, oral history, traditions—has a value that cannot be measured in dollars and cents. The majority of the Alaskan Natives still find that it is better to live off the land, despite its hardships, than to adapt totally to the Western way of life. But numerous forces, in addition to development that encroaches upon their villages, are making it increasingly difficult for them to sustain their varied and rich cultures. And many Natives fear that, ironically, their own corporations could be one of these forces. Thus, the conflict on Kodiak Island is more than a distant, inconsequential squabble. It is a drama that will be reenacted, with variations, in most of the eleven other regions of Alaska: whether profits or a way of life—or a healthy combination of both—will prevail. The conflict between profits and culture has been particularly striking because corporations were introduced so suddenly to a people so culturally remote from them.

To some of the unmitigated Boomers, the loss of the Natives' way of life won't be such a great tragedy. To people such as *Anchorage Times* publisher Robert Atwood, the Natives have a responsibility to use their lands to further the development of the state. So, until recently, Atwood, an opponent of the land claims act, was not very sympathetic to the Native cause. Not only were the Natives at the bottom of the economic heap, but demands for settlement of their aboriginal claims, in the Boomers' view, threatened to rob the state of land and capital desperately needed to harvest its vast store of riches. Today, however, the Natives—or at least some of their leaders—are the recipients not only of Atwood's powerful backing, but of his gratitude. "When the last legislature got into some of this screwball thinking that would have practically confiscated the oil industry, the Natives helped put a stop to that," he told us in 1976.

"They're becoming capitalists, more responsible, less inclined to knock over the apple cart."

This greening of the Natives is due in no small part to the sweep of the Native Calims Act—a measure as radical in concept as any ever passed by Congress and, at the same time, as American as the modern corporation. It followed a century of neglect by the American government.

* * *

The policy of the U.S. government toward the Alaskan Natives in the last half of the nineteenth century was one of malign neglect. For the first seventeen years after the U.S. acquisition of Alaska, with only about 300 non-Natives living in the territory, there was virtually no government at all. While the government's policy was to settle American Indians on reservations, in 1871 Congress prohibited the federal government from making new treaties, thus preventing the Alaska Natives from obtaining any land of their own.

In one of several schizophrenic flip-flops on Indian policy, Congress decided to abandon the reservation approach and to encourage assimilation into the white culture through passage of the General Allotment Act of 1887, which provided small farm plots to Indians. But the measure excluded Alaska Natives. Worse, whites were settling in southeastern Alaska and pushing the Tlingit and Haida Indians off some of their traditional hunting and fishing grounds. The Indians protested to the secretary of the interior, who told them the matter was outside his jurisdiction.

This pattern of unconcern continued until 1943 when, following another about-face during which Congress decided that the Indian culture was worth preserving after all, Interior Secretary Harold Ickes announced that Alaskan Native villages would be eligible to receive land for reservations. But, by the 1950s, before a significant number of Native villages received title to the land, assimilation was the fad again and reservations were out once more.

The U.S. government and white fortune hunters were not the only intruders into Native culture. A host of religious missionaries in 1885 launched an attempt to convert the Natives to Christianity. Under the leadership of Sheldon Jackson, a Presbyterian missionary and noted educator, the Baptists, Episcopalians, Congregationalists, Moravians, Methodists, and Presbyterians met to divide up Alaska and launch their mission into the wilderness. Many Natives were converted but many others successfully resisted. Their lives were stable and self-sufficient; they had all the material goods they desired, their way of life was in equilibrium with the environment, and their society stressed cooperation over competition.

These stabilities offered a certain immunity both from the missionaries' efforts and other intrusions. Their resistance was further aided by their natural hardiness. Journalist Lael Morgan writes:

> What saved some of the old ways was the same thing that had been the Natives' enemy of old—the harshness of the country. No matter how much the outsiders ridiculed their Native cultures, the Alaskans saw that by maintaining them they could survive in the country well beyond the endurance of the average newcomer.[3]

Formal education became more important to Native groups as the white culture impinged more upon them, and they felt it necessary to learn Western ways in order to survive. But education made further incursions into their way of life. Those Natives who had stuck with their nomadic ways were forced to give up some of their mobility so their children could attend school at specific times of the year. And most schools provided by the federal—and later the state—governments were sadly neglected, underfunded, and generally at some distance from their villages. Those Natives who felt compelled to send their children to distant Bureau of Indian Affairs boarding schools, often outside the state and as far away as Oklahoma, saw their children's ties to their culture diminish.

It wasn't until a suit was brought on behalf of a Native student in the early 1970s that the state finally agreed to provide high schools in, or very near, all Native villages. Such a plan was to begin in 1979. Still, so-called "quality of education" is not enough. Many Natives want to insure that their children are not merely taught the Western way of life but educated about their own cultures. In a plea for retention of the Yupik Eskimos' way of life, Yupiktak Bista, a nonprofit community assistance organization for southwest Alaska, articulated this central problem:

[3] There are many misconceptions about Alaskan Natives, particularly the Eskimos. For example, igloos: while Eskimos in Greenland, northwestern Canada, and other parts of the Arctic built ice houses, snow and ice have rarely, if ever, been used to build homes for Alaskan Eskimos. The Alaskan "igloo" is made of rectangular chunks of sod skillfully removed from the tundra. They are partly underground and usually consist of a single room, connected to the outside by a tunnel. Such is the misconception about igloos that in a 1930s Hollywood movie made in the village of Teller near Nome, the filmmakers had to teach the Eskimos how to build ice houses. Eskimos who later saw the film in Nome said they enjoyed *King Kong* more.

Today we have entrusted the minds of our young to professional teachers who seemingly know all there is to know. They are teaching a child how to read, write, repair a car, weld two pipes together. But they are not teaching the child the most important thing: *who he is,* an Eskimo or Indian with a history full of folklore, music, great men, medicine, a philosophy complete with poets; in short, there was a civilization, a culture which survived the harshest of environments for thousands of years. Now this culture and the subsistence way of life are being swept away by books, patents, money, and corporations.

It is not our intent to wage war on Western civilization. We merely want to come to terms with it—on our own grounds. We do not dislike Western civilization or the White Man. We simply treasure our young and our culture.

As the Alaska territory developed, and the percentage of whites increased, so did the ethnic consciousness of the Natives. As the push for statehood was gathering increasing support in the 1950s, many Natives hoped that in the process they might win back some of their lands from the federal government. That was a plausible hope, but a feeble one; the prime movers for statehood were Boomers who gave little thought to securing justice for the Natives. They were more intent on wresting economic control of the state from the federal government, the Seattle fish monopoly, Outside mining companies and the hated conservationists. *Anchorage Times* publisher Robert B. Atwood voiced the prevailing Boomer sentiment when he complained to a House subcommittee in 1953:

Alaska was closed to development under the guise of conservation. It remains for the most part today. The true meaning of conservation is controlled use and wise management. But in Alaska, conservation as it is and has been practiced means paralysis. . . . This so-called conservation is actually a waste of the worst sort.

Another misconception has to do with wife-swapping. According to James W. Vanstone in his book, *Point Hope,* " 'wife exchange' . . . was practiced . . . as a practical, not an emotional arrangement, serving to draw unrelated families together for mutual support and protection, and was a recognized method of extending the family membership. . . . Probably not common at any time, the last case of 'wife exchange' is said to have taken place around 1940."

But one conception about Eskimos is true: they do have a tradition of kissing by rubbing noses. In early 1971, at the National Congress of American Indians convention in Kansas City, Fairbanks Eskimo Laura Bergt taught Vice-President Spiro T. Agnew how to kiss Eskimo-style. This caused one Native leader to jest that each of the kisses was worth a million acres—a reference to the then pending land claims fight.

Several years later another Alaskan entrepreneur, Walter J. Hickel—the state's governor and later interior secretary in the Nixon administration—put it more succinctly: "We're trying to make a Fifth Avenue out of the tundra."

In many ways the Natives' and the Boomers' interests were in direct conflict because they were competing for that precious real estate the federal government, owner of almost all of the Territory's 375 million acres, was willing to relinquish. In testimony before the Senate Interior and Insular Affairs Committee, Atwood neatly disposed of the Native problem, at least in relation to statehood. "The Indians, with their aboriginal rights, are a federal problem," he told the senators. "We have no control over it and we cannot dispose of it and we have nothing to say about it. Whatever happens to Alaska it will still be a federal problem."[4]

The granting of statehood gave Natives their first impetus to achieve a land claims settlement for themselves. In principle, the Statehood Act had preserved the Natives' aboriginal title to the land, but its practical effect was to give them nothing. And there was additional reason for the Natives to be concerned: the Statehood Act gave the State of Alaska 102.5 million acres—more than one-fourth of the state's 375-million-acre land area. The state's land selections would undoubtedly include traditional Native hunting and fishing grounds and Native lands with valuable development potential. Thus, the Natives stood to lose some of their most prized land to the state if they did not begin to push for a land claims settlement for themselves. As former Interior Secretary Stewart Udall noted in retrospect when he addressed the Alaska Federation of Natives (AFN) convention in October 1976, the passage of the Statehood Act put the state and Natives on a "collision course."

It was awhile before that collision occurred. The diverse Native groups in the state, long separated by geography, cultural differ-

[4] The senators needed little persuasion to ignore the Native claims question. At an Interior Committee hearing in Ketchikan, one of the witnesses, Eugene Wacker, told the panel that he had been requested by a Chief Kaihan to bring the aboriginal rights problem before the committee hearing.

"Did he want it settled in the next hour?" sniped Senator Henry M. Jackson (Democrat, Washington).

"No," Wacker replied, "he has been waiting for eighty-some-odd years."

"I do not want to be unduly pessimistic," Senator Clinton B. Anderson (Democrat, Mexico) observed, "but it may still run that long again."

"He asked me to bring it up," Wacker explained apologetically.

The matter was quickly dropped.

ences, and traditional rivalries, were slow to get together. Although there had been a variety of small Native organizations for years, there was no truly statewide Native group with any collective political muscle until the AFN was formed in 1966. The AFN periodically went through convulsive internal battles, but it held together to become a potent political force in state politics. One of the first acts of the new organization in 1966 was to ask that the federal government ban further state land selections, permitted by the Statehood Act, until the Native claims issue was settled. Udall, sympathetic to Native concerns, quickly complied.

With the election of Richard Nixon as president in 1968, and his nomination of then Governor Hickel of Alaska to be interior secretary, the chance for a sizable land claims settlement favorable to the Natives began to look remote again. Nixon was not known to be a friend of any racial minorities, and Hickel, as governor, had vigorously fought Udall's land freeze, which was still in effect. Shortly after being nominated, Hickel commented at an impromptu press conference regarding the land freeze that what one secretary did by executive order, "another secretary can undo." But Hickel was soon eating his words when his nomination ran into trouble in the Senate, drawing especially heavy fire from environmentalists. Faced with the prospect of rejection, Hickel sought to appease Natives and environmentalists. He reversed his position and agreed to extend the land freeze until December 1970. This won him the endorsement of the Native lobbying delegation and helped secure his confirmation.

But it took the discovery of oil on Alaska's North Slope, and the controversy over construction of the trans-Alaska oil pipeline, to summon the Natives' most important ally in the land claims fight—the oil industry. In 1970, a federal district court judge ruled that the pipeline could not be laid across the Yukon River Valley until the aboriginal claims of the Yukon River Indians had been settled.

The oil companies saw that the Native land claims stood in the way of a pipeline permit, but they soon realized that many of the Native leaders also favored development of oil and minerals on land they might receive under a claims act. Accepting the reality that the pipeline would not be built until the claims issue was settled, the oil companies joined with the Natives to lobby for a just lands settlement. This unlikely coalition of oil and Natives over the claims fight also produced some unusual personal alliances. Charlie Edwardsen, one of the most militant and effective of the young Eskimos from the North Slope, was a close friend of British Petroleum's Washington representative, Hugh Gallagher, who later wrote a flattering biography of the Native leader. The khaki-clad Edwardsen (who once stalked out of a meeting with aides to Vice-President Spiro Agnew and other Native leaders after slamming his fists on the table and saying he could not compromise on a land claims settlement) seemed an incongruous figure in the lavish Washington office of British Petroleum, which he used as one of his bases of operation. Gallagher, in fact, had been close to many Natives, and had urged that the oil companies support the Natives' land claims fight even before any correlation developed between the pipeline and the Native Claims Act.

Starting in 1967, a number of land claims bills were proposed by the Interior Department, members of Congress, the state of Alaska, and the Natives themselves. Some proposals emphasized money, rather than land; others supported a village-level, rather than regional, settlement; the AFN, though, consistently favored a large land settlement in conjunction with the establishment of profit-making regional corporations. The Native leaders generally wanted to insure that any settlement left them in a strong enough position so that they could enjoy true self-determination over their own futures. Activists such as Edwardsen constantly reminded other Native leaders that any settlement based on the philosophies of antipoverty or welfare programs would lead to further dependence, rather than independence, for the Native peoples. Native self-sufficiency was the fervent desire, as AFN President Emil Notti told a congressional committee in 1968:

> I visualize Native businesses beginning to alleviate unemployment. I stand here before you to state in the strongest terms possible that the representatives of . . . Native people in Alaska do not want paternal guidance from Washington, D.C. We feel we have the ability to make our own way, and once we get a fair settlement for lands, it will enable us to run our own businesses.

The state of Alaska, for its part, wanted to limit the powers of any Native corporations that might be established and opposed creation of statewide or regional corporations in the first place. If there were to be regional corporations, the state said, they should not exert any powerful economic influence, but should rather perform public works or social welfare functions for the Natives. To this end, the state generally favored a village-level settlement which would substantially limit the Natives' political and economic clout. Hickel, for example, as governor, recommended in congressional testimony in 1968 that most of the money received by the corporations be required to be used for capital improvements—such as roads, hospitals, schools—in Native areas.

Once the oil companies decided to join in the claims fight in 1970, they vigorously pushed for a settlement that would give the Natives substantial land and would create regional corporations with broad discretion over land selections. The environmental organizations, for their part, worried that the Natives would select land that should remain as wilderness and gave lukewarm support to a meaningful Native land claims settlement. They also made various proposals which would have severely restricted how Natives could use their land. Environmentalists, for example, pressed for creation of a planning commission, with powers over Native land use, as a cornerstone for any claims act. (The act approved in 1971 did include a similar commission—the Joint Federal-State Land Use Planning Commission for Alaska—but with considerably limited powers.) Proposals such as this were viewed by the Natives as paternalistic.

Finally, at the long end of the legislative chain, the Nixon administration surprisingly supported the concept of a land claims settlement. In large part the turnabout came in 1970 when the Natives were able to catch the ear of Vice-President Agnew, then head of the executive branch's National Council on Indian Opportunity and a central lobbying target. After a meeting with Agnew and Interior Department officials in March 1970, Native leaders were asked by Interior officials to help them draft a new administration bill, a key breakthrough for the AFN. Senator Ted Stevens helped secure Nixon administration support for a generous settlement through the lobbying of presidential aide John Ehrlichman. By mid-1970, Nixon himself issued a policy statement on "Indian self-determination," declaring his support for a "fair and equitable" settlement for Alaska's Natives. After a long, complicated fight, Congress finally approved a sizable claims settlement, and Nixon signed the Claims Act into law on December 18, 1971.

* * *

And so, in one swoop, Alaska's Natives, as former Interior Secretary Udall said in October 1976, "got a bigger land settlement than all the Indians in the Lower-48" had received in their entire history of dealing with the federal government. The 1971 act, Udall said, marked the only instance in American history "when the United States government was generous—not too generous, not extravagant—but just" in its treatment of a Native American group.

Some 80,000 Alaskan Natives, 60,000 of them state residents, were enrolled in thirteen regional corporations.[5] Most Natives living in the state were enrolled in both regional and village corporations. The corporations all would share, according to their respective number of stockholders, $462.5 million from the U.S. Treasury's general fund, and $500 million from a 2 percent payment on all royalties, rentals, and bonuses received by the state and federal governments for exploration or extraction of oil, natural gas, and minerals in Alaska.[6] The prospects were awesome for the Natives as they assumed a heady new power and respect unknown to them previously.

They did owe some debts of gratitude for the settlement. Former Interior Secretary Udall's initial land freeze was a crucial catalyst of the settlement. When he had first examined the Native land claims issue in 1961, Udall had been skeptical. One of his aides who had assessed the prospects pessimistically reported that Congress would "never give Alaska's Natives even one acre of fee

[5] The thirteenth corporation consists of Alaskan Natives living outside the state. These Outside Natives had the option of either enrolling in the corporation from their former region, or going with the thirteenth corporation. The twelve regions, according to the Claims Act, were to be "composed, as far as practicable, of Natives having a common heritage and sharing common interests." The twelve regions, their approximate locations in the state, and their main Native groups, are: (1) Sealaska, southeastern, Tlingit and Haida Indians; (2) Arctic Slope, northern, Inupiat Eskimos, (3) NANA (Northwest Alaska Native Association), northwestern, Inupiat Eskimos; (4) Cook Inlet, south central (Anchorage area), urban Eskimos and Indians; (5) Chugach, east of Anchorage, coastal Eskimos, Aleuts, and Indians; (6) Calista, southwest, Yupik Eskimos; (7) Bristol Bay, south of Calista, southwest, Yupik Eskimos; (8) Bering Straits, northwestern (south and west of NANA), Eskimos; (9) Aleut, lower Alaska peninsula and Aleutian Islands, Aleuts; (10) Ahtna, eastern Alaska (north of Chugach region), Athabascan Indians; (11) Koniag, the Kodiak Island group and a portion of the upper Alaska peninsula, Aleuts; (12) Doyon, south of Arctic Slope region (spanning more than one third of the state's land area, with Fairbanks the major city), Athabascan Indians.

[6] Once the $500 million figure is reached, the two percent royalty provision ceases. The federal and royalty money is paid every three months into the Alaska Native Fund, the vehicle for distributing the money to the regional corporations. Under the act, individual stockholders were entitled to 10 percent of the federal money for the first five years of the act. During those years, the average stockholder who was a member of both a regional and village corporation received between $400 and $500 a year.

ALASKA NATIVE LAND OWNERSHIP

SUBSURFACE ESTATE

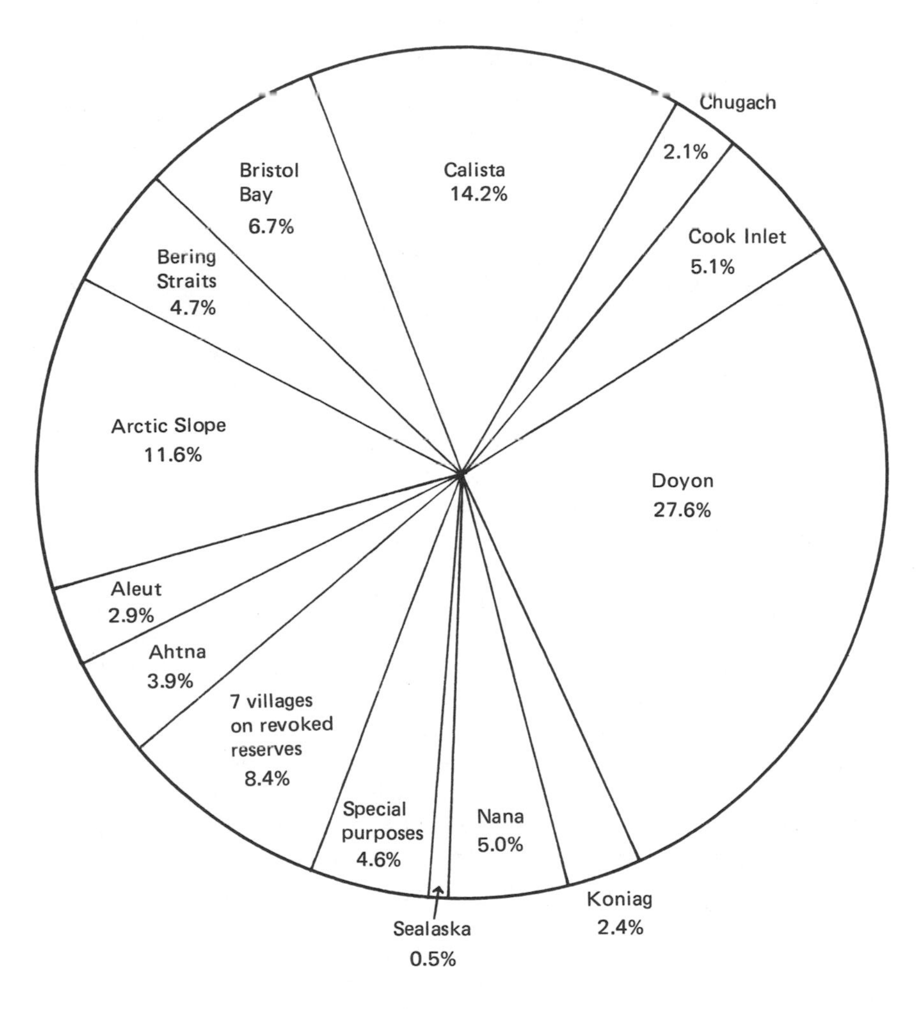

TOTAL ACREAGE – 43.7 MILLION

CREDIT: ALASKA NATIVE LAND CLAIMS
By Robert D. Arnold, Alaska Native Foundation 1976

title land." And when you consider "that in 1961, the Alaska Natives were not organized and had no voice," Udall said, shaking his head, the settlement's passage in 1971 was all the more amazing.

Of course, aggressive Native lobbying played an important role too. But most observers of the fight over the land claims believe it was the oil companies which turned the trick in the end. As Edward Weinberg, one of the Natives' attorneys, was to conclude later, the passage of the act was due "two percent to the justice of the case, ninety-eight percent to the need for oil."

Within three months of the act's passage, there already were arguments over what certain sections of the new law meant. This prompted Senator Lee Metcalf (Democrat, Montana) to comment: "That was a lawsuit we wrote." One Washington lawyer for a Native corporation called it "A litigious nightmare, but a lawyer's picnic;" and a Native leader termed it "The Bar Association Land Claims Settlement Act." Each of the regional corporations has found it necessary to retain Outside counsel, in addition to Alaskan lawyers. A seemingly endless stream of suits has been filed since inception of the act, and Native corporations have had to use millions of dollars of their claims money to pay local and Outside lawyers, primarily ones in Washington, D.C.

There were three major unsettled legal issues as of early 1977, the most bitter of which involved the Interior Department and concerned conveyance of the promised land. Under the act, about 22 million acres were supposed to be transferred to the villages in December 1974 after completion of their selections; the remainder was to be distributed to the regional corporations one year later. But as of a year after the second deadline, there had been few major land transfers to either village or regional corporations. By early 1977, only 5.5 million acres—one eighth of the total—had been conveyed to the Native corporations. Many Natives hoped the Carter administration and Interior Secretary Cecil Andrus would move faster than their predecessors.

One major cause of the delay in conveying land was Interior's insistence on reserving a 25-foot "continuous" easement[7] on all land fronting the ocean and other major waterways. Native lawyers

[7] An easement is basically the right for people to cross land owned by someone else. Easements under the Claims Act would allow the public, a government agency, or a public utility to cross Native-owned lands to get to federal and state lands, waters, resources, or facilities; to bodies of water, cemeteries, or historic sites and monuments; or to public utility, public transportation, or communications routes.

pointed out that the act empowers Interior only to retain easement rights at "periodic points" that are "reasonably necessary" for public access to the land, and they charged that Interior was flagrantly disregarding the act in a classic bureaucratic attempt to retain as much of its domain as possible for as long as possible.

Title transfer also was delayed by disputes over village eligibility to receive lands. The Claims Act provided that only villages with a population of at least twenty-five could select land. Because many Native peoples have lived a largely nomadic existence, determining what constitutes an "eligible village" under the act is open to wide interpretation, and Interior challenged a number of village applications. In 1976 some Natives on Kodiak Island were indicted for filing allegedly false affidavits concerning their village residence. Native lawyers charged harassment.

But the most disturbing legal issue was not the Natives versus federal government, but Natives versus Natives. The claims act provided that the twelve land-owning regional corporations own the subsurface rights not only to the land which they themselves selected, but to the land chosen by villages within their regions. Some regions therefore have access to much more underground wealth than others. One troubling question for the authors of the act was whether the mineral-laden regions should share their riches with their less endowed corporate cousins. A compromise was reached: a corporation would retain 30 percent of the revenues earned from mineral development on its own land, and the remainder would be divided among all the other regional corporations, according to their number of stockholders. This was provided in Section 7(i) of the Claims Act. But the 7(i) language is vague as to whether the word "revenues" means gross or net, what costs may be deducted by the mineral-producing corporation before pooling the revenues, and so on.

Native companies have predictably split on the 7(i) issue along "have" and "have-not" lines. The Arctic Slope Regional Corporation, for example, is a "have." The 84,000 square miles it spans stretch across the top of Alaska, straddle the Prudhoe Bay oil reserves, and almost certainly contain additional oil reserves. The corporation, after receiving $4.5 million from an exploration agreement with several oil companies, unilaterally decided that the other regional corporations were not entitled to share in the money, and spent it. It argued that 7(i) required shared mineral revenues only from "patented" lands, and that Arctic Slope had not officially obtained title to the leased acreage when it received its $4.5 million. It is a technical and dubious legal argument—one that will be resolved in court—and the kind of sneaky trick one might expect Hertz to pull on Avis.

Another major legal issue left unresolved by the Claims Act was what compensation, if any, was due to Natives whose lands were trespassed upon by the state of Alaska and oil and gas companies involved in North Slope oil development prior to the passage of the act. The North Slope Eskimos contended in a federal suit filed in 1973 that the state and the oil companies must pay damages for violating their aboriginal rights. The state argued that the 1971 act not only extinguished the Natives' aboriginal claims, but also eliminated the Natives' rights to file trespass suits. In a 1975 court ruling, a federal district court judge ordered the U.S. Justice Department to intervene and to file a suit (*Edwardsen et al.* v. *Morton et al.*)[8] on behalf of the Eskimos. A federal judge dismissed the suit in early 1977,[9] but the Eskimos said they would appeal.

Needless to say, these and scores of other legal issues have kept the corporations' lawyers quite busy, at the same time sapping the corporations' time and money. Because of the political and legal complexity of the issues, many of the Native corporation leaders we talked to felt it was essential that they hire lawyers who were intimately familiar with the act, or who were politically well connected in Washington, D.C. And so, many firms have retained Outside lawyers with big reputations or who were involved in drafting the claims act. They all command big fees. Although some Native corporations list legal fees in their annual reports, others closely guard the amounts of money they pay their lawyers. Koniag's annual report for fiscal year 1975 listed $185,700 paid in legal fees that year, while the Aleut corporation listed $79,026 for the same year. Roy Huhndorf, president of Cook Inlet Region, Inc. told us in October 1976 that legal and land selection costs for his corporation at that time were "approaching $4 million." Huhndorf said his corporation

[8] The key names in the suit are North Slope Eskimo activist Charles Edwardsen, and former Interior Secretary Rogers C. B. Morton.

[9] The case took an interesting twist in early 1976 when the Justice Department filed a motion asking U.S. District Court Judge James A. von der Heydt to disqualify himself from presiding over it because of discussions he had held with one of the defendants, Alyeska, regarding a possible job for him with the pipeline consortium. The judge withdrew from the case on January 12.

uses a number of attorneys, including F. Conger Fawcett of the firm of Graham and James, in San Francisco; Monroe E. Price, acknowledged authority on Indian law and law professor at the University of California, Los Angeles; and Terry Lenzner, of Washington, D.C., former assistant chief counsel to the Senate Watergate Committee.[10]

Huhndorf said it was conceivable that the corporations could get by with fewer legal expenses but added that because the stakes were so great, "we try to get the best lawyers we can." One other Native leader, who did not wish to be quoted by name, suggested that there was no need to have a big-name lawyer for every piece of litigation that the Native corporations faced. "This thing was designed to make lawyers rich," he concluded. "It has certain built-in conflicts. It's really a Bar Association Land Claims Settlement Act, because it requires so many attorneys to resolve the differences between corporations and government, between corporation and corporation. Once you hire a certain lawyer, you're stuck with him forever, because you become convinced that only he has the particular expertise to handle your problems."

Thus, outstanding lawyers, originally contracted for major legal fights, often end up handling a fair amount of routine legal matters—at a premium price. The Native leader quoted above cited Washington, D.C., attorney Edward Weinberg, a key figure in assisting the Natives in the passage of the land claims act. He noted that Weinberg, an attorney of high integrity, had done excellent legal work in the land claims fight and for Koniag Corporation, and that his remarks were not meant to be critical of him. But, he said, "I can't see having a Weinberg in the garage" on a big retainer, when much of the corporation's legal work could be handled on a more routine basis by someone with less experience. In some cases, he

[10] Among other Washington, D.C., attorneys for Native corporations are Edward Weinberg, former Interior Department solicitor under President Johnson; Arthur Lazarus, of Fried, Frank, Harris, Shriver, & Kampelman (Harris is Patricia Roberts Harris, the Secretary of Housing and Urban Development; Shriver is R. Sargent Shriver, the former Peace Corps director and vice-presidential nominee in 1972); Richmond F. Allan, of Weissbrodt & Weissbrodt; Jonathan Blank, of Preston, Thorgrimson, Ellis, Holman, & Fletcher; Wald, Harkrader, & Ross; Wilkinson, Cragun, & Barker. Stewart Udall recently became associated with Weinberg's firm (Duncan, Brown, Weinberg, & Palmer) and has picked up as clients the Alaska Federation of Natives (on the wilderness lands issue) and one of the firms vying for approval for its route for the trans-Alaska gas pipeline.

said, you want someone like Weinberg; in others the corporations could use younger, energetic, idealistic in-house counsel who could perform the same tasks for much less money.

Over the years, many civil rights, environmental, and consumer organizations have used such attorneys, rather than paying large retainers to more established lawyers. Some Native leaders to whom we posed this possibility agreed that it was probably a good idea, but added that they hadn't seen a flood of idealistic young attorneys clamoring to assist the Native corporations. But then, there was no great interest among the Native corporations to seek out such lawyers, noted one Native leader, because there was a feeling that if you were going to play in the big leagues, you had to have a big-name attorney.

* * *

Because the various legal battles put a cloud of uncertainty over the corporations' eventual land holdings, many of the Native firms as late as 1977 were still searching for a sound investment policy. The regional corporations' investments had run the full gamut: stock investments, trans-Alaska oil pipeline–related businesses, hotels, motels, joint ventures with established firms and with oil companies to seek onshore support bases for offshore oil drilling, and agreements with other private corporations for mineral exploration. By the end of 1976, at least seven of the twelve regional corporations had oil exploration contracts with major companies.

With pipeline construction winding down by late 1976, several Native corporation leaders said their firms were reassessing their investment possibilities. Typical was Cook Inlet's Huhndorf, who told us that his company eventually would move from pipeline-related businesses and property acquisitions to natural resource development. Huhndorf said Cook Inlet's investments eventually "would occur in timber, petroleum, gas, hard-rock minerals, hydrocarbons such as coal, hydroelectric power, cement manufacturing, gravel, possibly agriculture, possibly construction, real estate development, the fishing industry." When we interviewed Huhndorf in October 1976, Cook Inlet's major investments included the purchase in 1975 of five Anchorage-area hotels; the acquisition of a large, 120,000-square-foot commercial warehouse; the purchase of a 26,000-square-foot office building; the development as an investment property and regional corporation headquarters of a $9.5 million, five-story office building with 90,000 square feet of floor space; joint ventures to provide pipeline camp maintenance north of the

Yukon, and for human waste disposal service along the pipeline route; and two major joint ventures involving Native regional corporations—the United Bank of Alaska, and Alaska Consolidated Shipping, Inc., which hopes to get contracts to transport pipeline oil from Valdez to the Lower-48.

For one corporation at least, reassessment of its investment policy was long overdue. The most criticized of the Native firms was Bering Straits Regional Corporation, which had investments all over the state. After receiving its initial land claims cash payments, Bering Straits rushed out and bought twenty-seven corporations. Later it became obvious it had "no idea what's coming off," according to one prominent Native leader who preferred to remain anonymous. He noted the corporation's acquisitions included a trucking company, "even though none of the corporation's people know anything about trucking." So the corporation had "rows and rows of trucks going nowhere." Such investments as these, he said, had severely depleted the corporation's finances. An authority on the Native Claims Act told us that Bering Straits had been "taken for a ride" on many of their real estate transactions. A leader of another Native corporation said that Bering Straits had scattered its investments too widely to be effectively managed and had, through poor leadership and failure to communicate effectively with its stockholders, been unable to build its region into a cohesive unit.

Bering Straits officials themselves admitted some of the problems during their annual stockholders' meeting on April 3, 1976. They acknowledged that not only had there been some bad investments, but that some of the money that was to have been passed on to the village corporations was encumbered and thus was not immediately available to the village units. They also conceded that two of the firm's enterprises—Alaska Truck Transport, and Life Systems, Inc.—had been big money losers. Alaska Truck Transport was sold by the corporation later in 1976.

Stockholders voiced a number of other complaints at the meeting: officers, they said, were being paid too much and weren't communicating adequately with the stockholders; some complicated terms were never understood by Eskimo-speaking shareholders because some English words, like "corporation" have no equivalent in Eskimo languages. In general, the stockholders complained that the corporation was wasting money. The Sitnasuak (Nome) Village Corporation was especially concerned: it was planning to purchase some land in Nome, and wondered if the money held in trust by

Bering Straits for the village corporation was actually there. It was, and would be available soon, Bering Straits executives promised.

Bering Straits was also the target of a state antitrust suit. Three of its mobile home subsidiaries were accused of a policy of illegally tying the rental of trailer court spaces to the purchase of mobile homes. And the Alaska Public Interest Research Group Lobby, which had pushed the state to act in that case, gave Bering Straits yet another public black eye in late 1976. AkPIRG wrote Alaska's U.S. Attorney G. Kent Edwards to ask him to investigate political contributions by a Bering Straits subsidiary to seventeen candidates for the state legislature and one candidate for the Anchorage Municipal Assembly. The Native Claims Settlement Act bars Native corporations from using claims settlement money to contribute to political candidates. The contributions, according to records filed in the state, showed that more than $6,000 was contributed to the candidates by the subsidiary, Anchorage Trailer Sales.[11]

Despite its various investment and legal problems, Bering Straits still had time to acquire a tire recapping company; a franchise for modular buildings; seven mobile home outlets in Valdez, Kenai, Anchorage, and Fairbanks; 24 percent of the stock of Alaska National Bank of the North; and a construction firm with $20 million worth of road and airport contracts annually. Also, the corporation was building a Fairbanks hotel due for completion in 1977; had a working arrangement with the Lost River Mining Company for fluorite exploration; and was planning to talk with some major companies about coal and uranium exploration and of the possibility of providing onshore support for offshore oil drilling in Norton Sound.

Other regional corporations invested in a wide variety of enterprises. The Aleut Corporation, as befits its geography and history, emphasized fishing—unlike Koniag—and the harvesting of fur seals on the Pribilof Islands, the breeding ground for seals for all of the North Pacific. The corporation purchased two crab trawlers for fishing, and a 225-foot motor freight vessel which was leased to a Seattle firm; bought a building in Anchorage and a number of multifamily units in Fairbanks; and was involved with five other regional

[11] Curiously, one of the contributions of $250 went to state legislative candidate Harold Galliett, who had initially successfully challenged in court the legality of a land swap involving the Cook Inlet Native Corporation and the state. The exchange, which was upheld by the state supreme court in early 1977, will substantially benefit the Cook Inlet firm. Thus, Bering Straits was in the position of supporting politically an opponent of one of the other regional corporations.

corporations in the previously-mentioned venture to try to win contracts to ship Alaskan oil to the Lower-48.

Sealaska had big plans involving timber and forest products but was temporarily stymied by environmentalists' lawsuits challenging practices and policies of the U.S. Forest Service in southeastern Alaska, where Sealaska's land selections were to be made. In the meantime, Sealaska purchased a brick company and three subsidiaries—one which makes ready-mix concrete, another which operates a barge service between Anchorage and Seattle, and a third which operates an export-import business. In addition, the regional corporation was constructing a five-story office building, Sealaska Plaza, in Juneau.[12]

Ahtna, the smallest of the regional corporations, made good profits on pipeline-related contracts. One continuing contract was for revegetation and control of soil erosion along the pipeline route. It also had a contract to put into mothballs several pipeline camps at the southern end of the pipeline. In non-pipeline deals, Ahtna, in a joint venture with its village corporations, constructed a $1.5 million, thirty-room hotel in Glennallen, north of Valdez.

The Bristol Bay Regional Corporation was involved in the two major joint ventures involving Native regional corporations—the United Bank of Alaska and Alaska Consolidated Shipping, Inc. In addition, by late 1976 Bristol Bay had tentatively agreed to purchase the Anchorage-Westward, one of Anchorage's major hotels. Before the hotel deal, the major Bristol Bay undertaking was the purchase for $9 million in late 1975 of Peter Pan Seafoods of Seattle, a processing company with 180 vessels and real estate holdings in Washington, Oregon, and Alaska. The corporation was looking into the possibility of copper mining near Chignik on the Alaska Peninsula and had an oil and natural gas exploration agreement with Phillips Petroleum. Additionally, in late 1976, Bristol Bay loaned $70,000 to help the financially ailing *Anchorage Daily News*, then on the verge of bankruptcy.

Chugach was another of the regional corporations whose initial investments were heavily weighted toward pipeline-related work. But only one of its four major pipeline contracts—managing an oil-

[12] Sealaska received the smallest amount of land of any regional corporation, 200,000 acres, because the Tlingit and Haida Indians it represents had been awarded an earlier $7.5 million settlement for land claims by the U.S. Court of Claims in 1959. However, that settlement provided no land to the Indians and the $7.5 million was based on the worth of Tongass Forest lands at the turn of the century.

spill team—remained in operation as pipeline construction wound down in late 1976 and early 1977. The firm also was seeking contracts to operate part of the pipeline after its completion, and to remove snow for the pipeline terminal staff housing area in Valdez. It had an onshore oil exploration agreement with Phillips Petroleum, plus plans to develop Icy Bay into a drilling supply base for outer continental shelf oil development in the Gulf of Alaska, at a cost of $15 million. The onshore facility would supplement a supply base planned by the oil companies at Yakutat, east of the Chugach region. Chugach is also among the six Native regional corporations involved in Alaska Consolidated Shipping.

Calista Corporation involved itself heavily in land and buildings. The corporation broke ground in downtown Anchorage in 1976 for a fifteen-story, $25 million hotel, to be managed by the Sheraton Corporation, that will be the tallest building in the Anchorage area. Another multimillion-dollar venture for Calista is the development of Settler's Bay, a first-of-its-kind Alaska housing and recreational subdivision on 1,800 acres across Knik Arm from Anchorage; it has been mired in controversy and charges of mismanagement. Among Calista's land holdings are a number of parcels totaling 372 acres in the Matanuska-Sustina borough north of Anchorage. Two parcels totaling 173 acres border on the Willow site which Alaska voters in 1976 chose as the location of the state's new capital. Other corporate investments include the joint venture development for $500,000 of the Bay Port Mobile Home Park near the Valdez airport and a travel service with offices in Bethel and Anchorage. And like many of the other regional firms, it also has been strongly interested in oil and natural gas exploration.

* * *

One firm whose corporate mentality has been tempered by a steely commitment to improving the lives of its shareholders is the NANA Regional Corporation. "They haven't made any real bad investments and they have made some money," noted Emil Notti, the slightly built, highly respected head of the Alaska Native Foundation, a study group which publishes material on the Native corporations and the Claims Act. "The best thing is that many of their people are involved in management," unlike stockholders in many of the other Native corporations, Notti, now an executive with Doyon, told us in late 1976.

As John Shively, NANA's vice president of operations, explained to us: "We wanted to build a cadre of people with managerial skills." NANA, unlike many of the other regional corporations, saw one of its main functions as providing jobs for its chronically underemployed shareholders—occupations that are "oriented toward things which fit into the Native life-style and which involve short bursts of work," in Shivcley's words.

Thus, such enterprises as NANA Construction (which built a $7 million utility structure at Deadhorse for the North Slope borough), NANA Environmental Systems (which won a $12.5 million water and sewage contract from the borough), and NANA Security (which had a $15 million Alyeska Pipeline Service Company contract to provide security guards at pipeline camps north of the Yukon River) all employed a significant number of shareholders in temporary jobs. These jobs allowed them to work for periods of, say, ten weeks and return to their homes in the 36,000-square-mile region above the Arctic Circle, where subsistence hunting, fishing, and whaling are still the primary means of livelihood for the 4,900 Eskimo shareholders. NANA also sponsors a picnic each year near a herd of reindeer it owns. After the picnic, board members, staff, and other stockholders dehorn the reindeers. The horns are ground up and sold to Koreans as an aphrodisiac.

NANA also set a low priority on mineral development. It did sign a $3 million oil and gas exploration agreement with Standard Oil of California, but Socal had drilled only dry holes by late 1976, and thirty-seven-year-old NANA President John Schaeffer was not upset. "We don't need to develop the minerals at this time. And it would be in direct opposition to the life-style the people are living now," he told us.

The Eskimo firm showed its concern for protecting that way of life by using its corporate money and managerial skills to bring better or lower-cost services to the stockholders. It started a small company to buy and store low-cost bulk fuel for several villages, which had been purchasing fuel by the barrel at much higher prices. It has guaranteed, along with the village corporation of Kotzebue, the region's largest town and the firm's home base, a $700,000 loan to expand phone service into the smaller villages. And NANA has filed a protest against an application by the region's only freight company for an increase in its rates. Despite the fact that the cost of such life-sustaining staples as food, fuel, and housing in Alaska are among the highest in the world—especially in isolated Native communities—this sort of co-op concept has not been tried by many other Native firms.[13]

As previously mentioned, the Native corporations generally have split along have and have-not lines. Doyon, Ltd. is another have. The largest of the Native regional corporations, the Fairbanks-based firm embraces much of the Alaskan interior. Within the next several years it will receive the patents to 8.4 million acres of land, in addition to subsurface rights to the 3.6 million acres selected by the thirty-four villages in its region. Conservatively, Doyon's real estate assets will be at least $1.2 billion—in addition to $120 million in cash payments that will be paid to it over the next decade or so—which will place it somewhere around 125 on *Fortune*'s list of the 500 largest corporations. As its annual report boasts, "Doyon will become one of the largest private landowners in the United States." But there is little danger that cunning white men will rip off Doyon's 9,000 shareholders, predominantly Athabascan Indians, whose corporate leaders have exhibited considerable caution and savvy in the first years of the firm's existence.

Doyon's initial laborious task after incorporation in May 1972 was to assist the villages in its region in the selection of their allotted 3.6 million acres. The villages were mainly concerned with finding land suitable to sustaining their people's subsistence life-styles—and showed little interest in mineral-bearing land whose development might endanger their way of life. But Doyon used other criteria in selecting its own lands; it wanted to find the best possible oil and mineral real estate.

The villages had little problem in determining which lands were best for them; Doyon had more trouble. Geological surveys were a very expensive way to locate oil-rich lands. So Doyon did what a number of other Native corporations have done—it entered into a partnership agreement with oil and mineral companies. First,

[13] The Native regional corporations have entered into few business deals with one another. This is due mainly to the many previously discussed legal tangles in which all the corporations find themselves, as well as the disagreements among the various regional firms over the 7 (i) mineral revenue sharing issue. There had been two notable exceptions to this by late 1976. Five of the regional corporations—Cook Inlet, Calista, Bristol Bay, Doyon, and NANA—formed United Bank of Alaska, which was chartered in 1975. The bank is owned by Unicorp., Inc., a holding company in which all five corporations own stock. In 1976, six of the corporations—Calista, Bristol Bay, Cook Inlet, Koniag, Chugach, and Aleut—formed a joint venture with Seatrain, the East Coast shipping firm, to try to win contracts to transport pipeline oil to the Lower-48.

it struck a deal with Louisiana Land and Exploration, Ashland Oil, and Amerada Hess to explore jointly more than 2 million acres. Wary of a broad-based agreement under which Doyon would lose both control and profits, the agreement allows the oil consortium to develop a maximum of only one eighth of the land it explores. Doyon also took on five new partners—British Petroleum, General Crude Oil, Union Carbide, Ethyl, and McIntyre Mines—to explore for minerals. And it contracted with American Smelting and Refining Company to develop some asbestos reserves in Eagle, about 175 miles east of Fairbanks.

Doyon president Tim Wallis doesn't like Section 7 (i). That sort of revenue sharing is "unworkable," he told us, adding that "corporations, by their nature, are competitive." In any event, 7 (i) "impedes growth" because it removes much of a corporation's incentive to develop its subsurface estate. Let each of the corporations fend for itself, he said. After all, does Macy's share profits with Gimbel's?

Doyon's largest investment by early 1977 was a $2.3 million building in Fairbanks it used for its headquarters. In a joint venture with a Fairbanks construction firm, it also received a $14 million contract to service several hundred miles of the North Slope Haul Road that runs parallel to the trans-Alaska pipeline. It set up an engineering and surveying subsidiary, and committed $600,000 to the joint venture with four other Native corporations toward the establishment of the Native-owned United Bank of Alaska.

* * *

While the outlook for many of the regional corporations is uncertain, the future for most of the 220 village corporations is very bleak, according to many authorities. Their financial woes spring largely from their dependent status: under the Claims Act, the regional corporations exercise certain controls over village corporations, effectively creating a guardian relationship between the two. Most village corporations are like subsidiaries of the regional corporations. For example, all monies received from the federal government and from the 2 percent natural resources royalty goes first to the regional corporation. It, in turn, distributes about one half of the funds to the village corporations and individuals. Regional corporations have a certain supervisory role, and may legally withhold funds from village corporations if their proposed projects appear to offer little benefit to the entire region. Regional corporations also have the authority to review land selections made by the villages, which were granted one half of the land under the Claims Act. Regionals have a legitimate interest in those 22 million acres because the Claims Act gave them the subsurface rights to most village lands, and a total of 40 million acres of the entire 43.7 million awarded under the act.[14]

Many village corporations with limited resources face severe difficulties unless they merge their assets with other villages, or merge or enter managerial agreements with their regional corporations, according to consultant Lee Gorsuch. In an analysis prepared for the Alaska Native Foundation, Gorsuch said that a village corporation could not carry out its corporate duties for much less than $70,000 a year.[15] This would include a full-time manager and secretary-bookkeeper, limited legal fees, and some travel and office expenses. Expenses are often a problem simply because of the village's size: more than half the corporations have fewer than 200 shareholders, and more than one fourth of the village corporations have fewer than 100 shareholders. Depending upon their size, village corporations in fiscal year 1976 were receiving anywhere from $9,500 to about $875,000 a year. Though some of the larger villages would have enough funds to make it on their own, most smaller villages obviously would find it difficult, if not impossible, to be successful profit-making corporations. As Gorsuch told us, "The vast majority of these villages have no way in hell of making it" as corporations. "They are so removed, naive, and ignorant of what's going on that unless the regional corporations take any kind of interest, they're the most vulnerable of the whole group."

Despite all the investment activity and the precarious financial status of the village corporations, it is still too early to judge—more than five years after the passage of the Alaska Native Claims Settlement Act—whether the Native corporations are a financial success. An early, and very tentative, analysis by two officials of the Ahtna Native Corporation ranked the more profitable firms in these early

[14] The act provided that six of the regional corporations—Ahtna, Arctic Slope, Chugach, Cook Inlet, Doyon, and NANA—receive both surface and subsurface rights to 16 million acres. This land is not shared with village corporations. It was awarded under what was called the "land loss" provision of the act which enabled those six regions to receive land that Natives of those regions traditionally have used and occupied, rather than being awarded solely on the basis of population (as was the case with the 22 million acres). The regionals also have subsurface rights to another 2 million acres awarded under a number of miscellaneous provisions of the act.

[15] Under the Claims Act, the village corporations may opt for either nonprofit or for-profit status. Regional corporations are required by the act to be for-profit, but they also are permitted to set up non-profit arms.

years as Doyon, NANA, Cook Inlet, Ahtna, Sealaska, and Chugach. The less profitable corporations were Koniag, Aleut, Bristol Bay, Bering Straits, Arctic Slope, and Calista. As soon as the legal battles are settled and all 44 million acres acquired by the corporations, some long-range trajectories may be plotted, both for specific firms and the whole Native corporation experiment. In the meantime, any general assessments of the financial performance of the Native corporations are close to meaningless.

If it is difficult to assess the corporations' fiscal posture at this time, it is clear that the newfound wealth has made Native leaders generally more conservative. With several of the Native firms investing in banks, most Native legislators in the 1976 session of the House voted against a bill designed to prevent redlining. Redlining is a discriminatory practice by which banks mark off an entire neighborhood as being too risky for mortgage and home improvement investment. Its effect in metropolitan areas is to deny lower-income people, mainly blacks, the ability to purchase homes. Most Native legislators opposed the bill designed to prevent this unethical practice. It was defeated. One Native legislator argued, "What if our bank wants to redline?" In Alaska, of course, the most likely victims of redlining are Natives and the state's 15,000 blacks.

Mike Bradner (Democrat, Fairbanks), speaker of the Alaska House of Representatives when we interviewed him in August 1976, ticked off several other pieces of legislation defeated in the 1976 session largely through Native opposition. One measure would have allowed credit unions to perform many functions of a bank. Another was an anti-trust proposal which would have prohibited the "tie-in" of the sale of mobile homes to the rental of space at mobile home parks. Another would have raised taxes on oil and would, of course, have applied to oil discoveries on Native land.

Some Native leaders worry about the shifting political sands of the Native state legislators and corporate leadership. Eben Hopson,[16] former AFN president and one of the important figures in the Native Claims Act fight, sees a disturbing trend in the erosion of traditional Native commitments to "bush" legislation with social aims:

> Many of these regional corporations have signed exploration and option agreements with oil corporations and several of these regional corporations

[16] Hopson also ran unsuccessfully for Congress in 1976, losing to incumbent Republican Don Young after winning the Democratic nomination.

have begun to appear to be politically aligned with their oil corporate partners. Suddenly, Native members of the state legislature, who used to vote as liberal Democrats, now vote with conservative urban Republicans on oil and gas legislation, thus alienating the urban liberals whose votes we could count on [in the past] to pass bush legislation in such areas as health, education, and local government.

New coalitions are developing. I worry about this. I worry that while this new oil coalition may work well for the oil industry's tax avoidance, it won't work for the people of our villages. We have had to work many years to build the political friendships in the state legislature that we enjoy, and I would hate to see these friendships lost because of the oil boom.

I worry that, as the market value of Alaska's oil rises, the new oil-bush coalition will prevent oil taxes from being raised accordingly, denying all Alaskans their fair share of oil revenue. . . . I do not believe that letting oil corporations explore our land for oil obliges us to adopt the politics of oil corporations.

This Native-conservative coalition reached rather alarming proportions in the 1977 legislative session, at least as far as the Democrats were concerned, when several Democratic Native legislators almost decided to give the GOP control of the House of Representatives —including the committee chairmanships—by voting to allow the GOP to reorganize the House. To the great relief of the Democrats, negotiations between the Natives and the GOP minority leaders broke down at the last minute.

Many prominent non-Natives also were concerned with the new political directions of many Native leaders. Bradner worried that Native legislators "do not see the corporations as special interests but as broadly representative of the needs of their constituents, which they are not." Representative Joe McKinnon, a liberal Democratic state legislator from Anchorage, put it more sharply. The Native legislators "are getting into the corporate mentality," he told us, adding, "What surprises me is that it happened overnight." However, Doyon president Tim Wallis thought that was overstating it. "The changes in votes may reflect a better understanding of management rather than merely a reflection of our own interests," he said.

Former state senator and NANA official Willie Hensley sees a better explanation for the new conservatism of Native legislators. He said that the Native legislators' positions on issues were in line with the views of Native corporation stockholders. "Now that we have some land, we're not going to let the legislature take it away, we're not going to let them tax us to death. If we have some resources, we're not going to let them take it." And, he added: "That's the American system—to please the stockholders."

Unfortunately, a sizable number of stockholders are not pleased. In fact, one Native leader noted there is scarcely a region where there isn't an "out" group of Natives contending for seats on the corporations' boards of directors. In some cases, the outs merely want control; in other cases, they seem genuinely concerned that their corporations are taking the Native people away from their centuries-old life-style in their pursuit of profits.

The Sealaska Corporation, the southeast Alaska corporation that represents the Tlingit and Haida Indians, was one such corporation besieged by dissatisfied stockholders. The disgruntled Sealaska stockholders organized in October 1976 "Operation David and Goliath" in an effort to oust the corporation's board of directors. David Katzeek, one of the leaders of the opposition movement, said that Sealaska was too devoted to the profit motive and failed to recognize that the area's "greatest assets are not just dollars and cents." Katzeek also complained that the corporation's board of directors candidates are selected by a management-dominated screening committee, which leads to a self-perpetuating organizational hierarchy. "Operation David and Goliath" presented a seven-point platform that was widely distributed throughout the Sealaska region. One of the points the group made was that the Native people's control of their land and resources must be protected when current stockholders' shares are allowed to be sold on the open market in 1991. "There will be and are multinational corporations that are interested in our shares," the group warned in reference to Japanese corporations which are heavily involved in the forest products industry in southeastern Alaska. The group also warned that the corporation must be more socially responsible and must work to develop jobs for its people. "The greatest profit of the corporation will be to develop its human resources," and Sealaska must be "sensitive to the needs of the people."

A similar battle erupted in the Bristol Bay Native Corporation. The clash started in 1976 when a group of stockholders formally petitioned the BBNC board of directors to discuss a corporation plan to purchase Peter Pan Seafoods. Management threw out the petition, saying it did not contain enough valid signatures, and the special meeting was not held. The corporation then went ahead and purchased the seafood firm. The dissidents maintained that the corporation's officers did not attempt to communicate with the stockholders on vital matters of company policy and were not concerned with enhancing the village life-style. In response, the corporation filed a libel suit against some of the dissidents.

One of the dissident stockholders, Archie Gottschalk, commented that he agreed that BBNC has to be a profit-making corporation under the law. But, he added, "I'd rather make one dollar profit instead of two dollars if it would benefit the people of the villages in services." Robert Bacon, BBNC's vice president in charge of operations, countered that the Claims Act requires the corporations "to undertake profit-making ventures, not ones of social health. It is not a question of wanting to, but not being able to under the law." But Frank Woods, Jr., a BBNC director who sided with the dissidents —and who was among those being sued for libel—said:

> The regional corporations have got to have human concerns to survive. BBNC has never taught its children—the villages—anything. Someone said years ago, "Keep them in the dark and they're easier to lead."

Some observers believe the Sealaska and Bristol Bay battles presage similar struggles for other regional corporations, somewhat along class lines: the educated, professional management group being challenged by less well-educated Native villagers and urban blue-collar workers.

Many prominent non-Natives, including Governor Hammond and former Interior Secretary Udall, have urged Natives not to fall prey to the notion of putting profits above the concerns for their traditional way of life. Hammond told us:

> Now you've got an interesting potential conflict developing in the Native community where you have the boys with the horn-rimmed glasses and the college education and briefcases who, given the administrative structure of the corporation, are going to be development-oriented [in order] to sustain the bureaucratic structure that . . . has been imposed upon them [by the Claims Act]. . . . You're going to find that there are some Natives who aspire to the continuation of the life-style they now enjoy.

Like most Western innovations and ideas, the concept of a corporation has no equivalent in Native culture. As anthropologist Tony Vaska, a Yupik Eskimo from near Bethel, noted, "The majority of the Natives don't understand the corporate structure. It's totally alien to the way we've always lived. Everyone used the land. Nobody owned it." Not surprisingly, the annual shareholders meetings are poor mediums for debating policy, since few stockholders understand the principles of corporations and capitalism in general. Annual reports, which can be bewildering to college-educated people, are incomprehensible to most Natives, who have lived a life far removed from corporate boardrooms. As one prominent Native leader put it, "A guy in the village who gets up enough guts to stand up at the annual meeting and say something is confronted by a highly educated guy who's trying to explain something he doesn't understand. There's no communication. The Native is reduced to anger."

Kodiak's Ed Naughton tells a story which illustrated the dilemma of the average Native stockholders in the corporations. Naughton recalled the euphoric days of late 1971—"when we came back with the land claims settlement in our hands"— and he went to a Kodiak Island village to tell the Natives what the settlement would mean for them. He was deeply involved in "describing the village corporations, the regional corporations, the for-profit corporations, and all these fantastic corporate strata" when he suddenly looked up and noticed "a gal old enough to be my mother—in fact, she was a good friend of my mother—who's giving me the poker face." That is "an expression we Natives wear when we're listening to white people talk, and we don't want to admit we don't know what they're saying, or that we dislike them and don't want to let them know that we dislike them.

"Now when a Native gives a Native the poker face, whoo, look out, there's something wrong. And so I just stopped right there and said, 'what's gone wrong? Is there something you don't understand?' And she said, 'Yes—corporations.' She said, 'I heard that word for a long time and I don't know what it means.' Now how in the hell are these people who five years ago didn't even know what a corporation means going to know how to operate in them, particularly when the leaders in that corporation are playing very close to the chest and not even telling each other what they're doing?

"How easily they could be led down the path," Naughton said, "because for them at the outset it becomes just an article of faith. They're either going to trust the leadership or they're not, and they're going to have to hope that whoever's making the decisions until they are up to speed as stockholders . . . is going to do them right." Unfortunately, that number of aware stockholders is small. One Fairbanks lawyer estimated that there are no more than 400 Natives in the state who truly understand the land claims settlement, and almost all of them are in leadership positions.

*   *   *

The danger in this lack of understanding of the corporation by most Natives is that the Native community in Alaska is becoming corporatized. As with most economically disadvantaged minorities, the Native leadership pool is limited. And the action has switched from the political to the economic front. Former political leaders, many of whom were instrumental in getting the Claims Act passed, were naturally attracted by the economic clout of the corporations —as well as the $40,000 to $50,000 salaries many top officers are paid. Because of their former political status and because of the corporations' overwhelming importance to the Native community, the firms' officers are frequently still looked upon by their shareholders as broad-based community leaders, even though their perspectives and interests have narrowed somewhat.

With a few exceptions, the Native firms are corporations just like IBM and AT&T. And, while most of the corporate leaders say they realize that part of their mission is to help preserve the traditional Native life-styles, the ultimate success of a corporation is, as Koniag's Karl Armstrong noted, determined by that one quantifiable measure—profits and losses. And as corporations were designed more for stability than for democracy, they were also designed more to protect proprietary interests than to require disclosure and openness. It is not surprising that some of the Native corporations decline to disclose the salaries of officers, for example, or that some are reluctant to discuss negotiations with oil companies, even with their own shareholders.

Given the limitations and potential pitfalls involved in the modern corporate structure, it is somewhat surprising that, during the years of debate preceding the Alaska Native Claims Settlement Act, the focus was almost solely on the corporation as the vehicle for a settlement. Remarkably, the pre-settlement debate gave no serious consideration to developing a more democratic entity that would more nearly meet the economic and cultural needs of the Native peoples. As established, the Native corporations leave important decision-making power in the hands of a few corporate leaders. The individual shareholder's sole check on the corporation is a limited one: he or she can cast a vote at the annual stockholders' meeting for members of the board of directors. As the book *Alaska Native Land Claims*, the Alaska Native Foundation's detailed analysis of the Claims Act, puts it:

> Although a corporation's stockholders are its owners, the role of stockholders in the life of a typical corporation is a very limited one. . . . What the corporation sets out to do, and how effectively it accomplishes it, is dependent upon the qualities of judgment brought to the enterprise by corporate leaders.

Although directors are elected on the basis of one person, one vote, it is difficult for stockholders in most of the Native corporations to mount effective challenges to the group in power. This is due partly to a lack of political sophistication; partly to geographical factors which make it difficult for dissidents to get together to organize their opposition; and largely to the power of corporate incumbents to use the proxy.

The level of democracy in the corporations could be improved considerably, however, if the Native firms were organized in a different corporate form—along the lines of cooperatives. Such changes could be achieved through revisions in corporate bylaws rather than through amendments to the Native Claims Act. A key to the cooperative structure is maximum decision-making power by the stockholders, rather than by a few directors and corporate managers. Because the regional corporations all have more than 1,000 stockholders, it probably would be unwieldy for them to call full meetings every time there is a policy, or major investment, decision to be made. Instead, a representative assembly of, say, 100, could be established; this would not only democratize the corporate decision-making process, but also would involve more deeply a greater number of individual stockholders, thereby reinforcing the feeling that the corporation is really theirs. Art Danforth, secretary-treasurer of the Cooperative League of the United States, told us that cooperatives at their best "can be kind of like New England town meetings," in that they involve the nearest thing possible to direct democracy under the corporate structure. In a situation where the corporate structure is an unfamiliar one, such as is the case with many Alaska Natives, and where there are even language barriers, the cooperative system would be far preferable, because important decisions affecting the future of the culture would be made by a representative group of Natives rather than just by a small number of corporate managers.

During the battle leading up to passage of the Claims Act, the Native lobbyists stressed the need for a settlement that would enable the Native cultures to survive and would also allow the Natives to prosper financially. A per capita disbursement wouldn't have made a lot of sense, since the Natives treat land used to sustain their subsistence way of life as community property. Certainly, the paternalistic Indian policies of the past—a federal agency protecting the interests of its wards—have been discredited.

But there *are* problems with the Claims Act. Some Native leaders told us that one troubling aspect of the act is that Natives born after 1971 cannot obtain stock in any of the corporations except through inheritance. Even more worrisome is the provision that allows Natives to sell their stock after 1991, which raises the specter of eventual non-Native control. For example, in the case of Doyon, the largest of the regions,[17] the value of its land alone could make a stockholder's 100 shares worth more than $130,000 in 1992. With such value, many individual stockholders may be tempted to sell. Finally, there is an obvious built-in conflict between the goals of protecting a way of life and making profits. And some Natives have expressed the worry that the end result of corporatizing Alaska's Native people could be the same thing that happened when the Menominee Indians of the Midwest had their tribal status terminated and had land from their former reservation in the Menominee Forest turned over to them and corporatized. As the Native American Rights Fund described the aftermath of the Menominee Termination Act signed into law on June 17, 1954:

> The tribal assets were turned over to a new corporation, Menominee Enterprises, Inc. (MEI), and suddenly Menominee survival was based on knowledge of a complicated corporate style of living including: par value stocks, voting trusts, income bonds and shareholders' rights. . . .
>
> The effects of termination and corporate-style management of Menominee assets pitted brother against brother and parents against their children. It increased the poverty of most individual Menominees, created political turmoil, and brought on economic chaos. . . .

[17] The approximate amount of land due to each of the regions (including villages within the regions) under the Alaska Native Claims Settlement Act is: Doyon, 12 million acres; Calista, 6.2 million; Arctic Slope, 5.1 million; Bristol Bay, 2.9 million; NANA, 2.2 million; Cook Inlet, 2.2 million; Ahtna, 1.7 million; Aleut, 1.3 million; Koniag, 1 million; Chugach, 920,000; Bering Straits, 2.1 million; Sealaska, 200,000.

The approximate amount of federal and mineral royalty money that will go to each region under the Claims Act is: Sealaska, $200 million; Calista, $165 million; Doyon, $115 million; Bering Straits, $85 million; Cook Inlet, $75 million; Bristol Bay, $65 million; NANA, $60 million; Arctic Slope, $48 million; Aleut, $40 million; Koniag, $40 million; Chugach, $25 million; Ahtna, $12 million.

MEI, as well as individual Menominees, were forced to sell corporate shares and land in order to pay county and state taxes. As a result, acres and acres of the heartland of the magnificent Menominee forest were sold to non-Indians and Menominee reservation lands fell into the hands of non-Indian developers who destroyed religious sites and the cultural character of the community.

The report went on to note that unlike the Alaskan Natives, the Menominees did not have actual control of the corporation; this instead was handled by "non-Indian businessmen and so-called experts . . . to insure its success." Also, the Menominees faced immediate taxation of their lands, while the Alaska Native corporations have no such problem on undeveloped lands until 1992. Eventually, the Menominees asked restoration of their tribal status so that they could hold on to some of their financial assets, land, and tribal culture.[18]

Although there are differences in the Menominee and Alaska settlements, there are enough similarities to make the future uncertain for some of the corporations and the Native cultures. Yet, despite all the legal snafus and internal conflicts within the corporations, there still is no question that the Land Claims Act has given the Alaska Natives more political and economic clout than any minority group in the U.S. has ever commanded in one state. An orientation speech that was given by management for workers on the trans-Alaska oil pipeline illustrates this:

Now, then, you may come upon a small Indian village of twelve or fifteen families somewhere up along the Yukon. You are to treat these people with respect. When you see them you may wonder why you are to treat them with respect. Well, we can give you three very good reasons. First, because they are people. Second, because they were here first and they owned the land before we did. Third, because their Native Land Claims corporations have got the money to hire the best legal talent in the United States.

There is an old Native saying that, "The way to beat the white man is with the white man's tools." As NANA's Hensley put it: "Anything that came along that helped us survive, we took ahold of it." The corporation, he told us, is just another of the white man's

[18] In the event the Alaska Native corporations ran into financial difficulty, what would the federal government's responsibility be, if any? Law professor Monroe E. Price, of the University of California, Los Angeles, noted that the situation is unclear. "No one knows what continues to be the relationship between the Alaska Native and the United States after the implementation of the Alaska Native Claims Settlement Act."

tools which the Natives can use to survive. "To me, this kind of extension of the corporate tool is not much different than trying to pick up an outboard motor, or a steel-tipped spear, or a gun to survive."

But whether the white man's tools will shape the Natives, or whether the Natives will adapt those tools to fit their own distinct needs, is still an open question.

VI

Pipe Dream

MENTION ALASKA to non-Alaskans today and most immediately think of the trans-Alaska oil pipeline. Mention the pipeline to Alaskans, and most yawn. With oil flowing by mid-1977, the pipeline was already yesterday's issue.

But if the pipeline was yesterday's issue in Alaska, oil is not. One thing that the super-growthers and the environmentalists agree on is that oil will continue to be the focus of controversy in Alaska for many years, even decades to come. Even by conservative estimates, Alaska's onshore and outer continental shelf lands contain the equivalent of at least eight more Prudhoe Bays. It is no wonder then, that a headline in a late 1976 issue of *Advertising Age* happily trumpeted: "For Anchorage, Oil Pipeline Is Only Tip of Iceberg."

Indeed it is. A mid-1974 report by the energy resources section of the Alaska Department of Natural Resources estimated the "speculative recoverable" oil in the state, excluding Prudhoe Bay's 9.6 billion barrels, at 77 billion barrels, and natural gas at 440 trillion cubic feet. And the state agency called its estimate of 77 billion barrels "conservative," as much as 50 percent too low. Some industry authorities put the Prudhoe Bay oil reserves at as high as 100 billion barrels. (William A. Egan, during his most recent term as governor from 1970 to 1974, liked to say there were 300 billion barrels of recoverable oil in Alaska, in what was undoubtedly an excessive burst of state pride.)[1] Add those 100 billion barrels to the estimates of as much as 33 billion barrels in the Naval Petroleum Reserve No. 4 (renamed National Petroleum Reserve in Alaska, as of June 1, 1977), which is expected to be open to private development in a few

[1] State minerals official Gilbert R. Eakins gave an even more optimistic estimate of 600 billion barrels during a 1972 speech to the Northwest Mining Association convention.

years, and there is a potential of 133 billion barrels of oil—onshore—on the North Slope alone. Multiply this by a conservative $12 per barrel and the North Slope could contain $1.6 trillion worth of oil—not counting the billions of barrels that lie off Alaska's expansive outer continental shelf offshore!

It is clear that Alaska has been targeted by the industry as the singular oil state of the future. Interior Secretary Thomas S. Kleppe estimated in late 1976 that the entire nation had proven crude oil reserves of about 32.6 billion barrels and natural gas reserves of about 230 trillion cubic feet. This would mean that Prudhoe Bay, according to industry figures, contains about 30 percent of the nation's oil reserves and about 11 percent of the natural gas reserves. Using the more optimistic 100-billion-barrel estimates, Prudhoe Bay alone could have three times as much oil as the rest of the United States—and more natural gas reserves than all the other states combined.

But trying to pin down oil reserve numbers is like trying to nail jelly to a tree or, in the words of one oil writer, "a little like quoting Scriptures: anyone can find an estimate to support his argument." Oil companies, the source of almost all government statistics relating to oil reserves, are notorious for understating reserves. In Alaska and elsewhere in recent years it has paid them to continue to underestimate reserves in order to make national energy problems appear more severe than they actually are and thus justify vastly higher prices. Specifically in Alaska, oil companies fear that the go-slow-on-development policies of Governor Hammond, combined with some liberal legislators' zeal, will result in additional taxes on them if reserve estimates are put at higher figures. Regardless of which figures one uses, though, the one clear point that emerges is that there is a lot of oil in Alaska, and that the multinational oil companies are going to make a great deal of money from it. And even those who are accused by the Boomers of being no-growthers see the state tied to oil development for decades to come. As Hammond told us:

> Well, of course, now we're funding state government to the tune of sixty-three percent from oil revenues. We've become so dependent on them that if you in fact drove them out of the state it would be extremely traumatic.

Even before the start-up of the pipeline, Alaska had become an oil-producing state, thanks to discoveries in the Kenai Peninsula and in the Upper Cook Inlet in south central Alaska, in the late 1950s and early 1960s. In addition to Prudhoe Bay, other major areas being actively pursued by the oil industry as of 1977 were Naval Petroleum Reserve No. 4 (referred to as NPR-4 or Pet 4), federal outer continental shelf waters of southern, western, and northern Alaska; state offshore lands, particularly in the Beaufort Sea of northern Alaska; and additional onshore areas that either are, or will be, owned by the state or the Native corporations.

Add to that the oil potential of Alaska's neighbors Siberia to the west and Canada to the east—and one can come up with a scenario in which Alaska's unmatchable wilderness is immersed in, and surrounded by, all kinds of onshore and offshore oil development over the next couple of decades. Some federal officials have estimated that approximately 7,500 miles of additional pipelines and 6,000 miles of new highways will be needed to bring out Alaska's oil, natural gas and other mineral treasures.

* * *

To appreciate what Alaska's future as an oil storehouse could be like requires an understanding of the impact the largest private project in history has had on the second least populous American state.

On July 18, 1968, at a time when the Vietnam War was raging and a bitter presidential campaign was in full swing, the remote state of Alaska was suddenly front-page news across the country. For on that day, Atlantic Richfield Company (Arco) and Humble Oil & Refining Company (now the Exxon Company, U.S.A.) confirmed what had been rumored for months: that Prudhoe Bay, on Alaska's North Slope, was the site of a major oil discovery. The find was estimated by the companies' consulting firm of DeGolyer and Martin at some 9.6 billion barrels.[2] (In 1971, Arco suggested the Prudhoe Bay reserves were closer to 16 billion barrels but it, like the other oil companies, chose to stick with the lower estimate.)

Alaskans were ecstatic. A boom was at hand, and they wanted to cash in. Republican Governor Keith H. Miller, on September 9, 1969, undoubtedly spoke for many of his constituents when he stated: "Tomorrow we will reach our birthright. We will rendezvous with our dreams." The next day the state auctioned off 450,000 acres of Prudhoe Bay for what then seemed the astounding sum of $900,220,590—the largest oil lease sale in U.S. history.

Even before the lease sale, those oil companies already holding productive leases (for which they had paid a relatively modest $12 million) at Prudhoe Bay—Arco, Humble (later Exxon) and British

[2] DeGolyer and Martin estimated reserves for the entire North Slope at 25 billion barrels.

Petroleum, Ltd.—had announced plans in February 1969 to jointly build a trans-Alaska oil pipeline. On June 6, 1969, the three companies, operating as the Trans-Alaska Pipeline System (TAPS), an unincorporated venture, filed with the U.S. Interior Department an application for a permit to build an 800-mile hot-oil pipeline from Prudhoe Bay to the ice-free port of Valdez, a small picturesque fishing village on Prince William Sound in southern Alaska.

To get the permit, TAPS would have to receive a waiver from a federal land freeze—imposed two years earlier by then Interior Secretary Stewart Udall—that was then in effect for all of Alaska. Nonetheless, the oil companies asked Interior Secretary Walter J. Hickel to approve the permit by early July 1969. Even before seeking the permit, the oil companies, apparently confident that approval would be obtained quickly, had made several important decisions: that the pipeline would go to Valdez and nowhere else, that 48-inch diameter pipe would be used for the pipeline, and that, since no U.S. company made pipe of that size, it would be ordered from Japan. Most important, the companies had determined they would build a buried pipeline, just as they had done many times in the Lower-48, despite the risks to Alaska's delicate permafrost-covered tundra, which could be severely damaged from hot oil flowing through the pipeline at temperatures of up to 180 degrees.

After the state held its lease sales in September 1969, the original three oil companies in TAPS added five more partners. Eventually, these eight owners of the pipeline system—Arco, Exxon, British Petroleum, Standard Oil of Ohio (Sohio), Mobil, Phillips, Union, and Amerada Hess—formally incorporated as the Alyeska Pipeline Service Company, Inc.

Despite its optimistic expectations for the July 1969 pipeline approval from Interior Secretary Hickel, the group had to wait. Because of opposition from environmentalists during his confirmation hearings, Hickel had had to agree to extend the land freeze imposed by Udall. So the secretary was forced to go a little slowly on pipeline approval. Even so, the oil companies had good reason to be confident of approval. Hickel, governor of Alaska before being named by President Nixon to the cabinet post, was a strong booster of the pipeline; he was in fact one of the longtime Boomers.

The wait was not long. In October 1969, the interior secretary asked the House and Senate Interior Committees to make an exception and to lift the land freeze for the purpose of the pipeline project only. After Hickel gave assurances that he would not grant a permit until the oil companies had satisfactorily explained how they would deal with permafrost and other environmental problems, the Senate committee in early December gave its approval, and the House committee followed suit a few days later. While this was occurring, however, significant legislation was being enacted that would give further ammunition to environmentalists who wanted to block the pipeline. Within two weeks after the committees gave their approval to lift the land freeze for the pipeline, President Nixon signed into law the National Environmental Policy Act (NEPA), which required an environmental impact statement as a precondition for any federally funded project or project on federal lands. The law was to give crucial impetus to the battle against the pipeline beginning to take shape.

Critics first focused on the environmental havoc they felt would be created by a hot-oil pipeline passing through delicate tundra and the habitat of a rich variety of fish, birds, and other wildlife—some of which could be found in no other areas of the United States. They emphasized the dangers of oil spills to the land, to the lakes, streams, and rivers. They warned of tanker accidents that could damage the fishing industry and severely pollute the Gulf of Alaska and the Pacific and Alaskan coasts. They warned that the pipeline would traverse some of the worst earthquake areas in the world and pointed out that Valdez, the pipeline port terminal, had been wiped out by the 1964 earthquake, the mightiest ever recorded in North American history. (The entire town was later rebuilt four miles west of its old site.)[3]

Native groups and some environmentalists also expressed concern over the impact that the pipeline and its accompanying North Slope Haul Road would have on subsistence fishing and hunting for the Natives. Particular concern was voiced over the caribou which, it was feared, would be diverted from their traditional breeding grounds and migration patterns by pipeline-related activity—and thus would not be readily available to Natives who for centuries had depended on them for food.

Typical of the environmentalists' concern was the statement of Edgar Wayburn, vice-president of the Sierra Club, who testified in

[3] Of 115 persons killed in that earthquake, 31 died at Valdez. According to a 1975 publication by Exxon, called *Exxon and the Environment*, the 1964 earthquake "released the energy of 500,000 Hiroshima-size atomic bombs." See Chapter XII for more details on Alaska's earthquake potential.

Anchorage on February 24, 1971, at Interior's hearings on the draft environmental impact statement for the pipeline:

> The entire . . . statement seems to us an apology for acceptance of arbitrary decisions previously made. It presents a fairly rosy picture of what just might happen, but hopefully won't, to the terrain, to the wildlife, and to the Alaskan people and their environment, if the proposed pipeline is constructed. . . . Properly, it should not be entitled an "environmental impact statement" but a 'construction justification statement.' . . . It evades detailed discussion of major adverse impacts of such threats as devastating earthquakes, a single page summarizing that the entire southern two thirds of the pipeline is "subject to the occurrences of large earthquakes, magnitude seven or greater." It gives almost no consideration to the immense problem of . . . tanker traffic and the real and frightening possibility of oil spills from Prince William Sound to Puget Sound and San Francisco Bay and Los Angeles. . . . Although it admits the hazard of marine and inland oil spills, permafrost problems, and destruction of wildlife and wilderness values, it treats all of these very superficially. The statement simply fails to mention the impact of feeder pipelines and roads throughout the North Slope.

Some Alaskans were torn between their concern for Alaska's wilderness values and what they perceived as the majority will of the state's residents to remove Prudhoe Bay oil via a trans-Alaska pipeline. One such person was Lowell Thomas, Jr., son of the famous newscaster, a state senator at the time of the 1971 environmental impact statement hearings in Anchorage, later elected lieutenant governor. At the 1971 hearings, he testified:

> I am here basically because of the unique environmental qualities of Alaska, and the fact that it is an unspoiled land of opportunity, not only to make a living, but also to enjoy the good things in life, which are pure atmosphere and scenic wonders. But at the same time, . . . I would like to say that as a conservationist, I think Alaska must have a certain degree and amount of development of its natural resources if we are going to pay our bills as a state and meet the needs of our people, if we are going to do the right thing by our indigenous people.

The testimony of environmental groups and those on middle ground was challenged by Boomers advocating development-at-any-cost and by public relations—conscious oil companies, who gave soothing assurances. They said, in effect: trust us; sure, there are problems, but we are the wizards of the technological age and we can solve them.

Representative of the Boomers' testimony was that of Tom

Fink, then a member of the Alaska House of Representatives and later a columnist for the *Anchorage Times*. (Fink, who resigned his legislative seat a few years ago rather than file a financial disclosure statement, was regarded as a potential gubernatorial candidate in 1978.) He and the other Boomers took the position that it was patriotic to build the pipeline to help supply U.S. energy needs, and that private enterprise should not be unduly hindered. Fink told the Interior officials in 1971:

> I wish that you'd issue the permit because we need the energy in Alaska, as well as the rest of the United States. I want you to issue the permit because it has always been, and should continue to be, the American way that would develop our natural resources for the benefit of our people without unbearable and impossible restrictions.

Hickel basically agreed with this interpretation of the "American way," and in early 1970 intended to issue a permit for construction of a 360-mile North Slope Haul Road, from the Yukon River to Prudhoe Bay. The road would be used to bring machinery, equipment, and other supplies to construction crews on the northern part of the pipeline. But as Hickel was about to issue the permit, groups of Natives and conservationists took the matter out of his hands. First, two Native villages sued TAPS for breach of contract, alleging that TAPS had failed to live up to a promise to choose Native contractors for the projects and to give pipeline jobs to Natives living along the pipeline route. Then in March 1970, five Native villages located north of the Yukon filed suit in U.S. District Court in Washington, D.C., claiming ownership of land intended for part of the pipeline and Haul Road, under their aboriginal claims. The suit, filed against Secretary Hickel, sought to block him from issuing the construction permit.

As a federal judge was considering the Native claims issue, three conservation groups—the Wilderness Society, the Environmental Defense Fund, and the Friends of the Earth—filed yet another federal suit in Washington, D.C., to block pipeline construction. The suit contended that the pipeline project violated the 1920 Mineral Leasing Act and the recently enacted National Environmental Policy Act (NEPA). On April 13, 1970, federal district court Judge George L. Hart, Jr., granted a temporary injunction blocking the pipeline project. Hart said there was reason to believe that the project, as proposed, violated both acts—the 1920 law, because TAPS was asking for a far wider right-of-way than the law allowed;

and NEPA, because no environmental impact statement had been prepared for the entire project.

The lawsuits made it clear to the oil companies that, although there were environmental obstacles to overcome before construction could begin, the most nettlesome problem was the Native land claims. So, as discussed in Chapter V, the oil companies threw their lobbying strength behind the Alaska Federation of Natives' effort to secure a just land claims settlement, and their support proved invaluable.

With the land issue finally settled by the 1971 Alaska Native Claims Settlement Act, attention turned back to the environmental arguments over the pipeline. On August 15, 1972, Judge Hart dissolved the temporary injunction against the project, saying that by then the Interior Department had met the provisions of NEPA (by preparing an environmental impact statement) and of the 1920 Minerals Leasing Act. Hart said he agreed with an Interior Department interpretation that it could issue a special land use permit to allow the pipeline builders to have more than the 54-foot right-of-way permitted by the 1920 act. The decision was appealed to the District of Columbia federal appeals court, which heard the case in late 1972. On February 9, 1973, the appeals court overturned Hart's decision, ruling that the Interior Department had exceeded its authority in proposing to grant the special right-of-way and land use permits. Two months later, the U.S. Supreme Court refused to review the appeals court decision, thus letting its decision stand.

Successful court challenges notwithstanding, pressures were building for construction of the pipeline. The oil companies continued to issue public warnings of potential energy shortages. And in his April 18, 1973, energy message to Congress, President Nixon called for stepped-up production of new fields of U.S. oil and natural gas and urged swift construction of the trans-Alaska pipeline.

Some members of Congress were growing increasingly worried that the Alyeska consortium would further foster the anti-competitive practices of the oil industry. Only four companies owned 95 percent of the Prudhoe Bay oil. Standard Oil of Ohio (Sohio), through a merger agreement with British Petroleum, owned about half; and Arco and Exxon, as joint owners of leases in the Prudhoe Bay field, owned more than 40 percent. The remaining 5 percent or so was divided among Amerada-Hess, Mobil, Phillips, and Union Oil. Those same four companies—the BP-Sohio combination, Arco, and Exxon—also owned about 90 percent of the pipeline itself. Some members of Congress were concerned that, by controlling the access to the pipeline, the major North Slope oil producers could in effect determine who bid for future oil leases there; no smaller company would be interested in acquiring any of the leases if it had no assurance of access to the pipeline to get its oil to market. As Representative Donald M. Fraser (Democrat, Minnesota) commented, ownership of a pipeline could be the same "as if General Motors owned the Interstate Highway System and charged a special toll for all cars that it did not manufacture." In addition to major pipeline control, Exxon and Arco controlled much of the domestic oil production on the West Coast. With this across-the-board dominance of Prudhoe Bay oil, Exxon, BP-Sohio, and Arco could control production, transportation, refining, and marketing of Alaskan oil. As author Mary Clay Berry stated in her 1975 book, *The Alaska Pipeline*, Exxon, Arco, and BP-Sohio would be in the position "similar to that of the state of Texas in the days when it controlled the price of domestic oil prorationing. . . . These plans were designed to give the companies a stranglehold over one fourth, and possibly more, of the United States' proven oil reserves."

By mid-1973, though, with the warnings of an "energy crisis" being pushed by the industry, lack of competition was a secondary concern. For most members of Congress, the unanswered question was not whether the pipeline would be built, but whether it would follow a route entirely through Alaska to Valdez or through Canada to the U.S. Midwest, if negotiations for such a route were initiated with the Canadian government. After the Senate Interior Committee approved a bill clearing the way for a trans-Alaskan pipeline and giving the Interior secretary authority over the size of pipeline rights-of-way, the full Senate took up the bill in July 1973. One amendment proposed by Senators Walter Mondale (Democrat, Minnesota) and Birch Bayh (Democrat, Indiana), called for a National Academy of Sciences study of alternative routes in Alaska and Canada. The amendment was soundly defeated. The Senate passed another amendment to bar shipments of Prudhoe Bay oil to foreign countries—with oil-hungry Japan, particularly, on the minds of the senators. Another amendment, proposed by Senator Mike Gravel (Democrat, Alaska), waived the provisions of the National Environmental Policy Act and prohibited further court challenges to the pipeline.

This was the crucial issue. In tension-filled balloting, 49 had voted for the Gravel amendment and 48 against. Then, Senator

Alan Cranston (Democrat, California), an opponent of the Gravel amendment who had arrived too late to vote on it initially, came to the floor. After Cranston's vote evened the tally, Vice-President Spiro T. Agnew, the presiding officer, cast the dramatic deciding vote, making it 50 for and 49 against.

With Senate passage, the House Interior Committee took up the measure and also narrowly approved the waiver of the NEPA provisions, making yet another battle certain on the House floor. Representative John R. Dellenback (Republican, Oregon) proposed an amendment to delete the waiver provision and instruct the courts to expedite challenges to the pipeline. Speaking in support of the amendment during House debate, Representative Morris K. Udall (Democrat, Arizona) warned that "a lot of those who helped to write the National Environmental Policy Act into law are preparing to gut it." Udall charged that Congress was bowing to oil industry pressures, that "the oil companies are trying to panic this country and panic this house and this Congress." By a 23-vote margin, the amendment was defeated. The House then easily passed the pipeline authorization bill, which was signed into law on November 16, 1973, by President Nixon.

On April 29, 1974, almost six years after the announcement of a major discovery of oil at Prudhoe Bay, Alyeska began construction of the 360-mile Haul Road from the Yukon River to Prudhoe Bay. On March 27, 1975, the first mainline pipe was installed. By the end of 1976, all but a few miles of the entire 800 miles of pipeline—just over half of it above ground and half buried, despite the oil companies' original plan to bury it all—was completed. By mid-1977, the first oil was flowing through the pipeline. By late 1977, Alyeska expected the system to be moving 1.2 million barrels a day through the line at a speed of about 7.5 miles an hour to the terminal at Valdez. Eventually, the line would be able to handle two million barrels a day. At Valdez, the oil would be stored in tanks until it could be loaded aboard tankers for shipment to ports at San Francisco, Los Angeles, Long Beach, and Puget Sound.

With the flow of Alaskan oil beginning in 1977, Americans could gratefully sigh that "energy independence"[4] was just around

[4] Petroleum industry officials predicted that the U.S. would import 51 percent of its oil in 1977, the highest percentage ever, up considerably from 42 percent in 1976. Despite the opening of the pipeline, U.S. reliance on imports was expected to continue to increase in the years to come.

the corner and that a copious supply of cheap crude oil was easily accessible and invulnerable to embargo. Such was the impression well promoted by the oil companies when they first embarked on their odyssey for pipeline approval. Sadly, these expectations were far from reality.

The anticipated price for Alaskan oil of $14.50 per barrel, or more, made a mockery of the glowing predictions by Alyeska officials who, in the early days of the pipeline debate, touted the advantages of cheap, American-produced oil. In the February 1971 hearings in Anchorage on the environmental impact statement for the pipeline, Edward L. Patton, then president of Alyeska and later its chairman of the board and chief executive officer, cited what Alyeska viewed as the two compelling reasons for the pipeline: first, the economic advantages of oil to Alaska and, second, the pressing energy needs of the United States. He also gave assurances that the environmental standards would be of the highest quality possible, and downplayed any possibility of environmental disaster:

> In our view, the discovery of oil at Prudhoe Bay presents an opportunity, the best current opportunity, for economic independence for the people and the state of Alaska. And it represents a singular addition to the energy resources of the United States. . . .

Patton's statement is interesting for a number of reasons. For one, it gives an indication of how poorly Alyeska had calculated the ultimate cost of the pipeline. Although Patton mentioned no figure of expected cost in his testimony, other oil industry witnesses referred to an estimated cost of $1.5 billion, a figure which by late 1976 had ballooned to $9 billion. Part of this was a miscalculation of the eventual size of the work force. Patton had stated in his 1971 testimony that the construction effort would create 5,000 to 8,000 jobs. Alyeska employed more than 20,000 workers in both 1975 and 1976. Patton also assured citizens at the Anchorage hearing that "Preconstruction preparation far exceeds that for any other pipeline built anywhere in the world," and touched briefly on the trans-Canada alternative being advocated by some environmentalists, saying: "Because the Canadian route would be considerably longer and would contain far greater stretches of sensitive-type permafrost, it presents no advantages over the trans-Alaska route from either an environmental or an engineering viewpoint." As for the potential for a disastrous tanker accident, Patton argued that the total traffic at the Valdez port would amount to no more than "three or four ships per day. This is not significant when compared with tanker traffic along many established maritime routes."

Even if Patton's assurances were wholly plausible, some non-industry experts had a telling objection to a pipeline through Alaska instead of through Canada to the U.S. Midwest: the West Coast simply lacked the oil refining capacity to handle much of the Prudhoe Bay oil. Patton did not directly address himself to that point in his testimony; instead, he said that most of the crude would go to Los Angeles, some to Puget Sound, and possibly some "through southern California or across the Isthmus of Panama," depending "upon future supply patterns." But other witnesses—even pro-oil advocates—were more candid about West Coast oil needs and refining capacity. O. K. (Easy) Gilbreth, chief petroleum engineer for the Alaska Department of Natural Resources division of oil and gas, after emphasizing that the Prudhoe Bay oil was essential to the nation's energy needs, then acknowledged that a trans-Alaska pipeline would result in an oil oversupply on the West Coast. Said Galbreth:

> Projections of demands on the West Coast indicate most of Prudhoe Bay crude can be sold directly if production can begin by the end of 1974. By 1977, 1978, excess capacity would approximate five to six hundred thousand barrels per day. This volume could be sold to the Midwestern markets or transported to the East Coast [by tanker].

So there it was: a future oil glut on the West Coast. Then, why build the pipeline through Alaska if it would result in a West Coast oversupply? The answer, Gilbreth said, is that there was an emergency need for the oil now, that U.S. negotiations with Canada over a pipeline through that country would take time, and that a trans-Canada pipeline "would be subject to political instability and sharing of U.S. markets."

Other early warnings of a West Coast oil glut were given by trans-Alaska pipeline critics, notably Charles J. Cicchetti, an economist with the prestigious Washington, D.C., think tank, Resources for the Future, and author of an exhaustive analysis on the economics of the Alaska pipeline controversy. In his testimony on the pipeline's environmental impact statement, Cicchetti and John V. Krutilla, director of the natural environments program for Resources for the Future, made a passing reference to the likelihood of "an oversupply in the West Coast market relative to the markets east of the Mississippi." (In earlier testimony, economist Herbert Winokar also suggested a West Coast oversupply by 1980 if the trans-Alaska pipeline were built.) Cicchetti followed up this testimony with his written analysis, *Alaskan Oil: Alternative Routes and Markets.* His report methodically demonstrated that a pipeline across Canada[5] was economically and environmentally superior to a trans-Alaskan route. In addition, Cicchetti discussed in detail the potential for a huge oversupply of oil on the West Coast if the trans-Alaska pipeline were built:

> If TAP [trans-Alaska pipeline] were built, if the plan to ship Alaskan oil directly to the West Coast were carried out, and if import restrictions similar to those in the rest of the nation were imposed on the West Coast, the probable result would be an excess supply of oil on the coast that could average as much as one million barrels a day as late as 1985 or 1990.

The circumstantial evidence indicates that the oil companies knew there would be a West Coast glut, and that their real intention all along was to sell some of the Prudhoe Bay oil to Japan. This evidence begins with Japan's long-expressed interest in North Slope oil. The Japanese owned North Slope leases. The Japanese must import 100 percent of the oil they need. BP signed an agreement in 1970 with a group of Japanese oil companies, an agreement which included marketing an undisclosed amount of Alaskan crude oil in Japan. In those early pipeline planning days, Phillips Petroleum had proposed an export-for-import plan, one of those convoluted oil industry transactions in which the oil companies in Alaska would

[5] Canada's government had expressed considerable interest in the possibility of an oil pipeline from Alaska through the Canadian Mackenzie Valley. Various Canadian officials, including Jack Davis, minister of fisheries and later the nation's first minister of the environment, endorsed a trans-Canada line in 1971, out of concern that tanker traffic generated at Valdez by a trans-Alaska pipeline would pose a serious danger to Canadian fisheries and the British Columbia coastline. In addition, the Canadian government had then committed itself to development in the Canadian Arctic. Because Canada had substantial natural gas deposits in the Arctic, it was contemplated that someday there would be a gas pipeline through the Mackenzie Valley, and it would thus make sense to put it and the oil pipeline in the same corridor.

In 1975, a commission headed by Justice Thomas Berger, of the British Columbia supreme court, began holding hearings on a proposed Mackenzie Valley gas pipeline which could handle gas from both the Canadian Arctic and Prudhoe Bay. Many Canadians, particularly Natives, spoke against the Mackenzie Valley pipeline because it would cross land claimed by Indian tribes. Others objected on environmental grounds. In early 1977, Berger recommended against the Mackenzie Valley gas line. An oil pipeline route, obviously, would have faced the same objections.

trade their excess Prudhoe Bay crude oil for Japanese rights to Middle Eastern oil, which would then be delivered to the U.S. East Coast. Throughout 1971 and 1972, several Japanese officials publicly expressed Japan's interest in obtaining Alaskan oil.

Then there was the oil companies' single-minded, stubborn insistence on a trans-Alaska route rather than one through Canada. This seemed strange not only because the oil was clearly most needed in the Midwest and East but because, as Cicchetti convincingly documented, oil prices were higher in the East and Midwest than in the West, and a trans-Canadian route could transport the oil at a lower tariff than the Alaska route and would ultimately be far more profitable to the oil companies. To this day many critics of the trans-Alaska route don't understand Alyeska's insistence on the Alaska line, at least without the Japanese connection.

But the possibility of Alaskan oil going to Japan was apparently rendered moot when the 1973 legislation authorizing the pipeline also barred the export of any of the Prudhoe Bay oil. There was, however, one loophole: export *could* be permitted if the president told Congress it was in the national interest. Congress could then either go along with, or reject, such a proposal.

By late 1976, the issue was no longer moot. Some oil company executives were openly stating that there would be a substantial West Coast oversupply, and that they should be given the right to export the excess Prudhoe Bay oil to Japan. Some members of Congress, such as Senator Ted Stevens, publicly stated they favored the idea of trading Alaskan oil for foreign oil. The company most concerned about a West Coast oversupply was Sohio, which through its merger with BP controls about 50 percent of Prudhoe Bay production. In August 1976, Joseph D. Hartnett, vice-president of Sohio, testified before a subcommittee of the U.S. House Interior Committee that his company's study of West Coast demand "shows there will be a surplus of 300,000 to 600,000 barrels per day of crude oil on the West Coast beginning in early 1978." In November 1976 another Sohio official put the expected surplus at 500,000 barrels a day.

The Sohio analysis estimated western U.S. needs—California, Oregon, Washington, Nevada, Arizona, Hawaii, Alaska—at 2.3 million barrels daily by 1978. Under various existing arrangements, these needs would be fulfilled by some one million barrels daily from California and Alaska's Cook Inlet oil fields, 100,000 barrels from the recently opened Elk Hills Reserve in California, and 400,000 to

550,000 barrels per day imported from Indonesia.[6] Adding these together comes to 1,500,000 or 1,650,000. Thus, some 650,000 to 800,000 barrels per day from the pipeline could be absorbed on the West Coast and, based on Prudhoe Bay's initial production of 1.2 million barrels daily, the West Coast would have a 400,000- to 550,000-barrel oversupply daily, according to the Sohio estimates. As the Alaska pipeline output increased to 2 million barrels per day, the surplus would grow.

However, other partners in the Prudhoe Bay oil venture suggested in late 1976 that the oversupply was mainly Sohio's problem. Atlantic Richfield indicated it would have no trouble handling its share of the pipeline oil on the West Coast. It owns a 100,000-barrel-a-day refinery, which it built in 1972 on Puget Sound in Washington to handle its Alaskan pipeline crude oil, and another refinery at Long Beach, California. Exxon representatives, however, told a Senate committee in 1976 that the firms would not be able to accommodate its share of approximately 20 percent of the Prudhoe Bay oil on the West Coast. They said they could handle some of it in their 100,000-barrel-a-day refinery on San Francisco Bay, but would have to move the rest through the Panama Canal to U.S. Gulf of Mexico and East Coast ports.

But it was nonetheless true that Sohio faced the biggest excess on the West Coast. A Sohio spokesman suggested in late 1976 that the over-supply problem would be solved once the company received the necessary permits to build a pipeline from Long Beach to Midland, Texas. The pipeline could carry 500,000 barrels a day to Midland, where the oil would be transferred to the midcontinent pipeline system for marketing. The hitch was that California's Air Resources Board opposed granting the permit to build the Long Beach-to-Midland pipeline, contending that the eighteen to twenty tankers visiting Long Beach every month to deliver oil would contribute substantially to the Los Angeles area's already grave air pollution problem. Sohio, though, was putting on a happy face and saying that it was just a matter of time before some compromise would be worked out on its proposed pipeline.[7] Thus, the proposal to allow

[6] Sohio said that the Indonesian oil must be imported to meet low-sulphur crude and refined oil demand. Alaska's oil has a sulphur content too high to meet California's air pollution standards, and the oil companies lack desulphurization capacity in the state and elsewhere on the West Coast to handle all the Alaskan oil.

[7] In the meantime, Sohio said, it also would have to ship some of its anticipated oversupply on tankers through the Panama Canal to Houston.

Alaska pipeline oil to be shipped to Japan, which was rejected by the Carter administration in June 1977, was being pictured by its advocates as just a temporary solution that would make the best of a difficult situation. Many state officials and environmentalists we talked to had predicted that, if the precedent of sending Alaskan oil to Japan were established, the practice would not be abandoned. Indeed, that had been Cicchetti's warning: that only if much of the Alaskan oil was intended for export to Japan did a pipeline through Alaska make more economic sense for the oil companies than a Canadian line. That is the most plausible explanation raised in 1972 for the oil companies' singular determination to build the pipeline across Alaska. As Cicchetti explained:

> Under this plan, excess oil would be shipped in foreign tankers from Valdez to Japan. The oil companies would pay lower royalties to Alaska and save on transportation costs.[8] Moreover, they would avoid the restrictions of the Jones Act, which requires that [more expensive] U.S. ships must be used for cargo transported between domestic ports. The exporting company would be allowed to increase its imports of foreign crude oil [to the higher valued petroleum markets of] the East Coast—again, in less expensive foreign tankers—for sale at the highest possible profits in the world. . . . If approved, these East Coast imports would be in addition to the present permissible level of foreign imports and would reap extraordinary profits . . .
>
> A second plan calls for the use of foreign tankers to transport North Slope crude oil to Central America, where a new pipeline would be built to pump the oil to another fleet of foreign tankers that would carry oil to the Virgin Islands for refining. By selling oil to themselves or engaging in "swaps" at the world price, the companies would reduce the wellhead price and therefore the taxes to the State of Alaska. After refining, this domestic crude might then be shipped to the East Coast . . . reaping larger profits than a direct overland pipeline through Canada.

Cicchetti added that one other consideration for the oil companies in selecting the trans-Alaska route was fear of "endless delays" if negotiations were opened with Canada over a pipeline route. Since any pipeline would run at least partly in Alaska, both a United States and a Canadian route would require the oil companies to deal with the state of Alaska and the United States federal government. A line from the North Slope into Canada would also involve the Canadian government and the various Canadian provinces through

[8] An explanation of Alaska's royalty payment on Prudhoe Bay oil is contained in Chapter VIII.

which any line would pass, raising the possibility of additional taxes and a demand by the Canadian government for a guaranteed share in the throughput capacity of the pipeline. Delays, taxes, and loss of throughput control "could significantly alter the financial returns to the companies," Cicchetti wrote. In addition, he said, BP had an added incentive to get the pipeline operating without delays because it had a merger agreement with Sohio which entitled it to get 54 percent of Sohio's stock as soon as 1.2 million barrels a day begin to move through the pipeline.

Thus, by 1973, before Congress approved construction of a trans-Alaska pipeline, there were strong indications that it was the needs of the giant oil companies, rather than the needs of the public, that were dictating the construction schedule and the location of a pipeline from Prudhoe Bay. Had Congress looked deeply enough, it would have found evidence that:

• Some of the oil companies, notably BP and Sohio, had a strong incentive to get the pipeline constructed as quickly as possible and, because of expected long delays in negotiating for a pipeline through Canada, pushed for the pipeline that could be built the fastest—the trans-Alaska pipeline.

• Despite their denials to Congress, the oil companies had their eyes on the Japan oil market from the earliest days of the pipeline planning.

• There would be an oversupply of oil on the West Coast soon after Alaskan pipeline oil began to flow.

• Except for the possibility of sending oil to Japan, a Canadian route would have provided the oil companies with the most profitable pipeline operations.

• A pipeline through Canada was environmentally superior to one through Alaska. Even the Department of the Interior, in its final environmental impact statement on the project, acknowledged that the best arrangement from an environmental standpoint was to have a joint oil and natural gas transportation system through Canada.

So it is evident that, for their own corporate reasons, the key companies involved in the North Slope project wanted to build the pipeline entirely in Alaska, and that some of those oil giants wanted to build it as quickly as possible. And they did—in less than two years' time for the pipeline itself and just over three years for the entire project. But the question of more immediate importance today is how, and how well, did they build it?

VII

Pipeline: The Untold Story

No one ever said building the pipeline was going to be easy. Winding its way over hundreds of miles of permafrost, across scores of streams and rivers, through volatile earthquake zones and up and down some of God's most spectacular mountains, the pipeline was a formidable engineering challenge.

And no one ever said the pipeline was going to be cheap. Over 800 miles of thick 48-inch pipe, more than 20,000 workers earning up to $19 per hour straight time for 70-hour weeks, difficult environmental stipulations, and the world's least hospitable climate—it was a management nightmare of such proportions that simply to note that it was the most expensive private project ever is still to understate its complexity.

No one knew this better than Edward Patton, chairman of the board and chief executive officer of Alyeska. But Patton, a former Exxon executive, told us he believed that, despite a series of cost estimates that by late 1976 had skyrocketed to ten times the original projection, the pipeline was constructed efficiently and with little waste or theft. "The last time we attempted to quantify [waste]," he explained in August 1976, "we had less than a half-million dollars lost on the whole project. . . . I'm satisfied it's more difficult to steal from this project than ordinary construction projects. And our loss ratio is probably something less than one tenth of a percent, whereas with a building in Washington, D.C., the loss rate may be fifteen percent." In retrospect, there is little he would do differently if pipeline construction were starting over again.

Whether or not Patton's assessment is accurate is of more than passing academic interest, not only because consumers will bear the ultimate brunt of the pipeline's cost but because it reveals something about the methods of operation of one of this country's richest, most important, and most complex industries.

* * *

Fairbanks is a sprawling city of musty bars and, during pipeline construction, corner-to-corner prostitutes, where the temperature climbs toward 90 in the summer and plummets to minus 65 in the winter. Fairbanks is also the center of pipeline operations and a city where members of many families have worked on the pipeline.

It was an untypically pleasant August 1976 day when we talked with three pipeline workers in the living room of a modest Fairbanks house and heard about the Great Insulation Heist and other pipeline stories. The stories were later to have a familiar ring in interviews with more than 50 pipeline workers in Fairbanks, Prudhoe Bay, Anchorage, at the Chandalar Camp in the Brooks Range, and in other parts of Alaska.

BOB: A bunch of us were up in the pipeyard. My official duty was garbage trucks; I hauled out the garbage.

CARL: We hauled out the garbage all right.

STEVE: It's only great by amateur standards. When the Teamster trucks were loaded with this best-in-the-world insulation, they would just drive their truck to wherever they wanted the insulation and unload it there. That's the way the professional guys did it, with official Teamster trucks loaded with insulation. And they go right out the front gate looking like everybody, just truck after truck after truck.

REPORTER: Isn't there someone there telling them not to do it?

STEVE: Oh, no, that's the idea. All the trucks are hauling insulation off to the pipeline. But some of the trucks didn't make it to the pipeline.

REPORTER: But one would assume the normal procedure would be: "OK, Smith, go to gate number two, pick up X number of bales of insulation, and go up to camp number sixteen by one P.M." And if he didn't do it, it would be pretty easy to find out that he didn't.

STEVE: Yeah, except that you have to keep in mind the attitude of everybody is: "Gee, we live here and all the pipeline-related shit, that's the occupation forces, and they're fair game." So everybody from the dispatcher to the chief of the yard to the truck driver to the guy guarding the gate, everybody knows that truck was not going where it was supposed to go, and they just lose the paper. By that time, five truckloads have been re-routed elsewhere, and all the people involved have got their truckload of insulation out of the deal, so everybody's happy.

STEVE: The fools . . . were just writing out orders as fast as they could. There were lots of bogus purchase orders. People come in and say I'm from Alyeska and I need all of your widgets. And people give them all their widgets and suddenly find out that weren't from Alyeska.

BOB: I was working in Isabel [a pipeline camp south of Fairbanks], and I have a Ford truck. Of course, you just go over and ask one of your buddies: "Say, hey, my rear end is kind of sounding bad here," and he says: 'OK, I'll get you a new whatever-you-need.'

CARL: People didn't have that much to do, so that kind of thing would be real easy.

BOB: Everybody's just laughing and joking and jamming things into their pocket. And the rationale [is]: I ain't got no stock in this company, go ahead. I'd go there and I'd say, "Well, I need a battery." I live in the bush out there and a battery, you know, you can run a stereo, house lights . . .

BOB: They brought out all these batteries, just filled them with water and stacked them up. Of course, in two or three days they all froze, just a pile of useless material.

STEVE: See, this is what fostered the whole attitude of ripping things off. They were so incredibly wasteful because they were stupid. They didn't understand you take a battery outside and it's fifty below and it freezes and the end pops open. So here's fifteen thousand dollars worth of batteries destroyed.

REPORTER: But why didn't someone tell them?

STEVE: Nobody knows; they're all from Texas.

REPORTER: Well, I'm a dumb easterner and I know that batteries have problems at fifty below, too.

STEVE: OK, let's say their stupidity was incredible. If here you come walking by, here's some guy, he's from Texas, he's stacking all the batteries outside, and you say: "Hey, put them back because they'll freeze." But if you're twenty minutes too late, they've frozen. And there are so many things like that that happen. . . . So the attitude is, if we don't steal the stuff and save it, Alyeska is going to destroy it. You have a whole bunch of stuff coming up in packing crates [that are constructed] with perfect sheets of plywood. They throw it out and burn it, so you want to get it before they burn it. That's the attitude. They were destroying it, so we decided to see if we could salvage some of it. It was legitimate salvage too; they just didn't understand what was going on.

[Bob then recounted how Ford trucks were stolen from Alyeska while they were being unloaded.]

Bob: You just pick up the keys—all the paperwork is just sitting there in the envelope [on the seat] and you just drive the truck off

Reporter: Do you personally know guys . . .

Bob: Oh, yeah—I'm covered, right?—I personally know trucks driving around town that are official 1975 Ford four-wheel-drive trucks with an old pickup body stuck on it. . . .

Carl: I was offered tires once at five dollars each.

Reporter: A little fencing operation?

Carl: Not even fencing, it was just sort of to compensate him for his expenses. I'm sure it would be legally called fencing, but it wasn't like he was making a whole lot of profit off it. It was just more tires than he could use.

Reporter: I've never heard of anything like this.

Steve: You've got a big bureaucracy [in Alyeska]. Half the people are new in the state and don't care. They're ripping off the state basically, ripping off our jobs. The other half are folks from the state who think that Alyeska is ripping off the state by destroying the kind of life-style we have here. So that kind of attitude prevails.

* * *

That attitude was so pervasive that it was difficult finding Alyeska workers who didn't share it. One apparent exception was a woman we talked to who worked as a Teamster in Fairbanks.

"I think this ripping off is really wrong," she declared with some passion. "People think it's OK to steal from a big company but they forget that it was once a small company. And what they don't realize is that they're paying for it, that sort of thing causes prices to rise for everyone. It's amazing the intricate rationalizations they use to justify the theft. And if you're around that sort of attitude long enough, you're very susceptible to getting sucked in yourself."

We told her that one of the most interesting rationalizations we had heard was that, if you didn't rip something off, Alyeska would destroy it.

"Well, you know," she responded, "that *is* right. We live in a cabin that a carpenter built with perfectly good plywood that Alyeska was going to destroy. He would just pick up a little piece here and a little piece there. Our whole house was built by Alyeska.

I don't see anything wrong with that, though. They would burn perfectly good plywood all the time."

Another favorite rationalization was that pipeline subcontractors wanted to be ripped off. "On cost-plus contracts," noted one pipe fitter, a longtime pipeline worker, "the more money you waste, the more money you make. They want to get ripped off." He admitted to having stolen a 12-ton hydraulic jack, 4½-inch by 6-foot pieces of oak—"they just leave them on the side of the right-of-way"—mosquito nets, gloves, sleeping bags, a generator, a first aid kit, and stainless steel he used to make various kinds of "pipeline jewelry" on the job. "You've got to do something with your time," he explained.

Richard Fineberg, a Fairbanks-based reporter who has probably written more extensively and authoritatively on the pipeline than anyone else, said he knows about 200 pipeline workers and that "the amount of theft has been tremendous." It was, however, much worse in the first eighteen months of the pipeline's construction, which began in the spring of 1974. "There was a massive lack of security. The individual workman was just picking up and walking off with the job," said Mike Bradner, a Fairbanks Democrat, who was speaker of Alaska's House of Representatives when we interviewed him in the summer of 1976. "Their records were so screwed up they had a hard time determining what had been ripped off."

Eventually, the stories of rip-offs became so "fantastically embarrassing" to Alyeska, Bradner said, that it began to get its act together, at least somewhat. But he dismissed Alyeska's assertions that the laxity of the unions was responsible for much of the theft and inefficiency. "I don't think Alyeska could use that as an excuse—fear of the unions. It was just a flat, wide-open, phenomenal opportunity for anybody to rip them off," he said. Teamster boss Jesse Carr also didn't like attempts to blame his union for the waste and theft. "We've suggested to Alyeska on numerous occasions," Carr told us, "how to tighten up some of what we thought was bad management, such as the warehouse inventory control. When they first started there was no inventory control at all. . . . We asked that they tighten up the inventory control . . . and not let everyone and their brother run in and get parts."

* * *

"The biggest rip-off," one former pipeline worker told us, "is doing no work." Brian Rogers, a researcher for the state legislature, said he had "lots of friends who quit Alyeska because it was too hard looking like you're working when you're not." A conservative Democrat in Fairbanks running for the state legislature, someone not unsympathetic to the oil industry, began one of his television ads in 1976: "How many pipeline workers have you heard complain about getting a paycheck for doing nothing?" Tom Snapp, editor of the *All-Alaska Weekly* in Fairbanks, who initially looked forward to the coming of the pipeline, recalled, "It's private and I figured it's not gonna be like the army," in terms of waste. But he was wrong. "So help me, Hannah, it was incredible," he lamented to us. Some workers were paid for working 168 hours in a week, which means they "worked" every hour that week.

One of the examples of waste Snapp uncovered was the purchase of twelve Radmark backfilling machines bought by Alyeska for a total of $10 million. The machines, which were supposed to be used to backfill the buried portions of the pipeline, were never used.

A former pipeline worker reflected to us: "I've been in the marines and I've worked for the state in nice, soft jobs and the pipeline without qualification far surpasses anything I've ever seen. I've got two younger brothers and I didn't want them to go to work on the pipeline as their first job out of high school. I didn't want them to get the idea that's what work is really like. But they did, so now they're rich and spoiled and not worth nothing because what they think work is is sitting on a bus and playing pinochle. In a competitive, real-world job they'd be worthless." One of this former pipeliner's younger brothers, who worked at one of the pipeline camps as a pipe fitter, visited him in Fairbanks in late August 1976. The younger brother brought with him one of his most prized possessions—an elaborate, stainless steel hashish pipe he made on the job. He told us he spent most of his seventy-hour weeks making pipeline jewelry—belt buckles, rings, maps of the pipeline made out of pipe which are sold to tourists for as much as $75—and goofing off.

Mike Bradner also worried about his younger brother, Terry, a personable and quick-witted twenty-one-year-old who worked on the pipeline as a Teamster at Prudhoe Bay. His primary responsibility was to pump gas, which took up one or two hours of his 12-hour working days. Much of the rest of the time he spent in a little heated shack reading, especially the porn magazines that were available in profuse array at the camp's commissary. For 1975, Terry paid $20,000 in federal taxes. He grossed up to $1,200 per week.

Alyeska and other oil company executives, even while trying to minimize the amount of waste and theft on the project, dismissed

Alyeska board chairman Patton's tiny estimates. Said one BP executive: "It's just like in the army. There always seems to be a lot of standing around. In the first couple of years there was a lot of inefficiency." Peter De May, Alyeska's vice-president for project management, admitted to us, "It was a makeshift operation for quite a while. We did end up with inventory control problems. We did end up with cost control problems." Even Patton has contradicted Patton. He once conceded to the *Los Angeles Times* that "There's been more stuff stolen from this project than in the whole history of Alaska." A second BP official acknowledged to us that "there's a lot we don't know" about the amount of thievery.

But a lot is known. For the first year and a half of the project, Alyeska in many cases did not employ the inventory and security measures that a small businessman would have. Basic controls, such as ID's and authorization signatures, were not utilized. Large warehouses and other storage areas were often unfenced and unguarded, and when guards were present they were often more a part of the problem than of the solution. Expensive tools were left unmarked. Theft in Fairbanks was rampant and uncontrolled.

According to Larry Carpenter, an Alyeska public relations executive in Fairbanks, the pipeline's first security chief, Mel Personnett, "found there was great resentment [among top Alyeska officers] towards strict security. He didn't like what people were getting away with. . . . He said if you won't let me run it my way, I'll go." He went. Shortly after leaving in September 1975, Personnett complained: "I've got bumps all over my head from running into brick walls."

Personnett was replaced by Robert Sundberg, a former Fairbanks police chief. A friendly and open man, Sundberg also painted a very different picture from Patton's. "Paperwork was a relatively loose procedure for a while, no doubt about that," he noted to us. Of the woman Teamster's story that her cabin had been built with Alyeska plywood, he commented: "I would say in all probability it's true." After we related stories we had heard about duplicate and unauthorized purchasing, he responded: "It's very probable they were buying the way you said it." He pointed out that items worth less than $500 were not inventoried.

When the project first began—and to some degree still by late 1976—Alyeska officials worried that security measures and inventory measures would slow down construction of the pipeline. Above all, they wanted labor peace; they didn't want to risk the ire of workers subjected to such measures as baggage inspection. And if they were willing to pay a twenty-one-year-old kid $50,000 a year or more to pump gas a couple hours a day, they were not going to worry too much about some rip-offs and duplicate orders. But the Personnett resignation and the hundreds of stories of theft and waste that were circulating became intolerably embarrassing, and when Sundberg was hired he was told he would be given at least some freedom to do his job.

For example, Alyeska had set up a special mail service to and from the isolated construction camps. About 50,000 pounds just in packages were being handled by the special mail service each week; this system had become one favorite means of getting stolen items safely out of the camps. Sundberg took the simple step of requiring that all packages leaving the camps be sealed in the presence of a security guard. The quantity of outgoing shipments, he reported, dropped by 75 percent. Which gives some idea of the severity of the theft problem.

But the rip-off mentality among workers became so deeply etched during the first stages of pipeline construction that, despite tighter measures and increases in the number of security guards, stealing remained widespread. Workers merely became more inventive.

Sundberg related one mid-1976 incident when a guard spotted a yellow stick hammered in the ground beyond the gate where he was stationed. For some reason the guard became suspicious and started digging where the stick was marked. He uncovered a $2,000 hydraulic ram jack used for lifting equipment weighing up to 150 tons. To Sundberg, this illustrated "the devious measures some will take to thieve." He added, "This goddamn thing doesn't have any pattern. Things are being lifted all over."

As Alyeska executives became increasingly embarrassed by the theft they also grew concerned about at least some of the waste and mismanagement. Frank Moolin, Alyeska's senior project officer, wrote a letter in December 1974 to the Alaska general manager of Bechtel, the huge California-based construction and engineering firm which was then managing the building of the pipeline. Complained Moolin:

> The resources that can be dedicated to this project, as for any project, are limited. Unfortunately, an attitude of "gold-plating" has evolved. This attitude exists within both the Alyeska and Bechtel organizations and came

about because of environmental and quality control demands, and because of the weather, terrain, and location. This attitude manifests itself in "slugging" the project with people, facilities, equipment, etc. . . . The aura of "only the best and the most is good enough" must be dispelled by Alyeska and Bechtel management. . . . If the "gold plating" attitude is not wiped out . . . *we will never be able* to exercise cost control. It will get away from us and be too late." [Emphasis in original.]

Two months later, Moolin wrote another letter to Bechtel in which he pointedly noted that many of the major contractors were submitting invoices "many months after the fact (if at all) and when they do submit them, they are incomplete, inaccurate, or not even cost-coded. . . . You will recall the debacle we had at the end of 1974 when we were faced with several hundred million dollars of uncoded invoices. . . . We must get on top of this."

One more example of this gold-plating approach was food. During the first months of construction, steak and lobster were on the menu every night at the camps, many of which boasted first-rate pastry chefs. Workers going out into the field during the day were allowed to take virtually unlimited quantities of raw steaks with them to barbecue for lunch. When Alyeska tried to terminate this costly privilege in the summer of 1974, a group of thirty welders at Tonsina Camp, south of Fairbanks, wrecked $3,000 worth of equipment in the camp mess.

* * *

But how inefficient can we be, Alyeska executives asserted. After all, the pipeline was built, and on schedule.

But that's the very point, critics responded. Alyeska was willing to pay almost any price[1]—even a 900 percent cost overrun that would make the Pentagon blush—to begin pumping out some of the billions of barrels of oil from beneath the frozen Prudhoe Bay tundra as soon as possible. It was an approach frequently described by pipeline observers in military terms. Said former House Speaker Bradner, considered a moderate on oil issues: "Alyeska used a military invasion technology: If you're not sure you need it, order it; if you're not sure you have it, double-order it."

The same approach was applied to manpower. In 1971, Alyeska was talking about employing 5,000 to 8,000 workers. As late as the end of 1974 it estimated that peak employment on the

[1] At the height of pipeline construction, Alyeska was regularly spending more than $10 million a day—or more in one day than was paid for Alaska by the U.S. government in 1867.

line would hit 15,600 workers in 1975, dropping to 12,000 to 1976. But labor productivity continued to fall far below even the revised estimates and the solution was to throw more manpower at the problem. In 1975, the number of pipeline employees was 21,600; in 1976, it also topped 21,000.

So, one of the most important and elusive questions becomes why Alyeska was willing to pay almost any price to get the Prudhoe Bay oil to market as soon as possible. State pipeline coordinator Charles (Chuck) Champion, himself a former oilman, told us in late 1976 that the failure to hold down costs was primarily due to the oil companies' attitude that the sooner they finished the pipeline the quicker they would begin to reap the profits from oil production. Said Champion:

> There is no amount of money you can spend in any given day on this project that will come anywhere near the profit to be made by completing it one day earlier. . . . They want to get their money out of this thing. So, in a project where you have billions of dollars on the table, you go as fast as you possibly can. That is the nature of the beast, that is the nature of any construction project: time is money, time equates to money, and especially at the end when you'll have ultimately probably some twenty-some-odd million dollars a day from the production at Prudhoe Bay. So in any given day on this project, you're spending probably ten million dollars to 12 million dollars a day. If you can spend that much and complete this thing one day earlier, you're still ahead. . . . The stakes are extremely high, but the payoff is even higher.

That explanation is true, at least as far as it goes. But it is too simplistic. Another—and one heard repeatedly in Alaska—is that the pipeline was one big cost-plus project. The pipeline subcontractors had cost-plus contracts with Alyeska and the owner oil companies have a cost-plus arrangement with the consumer.

The oil companies filed tariff applications with the Interstate Commerce Commission in 1977. The requested tariffs consisted of the pipeline's cost—including any waste—and a "reasonable return on investment." Since the companies that own the oil also own the pipeline, they are essentially paying themselves for the right to use the pipeline. The Federal Energy Administration sets the market price of the oil itself. That price is based on the cost of bringing the oil to market—including the pipeline tariffs—and, of course, includes reasonable profit.

But the explanation of the pipeline's urgency is more complicated than that because the oil companies still do care—at least somewhat—about the total costs of bringing the oil to market. A major part of the answer, as previously noted, is that two of the four largest owners of the Prudhoe Bay Reserve—BP and Sohio—have become intimately linked. BP is a huge multinational with large worldwide reserves which has been looking for ways to expand its marketing potential within the United States. Sohio is a relatively small oil company which owns little crude but whose strength has been in marketing. To fulfill their respective corporate needs, a merger was agreed upon: Sohio would get Prudhoe Bay oil owned by BP, and BP would get a share in Sohio (and, in the process, entry into the American retail oil market). BP's share initially was 26 percent of Sohio, but it was to climb to 54 percent, as Prudhoe Bay production reached about 1.2 million barrels per day. Hence, BP had a special interest in seeing the pipeline completed quickly.

Sohio's concern was even more pressing than its partner's. "Sohio is stretched from pillar to post," State Commissioner of Revenue Sterling Gallagher, previously an Anchorage banker, noted to us in late 1976. "You look at that balance sheet and it scares you to death. . . . Who would underwrite that company if it were not for Prudhoe Bay oil?" It was obvious that Sohio's financial problems, and BP's arrangement to gain control of 54 percent of Sohio stock, made it imperative for the two companies to "get out the oil as quickly as possible" from Prudhoe Bay, Gallagher observed.

Sohio's assets at the end of 1975 were about $1.8 billion and its initial share of pipeline costs was expected to total about $2.8 billion. Its debt structure—most of it short-term—was so unfavorable that it was forced to pay as much as 10⅝ percent to finance its share of the project. But with rapid construction of the pipeline, Gallagher noted, Sohio could get out from under "this terrible financial burden by 1982 or 1983." Sohio's overriding concern was simply "the sooner the better."

One interesting sidelight here is that apparently not all of the Alyeska partners were so anxious to get the oil flowing. Some observers have suggested that at least one of the major partners in the Alyeska venture—Exxon, with its 20 percent ownership—may have been concerned over the potential domestic competition offered by the BP-Sohio combination. As Mary Clay Berry wrote in her book, *The Alaska Pipeline*, concerning the period in 1970 when the Trans-Alaska Pipeline System (TAPS) was reorganizing into Alyeska:

One of the striking things about TAPS had been its inefficiency. Sometimes the major companies in the venture seemed to be operating at cross purposes. In fact, they may have been. BP had every reason to want the pipeline built as quickly as possible. . . . On the other hand, Humble Oil seemed to be dragging its feet. It is possible that Humble and its parent, then Standard of New Jersey (now the Exxon Corporation), did not welcome the kind of domestic competition the BP-Sohio combination would provide. At any rate, Interior Department officials who had to deal with TAPS and the parent companies regularly during this period generally agree that Humble was the least cooperative of the companies involved.

In his book, *The Seven Sisters: The Great Oil Companies and the World They Shaped*, Anthony Sampson wrote that BP suspected that Exxon was deliberately delaying the pipeline. BP, which struck oil at Prudhoe Bay nine months after Arco's historic strike there in June 1968, had, as previously noted, a problem of finding U.S. outlets for its Alaska oil. When its proposed merger agreement with Sohio was challenged by Justice Department anti-trust chief Richard McLaren, BP chairman Eric Drake complained about McLaren to Attorney General John N. Mitchell. BP officials also threatened overseas reprisals against U.S. oil companies if the merger were not allowed to go through. The merger was allowed to go through. But Exxon, meanwhile, appeared to be in no rush to get its Alaska oil out of the ground because it had substantial and far cheaper oil available to it from the Middle East. When Exxon experimented with using an icebreaker, the S.S. *Manhattan*, rather than a pipeline, to transport its Prudhoe Bay oil, BP suspected this was just another delaying tactic. Wrote Sampson: "Drake became so impatient that, as he told me, he threatened the chief executive of Exxon, Ken Jamieson, with bringing an anti-trust suit."

Another piece in the pipleline puzzle is the 1973 Arab oil embargo and the profitability of the Prudhoe Bay oil. Alyeska's top officials all asserted to us that, as the original cost estimates of pipeline construction began to escalate, had it not been for the embargo —which quadrupled the price of newly discovered oil—the pipeline would not have been built. "If, indeed, we were at this point talking about $2.40 a barrel of crude we would have shut up shop a long time ago," Alyeska president William Darch told us in late 1976. While others are highly skeptical of this, there is no question that the Alaskan oil venture will *now* be a highly profitable one.

Prominent oil economist Michael Tanzer, hired as a consultant by the Alaska legislature, estimated in 1976 that even at then current oil prices (which are expected to rise over the next twenty years) the oil companies would realize *net* profits from 1977 to 1995, the predicted life of the Prudhoe Bay field, of $26 billion at 1976 state and federal taxing levels. And this assessment is based on the oil companies' very conservative 9.6-billion-barrel estimate of the Prudhoe Bay reserves; non-industry estimates have gone as high as 50 to 100 billion barrels. It also does not assume the production of additional Alaska crude—a virtual certainty—which might be transported via the Alaska pipeline and thus increase the line's profitability.

A more realistic profit assessment was made by a Wall Street investment research analysis company in 1977. The firm, Wainright Securities, Inc., predicted in an eighty-five-page copyrighted industry review that the oil companies would earn $98 billion—*net*—through the year 2005, a return of almost $4 billion annually! The firm advised investors that the "uniqueness of [the] long-lived Prudhoe Bay reserves cannot be emphasized enough in today's industry environment. With most companies facing the difficult tasks of replacing depleted low-cost reserves, access to substantial North Slope reserves affords the luxury of a stable underlying basic cash flow on which to launch new corporate investment for future growth." The oil industry's own analysis, based on conservative assumptions, estimated annual net profits at $1.8 billion—$600 million from the pipeline and $1.2 billion from the oil—or an 18 percent return on investment. But, regardless of which profit estimate is relied upon, as state Attorney General Avrum Gross told us: "The cost of the line is peanuts compared to the staggering profits."

The state of Alaska won't be doing badly either. With its 12½ percent royalty, plus severance taxes, the state in effect owns about 25 percent of the Prudhoe Bay crude, and its net income over the lifetime of the field is estimated at more than $1 billion annually.

Despite the state's good fortune, it has been played for a patsy by the oil companies, and it has come to realize it. Unlike the other owners of Prudhoe Bay, the state has no share in the pipeline itself, only the oil. Yet what the state receives for its one-eighth royalty share of the oil is based on the wellhead price: that is, the market price of the oil minus costs of transportation, which, in the case of Prudhoe Bay crude, includes the pipeline tariff and tanker fees. Alaska had a direct stake in keeping down the pipeline's construction cost—on which the tariff is based—because, unlike the oil companies, it will not merely be transferring money from its left to its right pocket.

Realizing this, the state established the Alaska Pipeline Commission several years ago under the pro-oil administration of Democratic Governor William Egan. Its charter was to closely monitor the economics of the pipeline and gather data on any waste and inefficiency for a possible challenge by the state to an ICC tariff applications. The commission failed miserably—Patton told us the state doesn't have any right to audit Alyeska anyway—and became mired in a political struggle. After months of legislative wrangling in 1973, it was stripped of much of its authority, which was transferred to the attorney general.[2]

Attorney General Gross told us in late 1976 he had few illusions over how much he could accomplish in the remaining months before the pipeline began operating and the ICC opened tariff hearings. He said he knew that much vital data was irretrievably lost by inaction under both the Egan and Hammond administrations. "The state did zilch, absolutely nothing," Gross lamented. "From day one, the lawyers and the accountants should have been all over them. That wasn't done and I don't know why." He added: "It's like the eleventh hour; it's five minutes to midnight." He thought for a moment. "My guess is that it may already be midnight."

Despite its weakened role and its sorry past performance, the revamped Alaska Pipeline Commission by late 1976 got some new members and was attempting to recoup as many of its losses as possible. Still empowered to represent the state's interest in tariff proceedings before the ICC, the commission hired attorney Terry Lenzner at an initial cost of $150,000 to probe the costs of the pipeline to determine if they were excessive.[3] Lenzner, former director of the federal Office of Legal Services in the Office of Economic Opportunity and later assistant chief counsel to the Senate Watergate

[2] Governor Hammond told us that legislation in effect until 1973 would have enabled the state to constrain Alyeska's cost overruns and thereby assure the state greater revenue. Under that pre-1973 legislation, the state had the right to alter leasing arrangements where the pipeline crossed state lands, so that the state could guarantee itself a certain rate of return no matter what Alyeska's costs in building the pipeline might be. This legislation offered Alyeska incentive to hold down costs, Hammond said, because it barred Alyeska "from writing costs off on a cost-plus basis." But the 1973 legislature, under pressure from the oil industry, repealed this legislation in a special session. Governor Egan, although he denied it, was accused of selling out to the oil companies. The 1973 legislation kept alive the pipeline commission, but with severely limited authority.

[3] The growing influence of the oil companies in state politics is best illustrated by a 1977 legislative battle over a proposal to provide an additional $800,000 for Lenzner's investigative team. Leading the fight against the funds increase was Representative Larry Carpenter (Republican, Fairbanks), who is a public relations official for Alyeska.

Committee, began to look into a number of areas that previously had been cited by state Pipeline Coordinator Champion as wasteful or excessive. These included the controversial $55 million weld repair program which received nationwide attention; repair work at nine river crossings; repairs to big game crossings; and various poor management practices, including the failure to pay bills within a certain period of time, which cost Alyeska discounts it would have been entitled to. Although Champion estimated to us that there was waste of $2 billion on the project, one interesting question was whether the ICC would buy the state's argument that certain costs should be eliminated from the tariff, since the ICC has had a reputation for never excluding incurred costs, regardless of waste. Alyeska had, of course, made it clear it would seek inclusion of all of its costs—including those for repairing defective welds.[4]

By the spring of 1977, the Alaska Pipeline Commission was charging publicly that Alyeska was not cooperating with its probe. In fact, the oil consortium was playing a transparent game of stonewalling. At first, in mid-1976, Alyeska's Patton asserted that the state had no right to examine its private records. Later Alyeska said it would be happy to cooperate with the state—as long as its requests for data were not too burdensome. By the winter of 1977, however, Alyeska had reverted to its original position, arguing that the Alaska Pipeline Commission had not been given statutory authority to subpoena the company's records and personnel. Its argument had little legal substance. But, in order to avoid a protracted court fight, a bill granting the commission crystal-clear authority to obtain the information was rushed through the legislature and signed by the governor. Alyeska then asked the state to negotiate a "good faith" agreement so that subpoenas and formal legal steps could be avoided.

In addition to obtaining cost data, the state commission wanted to question top Alyeska officials under oath. Alyeska balked at this in the spring of 1977, maintaining that its executives were too busy, just prior to the start-up of the pipeline, to talk to the state. This prompted Lanzner to observe that Alyeska had "plenty of time for public relations but no time to answer crucial questions." After protracted discussions, the negotiations broke down—the state charging the oil companies with a "lack of good faith." The commission then

[4] One encouraging sign occurred in late June 1977. A possibly rejuvenated ICC, under sharp attack from both Congress and the Carter administration for its generally pro-industry bias, set temporary pipeline tariffs, pending formal hearings, about 23 percent lower than those requested by the oil companies.

went to state court, where it won. Alyeska, using all possible delaying tactics, then took the case into federal court. By the end of June and the start-up of the pipeline—and after the oil companies had already filed their proposed tariffs with the ICC—the state had obtained too little data but a massive case of indigestion from the oil firms. The pipeline owners, a frustrated Lenzner complained, "have obstructed efforts to obtain explanations . . . of extensive cost overruns and management problems on the trans-Alaska pipeline project."

As unfortunate as the lack of fiscal scrutiny of the pipeline was for Alaska—Governor Hammond estimated it may have cost the state hundreds of millions of dollars—it was even more of a loss to the rest of the country, which will have to pay the pipeline bill. Perhaps more importantly, the trans-Alaska pipeline presented an unparalleled opportunity to observe in minute detail the oil industry in action on its most important undertaking. Without specific data, it is impossible to make a good estimate of the money squandered on the job that, as of early 1977, was estimated preliminarily by the ICC to have cost $9 billion. It will probably remain a matter of speculation whether the largest private construction project in history was also the most wasteful one.[5]

Despite the absence of the kind of detailed data an alert state of Alaska could have gathered, a project as elephantine as the pipeline could not pass through our last great wilderness without leaving some distinct footprints in the tundra. And those footprints may reveal more about the way the oil industry does business than the oil industry would care to have the public know.

* * *

Theft, poor productivity, and mismanagement are not the only reasons for the bloated cost of the pipeline. Another avoidable expense was the repeated violation by Alyeska and its subcontractors of right-of-way and environmental stipulations, which meant many

[5] Thornton B. Bradshaw, the Arco president, scarcely seems to have noticed the pipeline's cost overruns. During an October 1976 speech to the Pacific Area Young Presidents Organization, Bradshaw, in an across-the-board defense of U.S. corporations, called the trans-Alaska oil pipeline and Prudhoe Bay oil development "big business at its best—enterprising, courageous, and above all, successful." Then without making any reference to the runaway costs that boosted the price tag for the pipeline from $900 million to $9 billion in seven years, Bradshaw told the business group that because the traditional private enterprise system was building the pipeline America would get the oil at far less cost than if the project had been handled by the government.

facets of the project had to be ripped up and done over again. Oftentimes, it was difficult, if not impossible, to assess specific blame for foul-ups because of the many layers of bureaucracy Alyeska had imposed on the project. And, according to environmentalists, the federal monitoring agency did a poor job and generally kept its operations hidden from public view, while state monitors did a reasonably good job and made records available to the public. To get some idea of the bureaucracy involved in monitoring pipeline construction, consider that there were six federal and state agencies—none of which had full responsibility—that oversaw different aspects of pipeline construction or handling of oil in connection with the project. These were:

- The Alaska Pipeline Office (APO), the federal agency under the Interior Department which was responsible for enforcing the right-of-way agreement on federal land—about 68 percent of the pipeline route.
- The State Pipeline Coordinator's Office (SPCO), the state agency with responsibility for enforcing right-of-way lease stipulations on state land, which included about 32 percent of the project.
- The U.S. Environmental Protection Agency, the federal agency with statutory authority to protect navigable waters from oil pollution.
- The Joint State-Federal Fish and Wildlife Advisory Team (JFWAT), a combined federal and state unit that advised the APO and SPCO concerning protection of fish and wildlife. The unit included personnel from the U.S. Fish and Wildlife Service, the National Marine Fisheries Service, and the state Department of Fish and Game.
- Alaska Department of Environmental Conservation (DEC), the state agency with statutory authority to protect the environment from oil pollution.
- The Alaska Department of Labor (ADL), the state agency empowered to protect worker safety, whose authority also included control over storage of flammable liquids.

Clearly, one of the significant factors contributing to the pipeline's escalated cost was the difficulty of managing a complex engineering project in the little-known, inhospitable Arctic. As State Pipeline Coordinator Champion noted:

> The mistakes were made simply because anytime you put 20,000 people, most of whom don't know the first damn thing about Arctic construction,

on a project as totally unique in its concept and construction—its severe weather conditions, the logistics, everything else about Alaska is strange—then you'll have costly mistakes.

But Champion strongly disputed Alyeska's contentions that it was entirely unforeseen problems that caused pipeline costs to escalate. The fact is, said the former oil executive, that if the oil companies didn't know about Alaska's special environmental and construction problems, they should have.

The problem is that the oil industry runs very much the way it did in 1935. If you do something and it works, you tend to do it over and over again because the oil industry involves very, very high capital investments. Risks are not things that people like to do with that kind of money, so as a result of all of this, the oil industry tends to rely on tried and true practices, and they tend to be somewhat behind advanced technology.

Well, here the entire project was advanced technology. My God, when they first came up here they argued ninety-five percent of this pipeline could be buried in conventional pipeline construction technique, the most asinine thing in the world. We have [Alyeska's] Ed Patton on the record at the time when the U.S. Geological Service was arguing for an above-ground pipeline because of the inherent danger in burial of thawing stable permafrost. Ed Patton said, 'Well, OK, we'll go above with eighteen percent, not because we need to do that but only to satisfy you guys so we can get this project going.' Well, now it's fifty, fifty-one percent [above ground]. It's just that everybody came here not understanding the Arctic.

Another example was Alyeska's plan to use a standard oil industry welding rod that could withstand temperatures of only 20 degrees Fahrenheit below zero. Champion said he told the firm's executives that the standard had to be 50 degrees below zero. "So we fought Alyeska tooth and nail," Champion said, "and they finally—I had to threaten them with court but they finally gave in and said, all right, and they upgraded to a higher standard." Given the controversy that arose in 1976 over faulty welds on the pipeline, Champion said, "Alyeska has definitely got to be thanking us for having done that, because the only thing that's saving their bacon on the welding program is the fact that the ductility of the weld material in the steel is such that even the questionable welds would never fail under the lifetime of the project." The alternative, Champion asserted, would have resulted in the welds' becoming brittle and then breaking as temperatures dropped, causing "an almost certain catastrophic oil spill."

As the state official responsible for seeing to it that Alyeska complied with environmental and construction stipulations during pipeline construction, Champion was often at the center of controversy. At one point in early 1975, Alyeska officials sharply assailed a private memo which he had written to Governor Jay Hammond, and which later received much press attention in the state, warning that the pipeline eventually would cost $7 billion to build. At that time, the builders were estimating the final cost would be $5.98 billion. Champion's report to the governor also noted that construction was running behind schedule and, in order to catch up, Alyeska would have to pour more workers—and therefore more money—into the project. Champion recalled with obvious satisfaction that "there were screams and howls of anguish and rebuttals and denials" by Alyeska of his estimates, "and I was pretty badly hammered with quotes from Alyeska that there was no possible way the pipeline could cost that kind of money." Champion also was accused of hurting Alyeska in the stock market. Since then, he said, he had "maintained a low profile" concerning costs "because I don't think it's our business to shake up Alyeska's money."

Despite this statement, Champion was certainly not overly circumspect in his statements to us. We asked him what he knew that Alyeska didn't about pipeline costs; why he could more closely estimate their costs than the company could. He responded:

> Well, we rebuilt their schedule and, quite frankly, there's no secret to it. I just figured out how long it was going to take them because of the failure rate they were having. We reworked their schedule and I came out with a time overrun and I knew they weren't going to allow a time overrun. So, I knew that additional people would have to be put in on the project—material and manpower—so we built that back in. I used to do a lot of this. I worked for oil companies all my life in construction projects so I happen to be fairly adept at outguessing. . . .

Champion estimated that there was "approximately" $2 billion in waste on the pipeline construction. He said that the project "under reasonably designed criteria and reasonable project management, with reasonable knowledge of the art, should have cost in the region of $5.8 to $6.2 billion."

William Darch, president of Alyeska, responded in a late October 1976 interview that Champion had just made a lucky guess in 1975 in estimating the costs of the pipeline more closely than Alyeska. We asked Darch why Alyeska had so severely criticized

Champion for his 1975 estimate of an eventual pipeline cost of $7 billion, since as it turned out even Champion's estimate was actually too low. Said Darch:

> Unless Mr. Champion has a crystal ball which he keeps in his bottom drawer, which I would like to get ahold of . . . it's an extremely time consuming process to make accurate estimates. For instance, I think the Society of American Estimating Engineers says that it is an art, a science . . . that to put forward an estimate which is going to be plus or minus twenty percent accuracy is going to involve you in about four percent of the capital cost of the project itself. And so if Mr. Champion can do that on the back of an envelope—you can well see these rash public statements can be extremely deceiving.

Alyeska did not make annual estimates of the project's costs but rather did them at irregular intervals. According to a summary provided for us by Alyeska, here is the schedule of the escalating costs and the company's stated public reason for the higher estimates:

- February 1969: plans announced for the pipeline. Preliminary cost estimate for construction was $900 million. "It was a budgetary figure based on general information available at the time. It reflected the estimated cost of a conventional pipeline of the size and length contemplated, plus an increment to cover the additional estimated costs required because of the remote location, the terrain and the harsh environmental conditions in Alaska. At the time, the pipeline had not been designed or engineered," Alyeska said, in a prepared statement.
- February 1971: $1.5 billion. Alyeska's information sheet does not list this figure, but the oil companies used this estimate at the environmental impact statement hearings. This figure was widely viewed at the time as a more realistic assessment of its eventual cost than the earlier estimate.
- March 1972: $3 billion.
- October 1974: $5.982 billion. "Increased costs from 1969 due primarily to three major causes," Alyeska said. "Increased cost of material; increased cost of labor; and more sophisticated design and engineering, due to more precise project definition and to compliance with the strict technical and environmental stipulations contained in the right-of-way permit issued by the Department of the Interior in January 1974." These design changes, Alyeska said, "have been substantial," including: construction of the North Slope Haul Road to secondary highway standards, rather than for temporary use; construction of about half the line above ground (instead of

the company's plans for a totally below-ground line) "entailing massive amounts of additional materials for pipe supports; special designs to meet the strictest seismic criteria ever imposed on such a structure; and construction of a ballast treatment plant at the terminal to meet stricter water quality standards." In addition, the increases resulted partly from inflation, Alyeska said.

- June 1975: $6.375 billion.
- January 23, 1976: $7 billion. The new estimate was made "on the basis of trends developed from the construction experience to date."
- June 30, 1976: $7.7 billion. Increase due to "the effects of lower productivity than previously anticipated, additional materials and associated freight and transportation . . . additional construction equipment . . . anticipated reinspection or repair costs for resolution . . . welding—X-ray problems . . . contingency allowances based on the extrapolation of cost trends experienced in scope and design changes over the past years," Alyeska said at the time.

Darch blamed the increased costs on lack of worker productivity, environmental stipulations and inflation:

> Basically, when the original estimates were made on this, one assumed that it would take twice as long to do the same job on the pipeline like the one that was done on the West Coast, which is the usual standard of criteria used in the construction industry. So, you've set your West Coast rates in terms of productivity and we had assumed we would achieve something like fifty percent of that. In actual fact, we haven't achieved that on the pipeline itself.

Champion said that it was undoubtedly true that environmental stipulations had added to the pipeline's costs but that much of that was Alyeska's fault. For example, he told us that Alyeska improperly buried many river crossings, some of which later floated to the surface, and failed to provide some of the agreed-upon 10-foot clearance for game crossings along sections of the above-ground portion of the pipeline. Some 40 percent of the game crossings built in 1975, and 21 percent in 1976, were found to be too low. He said some game passages were not even provided "because of survey errors, because of terrain variations, because of a general lackadaisical attitude . . . and incompetence on the part of [Alyeska's] quality control." As a result, many game crossings had to be reworked, as did many of the river crossings. We sat in on one session, with Alyeska and Fish and Wildlife officials in Champion's office, of a discussion of inadequate game crossings. The Alyeska representatives often made light of the entire issue, at one point asking: "Who knows what a moose thinks, anyway, when he approaches the pipeline?"

Champion disclosed that Alyeska, during the construction phase, had "some pretty major oil spills.[6] We called them in and explained to them what these problems were and that we wanted them corrected. Well, in many cases they did not correct them—and other spills were incurred which cost a lot of money. . . . That is a case where again it was stupidity. We warned them . . . but there was incompetence and lack of ability to solve problems simply because they didn't want to do it." (One such spill, discovered in June 1975, dumped 60,000 gallons at the Galbraith Lake construction camp in the beautiful Brooks Range 130 miles south of Prudhoe Bay. According to the pipeline coordinator's 1975 report, "significant oil reached Galbraith Lake, causing a visible sheen and a detrimental environmental impact." Alyeska initially reported that only 100 gallons had been spilled.)

The reports by Champion's office for 1974 and 1975 described a number of environmentally damaging activities during pipeline construction—oil spills, siltation and erosion problems, water pollution due to improperly run sewage treatment plants, fish entrapment due to improperly placed culverts and poorly constructed low water crossings, and, in what was later to become a major controversy, inadequate and falsified weld X rays. The 1975 report bluntly stated that Alyeska and its contractors showed "an almost consistent lack of adequate quality control–quality assurance attention to environmental concerns and constraints." Too often, the report said, Alyeska's quality control people failed to issue work stoppage orders when they should have or, if they issued orders, they were ignored.

The welding problems on the pipeline received more attention in the national news media than any other construction or environmental aspect of the project. Perhaps the issue would never have been made public had it not been for Peter Kelley, a former employee of Ketchbaw Industries, Inc., a Texas firm which had the welding monitoring contract. Kelley, in September 1975, filed a civil suit alleging he was fired by Ketchbaw after he complained

[6] The spills by Alyeska and its contractors of diesel fuel, gasoline, hydraulic fluid, crankcase oil, and transmission grease officially totaled almost 550,000 gallons along the pipeline route by early 1977. Some critics said even this figure was too low, contending many spills went unreported. For example, a February 13, 1976, memorandum by a state inspector noted that of 262 "readily visible" spills that investigators had come across, only nine had been reported as required.

about the company's falsifying X-ray records of pipeline welds. Kelley then assisted Alyeska officials by pointing out to them cases where X-ray welds were faked. At any rate, the weld problem was well publicized in Alaska's newspapers in the last few months of 1975 and, according to Champion, pretty well resolved before Congress and Lower-48 newspapers latched onto the issue. An internal audit by Alyeska eventually reported finding 3,955 "questionable welds." These were ones for which X rays were missing, for which copies of X rays from one weld had been put in the file for the wrong weld, for which X rays were unreadable, or for which a reading of the X ray showed that the weld failed to meet federal safety standards.

Well into 1976 stories about the weld problems appeared in major publications in the Lower-48, prompting congressional and U.S. Department of Transportation investigations. In July 1976 a team headed by John W. Barnum, deputy secretary of DOT, visited Alaska. Barnum promptly reported that the questionable welds had occurred in 1975 and were no longer a problem. However, a visit to Alaska during the same period by the staff of the Energy and Power Subcommittee of the House Interstate and Foreign Commerce Committee, produced different findings. The staff report submitted on September 8, 1976, stated that "every one of the major 1975 problems has been repeated in 1976." The staff also found, contrary to Barnum's findings, that Alyeska quality control was not always present as required before welding began; that radiographers were not completing the required X-raying of 75 percent of each day's X rays by 7 A.M. the next day. The report, which also listed many nonwelding problems during pipeline construction, also contended that Barnum's report was "uncritical" and "accepts Alyeska's representations of fact without independent evaluation." Perhaps even more troubling than the welds was the staff's statement that Alyeska's leak-detection system would not spot leaks of up to 500 barrels—21,000 gallons—a day. Some environmentalists estimated the system wouldn't detect leaks of up to 1,700 barrels—71,400 gallons—a day.

Darch told us in late 1976 that the environmental protections provided by Alyeska during construction of the pipeline were of the highest caliber. "Certainly you cannot build a pipeline without disturbing the environment. We hope that when it is completed it will fade into the background and will not be a disturbance. I think its appearance does enhance—or it does in my eyes—the environment, quite frankly. . . . because when I see sections of the line which are now being constructed, I think they're beautiful. I mean that esthetically. I mean it's not an eyesore."

Champion, although disagreeing sharply with Alyeska on many aspects of pipeline construction, maintained that the 1976 criticism of the pipeline firm over the welds issue was blown out of proportion by Congress and the national press. Certainly, dozens of memos and letters which Champion made available to us indicate that his office was working to correct a variety of weld problems long before the issue of phony X rays was first raised in the Lower-48 press. A March 1976 report from Champion's office noted that the state had for many months pushed Alyeska to correct incompetent management practices "which permitted an unprecedented quantity of weld defects, and did contribute to clouding the integrity of the welding by failing to monitor the X ray of welds."

Nonetheless, Champion noted, because of pressure by Congress and the attention given the issue by the national press, Alyeska was required by the federal government to repair all 3,955 questionable welds. This, despite the fact that his staff had determined that probably "70 percent of those welds were acceptable as they stood." Instead of having to dig up only 30 percent of the welds Alyeska had to dig them all up, resulting in "an economic tragedy and an environmental travesty." The digging, he said, had contributed to environmental problems because it means "3,955 more holes in the ground." In a September 1976 inspection trip, the state pipeline coordinator said he observed work crews pumping silt out of one of those holes "right into the Tonsina River, completely silting up two miles of salmon beds" in an important salmon spawning area.

Although Champion received generally good marks from environmentalists for his monitoring activities on state land, such was not the case for his federal counterpart. In December 1976 syndicated columnist Jack Anderson reported that Andrew P. Rollins, who headed the Interior Department's Alaska Pipeline Office, had accepted chartered plane rides, free fishing vacations, a rent-free vacation house in Hawaii, and other favors from the Morrison-Knudsen construction firm, the Alyeska subcontractor which built the southern portion of the pipeline. Anderson reported that Rollins first denied and then acknowledged receiving the gifts from Morrison-Knudsen. But, Anderson reported, Rollins said the fishing trips with Jean Beard, Morrison-Knudsen's vice president in charge of pipeline operations, were (in Anderson's words) "nothing more than old friends getting together." Rollins was removed from the key federal monitoring post within a few days after Jimmy Carter was sworn in as president.

Rollins's dismissal was cheered by many Alaska environmentalists. The Fairbanks Environmental Center, four months before Rollins's discharge, had asked Thomas Kleppe, then the Interior secretary, to fire him. The organization charged that the pipeline office under Rollins had failed in its responsibility for surveillance of the pipeline on federal lands. In a 200-page assessment of the performance of Rollins's office, the environmental center alleged that the office had persistently failed to enforce stipulations and regulations; had been too lenient in imposing penalties for violations of regulations and stipulations; had allowed construction to begin "before an adequate quality assurance program was approved or implemented"; and had placed obstacles in the way of citizen access to data on pipeline construction.

This last allegation was a serious one. G. M. Zemansky, a board member of the Fairbanks Environmental Center, commented in August 1976 at the Twenty-seventh Alaska Science Conference that Rollins's office and Alyeska had effectively barred adequate surveillance of the pipeline construction by private environmental groups. As Zemansky reported, and as others told us, the private conservation groups generally did a poor job of monitoring the environmental impact of the pipeline while it was being constructed. Part of this, though, was no fault of theirs. For one thing, trying to monitor pipeline construction presented difficulties similar to those encountered by a journalist covering a war: the military decides what you see and when you see it. News reporters were always escorted by an Alyeska representative when doing stories at pipeline construction sites. Since access to the Haul Road was barred to private parties, those citizens wishing to see the pipeline had to go as guests of Alyeska or with one of the people from state and federal monitoring teams.

Early in 1974, a coalition of environmental groups, including the Sierra Club and the National Wildlife Federation, formed the Arctic Environmental Council, which was backed by the prestigious Arctic Institute of North America. Its purpose was to monitor pipeline construction. The Arctic Institute, in explaining early on the need for such a council, said that, "it might be timely to attempt to bring together the environmentalists-conservationists with the pipeline owners to begin serious discussions of their basic differences, looking toward finding solutions—or at least identifying areas of mutual concern. It must be said at the same time that a number of persons consulted felt that any such effort would likely be entirely fruitless." Initial funding came from the Laurel Foundation and the Rockefeller Foundation.

The effort, from an environmental standpoint, was a disaster. For Alyeska it was a public relations coup. Although the council was set up with the aim of having no direct link with government or industry, it was disclosed after the group's first pipeline visit that Alyeska picked up the travel fare. Worse, the council didn't have the funds to publish a report on its trip; incredibly, the environmental group approached Alyeska and *asked* it to pay the publication costs. Apparently delighted, Alyeska agreed to print the report free of charge. In addition, the Atlantic Richfield Foundation provided a $10,000 grant to the Arctic Institute for the specific purpose of funding the council's activities. Arco, of course, is one of the major members of the Alyeska consortium.

Although the council's report contained some criticisms of Alyeska's performance, it generally gave the firm high marks for protecting the environment during pipeline construction. Alyeska then began quoting in its own publications those excerpts from the council's report which put Alyeska's environmental performance in a good light. One such statement by the council read, in part: "The council notes evidence of environmental consciousness at all levels and observed that with only a few exceptions the work is proceeding according to good environmental engineering practices." On top of everything else, one of the council members, Larry Bliss, a University of Alberta (Canada) botanist, had previously worked as a consultant to Alyeska.

The council's director, Dr. Fred G. Armstrong, defended the council's questionable links to Alyeska in an August 1976 interview with the *Anchorage Times*. Armstrong said that "Alyeska agreed to print it in [its] facilities exactly as we wrote it. There's criticism of Alyeska in there; there's criticism of the Department of the Interior in there; there's criticism of the [federal] Alaska Pipeline Office in there. I don't think it benefits anyone except the public."

But the council's lone Alaskan member, David R. Klein, of the University of Alaska's Cooperative Wildlife Research Unit, as well as other environmentalists not associated with the council, didn't see it that way. In July 1976 Klein resigned from the council, complaining that the group's credibility was negligible since it had close ties with the organization it was supposed to be investigating and had failed to publish any report dealing with later stages of pipeline construction. Before he resigned, in a letter to the council's Armstrong, Klein protested that "Alyeska has gained considerable public relations benefit from our previous trip by quoting, for their own press releases and brochures, only those portions of the news releases which cast them in a favorable light and by stressing that the council was a group getting the true picture of the pipeline project out to the public. Frankly, I do not appreciate being part of such an image."

Zemansky, the Fairbanks Environmental Center board member, commented in August 1976 on the council's failure, as well as another unsuccessful attempt organized by Alaska ecology groups to survey construction practices. This latter effort failed because of a lack of both financial support and cooperation from Alyeska and the federal APO, which denied the local groups access to the pipeline. Said Zemansky:

> The council has enjoyed the cooperation of government and industry, possibly because it was realized early on that the council would be an impotent and ineffective group, but that it might serve for some public relations value. . . . The council has no permanent staff and since the protest resignation of its only Alaskan member is composed entirely of "Outsiders." Eminent as they are, these men simply have no time to really investigate what is occurring on the pipeline even if they were well intentioned. The council is now supported financially by Alyeska and, although it has made three trips to Alaska in three construction years, has only published a report for its first trip. The report contained little more than "canned" speeches and a reprint of the stipulations.

Zemansky also noted that the national environmental groups that had been plaintiffs in the 1970 suit delaying pipeline construction—Friends of the Earth, Wilderness Society, Environmental Defense Fund—had declined to participate in the council, "perhaps sensing that . . . [it] would be ineffective." He added that the three national organizations supported an attempt by his organization and the Alaska Center for the Environment and several other Alaska organizations to monitor the pipeline. "Although this effort was never able to obtain the necessary financial support, it did determine two things," Zemansky said. "Alyeska was not going to cooperate and neither would the APO. Non-cooperation from Alyeska and the APO effectively meant no access to the pipeline either physically or in terms of information." Zemansky said that Champion's office had provided "excellent cooperation," but such was not the case with the APO or the state's Department of Environmental Conservation, against which he had filed a Freedom of Information Act suit.

The upshot of all this was that on this most massive construction project ever undertaken, the major conservation groups and the public interest generally were not represented in pipeline monitoring. Jack Hession, of the Sierra Club, told us in late 1976 that the pipeline issue was in the past and that his and other environmental organizations were concentrating on the next big fight to get some 116 million acres of Alaska wilderness permanently protected as federal parks, monuments, and fish and wildlife refuges.[7]

As important as that effort may be, it is indeed startling that the major environmental groups failed to monitor pipeline construction. After spending years and hundreds of thousands of dollars fighting against construction of the pipeline and for tough environmental stipulations, the major organizations failed even to set up a truly independent task force with a staff adequate to monitor construction and publish reports. Granted, Alyeska and the federal Alaska Pipeline Office were blocking environmentalists' efforts. But such obstructions have not deterred these organizations in the past. Had the environmentalists taken their case to the public through the press and through lawsuits designed to give them access to the pipeline, they probably would have prevailed. Such monitoring not only might have headed off environmental problems but would have set an important precedent for citizen monitoring of future pipelines in the Arctic.

Pipeline construction clearly had an adverse impact on the environment. But the pipeline also had many other types of impact—on life-styles, pocketbooks, and psyches. To many Alaskans, the physical fact of the pipeline is not nearly as important as the feeling that somehow the state will never again be quite the same.

* * *

Construction of the pipeline brought with it a population explosion, an economic bonanza for many Alaskans, runaway inflation, and disruption of a way of life for many state residents. In just two years of pipeline activity, Alaska's population shot up by 25 percent, topping 400,000 in 1976. Anchorage-area workers, who had been the fourteenth highest-paid in the nation in 1973, moved up to number two in 1974, due chiefly to pipeline impact, according to a

[7] This is known as the D-2 wilderness lands issue. See Chapter XI.

U.S. Commerce Department report released in late 1976. Under union contracts negotiated for the pipeline, laborers and skilled craftsmen pulled down paychecks of $1,000 to $1,500 a week, usually on "seven-ten" shifts (seven days a week, ten hours a day) or "six-twelves," for seven- to nine-week periods, with rest and relaxation breaks for one or two weeks between work periods.

The whopping paychecks of pipeline workers forced many other private employers and the state and local governments to raise their workers' wages substantially—or else lose many of them to pipeline construction. Anchorage police, for example, averaged $40,000 a year in 1976—only slightly more than the wage of an average Fairbanks worker, according to a 1976 survey. Commerce Department statistics showed that per capita income in Anchorage in 1974 had increased 22.9 percent over the previous year, to $7,159—or 43 percent above the national per capita personal income figure. Overall, according to the Bureau of Labor Statistics, Alaska ranked first among the states in per capita income in 1974 with $7,062. By 1976 this had grown to $10,178. Somewhat offsetting this, however, was the cost-of-living factor which, for the Anchorage area, was 40 percent higher than in the Lower-48 states in 1976.

Nowhere was the impact of oil-induced change felt more keenly than in Fairbanks. In that central Alaskan city, located below the Arctic Circle, residents saw their area's population increase from 45,000 in 1970 to an estimated 70,000 in 1976, public and private services spread thin, prices spiral upward, and social problems increase. At the same time, wages soared and the welfare and food stamp roles decreased dramatically as pipeline jobs became available.

Located just off the pipeline route, Fairbanks was the logical jumping-off point for the colossal undertaking, and the city's business and political leaders eagerly sought what they felt would be the blessings of the pipeline project. Fairbanks thus became the supply and transportation center for the pipeline, as well as the rest and recreation spot for many pipeline employees. This resulted in a constant flow of highly paid workers into and out of the city. For some Fairbanks residents, the newfound wealth was indeed a blessing; for others, the pipeline turned into more of a nightmare.

This dichotomy was documented in a pipeline impact study of 400 Fairbanks residents that was conducted by Jack Kruse, assistant professor of survey research at the University of Alaska's Institute of Social and Economic Research. As Kruse told us in late 1976:

> The positive aspects of the pipeline are all economic, while the negative aspects are seen as a higher cost of living, a scarcity of goods—particularly housing—a deterioration of services, poor utilities, long lines, loss of friendliness, loss of privacy.

With the influx of people and money, the cost of housing soared out of sight in Fairbanks. A March 1976 survey by the Pipeline Impact Information Center in Fairbanks showed, for example, that available two-bedroom, furnished apartments, without utilities included, were renting for $668 a month, compared to $324 a month in December 1974. But at least by March 1976, some units were available. A Pipeline Impact Information Center report in March 1975 found there were only 18 apartments advertised for rental in that month in an area of 60,000 people; one year later the crunch had eased, and 133 units were available. This housing shortage resulted in a mobile home boom: an estimated 25 percent of all Fairbanks residents, and 12 percent of all Anchorage residents, were living in mobile homes in 1976.

Fairbanks residents throughout the pipeline construction period found themselves faced with higher prices for virtually everything, telephone problems, traffic jams, more traffic accidents, far more crime, an influx of prostitutes, and longer lines in grocery stores, banks, restaurants, post offices, and other commercial shops. As Tom Snapp, publisher and editor of the *All-Alaska Weekly*, put it in late 1976: "Waiting in line has become a way of life."

Not only is Fairbanks cold and expensive, it also suffers from one of the most serious air pollution problems in the United States: ice fog. During the extremely cold season when temperatures are regularly well below zero, the water vapor in the air that comes chiefly from auto exhaust forms into a dense ice fog. This ice fog can be so thick that driving becomes extremely dangerous and community activities must be canceled. The fog results from temperature inversions, often more severe than those experienced by many large metropolitan areas, such as Los Angeles, on hot summer days. In Fairbanks such inversions easily linger because the city is situated in a basin surrounded on three sides by hills and ridges, creating a stable air mass. Inversions occur more than half of the days of the year, and about 80 percent of the days during the harshest winter months when temperatures plunge to as low as 60 to 70 below zero. The increase of vehicles connected with pipeline construction seriously exacerbated the problem.

Fairbanks abounds in other air pollution problems. A 1974 study by the Council on Municipal Performance placed the city first in the county in the level of particulate pollution, and sixth in carbon monoxide levels. Another recent study ranked Fairbanks first in the concentration of lead in the air. Carbon monoxide wastes are at such high levels in Fairbanks that the city exceeds most major pollution-choked areas of the Lower-48 in this category, according to federal statistics. Blood samples taken in 1974 revealed that the level of carbon monoxide saturation in the hemoglobin[8] of Fairbanks residents rose during that year from 2.2 to 3.1 percent. This compared most unfavorably to the national average of 1.4 percent, and to the 1.5 percent maximum allowed by the Clean Air Act, as well as to such major metropolitan areas as Los Angeles (2.7 percent), Brooklyn (2.1 percent), and Denver (2 percent).

William Zoller, a University of Maryland environmental scientist who was in Fairbanks on a sabbatical in early 1977 to study the city's air pollution, likened the community's foul air to that found in the Baltimore Harbor Tunnel. Zoller, who had monitored air pollution in Antarctica and in industrial regions of the United States, said that the air quality in Fairbanks was so bad that, "If we asked the National Institutes of Health to set up a case like this to study the effects on humans, they wouldn't do it." With the carbon monoxide level running as high as twenty parts per million parts of air in Fairbanks, there was a danger to the health of persons with heart troubles or respiratory conditions, while healthy persons could be afflicted with headaches, nausea, fatigue, and impaired reactions.

Automobiles are the major cause of Fairbanks's air pollution. But it's not just cars moving in traffic or stuck in traffic jams that cause the pollution; it's also parked cars left running. Fairbanks residents, faced with so many bitterly cold days, naturally have a hard time getting their cars started. Once their cars are started owners don't want to risk not being able to start them again, since engines can freeze up in twenty minutes or less. So, when residents go into stores, they leave their cars running. This, of course, not only wastes gasoline, which costs 15 to 20 percent more than in the

[8] Hemoglobin is the protein coloring matter of the red blood corpuscles, which serves to convey oxygen to the tissues. Carbon monoxide adheres to hemoglobin, thus impairing the capability of the blood to carry oxygen.

Lower-48, but poisons the air even more. Despite the city's dangerous air, many Fairbanks civic leaders have proposed that the community work to attract construction of petrochemical plants as an additional way of cashing in on the North Slope oil and gas bonanza. Zoller's assistant, William Keifer, noted to an interviewer that such plants are major polluters and that to establish them in an area that already has some of the nation's most dangerous air "would be disastrous."

Fairbanks also experienced other less dangerous, but still annoying, problems during pipeline construction. For example, residents ordering new telephones found they had to wait up to a year or more to get them installed. Those with telephones found they often had long waits for dial tones. More frequently, the circuits were just busy. One government worker told us of dialing Alyeska 103 times before finally getting through.

For many Fairbanks residents, their newfound wealth was ample compensation for the inconveniences their jobs indirectly caused. But there were many other Fairbanksans who were not as fortunate. Older residents on fixed incomes and persons in lower-paying jobs who were physically unable to perform pipeline work were the victims of the city's high cost of living, fueled mostly by the huge influx of money doled out by the pipeline project in wages or purchases. As of 1976, the cost of living in Fairbanks was 50 percent higher than in the lower-48. The average Fairbanks family of four was spending about $1,500 a month just on its basic needs.

In the quality of living survey by Professor Kruse, 40 percent of the 400 Fairbanks residents surveyed had been in Fairbanks less than three years, and 22 percent of the households had someone currently working on the pipeline. Kruse's study showed a dramatic upsurge in wealth: in 1973, only 6 percent of those surveyed were earning more than $40,000 annually; by 1975, with the pipeline boom well under way, the figure had soared to 27 percent. On the lower end of the economic scale, 35 percent were earning less than $12,000 a year in 1973; by 1975, that figure had plummeted to 14 percent. The median income per household was an incredible $35,000.

Nevertheless, perhaps the most telling figure was one that showed that only 14 percent of those surveyed felt Fairbanks had improved for the better since the start of the pipeline era. Just 17 percent of those who had been residents for ten years or longer said they were receiving benefits from the pipeline, while 39 percent of those living there for less than three years said they were benefiting from it—indicating something of a split between the old and the new Fairbanksans.

Some old-timers, though, were pleased with what was happening to Fairbanks. Dr. William Wood, former president of the University of Alaska in Fairbanks and head of the Fairbanks Industrial Development Corporation, likened Fairbanks's problems to those that people experience for a period while the interior of their houses are being painted. The painting causes some temporary disruptions and problems but, once it's finished, it looks very nice, "and you're proud of it." So it will be with Fairbanks, he said. Even such severe problems as inflation are not really due to the pipeline, he said, but rather to shoddy economic policies formulated in Washington, D.C., and Juneau.

Still, it was obvious that a lot of Wood's fellow Fairbanksans didn't agree with him. The unhappiness of many with the pipeline's impact, and the influx of workers from the Texas and Oklahoma oil fields, was evident in a popular bumper sticker that appeared on cars in the city in 1975 and 1976: "Happiness is . . . 10,000 Okies going south with a Texan under each arm." And there was the incident mentioned earlier of the Fairbanks resident arrested for going around town painting "Alaska for Alaskans. Yankee Go Home" on out-of-state cars. At a University of Alaska–sponsored symposium on state social problems in Anchorage on October 30, 1976, one Fairbanks resident, after reciting some pipeline impact horror stories, said: "Construction is just about finished. Maybe, just maybe, we'll be lucky and they'll all go home."

At the southern end of the pipeline, at the port of Valdez, residents voiced similar complaints about deterioration in all kinds of public and private services as the result of construction of the pipeline port facility. Valdez, strategically located in Prince William Sound off the Gulf of Alaska, was known as the "Switzerland of Alaska" because of its natural beauty. It had been a major port of entry during the Gold Rush days at the turn of the century, but its boom-town existence was short-lived, and even its fishing industry deteriorated. Major employment opportunities—trucking, construction, tourism—were available in the summer, but with the winter came large-scale unemployment. The 1964 earthquake, which destroyed the town and caused the community to be relocated, was almost the final blow. By 1969, just after the discovery of oil at Prudhoe Bay, a U.S. Department of Labor study showed 40 percent of

The Alatna River, winding southward out of the Brooks Range *(National Park Service/M. Woodbridge Williams)*

Crater of Aniakchak Caldera National Monument on the Alaska Peninsula *(National Park Service/M. Woodbridge Williams)*

The Arrigetch Peaks in the Brooks Range overleaf *(National Park Service)*

Fishing in Walker Lake in the Brooks Range *(National Park Service)*

Iniakuk Lake in the Brooks Range *(National Park Service)*

Margerie Glacier in Glacier Bay National Monument *(National Park Service)*

Mount McKinley seen from the southeast, with Buckskin Glacier at right *(National Park Service/Norman Herkenham)*

Thick-billed murres nesting on the shore of the proposed Chukchi-Imuruk National Reserve on the Seward Peninsula *(National Park Service/Robert Belous)*

Peregrine falcon *(National Park Service)*

A baby hair seal in Glacier Bay *(National Park Service/Janda)*

Grizzly bear fishing for salmon in the McNeil River near the proposed Katmai National Park on the Alaska Peninsula *(National Park Service/Keith Trexler)*

Walrus *(National Park Service)*

Edward Patton, Chairman of the Board and Chief Executive Officer of Alyeska Pipeline Service Company
(Alyeska Pipeline Service Company)

Jesse Carr, Alaska Teamsters' boss
(Anchorage Daily News)

Native leader Willie Hensley

Governor Jay Hammond

Moose under the pipeline *(Alyeska Pipeline Service Company)*

Welding two sections of the 48-inch diameter pipe *(Alyeska Pipeline Service Company)*

A section of above ground pipeline zigzags over the tundra of the North Slope, about 120 miles south of Prudhoe Bay *(Alyeska Pipeline Service Company)*

Detail of pipeline
(Alyeska Pipeline Service Company)

Pipeline construction at Thompson Pass
(Alyeska Pipeline Service Company)

Eskimo woman preparing seal intestines *(National Park Service)*

The blanket toss *(National Park Service)*

Eskimo girl in Elim, on the Seward Peninsula *(National Park Service/Arthur Mortvedt)*

Eskimo family in Mary's Igloo on the Seward Peninsula *(National Park Service/Robert Belous)*

An Eskimo woman prepares the traditional meal in the proposed Chukchi-Imuruk National Reserve on the Seward Peninsula *(National Park Service/Robert Belous)*

Eskimo hunters hauling a seal kill in proposed Cape Krusenstern National Monument near Kotzebue *(National Park Service/Robert Belous)*

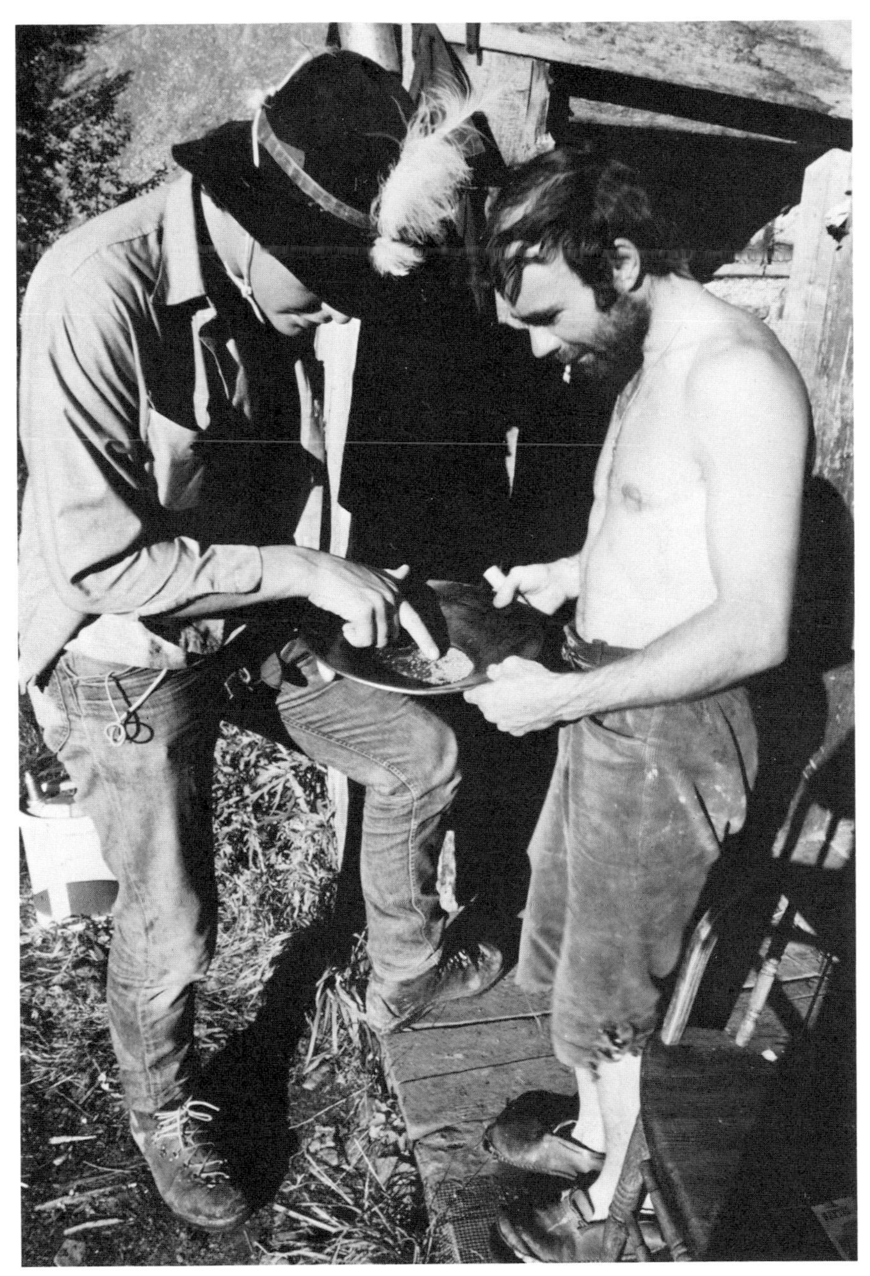

Gold miners *(National Park Service)*

Dog team traveling at −55°F *(National Park Service)*

the Valdez labor force was unemployed. Under these circumstances, many Valdez residents were understandably eager to have their town become the port terminal for the pipeline. A University of Alaska study reported that Valdez residents generally remained pro-pipeline despite an almost 400 percent increase in the town's population between January 1974 and July 1975 (to 6,512 people), and a decline in the quality of a number of consumer services. As Dr. Michael Baring-Gould, one of the authors of the study, told us:

> What you have in Valdez is basically a white, middle-class town, with a lot of high seasonal unemployment, that had been looking for some new economic stimulus. They had had a boom period before in their history and they wanted to return to those days. They had been shot down on a number of projects before. Then, the 1964 earthquake almost wiped them out and they had to be moved to a new site. So, the majority of the people there jumped at the chance to be the port terminal for the pipeline.

By mid-1976 some 3,900 people were employed on pipeline port work in Valdez. One Alaskan said the town's sudden boom had "been like moving Los Angeles to Lake Tahoe."

The pipeline also affected smaller communities, particularly Eskimo villages in the Arctic. In hearings and public forums on whether to open the Haul Road to the public, some Native representatives said that pipeline construction and use of the road had diverted caribou[9] from their normal migrating patterns, forcing the Natives to travel greater distances from their villages to hunt this vital source for their food supply. While the ultimate impact of the pipeline on the caribou and other animals was unclear, one experiment in late 1974 wasn't very encouraging. Wildlife researchers set up a simulated pipeline at Prudhoe Bay before the actual pipeline was built. Of the 5,599 animals that approached the two-mile-long simulated barrier, about 10 percent crossed over two gravel ramps that spanned the structure, fewer than 5 percent used four underpasses, and a few crawled under it. About 42 percent went around the barrier, but 34.4 percent turned back after approaching the structure. Environmentalists said this showed that caribou and other animals would be affected by the pipeline and other development.

[9] The caribou's numbers have been tragically depleted in recent years because of a variety of factors, including wolves and overhunting by non-Native sportsmen. In the western Arctic in 1970 there were an estimated 242, 000 caribou. By late 1976, about 50,000.

In addition to the life-style, environmental, and economic impacts of the pipeline, there was also a more subtle kind of influence at work. Alyeska and the oil companies, through a sophisticated advertising and public relations campaign, lulled many Alaskans into the feeling that what was good for Big Oil in Alaska was good for Alaska. Some 22,000 Anchorage school children in 1975 saw an Alyeska slide presentation on the benefits of oil to their state. And, of course, the *Anchorage Times* helped spread the oil companies' message in its news and editorial columns. Many Alaskan activists, such as Peg Tiletson, of the Alaska Center for the Environment, saw the oil companies as subtly overwhelming the community. "Look at the lovely ads they run on television," Tiletson said in August 1976. "The Arco ads, the bringing of programs to Alaska, the supporting of the arts. They have the money to become associated with all the good things of a community. This certainly does not buy goodwill, but it casts their presence in a favorable light to a lot of people."

Pipeline worker and free-lance writer Ron Rau, in an article in *National Wildlife* magazine (October–November 1976), described the impact that the oil companies' public relations campaign had had in the state:

> . . . [It has created] a climate in which the company [Alyeska] feels safe in making a statement like this, taken from their glossy October 1975 report: "Between Prudhoe Bay and Valdez, more than 800 streams cross the path of the trans-Alaska pipeline. . . ." "Wait a minute!" I shout. Who is crossing whom? I thought the 800 streams were there first. I *know* they were. They haven't gotten my mind yet. I can still recognize *doublethink*. But it's getting harder all the time. Two years ago that statement would not have been possible. Two years ago everyone knew it was the pipeline that crossed the streams.

In addition, as mentioned earlier, the oil companies are stepping more actively into the political arena. Oil lobbyists received $382,902 in fees, expenses, and lobbying expenditures at the 1976 state legislative session, to make them by far the biggest single lobbying force. In all, $935,348 was spent by legislative lobbyists that year. Common Sense for Alaska, a pro-development organization established before the 1976 state political campaign, received financing and membership from the oil industry, and acted as a front group for the oil companies. Such activity can be expected to increase in the years to come, particularly in the crucial 1978 gubernatorial election in which the super-growth forces would like very much to unseat

Governor Hammond. One Alaska politician already benefiting from the oil firms' largesse was Senator Mike Gravel. After reelection in 1974, the Democratic senator found himself personally in debt for about $65,000 to $75,000. So he instructed his top aide to "go to the oil companies" and collect some gratitude for his work on their behalf. At the aide's suggestion, oilman Leon Hess, head of the Amerada Hess Corporation, raised $30,000 for Gravel, and two other oil fund raisers gathered in over $40,000 for the financially beleaguered Gravel.

VIII

Son of Pipe Dream

As the construction of the most famous pipeline in history was winding down in early 1977, the battle over yet another pipeline—this one to transport an estimated 26 trillion cubic feet of Prudhoe Bay's natural gas to market—began to heat up. And that conflict was being fought along much the same lines as the controversy over the oil pipeline, with the dispute centering on the best route for getting the gas to market. This time around, three proposals were up for consideration by the Federal Power Commission, the president, and the Congress. Only one of the proposals was for an all-Alaska route; the other two were Alaska-Canadian hybrids.

Given the many battles Governor Hammond had fought with the super-growth interests in the state, it seemed curious to some that on the natural gas pipeline issue Hammond linked arms with the El Paso Alaska Company, the Alaska Teamsters Union, the *Anchorage Times*, the state's three members of Congress, and the Alaska business establishment in supporting the all-Alaska route. The environmentalists, usually aligned with Hammond on development issues, favored one of the routes through Canada.

The proposal by El Paso (made up of El Paso Natural Gas Company and Western LNG Company) was for a 42-inch diameter pipeline along an 809-mile route generally parallel to the trans-Alaska oil pipeline, running from Prudhoe Bay to Point Gravina, near Valdez, on Alaska's south coast. Its major deviation from the oil pipeline route was that it would cut through the Chugach National Forest—which was a matter of concern to environmentalists. At Point Gravina, El Paso proposed to build a gas liquefying plant from which the liquid gas would be shipped some 1,900 nautical miles in eleven pressurized tankers through the Gulf of Alaska and the Pacific Ocean to Point Conception on the southern California coast.

There a natural gas regasification and storage facility would be constructed from which 2.4 billion cubic feet per day of Alaskan gas would be channeled into existing pipelines to markets in the Midwest and East.

A second proposal called for a pipeline from 30 to 48 inches in diameter running 195 miles from Prudhoe Bay to the Canadian border. This line, proposed by the Alaskan Arctic Gas Pipeline Company, a consortium of Canadian and U.S. energy companies,[1] would cross 162 miles of the environmentally valuable Arctic National Wildlife Range. In Canada, the pipeline would veer to the southeast at the Mackenzie River Delta to hook up with a proposed pipeline to carry gas from that oil- and gas-rich area of Canada. The route, involving 4,175 miles of new and looped pipelines (connected and parallel to existing lines) would eventually join existing gas pipeline networks in Alberta, where the gas would then be carried to various U.S. and Canadian destinations. It would supply 2.25 billion cubic feet of Alaskan gas a day to the U.S., and 1.5 billion cubic feet a day of Canadian gas to Canada.

The third proposal, by the Alcan Pipeline Company, the Northwest Pipeline Corporation of Salt Lake City, and several Canadian companies, was a late arrival in the gas pipeline sweepstakes. It would use the trans-Alaska oil pipeline corridor from Prudhoe Bay to a point south of Fairbanks, and would then follow the existing Haines pipeline corridor and the Alaska (Alcan) Highway into Canada, where it would connect to existing British Columbia and Alberta distribution systems capable of transporting the gas to various Canadian and U.S. locations.[2] This route was much preferred by environmentalists because it totally avoided crossing the Arctic National Wildlife Range in Alaska and adjacent rangeland in Canada, which environmentalists hoped some day could be joined with the U.S. portion to form a protected international wildlife range. The Alcan proposal initially called for 4,600 miles of new 30- to 48-inch pipeline, which would run for 730 miles in Alaska and 936 miles in Canada and provide 2.4 billion cubic feet of gas a day to the U.S.

[1] At Caroline Junction, Alberta, the system would divide, with one leg going to the Pacific Northwest and down to California; the other section would cross the border into Montana and then go southeast into Illinois. Other pipelines would carry the gas to eastern markets.

[2] It would also divide into legs which would deliver the gas to the Pacific Northwest and to Illinois. The gas then would be transported to some eastern markets through existing pipelines.

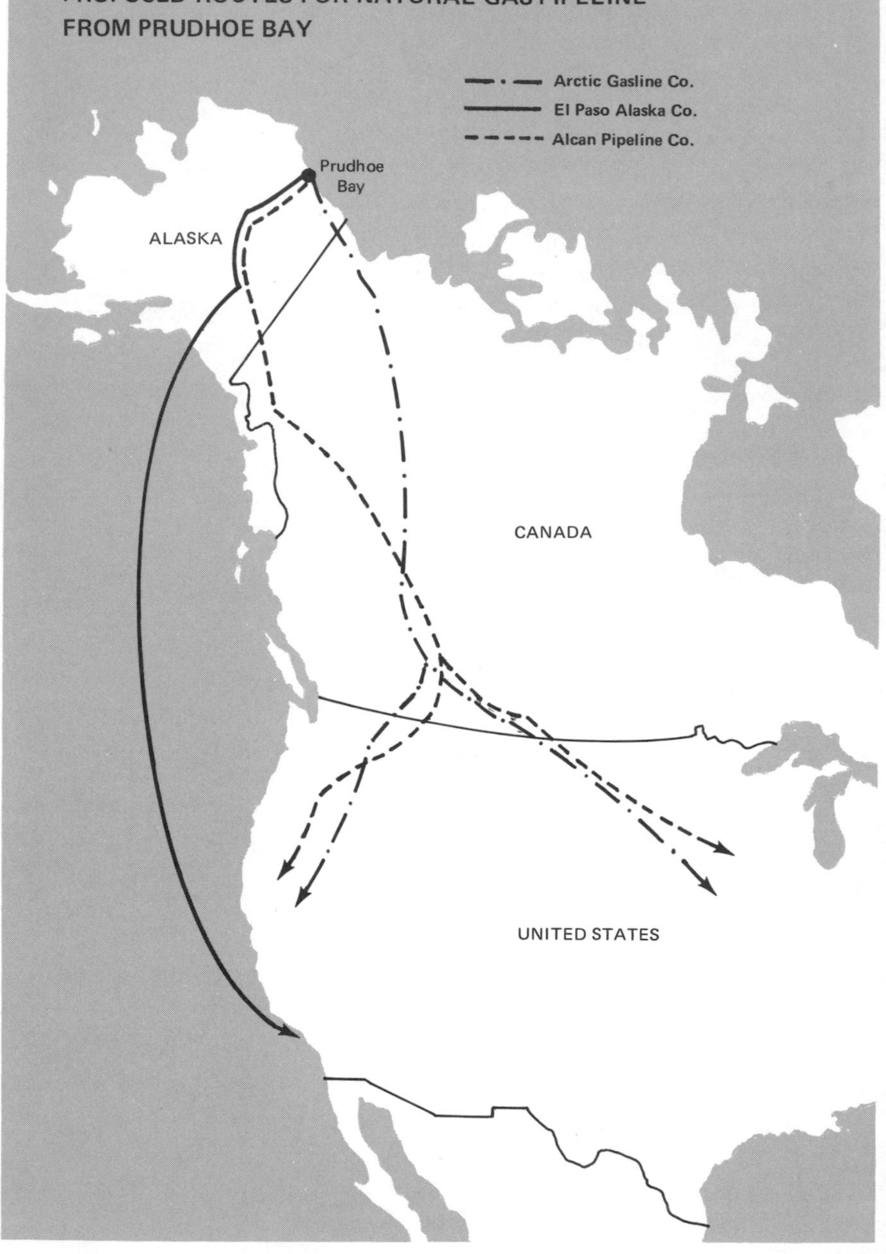
PROPOSED ROUTES FOR NATURAL GAS PIPELINE
FROM PRUDHOE BAY
Arctic Gasline Co.
El Paso Alaska Co.
Alcan Pipeline Co.
Prudhoe
Bay
ALASKA
CANADA
UNITED STATES

A number of cost figures were put forward for the various proposals, with most of the industry estimates in the $6 billion range in early 1977. However, a Federal Power Commission administrative law judge, Nahum Litt, in early 1977 placed the cost for the Arctic Gas proposal at $8.5 billion. Some skeptics in Congress, having seen the trans-Alaska oil pipeline increase 900 percent over a seven-year period, suggested that the eventual costs of the gas pipeline could be double or triple the industry estimates. In any event, it seemed likely the gas pipeline would supplant the oil pipeline as the most expensive private undertaking in history. The potential cost overruns concerned representatives of the three gas pipeline applicants who worried that unsympathetic moneylenders might turn their backs on them in the face of staggering costs.

A bill passed by Congress and signed into law by President Ford in October 1976 set up the procedure for choosing the route for the gas pipeline in 1977–78. The measure instructed the Federal Power Commission to recommend its choice of routes by May 1, 1977. President Carter would then have to make his recommendation by December 1977, and Congress would have to act on Carter's recommendation within sixty days after that. A choice of one of the two Alaskan-Canadian routes would, of course, necessitate negotiations with the Canadian Government and involve at least some additional delay. Nonetheless, the FPC, in a split vote, reported to the President in May that either of the Canadian routes was preferable to the El Paso proposal.

The procedural legislation for selecting the gas pipeline route reaffirmed a precedent established in the 1973 law authorizing the trans-Alaska oil pipeline. Court challenges to the gas pipeline on the basis that the National Environmental Policy Act had not been complied with were prohibited. Brec Cooke, Washington representative for the Wilderness Society, told a U.S. House subcommittee in August 1976 that this provision was a "breach of faith" of the environmental principles embodied in NEPA "for the sake of mere expediency." The expediency was the need, as seen by Congress and the industry, to bring the natural gas to market as quickly as possible.

On the plus side, the procedural measure allowed the Alaska government to ship its royalty gas in the pipeline for use within the state. The state's royalty amounts to a one-eighth share of all gas produced at Prudhoe Bay[3] under terms of the original 1969 lease

[3] Using industry estimates, this means the state would get some 3 trillion cubic feet of natural gas from Prudhoe Bay. An April 1976 study by the Alaska Department

sales to the industry. The legislation also directed the president to insure that, whichever line is built, there is the capability for direct pipeline delivery to points both east and west of the Rocky Mountains.

Before Alcan submitted the third pipeline proposal in mid-1976, Hammond's state administration had already hitched its fortunes to El Paso's all-Alaska route proposal. As Hammond told us in late 1976, his administration had studied the alternatives and concluded that "environmentally and economically, the all-Alaska route best meets Alaska's collective interests." This despite the fact that the natural gas would be transported to California in a highly volatile liquefied state aboard a fleet of tankers. In the event of a tanker collision or other accident, one spark or flame could ignite the gas.

In November 1976, the Hammond administration stepped up its support for the El Paso proposal with the announcement by the governor of an unorthodox plan: the state would aid El Paso's massive lobbying effort by selling 2.6 trillion cubic feet of its Prudhoe Bay royalty gas over a twenty-year period to Tenneco, Southern Natural Gas, and El Paso. In exchange for their inclusion in the sale, Tenneco and Southern Natural Gas agreed to throw their political support and lobbying efforts into winning federal approval of the all-Alaska route. Two weeks later, the state's Royalty Oil and Gas Development Advisory Board approved the contracts. The contracts required state legislative approval, however, and would be invalidated if some route other than the all-Alaska one was eventually selected.

The proposed sale was assailed by former lieutenant governor H. A. (Red) Boucher, as well as by a state senator, a Northwest Pipeline official, and the Wilderness Society during hearings before the advisory board. Boucher, expected to run for governor in 1978, said that while he had previously served as a marketing consultant to El Paso he nonetheless opposed the proposed royalty gas sale. "I believe strongly in the separation of government and industry," he said. "To commit the public's resources as a political bargaining tool, if not legally wrong, is at least morally wrong." Peter Scholes, Alaska regional representative for the Wilderness Society, warned

---

of Natural Resources, for the state's Royalty Oil and Gas Development Advisory Board, said that the state would be able to meet its own natural gas needs and still have "a surplus above 90 percent of royalty gas" for a twenty-year period, which the state would be able to sell.

against the all-Alaska route, saying it could result in thermal pollution problems from the gas liquefication plant at Point Gravina and would increase the possibility of collisions between gas and oil tankers in Alaskan waters.

Hammond's decision to support the El Paso proposal on such enthusiastic terms seemed inconsistent with his stated intention of supporting only that growth that pays its own way and is environmentally prudent. As we shall see later in the chapter, the Alcan proposal was far superior from an environmental standpoint; both the El Paso and Arctic Gas proposals posed grave environmental risks. But Hammond's support for the El Paso route was based on an inescapable political reality: as with the oil pipeline route, virtually every special interest group in the state—except the environmentalists—was supporting an all-Alaska route. To oppose a consensus on such a motherhood issue would be taking a risk not acceptable even to the usually independent governor.

El Paso helped cultivate acceptance of the all-Alaska route through an intensive lobbying and publicity effort which, by the end of 1976, had cost $18 million in two years. The Organization for the Management of Alaska's Resources (OMAR), an Alaskan business group, also invested heavily in El Paso's cause. This included direct lobbying activities in Washington, D.C. One such effort in May 1976 involved 60 Alaskans who lobbied more than 200 members of Congress and staffers (Alaska's Gravel, Stevens, and Young were already firmly in the El Paso camp). El Paso also hired former Senator Marlow Cook (Republican, Kentucky) to lobby on Capitol Hill for its proposal while Tenneco retained former Interior Department official Jared Carter as a lobbyist.

Alaska Teamster chief, Jesse Carr, made no bones about it: the major consideration for his union was that an all-Alaska route would provide more jobs for Teamsters. Estimates of jobs that would be created in Alaska ranged from about 20,000 for the El Paso proposal, 9,000 for the Arctic Gas proposal, and 15,000 for the Alcan plan. By early 1977, when oil pipeline construction had ended, Carr's concern for jobs for Teamsters was understandable in the face of the massive oil pipeline layoffs and a state unemployment figure of 14.1 percent in March and 15.5 per cent in April.

The environmentalists, for their part, were urging approval of the Alcan route proposal. The El Paso route troubled them but the Arctic Gas proposal was downright alarming. The Wilderness Society warned that the Arctic Gas route, in cutting across the Arctic

National Wildlife Range for 162 miles and then into the adjacent Canadian range, would endanger the calving grounds of one of North America's last caribou herds, harm nesting waterfowl, and leave a scar upon "a magnificent landscape of mountains, wild rivers, tundra, and seacoast, one of our planet's last few truly remote, superbly uncivilized places." The Arctic Gas route also could dash hopes "of creating a Canadian counterpart to the Arctic Range, forming in effect a great binational sanctuary," the Wilderness Society declared.

Another force was working against the Arctic Gas route: Canada's Northwest Territories' Indians, who had assailed the route with growing militance in recent years, following the example of the Alaska Natives and their push for a land claims settlement. British Columbia Supreme Court Justice Thomas R. Berger, who began holding hearings in 1974 on the Mackenzie Valley pipeline proposal, also suggested a land claims settlement must precede any construction. The Indians indicated they would use the courts to block the pipeline if it were approved before a land claims settlement. Some of the more militant Indians even suggested they would take extralegal means to prevent pipeline construction if a just land claims settlement were not first reached. El Paso lobbyists often cited Indians' threats to blow up a Mackenzie Valley pipeline if their land claims were not first satisfied.

Nonetheless, despite the environmental and Native claims problems, the Arctic Gas proposal seemed to be the one most favored by Congress in early 1977. And the Arctic Gas proposal got a substantial boost in early February 1977 when FPC Administrative Law Judge Litt designated it the preferred route. Governor Hammond, commenting that the judge had chosen "the route which nearly all Alaskans agree is the worst," said the state would appeal to the full FPC. But the FPC recommended approval of the Arctic Gas proposal as well as the Alcan route—but not the all-Alaska route. In May 1977, Justice Berger recommended that no Mackenzie Valley pipeline be built for at least ten years, but suggested that the Alcan proposal could be acceptable. In July, Canada's National Energy Board recommended the Alcan route. The same month, both the U.S. Council on Environmental Quality and a special presidential task force endorsed the Alcan route. Canada's Prime Minister Pierre Trudeau was to announce his decision by late 1977, prior to action by President Carter and Congress on the U.S. choice of routes.

While there were many parallels between the oil and natural gas pipeline debates, one departure was the contention—put forth by all three gas pipeline companies—that regardless of which route was selected, the government would have to be willing to bail out the project if it ran into financial difficulties. This was made abundantly clear in an August 1976 interchange of letters between Representative John D. Dingell (Democrat, Michigan), chairman of the Energy and Power Subcommittee of the House Interstate and Foreign Commerce Committee, and top officials of each of the three pipeline companies that were seeking approval of a Prudhoe Bay natural gas pipeline. Dingell confessed his unsettling doubts about cost controls of the proposed pipeline and his fear that the federal government would be euchred into helping finance it. His letters brought mostly unresponsive answers from the pipeline companies.

In his letter to John C. Bennett, vice-president of El Paso, Dingell wrote:

> There is a good chance that the taxpayers of this country will be asked to bear a good deal of the risk and, in some cases, costs in the form of federal financial assistance. . . .
>
> Both El Paso and Arctic argued that their almost identical cost estimates of $6.5 billion are reasonable and, in fact, include a built-in cushion for cost overruns. As you are well aware, the costs of every major construction project in this country in the last ten years have mushroomed once the contract got underway (e.g., the Trans-Alaska Pipeline, virtually every major weapons system purchased by the Department of Defense, etc.). Extrapolating from these experiences, I would not be surprised to see your estimates double or triple. . . .
>
> We do not want to get into a situation where the construction of this system is 75 percent completed and the Congress is faced with the choice of providing substantial government subsidies to complete the system or not having any gas delivered. . . . Why should the government leave the option open for bailing out an economically unjustifiable project?

Bennett's answer to Dingell, for the most part, danced around the issue of a federal bailout. Bennett did say that El Paso felt "that its proposal can be financed without federal assistance," but added that "no one can guarantee circumstances beyond our control, such as labor and material cost increases, availability of supplies, government policies affecting the economy and a myriad of similar variables. . . . The concern expressed by some parties about possible need for federal assistance is not predicated upon lack of economic justification, but rather the unique nature of the project and the tremendous capital requirements."[4] William W. Brackett, vice-chairman of Arctic Gas, in his response to Dingell, wrote that he did not anticipate the need for federal assistance, but stated that: "I cannot rule out the *possibility* [his emphasis] that some form of federal assistance will be needed. . . ." Brackett said that "governmental backstopping" for the project would be justified based on "the importance of Alaskan gas to the nation's energy supply . . . the inability of private firms to provide absolute completion and noninterruption guarantees which are required for financing large projects; and . . . the necessarily huge size of 'frontier' energy projects (at a time when conventional energy sources are inadequate and/or too unstable and actually or potentially too expensive.)"

John J. McMillian, chairman and chief executive officer of Northwest, was considerably more frank than the other two companies' representatives. McMillian stated that private financing for the Alcan project might be difficult to come by, particularly in light of the huge overruns on the trans-Alaska oil pipeline. Wrote McMillian:

> An Alaska gas transportation system is an indispensable national undertaking . . . to satisfy a significant portion of the nation's gas supply needs. . . .
>
> We have here a rare instance where the public interest is clear. This simply means that government must, if necessary, act to assist the private sector in financing this project. . . . The inability to obtain private financing because of the size or the special characteristics of a project does not necessarily condemn it in terms of the public interest.

The natural gas pipeline, of course, had not sparked nearly the controversy that the trans-Alaska oil pipeline had. Part of this was due to the "camel's nose under the tent" principle. Since Alaska's Arctic had already been penetrated by one pipeline, it was increasingly difficult to get as upset over a second project. Nonetheless, much was at stake. The Arctic Gas proposal, by breaking open the Arctic National Wildlife Range, was an environmental monster. The El Paso plan carried with it the potential for a liquefied natural gas explosion at sea. The Alcan plan posed far fewer environ-

[4] Indeed, since many people feared that the cost of bringing North Slope natural gas to market would be too high to justify construction of the El Paso route, and thus too high to get private sector financial backing, State Revenue Commissioner Sterling Gallagher proposed in early 1977 that the state guarantee $1 billion worth of financing for the El Paso route, an amount *four* times more than the controversial federal loan guarantee for Lockheed Aircraft Corporation in 1971.

mental problems than either of the other proposals—although it appeared more costly because it covered a longer route.

In addition to the environmental issue, it was especially troubling that, as of mid-1977, appropriate congressional committees had not fully addressed themselves to the financing of the natural gas pipeline. Given the record of waste, inefficiency, and environmental damage during construction of the oil pipeline, it was the height of folly to permit the risk of having the company building the natural gas pipeline to run up the project's cost—with the government (and consumers) waiting in the wings to rescue the company should its finances fail.

* * *

Just fifty miles to the west of the rich oil fields of Prudhoe Bay, also on the North Slope, lies an area of more than 23 million acres—approximately the size of the state of Indiana—that some government officials believe has recoverable oil reserves of anywhere from 10 billion to 100 billion barrels.[5] If the higher figure is correct, that would be the equivalent of ten Prudhoe Bays, using the industry estimate for Prudhoe Bay of 9.6 billion barrels. This potential bonanza area is the Naval Petroleum Reserve No. 4 (NPR-4 or Pet 4, for short), which had been administered by the navy since 1923. On June 1, 1977, however, under legislation passed the previous year, the reserve was transferred to the Department of the Interior and renamed National Petroleum Reserve in Alaska. The transfer was part of a long-range plan to bring Pet 4 into production, thus further entrenching Alaska as the nation's number one energy-producing state.

To many members of Congress, the decision to transfer Pet 4 from the navy to the Interior Department was the first step in an eventual giveaway of the reserve's riches to powerful multinational oil companies. As the most outspoken of these critics, Representative John E. Moss (Democrat, California), put it during 1974 hearings on production of oil and gas on public lands, "The oil industry lusts after these riches, and will find a way to get them." To students of history, efforts to open up the navy's petroleum reserves to private development recall the days of the Teapot Dome scandal of the 1920s. As Senator Adlai Stevenson (Democrat, Illinois) stated during 1974 hearings on opening up the Elk Hills Reserve in California: "History is repeating itself, except that the stakes could make the

[5] Estimates of recoverable natural gas for Pet 4 have ranged as high as 32 trillion cubic feet, enough to supply all U.S. users for about a year and a half.

raid on Teapot Dome a petty misdemeanor by comparison." The stakes are indeed far greater than they were when oil executives bribed a cabinet officer to get at the oil in the Teapot Dome and Elk Hills reserves five decades ago. For if some of the optimistic estimates by government officials are correct, Pet 4 could rank second only to Saudi Arabia's reserves of 177.5 billion barrels.

Ever since the concept of naval petroleum reserves was established in 1912, the oil industry has attempted to open them up for private development. The impetus for creation of naval petroleum reserves came as the navies of the world began to switch from coal to oil and a worldwide shortage of petroleum appeared imminent.[6] The initial purpose of the various reserves was to provide the navy with the necessary oil in the event of war. Reserves administered by the navy were established first at Elk Hills and Buena Vista in California, and at Teapot Dome in Wyoming. NPR-4 was established in February 1923 by President Warren G. Harding, whose administration was shortly to become engulfed in the Teapot Dome scandal.

The scandal, which started to heat up early in 1924, shortly after Harding's death in August 1923, involved payment to Interior Secretary Albert B. Fall of $100,000 in cash by Edward L. Doheny of Pan-American Oil Company, and $300,000 in Liberty Bonds and cash by Harry F. Sinclair of the Mammoth Oil Company. In return, Fall secretly turned over to Doheny and Sinclair noncompetitive-bid leases on the Teapot Dome and Elk Hills reserves. Fall was convicted of bribery but, in a strange twist, the oilmen were acquitted. Sinclair, however, did go to jail in 1929 for contempt of the Senate after refusing to answer questions concerning the scandal, and for contempt of court for hiring Burns private detectives to shadow jurors during his trial. In 1927, the Supreme Court ordered the

[6] Oil industry representatives opposed the reserves from the very beginning with dire warnings that the nation was about to run out of oil. Such predictions, coupled with the industry's involvement in the U.S. war effort in World War I, helped win the industry passage of the oil depletion allowance in 1918. The warnings of an imminent end to the nation's oil supply continued until shortly after the war. As one petroleum geologist was to write later about the period: "Incredible as it may seem, in 1920 we thought we were facing the beginning of the end of crude-oil resources in America, drilling what we thought were our last known structures and frowning—can you imagine it?—upon the rambling motorist who drove into our stations and demanded gasoline." In the 1920s some of the world's richest oil fields were discovered in Texas. Coupled with sizable reserves in Oklahoma, California, and Arkansas, the Texas discoveries transformed this earlier version of the "energy crisis" into an oil glut.

lands returned from the administration of the Interior Department to the navy, characterizing the switch to Interior in 1921 as having been achieved by conspiracy, corruption, and fraud.

The Teapot Dome scandal didn't represent an isolated effort by Big Oil to get the reserves opened for private development. Before that scandal, Josephus Daniels, secretary of the navy under President Woodrow Wilson, stated:

I have been compelled to fight almost every day of my incumbency in office to prevent the dummy entrymen and illegal operators from taking the Naval Reserves, the only hope for the Navy when the all too rapid use of American oil will leave it the only available supply.

Daniels also recalled how, during World War I, West Coast oilmen promoted an oil shortage scare and tried to mobilize influential citizens behind an effort to open up the naval reserves. In later years, at the Elk Hills Reserve, which was one-third owned by Standard Oil of California, the navy was forced to drill offset wells to prevent its reserves from being drained by Standard. As Representative Carl Vinson (Democrat, Georgia), a longtime defender of the reserves, stated in 1953 concerning efforts to open up the Elk Hills Reserve:

I have no criticism of Standard for wanting the oil out of the ground. They are in the business. What I am up here for is to watch the government's interest, and follow out what President Taft set out as a conservation program. And from that day down to this, there has been a constant raid—geological, scientific, and engineering—on the reserve.

Support for the federal oil reserves concept over the years has come from both members of Congress who viewed the reserves as having national defense value in the event of war and those who felt that the oil companies should not be allowed to make vast profits from federal oil land that rightfully belonged to all the people of the United States. This has produced some strange bedfellows: for example, ultra-conservative former Representative F. Edward Hebert (Democrat, Louisiana), the longtime House Armed Services Committee chairman, and liberal Senator Adlai Stevenson (Democrat, Illinois), both opposed turning over the reserves to the oil companies. California's Representative Moss was one liberal member of Congress who viewed energy-crisis arguments applied to the reserves as just a new twist in the old oil company game of trying to reap windfall profits from petroleum on federal land. Said Moss during 1974 congressional hearings on production of oil and gas on public lands:

> Pet Four alone may double our known existing reserves. Elk Hills is a $10 billion property. The oil industry lusts for these riches, and will find a way to get them. In no way can we depend upon the Interior Department to safeguard the public interest, for it has shown itself to be an adjunct of industry in such a manner as to constitute a public disgrace. The navy is too intimidated to act aggressively against encroachers. The Justice Department is at best a bulldog with rubber teeth . . . The solution is to allow the Navy to retain control of the reserves, with adequate funding to fully explore and map them, reporting annually to Congress on what these reserves contain. In no way should the Interior Department be allowed to approach or have any say in management of the reserves.

Moss expressed support for pending legislation that would have established a National Oil and Gas Corporation to work with the navy in preparing the resrves "for whatever eventual, inevitable exploitation the nation may desire." The corporation, Moss said, would provide a "yardstick . . . against which to measure behavior and performance of the private oil industry, which I believe today requires more careful control and scrutiny than any other area of American business. Its recklessness, drive for profit, greed, readiness to subvert and ignore the public interest, and willingness to bend law for its interests match and surpass any excesses of the Gilded Age. This industry must be brought under control."

The Oil and Gas Corporation proposal posed an enormous threat to the industry and, not surprisingly, failed to win congressional support. The proposal raised the possibility of the government taking what for it would be a novel approach of keeping the profits from oil on government land, rather than turning them over to private multinational oil companies. Pet 4, with its vast potential, seemed an appropriate place for such an experiment to be undertaken.

The oil companies had some twenty years earlier fought off another possible move by the federal government into the oil business at Pet 4. Kirby Brant, who was the former counsel and then deputy director for the Office of Naval Petroleum and Oil Shale Reserves for most of the period from September 1968 until 1974, told us in late 1976 that the navy was on the verge of undertaking intensive exploration of Pet 4 in 1953 when President Eisenhower took office. Brant, a lieutenant commander who had thoroughly studied the files and records pertaining to the reserves from 1912 until he resigned from the navy in protest of policy over the reserves in 1974, said that the oil industry pressured Eisenhower to drop the tests.

Brant explained that between 1944 and 1953 the navy and the U.S. Geological Survey spent some $50 million exploring the entire North Slope area, including NPR-4 and Prudhoe Bay. The wells were all shallow ones and not of the depth that later resulted in the giant discovery at Prudhoe Bay. When Eisenhower came into office, Brant said, "The navy had a rig in place, ready to do deep testing, when the oil companies came down hard on Ike with cries of 'socialism.' The oil companies said that such tests should be done by private enterprise."

The significance of this, of course, is that if the navy had gone ahead with its deep tests, it could have discovered North Slope oil fifteen years before the oil companies did in 1968. In fact, the basic data from the navy tests were later used by private corporations to find the North Slope areas with the most oil potential, Brant said. Had the navy been allowed to proceed with its deep drilling in 1953, he added, the energy shortages that surfaced in 1973–74 might have been averted, because North Slope oil would have been available for production before that time.

Just as Secretary of the Navy Robert B. Anderson in the Eisenhower administration favored leasing NPR-4 to private corporations, a number of other Defense Department figures over the years took similar positions. The most serious such effort, though, did not occur until the Nixon administration, when Deputy Secretary of Defense William D. Clements, Jr., set up in 1973 a departmental Energy Task Group that reported directly to him. In an internal memorandum he wrote a few days after establishing the unit, Clements urged that the navy "aggressively pursue" an "accelerated program" to permit private oil companies to produce NPR-4's oil. Clements set up the task group after receiving a report from an oil industry consultant he had hired who took just two weeks to compile his handwritten proposal calling for the navy to open its reserves. Given this consultant's report, and Clements's obvious leanings as revealed in the memo, the recommendation of his task group in late 1973 pertaining to NPR-4 was a foregone conclusion: the secretary of the navy should take forceful steps toward exploration and ultimate development of NPR-4. The task group also proposed construction of another pipeline to carry the NPR-4 oil.

One of the incidents that led him to decide to quit the navy, Brant said, was when he was asked to assist the Senate Armed Services Committee prior to hearings on proposals to open up NPR-4 for development. Two days before any hearings had even begun, he was called by a committee staffer. When he went to the staffer's office, he found the staffer, assisted by a representative of Clements's task group, already writing up the committee report. The report called for full support of the task group's recommendation. Brant said he refused to participate and walked out. "To put it bluntly, one house of Congress was being controlled by the Southeastern Drilling Company [SEDCO]."

And so it seemed. Clements owned about $100 million worth of shares in SEDCO, making him the company's chief stockholder. SEDCO, a Dallas-based firm that performed work for major oil companies throughout the world, was headed by his son, B. Gill Clements. SEDCO is in the business of drilling wells, building pipelines, and giving engineering advice on opening up new oil fields, both onshore and off. It performed work for the major companies at Prudhoe Bay and also had a one-half interest in a contract to build part of the North Slope Haul Road. Even more to the point, SEDCO was likely to benefit from development of NPR-4 through contracts with oil companies. Clements, when he took his defense post, did resign as chairman of SEDCO's board but he retained his stock. After his memo on the defense energy task group was publicized by syndicated columnist Jack Anderson, Clements said he would remove himself from "the decisional chain of command" on energy matters. Defense Secretary James Schlesinger at first said Clements would continue to be available to offer "technical advice" on energy matters, but Clements later promised not to do even that. Still, his goal was already accomplished, for the task group had given its stamp of approval to the idea of putting the Alaska reserves in private hands for development.

The legislation signed into law by President Ford in 1976, transferring NPR-4 to Interior's jurisdiction, provided that exploration previously contracted for by the navy could continue and that Interior could contract for more exploration—but not development. Initial exploration was being conducted by the Husky Oil Company, which contracted to drill twenty-five to thirty wells on NPR-4 over a five-year period. The law provided for establishment of a task force—including representatives of the state government, the Arctic Slope Native community, and various federal officials—to make recommendations by April 5, 1979, concerning the best uses for the land in NPR-4, including the possibility of oil development. The Interior Department was to submit a study and make recommendations to Congress by January 1, 1980. Whether, and how, NPR-4 is developed is then up to Congress.

James Coan is federal project coordinator in Alaska for the Bureau of Land Management, the agency of the Interior Department which was assigned surface management of NPR-4. He is careful not to talk as if development is inevitable, although it's hard to find anyone in Alaska not connected with BLM who thinks NPR-4 is just going to sit undeveloped for very long. Coan, however, stressed to us that BLM was giving special considerations to wildlife, environmental, archeological, and Native cultural values during the drilling and seismological testing on NPR-4.

Although some of the Alaskans we talked to in late 1976 were extremely wary of further development on the North Slope and the impact it could have on the environment and the Native culture,[7] many said the federal government had done a better job than usual of involving the public in its NPR-4 study. Unlike the battle over federal leasing of Alaska's outer continental shelf, the Interior Department had been consulting the Alaska state government and the Native community every step of the way over NPR-4, various concerned parties told us. "If the federal government had handled OCS the way they've handled NPR-4 thus far, we'd have few worries," Guy Martin, the state commissioner of natural resources, told us in late 1976.[8]

Despite this, many North Slope residents and environmentalists were fearful of what NPR-4 development would bring. As Barrow resident Chuck McIsaac told a reporter in early 1976 concerning Pet 4 development: "Pow. Here's a package; you open it up

[7] The initial draft environmental impact statement for Pet 4, released in March 1977, said that *exploration* would have no adverse lasting effects on the North Slope. However, the navy statement added that a separate environmental impact study would be needed to determine if *development* of Pet 4 oil would have an adverse impact.

[8] In March 1977, Martin was appointed by President Carter to be assistant secretary of the interior for land and water resources. In this post, Martin had responsibility for the Bureau of Land Management, Bureau of Reclamation, and land and water planning and research. The appointment was of special significance for Alaskans because the BLM is the state's biggest landholder. And Martin's new post gave him a voice in major decisions affecting Alaska—including the route for a gas pipeline, outer continental shelf oil and gas exploration and development, implementation of the Native Claims Settlement Act, and the setting aside of lands for wilderness purposes.

and it eats you." McIsaac said that Barrow already had problems with health service, water supply, and air service, and that heavy use of these by oil workers would severely burden the community. Some North Slope Eskimos told reporters they thought that seismic tests utilizing explosives were affecting the availability of fish and game. "They're really going to start screwing up the land," commented Billy Neakok of Barrow, concerning oil development and the Eskimos' reliance on whale, walrus, polar bear, and a variety of fish for their meat supply. Some residents also expressed concern that an influx of a great many non-Native workers for the Pet 4 project could exacerbate racial tensions in the community.

Interestingly, the government of the North Slope Borough favored the transfer of authority over NPR-4 to the Interior Department. North Slope Borough Mayor Eben Hopson explained that if there were to be oil development, the borough wanted to be able to tax it. If development were done by the navy for military use, he noted, the borough would not be able to tax the equipment the navy used or contracted for. However, if Interior proposed to develop the reserve for sale to the public, this would mean private oil companies would develop the resources and that the borough would be able to tax their equipment. Some environmentalists also had supported the transfer on the grounds that Interior would do a better job of protecting the land than the navy. (Brant told us such thinking ignored the lessons of history—such as the Interior Department's involvement in the Teapot Dome scandal and the fact that the navy had persistently resisted the encroachments by private companies on the reserves. Under the navy, NPR-4 was a de facto wilderness; under Interior, he said, the reserve was likely to be exploited to its maximum.)

With NPR-4 in Interior's hands, many environmentalists began pushing to have a substantial portion of it permanently set aside as national parks and wildlife refuges, or as part of the wild and scenic rivers systems, thereby protecting it from development. Especially vital, said the environmentalists, is the need to protect areas of critical habitat for the dwindling Arctic caribou herd, millions of migratory birds, and the endangered peregrines and gyrfalcons. These key areas include the Utukok River and Teshekpuk Lake areas and the Colville River Valley.

Once the decision is made to develop the reserve's oil, the question becomes how. That decision won't be made for some time, but the possibilities range from one or more new pipelines or a short linkup to the existing trans-Alaska pipeline, to the use of tankers—a proposal that was dismissed by the oil companies for Prudhoe Bay because northern Arctic waters are ice-free only two to three months out of the year. Regardless of the method of developing NPR-4, it is widely assumed that private industry, rather than government, will do the developing—mainly because of the old bugaboo of "socialism." As Assistant Interior Secretary Jack Horton put it in August 1976, the government "does not plan to federalize the oil and gas industry."

Nonetheless, a massive study on NPR-4's oil and gas potential, prepared by a planning consultant (Resource Planning Associates, Inc., of Cambridge, Massachusetts) for the Federal Energy Administration in July 1976, took note of countervailing arguments:

> Private-sector development of NPR-4 is favored by some because private companies are usually thought to be more economically efficient than government since, unlike government, private firms must be profitable to remain in business.
>
> However, the tripling of oil prices during and since the 1973 Arab oil embargo has prompted proposals that would involve government directly in oil and gas operations. Support for more direct government involvement is generally based on a belief that the existing tax structure and royalty and bonus procedures cannot capture for the public the windfall benefits industry realizes from such market aberrations. . . . [S]upport is also based on national defense considerations. Specifically, because national defense is and will continue to be dependent on petroleum products, some argue that the government should ensure that its basic needs are met before private entities are allowed to produce resources for general consumption.

There are additional arguments for more government involvement in petroleum production on public lands. The public is now almost totally at the mercy of an energy industry that is becoming increasingly concentrated in the hands of multinational corporations able to manipulate the market; the oil shortage scare of 1973–74, and the natural gas shortages of 1973 and 1977, demonstrated just how much control the oil companies have over the government and the public; the energy companies, by keeping their business operations secret, force the public to accept as an act of faith their projections of reserves, shortages, and future energy prospects.

In a sense, we have put the cart before the horse in discussing who should develop NPR-4. The necessary preliminary question is whether these reserves *should* be developed. With the West Coast oil glut the Prudhoe Bay oil will produce, and the potential high cost of building a second pipeline through Canada to bring the oil to the Midwest and East, it would seem a wise policy to delay marketing NPR-4 oil for some years to come. There is some persuasive logic in retired naval officer Brant's argument: "Why not keep them shut in—or produce the reserves and store them until the day we need them. . . . As we come to rely more on foreign oil, we can only truly protect our national security by having large domestic reserves."

Brant believes that although the original rationale for the reserves has changed—that is, the need for oil to replace coal to power navy ships—it is still a valid concept in terms of the broader national interest. That concept lost some of its force when the navy was unable to get more funds to explore Pet 4. As a result, the government for years has had no true picture of the exact amount and worth of the oil on NPR-4. The oil industry, he said, prefers a situation where it can say about public lands it wishes to lease, "We don't know what's there, but neither do you, Uncle Sam." If the government did know and decided to allow private leasing, it would be in a better position to get its fair share. Whether the government will get that fair share when NPR-4 oil is eventually marketed is, given the historical precedents, questionable.

* * *

Imagine yourself governor of, say, New York and discovering one day that one of your biggest problems will be deciding what to do with a budget surplus—projected over the remainder of this century—that is the equivalent of $2,500 per capita *annually*. Ridiculous, of course. At a time when chief executives of states, and cities, across the country are scraping for every penny in order to maintain even minimal governmental services, only a governor who believed in Santa Claus could have such hallucinated visions of fiscal sugarplums dancing in his head.

Except one. "This is an absolutely unique situation in that the state has money it doesn't know how to spend," explained Arlon Tussing, a University of Alaska economics professor. "It is more comparable to what's happened in Libya and Kuwait than to anything that's ever happened in the United States. It's mind-boggling." The word is apt. For the State of Alaska will soon be wealthy enough to make every one of its 400,000 residents, if not rich, very comfortable. The source of this unprecedented prosperity will be the state's share of the revenues from the sale of the billions of barrels of Prudhoe Bay oil that began their 800-mile journey south to Valdez through the Alaska pipeline in mid-1977.

Alaska's share of that oil field is sizable—25 percent in royalties and severance taxes. Unless it decides to take the advice of its economic consultants and its state Department of Revenue and greatly increase oil taxes, state revenue will average $1 billion a year from Prudhoe Bay alone—enough to provide every family of four residing in the state with a $10,000 a year subsidy. The state Department of Revenue estimated in October 1976 that Alaska's total annual oil and gas revenue will climb to $1.5 billion by 1985.

So it is understandable that Alaskans would be euphoric over their imminent bonanza. Except most weren't. In our travels throughout the state in 1976, few Alaskans we talked to were even remotely excited over the new wealth. Most were either bored by the subject, cynical about where the money would wind up, or just generally unaware of the sums involved. As the *Anchorage Times* noted on November 21, 1976: "The impact of the new oil money . . . has hardly begun to sink into the public consciousness." Some recent Alaskan history helps explain this monetary malaise.

In 1969, when the state received $900 million in oil lease bonuses, Alaskans were euphoric. To an undeveloped state with an annual budget of less than $300 million and an area twice the size of Texas, which had been run as a virtual fiefdom of the Interior Department for almost a century, $900 million represented not only wealth but independence. Almost everyone was enthusiastically pro-pipeline; dissent was considered un-Alaskan in a state in which local pride is so openly paraded that social status is carefully calibrated by the number of years one has lived in the state. But the $900 million quickly disappeared, gobbled up by an undernourished government intent on upgrading various social programs and a poor education system, and providing sewers and other basic services and public works projects to outlying towns.[9] And, as we have seen, neither the state government nor the residents was fully prepared to deal with the impact the billions expended on pipeline construction have had on the Alaskan economy and its frontier life-style. The

[9] Although many Alaskans contend that the $900 million was squandered, others told us that the state's economy had been so depressed for so long that state spending was absolutely vital to prop up many sagging local businesses and to create (and maintain) jobs for Alaska's work force, which is chronically plagued by a high unemployment rate.

pipeline pay of up to $60,000 and more per year forced other wages up, and prices soared. The invasion of Texas oilmen was greeted by most Alaskans with the kind of warmth with which the Pharaoh welcomed the ten plagues. Alaskans came to understand the limitations of wealth, particularly when that wealth comes too suddenly. Perhaps, in fact, they learned this lesson too well and forgot that money can be fun.

On November 2, 1976, the voters approved an amendment to the state's constitution which generated little discussion and less controversy. The amendment created the Alaska Permanent Fund and designated it the repository for at least 25 percent—and conceivably all 100 percent—of mineral lease rentals, royalties, royalty gas and oil sale proceeds, federal mineral revenue sharing payments, and cash bonuses from oil and gas lease sales received by the state. The Permanent Fund, which will invest, not spend, these revenues, is an attempt to insure that there are some long-range benefits from the sale of the state's non-renewable resources, and that at least some of the receipts are not squandered. But the amendment is vague and leaves it to the governor and legislature to decide precisely for what purposes, and how, this money is to be invested.

To stimulate some ideas and some interest in how Alaska should develop and manage its incredible potential wealth in non-renewable resources worth tens of billions of dollars, Governor Hammond created the Alaska Public Forum in 1976. The Forum sponsored a series of public workshops throughout the state to tap citizen opinion on these vital questions. In addition, Hammond expanded an existing investment advisory committee to twenty-one members and instructed it to submit proposals to him on how the Alaska Permanent Fund should operate. Hammond, in turn, would then make recommendations to the legislature.

The proposals for operation of the Permanent Fund were diverse. One would have had the Fund make loans to small businesses and other marginal enterprises in order to stimulate commerce within the state. Another would have provided financing of community development projects and private housing needs. Another would have had the Fund invest in Outside blue-chip stocks to insure that the money would be there when needed sometime in the future. And much of the business community was sympathetic to a proposal that would have had the Permanent Fund set up a development bank, similar to the World Bank. This plan, which some critics called a scheme to subsidize big business, would funnel loans through private banks to finance long-range projects in the state, such as mining ventures and petrochemical plants.

Whatever percentage of oil and mineral doesn't go into the Permanent Fund will go into the general treasury, and what will happen to these revenues is even less clear, particularly since Alaska today is not the impoverished land it was in 1969. Over the last eight years the state budget has tripled. Clearly, the state government's claim to the oil revenues is far less compelling than it was in 1969.

The state's rosier financial picture gave rise to the proposal of a number of grandiose and expensive plans, the most popular of which involved moving the state capital at a cost of up to $2.5 billion (see Chapter XI). Curiously, until early 1977, the solution to the money quandary that might have made the most sense, both politically and philosophically, had been the least discussed option: giving the money back to the people of Alaska. After all, it was the people's land that was leased to the oil companies; the state government merely acted as a collective bargaining agent for its citizens. Why shouldn't Alaskans receive direct payment for their land, just as the Texas farmers who sold their land to the oil companies did? Moreover, distributing the Prudhoe Bay revenues to the state's residents on some per capita basis would be consistent with the democratic principles of appropriating funds for government and making government accountable. Presumably, it is the people, not the government, who should decide what the legitimate needs of government are, and how much of their money they are willing to allocate to it. One need not be a fiscal conservative to believe that taxes should hurt, and the billion dollars that will annually flow to the state from the Prudhoe Bay sales is an arbitrary amount that bears no relation to the needs of the state government.

But the only prominent politician in the state whom we found thinking along these lines in 1976, however, was Hammond.[10] And it was as a fiscal conservative that Hammond worried that a political corollary of Parkinson's Law would assert itself in relation to the Prudhoe Bay revenues—that government would expand to consume whatever funds were made available to it. "I would far rather," he said in a late 1976 interview, "take that oil money—money from nonrenewable resources—sail it back out to the people in the form of a dividend, and then, through the normal taxing process, provide for the

[10] Former senate president Chancy Croft (still a member of the Alaska Senate in 1977) said he favored oil tax legislation which included a revenue-sharing plan to redirect money back to citizens, but no details had been worked out as of early 1977.

funds for normal state services." Hammond envisioned a revenue-sharing state corporation, Alaska, Inc., to perform this function. In his State of the State message on January 11, 1977, he told the legislature that he would formally submit legislation proposing creation of Alaska, Inc. At the same time, he announced his proposal to put 50 percent—rather than the minimum 25 percent required by the constitutional amendment—of oil, gas, and mineral revenues into the Permanent Fund. (Later, he said that the full 100 percent should go into the Fund.) Reaction from legislators to Hammond's announcement was far from enthusiastic. Typical was the comment of Senator Bill Ray (Democrat, Juneau) who said Hammond's Permanent Fund and Alaska, Inc., proposals were "well intentioned, but misguided." He termed Hammond's Alaska, Inc., revenue-sharing plan "very appealing, but there's not much chance of passage."

Despite the appeal of the Hammond plan, it did have several drawbacks. The most serious was its lack of progressiveness. A millionaire and an unemployed Native who had lived in the state for the same length of time would receive equal payments. Additionally, it gave the individual Alaskan a personal stake in accelerated oil, gas, and mineral exploitation of the state. The more leasing, the greater the revenues to Alaska, Inc., the larger the dividend check each year to shareholders; there were to be no annual dividend checks for conserving the wilderness. Also, money paid out by the state to residents would be subject to the federal income tax; if retained by the state it would not be.

Nevertheless, these last two drawbacks were really the unavoidable consequences of affluence. And progressiveness could be built into the Alaska, Inc., concept—as Hammond himself suggested—so that needy residents would receive larger checks than the richer shareholders. What really seemed to bother many Alaskan politicians was the very concept of Alaska, Inc.; it seemed somehow daffy and vaguely un-American for a state to be writing out checks to its residents each year. It's the citizens, after all, who usually do the check writing. Yet, when one considers it, it really isn't the concept of a state government funding its residents that's so strange; it's the uniqueness of the Alaskan condition. So few people living atop such vast wealth.

With Hammond thinking unique thoughts about what to do with some of the money the state receives from oil, natural gas, and mineral leasing and production, many other Alaskans were thinking that the state should move toward a position of developing its own oil. "Why don't we have state-owned oil?" asked Anchorage attorney Warren Matthews. "Why doesn't the state do its own drilling and operate the wells? Why shouldn't the state get the money that's going to the oil companies?" Matthews's comment was typical of that of many Alaskans we talked to who felt the state was being shortchanged in its dealings with the oil companies.

A number of Alaskans recognized the unique opportunity to alter state government dealings with multinational oil corporations. Patrick Dobey, petroleum manager for the state's division of Minerals and Energy Management, himself a former oilman, thinks the state and federal governments should assume more direct control of oil development on their own lands. "The federal government and the state are in the oil business whether they like it or not," Dobey told us. "When we lease, we're selling the taxpayers' oil; that's oil that the people, the taxpayers own. . . . The government could exert better environmental controls [than private industry]. . . . [And] government is just as capable of contracting experts as the oil companies are." Dobey said that the federal and state governments must start using a little imagination in dealing with the oil companies. The federal government thus far has "adopted the role of the Texas rancher" in using the same basic lease policies that small landowners did in the Lower-48. Such a posture is most favorable to the oil industry because all the individual landowner gets out of oil exploration is "a front-end deal, a bonus, and a low royalty for his former 100 percent mineral rights—that is, a small percentage of the profits." But while the farmer does not have much negotiating leverage, the state and federal governments do.

Dobey's boss, then state Natural Resources Commissioner Guy Martin, told us in late 1976 that while he expected the state to take an increasingly active role in oil and gas management over the next couple of years, the immediate prospects for a state-owned oil and gas company were not great.

> . . . In order to start a state-owned oil company, what you'd have to do is devote everything we have now in bringing Prudhoe Bay on line—plus create a whole other organization over here that has no other responsibility whatsoever except to set up a state oil company. . . . Quite frankly, just doing the things necessary to cope with the oil field coming on is an overwhelming job.

When he took over his state cabinet post in 1975, Martin discovered that his agency, as the department responsible for oil and gas management, had just four people handling this enormous undertaking. The original Prudhoe Bay lease sale in 1969 was put together by an ad hoc group of state officials and employees of the mineral leasing division, most of whom lacked any professional qualifications in oil and gas management. So in order to establish more expertise in this vital area, Martin set up a new division under Dobey. "I tell you all this to show you that the step from there [four people handling oil and gas management] to a state-owned and operated oil company is such a mammoth step, putting philosophical implications aside, that at least at present it's sort of something to think about and look toward. But it's not realistic in the short run."

What is realistic, Martin said, is "dramatically expanding the state's role in oil and gas operations." This could be done in a number of ways, he said, such as:

- Increasing the tax burden on the oil and gas industry.
- Revising leasing methods so that the state would take a much greater royalty than the one-eighth share it currently gets for Prudhoe Bay and Cook Inlet oil and gas.
- Alaska "could invest and seek an equity position in oil and gas operations," Martin suggested. "For instance, we could buy a share of one of the pipelines—actually use state money through bonding, or use royalty gas money, or money from the Permanent Fund—to invest in an equity share in some of these facilities which would give us some control, influence, and access to the information that is traded inside the organization, rather than just what you can get as a government."
- Alaska "could take on certain aspects of an oil and gas company. For instance, we could contract for a major exploration effort, so when we sell oil and gas we know what we're selling."

Major studies by state agencies and Outside consultants on oil and gas leasing and taxation were released in early 1977. One of the studies concluded that the state, through inadequate leasing procedures at the time of its 1969 Prudhoe Bay sale, lost out on billions of dollars in lease bonus money. Richard B. Norgaard, a member of the Energy and Resources Group at the University of California, Berkeley, wrote that "Prudhoe Bay is clearly a 'tough luck' story for the state . . . Had the state known about the Prudhoe Bay field in advance, between $5 billion and $10 billion more would have been collected in bonus bids." Norgaard added that, if there had been exploratory drilling before the lease sales, the state would have known the true value of the Prudhoe Bay fields and could have required higher bids for the leases. One consultant's report called for a revamping of the state's taxes on the oil companies. That study, by Jerome M. Zeifman and Kenneth G. Ainsworth,[11] pointed out a number of loopholes in existing state taxation policy. Especially inadequate, they said, was the state corporate tax as applied to oil companies because it uses federal taxable income as the base for figuring the state tax. Because federal taxable income is arrived at after figuring in various federal tax breaks, the tax base is considerably eroded. Thus, although the federal statutory corporate tax rate is 48 percent, the effective tax rate in 1975 was 21.3 percent for all corporations, and even less for the oil industry. With Alaska's 9.4 percent statutory corporate income tax rate, Zeifman and Ainsworth calculated the *effective* state oil tax rate at just 0.28 to 5.0 percent. The consultants' study of ten oil companies doing business in Alaska showed that in the three-year period of 1973 through 1975, those firms' book income figures (income reported to shareholders) exceeded taxable income by $1.6 billion to $3 billion a year. The consultants noted: "It is this eroded tax base which Alaska has relied upon for its corporate tax revenues."

Based on this report, and another from the state Department of Revenue, Hammond submitted legislation to the 1977 legislature that would have raised taxes on Prudhoe Bay oil by $200 million annually. But the legislature agreed to an increase of only $115 million. Hammond's fairly hard-nosed attitude about oil company taxation was also expressed in one of our interviews with him in October 1976:

> People ask how much do you intend to tax your oil companies. I say, just as much as we can get. Now there is a point of diminishing returns. Unfortunately, that's hard to determine, frankly, because we went about taxing them initially all wrong in my view, and at the time I protested. . . . We ought to be talking about a ninety-nine percent severance tax. No takers. You move down to ninety-eight, ninety-seven, ninety-six, somewhere you're going to get some vibration. Then you know you're in the ball park. We had no idea. We didn't know whether to extract twice as much from oil companies, or half as much. . . . I think it's appropriate for the state to re-

[11] Zeifman is an associate professor of law at Santa Clara (California) University. He formerly was general counsel to the U.S. House Judiciary Committee, as well as chief counsel to the Special Subcommittee on State Taxation of Interstate Commerce. Ainsworth is chairperson of the economics department of Allegheny College, Meadville, Pennsylvania. He formerly served as an economist on the Special Subcommittee on State Taxation of Interstate Commerce.

ceive on their non-renewable resources a certain percentage return on the value of the product and, by George, if they can't produce it from that, they ought to leave it in the ground. Then, on top of that I think we ought to consider something like the excess profits tax or something that relates to when they make it much bigger, then presumably we get a little piece of the action as well so we don't end up with just a very modest return when we could at least prosper alongside it.

Many consumer advocates in the state support an increased state role in development. James Love, of the Alaska Public Interest Research Group, told us in early 1977 that his group was drafting a bill which would set up a state energy corporation. The corporation would do preliminary exploration and possibly some development of oil and gas reserves on state-owned lands.

The increasing public discussion of a greater state role in oil and gas exploration and development clearly has some of the state's super-growthers worried. Anchorage businessman Tom Fink, a former legislator and now an *Anchorage Times* columnist, commented in late 1976 that some Alaskans have for the last several years been talking about "the state controlling the oil development. I'm very much opposed to that." Fink said he also was concerned about suggestions by some Alaskans and Outsiers that the federal government, rather than private enterprise, explore federally owned lands in Alaska. "Whenever the government gets involved, it costs more than the free enterprise system," Fink said.

The oil companies, for their part, have resisted both encroachments on what they regard as their private prerogatives and any additional taxation. In 1972, for example, seven oil companies filed a lawsuit in Anchorage Superior Court challenging the right of the North Slope Borough to incorporate. The suit was filed after the state's Local Boundary Commission, following a series of public hearings, approved the Natives' petition to incorporate. The seven companies—Mobil Oil, Humble Oil (now Exxon), Phillips Petroleum, Union Oil, Amoco, BP, and Amerada Hess—alleged a number of technical errors in the commission's decision, but their key objection was that the newly created borough could impose taxes and regulations on them. The firms also tried unsuccessfully to get the courts to block an incorporation election; 95 percent of those casting ballots voted for borough incorporation. The Arctic Slope Eskimos viewed the lands which the oil companies were using as traditionally belonging to them and saw incorporation as a way to tax the oil companies, provide needed community services, protect their subsistence life-style, and at the same time gain some measure of control over potentially damaging development. The oil companies pursued their legal challenge to incorporation of the borough, but in March 1974 the Alaska Supreme Court upheld the legality of the borough's incorporation. Since then, the borough has been involved in a series of battles with the oil companies over taxation. One such dispute was settled out of court in October 1974 when twenty-six oil companies agreed, among other things, to pay $5 million to the borough. The borough, among other things, agreed not to levy a 3 percent sales and use tax until 1979, and promised not to challenge the constitutionality of certain laws passed by the legislature in 1973 which limited boroughs' taxing authority. Nonetheless, other tax disputes between the oil companies and the borough followed.

In his 1976 consultant's report to the legislature, oil economist Michael Tanzer said that oil company earnings from Prudhoe Bay would be so huge that Alaska could tax at 50 percent, or even 80 percent, of the value of the oil and the companies would still make substantial profits. Tanzer, whose report was widely denounced by the oil companies and the super-growthers, stated that such a tax was possible not simply because

> the companies have already invested such a large amount in Prudhoe Bay that they couldn't afford to switch away from it now. Rather, it is a conclusion based on the belief that even if the companies had the opportunity to pull out from Prudhoe Bay, with full recovery of their recent investment plus a "reasonable" profit, they would still prefer to stay even under the higher tax rates considered here . . .

Tanzer compared Alaska's position to that of the Middle East oil-producing countries thirty years ago "when essentially they were passive collectors of small amounts of royalties, and had little information about, let alone control of, their most crucial industry." The state, he suggested, could cease leasing potential oil lands and "instead undertake exploration itself . . . either on a joint venture basis with other oil companies, or by the state hiring the specialized oil drilling companies which do much of the drilling for the major oil companies." He continued:

> We recognize that the idea of such an active role may seem strange to Americans who are conditioned to thinking that only the big oil companies are capable of carrying out such projects in the oil sector. However, the people of Alaska and their representatives need to see that events have moved rap-

idly in the oil industry in recent years, and in particular there has been a wider dispersion of knowledge and technological capability. Hence, many functions in the industry which were once largely the preserve of the big oil companies can now be carried out by smaller firms who work "for hire," and the big profits then go to the purchaser of the service.

The Tanzer report offered a good starting point for the state to move toward getting more of the benefits from its own oil wealth.

IX

Boss Carr

If Jess Carr told me to hook a chicken to a plow, I wouldn't tell him, "Mr. Carr, you can't hook a chicken to a plow." I would just do it.

—Alaska Teamster official Fred (Freddy the Fix) Dominic Figone.

THE COUNTENANCE of Jesse L. Carr beams down from a portrait above his chair in a conference room so lush with fine wood and leather it would bring a flush of pride to the cheeks of the chairman of IBM. Adjacent to the conference room is Jess Carr's equally lavish private office in which the prized possession is a $10,000 desk. Although Carr is a high-school dropout and has probably never even harbored a thought of becoming a corporate mogul, he does not feel overwhelmed or embarrassed by the ornate ambiance of his office. Far from it. Jess Carr—and his surroundings—radiate control, authority, and money. And if these are the elements of power, then Jess Carr is one of the most powerful people in the United States today.

Carr is secretary-treasurer of the Teamsters' Alaska-wide Local 959. It is a deceptive title, for he is no mere note-taker and money-counter. Jess Carr is *the* boss of the Alaska Teamsters and a man who not only sets the course for labor in the state but whose support and opinions are eagerly sought by the leaders of the state's business establishment. In fact, Carr's special brand of conservative politics and Boomer philosophy often make it difficult to distinguish his views from those of the Chamber of Commerce, the oil companies, and the *Anchorage Times*.

In at least one important sense, Carr is to other labor leaders what Hammond is to other governors: atypical. With membership at 25,000, distributed among more than 200 occupations covered by 80 contracts; with pension fund reserves well over $100 million by early 1977; with a seat on the board of the state's major bank; with Teamster workers having taken home $1,500 a week and more on pipeline work; as one of the state's largest private property owners and landlords; and with a potent lobbying apparatus and increasing political strength, the Alaska Teamsters union under Jess Carr has grown from a small, struggling local two decades ago to a position challenging the oil companies as the most powerful economic and political special interest in the state. And with its growth continuing, even accelerating, Carr is daily moving closer to the time when he may be able to tell the governor of Alaska to hook a chicken to a plow.

Because of the unique circumstances in which the Teamsters find themselves in Alaska, Carr is in a position, unmatched by any leader of a single local union anywhere in the United States today, to control the state's economic and political affairs. In such a sparsely populated state, a relatively few people can have a decided impact on the state's political and economic fortunes. With 25,000 members in early 1977—amounting to 15 percent of the state's total work force (both union and nonunion)—the Alaska Teamsters were a formidable force indeed. With all AFL-CIO–affiliated unions in the state having just 23,000 members scattered among more than seventy-five locals, the Teamsters clearly were the dominant union in the state. Excluding traditionally non-union white-collar jobs, the Teamsters represented one of every three workers in the state. And that is extraordinary.

"That's very definitely a lot of members for one labor organization to have in a state with the population of Alaska," Frank Emig, assistant director for the organizing and field services department of the international AFL-CIO, told us. "In other states where one local has a lot of members, there is an industry which itself hires a disproportionate percentage of the work force. That's the case with the United Auto Workers in Michigan and the United Steelworkers in Indiana. But in Alaska, the Teamsters aren't limited to one basic industry."

So, it's not just sheer numbers, but diversity, that makes the Teamsters a dominant force in Alaska. Police officers, longshoremen, stevedores, nurses, high school principals, office workers, warehouse workers, municipal employees, telephone operators, construction workers, building supply personnel, delivery drivers, taxi drivers, bus drivers, fire fighters, and dairy workers are among those represented by Local 959. In addition to oil-related employees, the

Teamsters represent workers at the state's telephone company, RCA Alaska Communications, Inc. (1,000 members); a major in-state airline company, Wien Air Alaska (800); Sea Land Freight Services, Inc., a major transportation firm (300); ITT Continental, which operates Sunshine Bakery in Anchorage (150); and a large wholesale grocery operation, J. P. Gottstein & Co., Inc., in Anchorage (over 100). Name an occupation or industry vital to the state and the chances are Local 959 represents the workers—or expects to in the near future. "The butchers are Teamsters, the bakers are Teamsters, and would you believe, the candlestick makers are *not* Teamsters," Dan Rather said of Local 959 on the June 6, 1976 broadcast of CBS Television's "Sixty Minutes" program. Laughing, Carr responded, "I've missed those, I guess. But we'll look into it tomorrow morning."

Carr, though, hasn't had to do much looking lately. Prospective Teamsters have been beating a path to his door in recent years in an effort to join up and share in the pay and benefits, unprecedented in the history of U.S. labor, which the Alaska Teamsters have won for their members. Dues collected by Local 959 jumped from $3.9 million to $10.9 million between 1974 and 1975. Carr and other Teamster officials even say that Local 959 has turned potential members away because of a lack of union personnel to handle new bargaining units. Thus, yet another source of Teamster power is that Local 959 delivers the goods for its members—or at least is perceived as delivering the goods.

The trans-Alaska oil pipeline contract was Carr's crowning achievement. Known as a tough, no-holds-barred negotiator, Carr won contracts that provided pipeline workers with weekly paychecks of $1,000 to $1,500, and other outstanding benefits. Truckers who drove north of Fairbanks on pipeline work, for example, were paid for 18 hours of work a day, regardless of how much time they actually put in. And wages are far from the whole story of the Teamsters' success in attracting new members: through its contracts, Local 959 provides what the *Anchorage Daily News* terms "womb-to-tomb" benefits for its members. Being a Teamster in Alaska means you have free dental, medical, and optical care, prepaid legal services, the possibility of retiring at age 45 on a pension of $500 a month, at age 50 at about $750 a month, or at age 62 at $1,500 to $2,000 a month. And there is more to what Carr calls providing "freedom from forseeable disaster for every Teamster and his family." There are Teamster tennis courts, swimming pools, and other recreational facilities, hospitals, a credit union to provide housing and car loans, low-cost group vacation programs, college scholarships and vocational training for children of Teamsters, and death benefits. Thus, from prenatal care to death, an Alaskan Teamster is covered. At least in theory.

The more Teamsters there are, of course, the more money and power Local 959 has to wield. By early 1977, the union's four primary trusts—pension, health and welfare, prepaid legal, and training—totaled more than $120 million. And with employers paying $3 into just the pension fund for every hour worked by a Teamster, the fund was growing in almost geometric proportions during the busy pipeline years. Yet few Teamsters have benefited from the pension fund, and relatively few will.

Most significantly, to become eligible for a pension, a Teamster must put in ten years of service, based on 2,000 hours of work a year—in Alaska. If workers leave the state before they earn the right to a pension, as was the case with many pipeline workers, their pensions are not transferable to any other Teamster jurisdiction in the Lower-48 and are lost to them—unless they come back to Alaska within three years and earn at least another 1,500 hours of retirement credits. Similar rules applied to the health and welfare plan, with the result that only 38 percent of all Alaska Teamsters were eligible for the plan in late 1975.

This illustrates two important points about the Alaska Teamsters. One is their independence from the Teamsters International. With their own pension and other funds and relative autonomy, one wonders, in fact, what the Alaska Teamsters have in common with the International Teamsters other than a name and some personal alliances. It is certainly unusual, and unfair, that pension credits accrued in one local of a national union are not transferable to another local. The other point is that Local 959's pension fund was designed to keep withdrawals to a minimum. By late 1976, there were just 302 retired Alaska Teamsters who were receiving pensions, which averaged $583 a month. In other words, about $2.1 million a year was being paid out in pensions to these retirees—an amount easily covered by just the interest on Local 959's investments of the fund. The rest of the pension funds remained under the control of the trustees—most notably, Jess Carr.

The financial well-being of Local 959 has helped make it one of the major political forces in Alaska, with the potential for being the most potent political entity in the state. Perhaps the best indication of Local 959's power is the lack of criticism of the union by politicians. In our interviews with them, all three Alaskan members of Congress—Representative Don Young, a conservative Republican; Senator Ted Stevens, a moderate Republican; and Senator Mike Gravel, a liberal Democrat—all had nothing but good words to say about Local 959 and Jess Carr. All three said they saw no danger of the Teamsters' exerting too much power over the state's economic and political life. During the 1976 primary and general election campaigns, many legislative candidates, particularly liberals, privately grumbled to us about the growing power and the ultraconservative politics of the Teamsters, but none of them was willing to make a major issue of Local 959. For to do so was regarded as political suicide, particularly in a close contest. Candidates who failed to receive Teamster endorsements told us this would hurt them in an election. An even worse fate, they said, was to be attacked by the Teamsters.

Although the Teamsters are among the state's leading conservative forces, Local 959 is by no means tied to one political party. In 1976 its political arm, Teamsters-ALIVE (Alaska Labor Independent Voter Education), endorsed both Republicans and Democrats, even some generally considered to be liberals. This was consistent with the union's previous practices. In fact, state Representative Bill Parker (Democrat, Anchorage), who was singled out by the Teamsters and other conservative and business-oriented forces for special attack in the 1976 campaign—and who lost in the general election—had received the Teamster endorsement and political contributions in the 1974 election. Parker's apparent sins, were his opposition to the capital move, his strong record of support for environmental safeguards and consumer protection legislation, and his close ties to the Alaska Public Interest Research Group, a lobbying force for progressive legislation.

In addition to endorsements, the Teamsters provide campaign contributions to favored candidates for Congress and state and local offices. Both Representative Young and Senator Stevens have benefited from Teamster contributions. In 1974 the union's political arm reported contributing more than $21,000 to election campaigns in Alaska, and in 1976 raised more than $30,000. In the 1976 campaign, Local 959 also added the new wrinkle of being the top contributor to a new organization, the Jeffersonian Democratic Committee, which was widely regarded as a Teamster front group. The union also helped candidates produce television spots in a sophisticated studio in its Anchorage headquarters.

In addition to its campaign activity, Local 959 had available the high-powered lobbying talents of Lewis M. Dischner, a controversial figure with political connections and a reputation for exerting muscle. A former Egan administration cabinet member and ex-Teamster official, as well as a close personal friend of Carr, Dischner was so highly thought of by Local 959 that he received $25,000 in 1976 for part-time work as the union's lobbyist the state legislature. (Another Teamster lobbyist, Emmitt Wilson, also a state cabinet official under the Egan administration, received $14,140 on a five-month retainer for legislative lobbying in 1976.)

All these factors—the ability to deliver votes, to make campaign contributions, to endorse candidates, to lobby heavily—have made Local 959 an effective political force which many observers feel has yet to reach its maximum potential. As the *Anchorage Daily News* noted in its 1975 Pulitzer Prize–winning series on Local 959, "Despite an occasional upset, no other group has displayed such consistent political power here as the Alaska Teamsters. Spanning as it does both party and ideological boundaries, the union outstrips either political party in this respect." Noting that Local 959's support for Democratic incumbent Governor William Egan was not enough to defeat Republican Jay Hammond in 1974, the *Daily News* pointed out, "While Hammond's victory in some measure refutes the union's reputation as kingmaker, the Teamsters are yet a force with which any political candidate must reckon." And, as more and more Alaskans become Teamsters, the union will be even more of a political force to reckon with.[1] More disturbing is the strong likelihood that, as its power does increase, politicians will be even less likely to speak out against Local 959 than they are now for fear of the kind of political retribution that was visited upon Bill Parker in 1976.

Some of the Alaska Teamsters' power can be traced directly to

[1] The Teamsters' political clout, as noted in Chapter III, has become so great that, although some of the stuffier Boomers feel uncomfortable with Carr's basically blue-collar cadres, the pro-development *Anchorage Times* suggested in an early 1976 editorial that Carr would make a good next governor of Alaska. Although Carr pooh-poohed to us the *Time*'s suggestion that he run for governor, some Democratic state legislators told us in late 1976 that they knew personally of a poll taken by the Teamsters that, among other things, tried to assess Carr's gubernatorial chances. One of them wondered, only partly in jest, why Carr would want to be elected to a less powerful job than the one he holds.

Carr himself. Through a combination of bargaining skill, a style that limits criticism from the rank and file, and an unusual degree of independence from the Teamster International power structure, Carr has risen to a position of unchallenged authority within Local 959. Because of some recent national media attention given to him, because of the Teamsters' growing power in Alaska, and because of his energetic efforts in building Local 959, Carr has become something of an Alaska legend—even among those who regard him as a danger to the well-being of the state. It wasn't always that way.

* * *

Carr was born in Upland, California, in 1925, the son of a forty-nine-year-old immigrant from Germany. After dropping out of high school in his junior year, he served in the marines in World War II. After the war, he worked as a truck driver in Pomona, California, and became a Teamster. By 1950 Carr had moved to Alaska, and in 1951 became business agent for Local 959. During the next few years he was to develop a close association with Dave Beck, who then headed the West Coast Teamsters and was later elected president of the International Brotherhood of Teamsters in 1952. After Beck was convicted of federal corruption charges, a union convention was called in 1957 to elect a new president. Carr was a delegate to that convention and was committed to vote for Bill Lee of Chicago, even though Jimmy Hoffa was the clear favorite to succeed Beck. The 1957 convention, according to Carr's admirers, proved that Carr was a man of principle who kept his word even when it was to his advantage to do otherwise. As Dave Beck told the *Anchorage Daily News* in that newspaper's 1975 Teamster series:

> Long before it was Carr's turn to vote, it had been demonstrated by an overwhelming percentage that Lee was defeated and Hoffa was elected, but Jess still stayed with Lee because of his commitment.
>
> Now when the election was over and Hoffa was elected, Jess came to me and he said, "Dave, I'm positive in my own mind that Hoffa is going to take action against me because of the fact that I voted against him."
>
> I said, "Now wait a minute, let me go talk to Hoffa." So I went over and I said to Hoffa, "Now wait a minute, Jimmy, I hear this rumor, I don't know if there's anything to it or not, but I'm telling you this would be the goddamndest monumental blunder you ever made in your life, and I'm making a specific request of you not to interfere with Jess Carr." And he said, "Dave, you've made that request and I'll go along with you a hundred percent."

Carr, in his interview with us, gave a much more precarious picture of the situation after the 1957 election. Local 959 was under the international union's trusteeship at the time, which meant that it had no local autonomy and that its leadership could be replaced by the international president. Because of the lag in time between the election and the time when Hoffa could take office, Beck remained as president. It was during this transition period that Beck granted Local 959 autonomy and gave it statewide jurisdiction with Carr as secretary-treasurer. As Carr told us:

> We lucked out. I knew when we voted against Hoffa that it would be so long, Charley. The proper thing to do at the time—rather, the political thing, I shouldn't say the proper thing—was to go ahead and vote for Hoffa because he was elected. But we committed ourselves and we went and voted for Bill Lee. And just because the monitors, or the government, said Hoffa couldn't take office for a few weeks, Dave Beck's still the president at the time and so, consequently, we got our own charter. . . . We were lucky Hoffa didn't take over sooner, because I was on trusteeship then and he could have fired me. On local autonomy, the members elect me. He can't get rid of me. Things weren't on the friendliest terms for awhile but . . .

Carr readily acknowledged his differences with Hoffa and said that at one time he considered pulling his union out of the Teamsters International. But, the differences were ironed out, he said, after the international union discovered "that Alaskans were a different breed of cat." Carr says that he "gets along well" with Hoffa's successor, Frank Fitzsimmons, who visited the state along with elder statesman Beck in the summer of 1976 and was given a grand tour by Carr.

That initial grant of autonomy by Beck marked the beginning of the Alaskan Teamsters' relative independence from the international union. Ever since taking over in 1957, Carr has kept the international at arm's length while building Local 959 into an organization that is the envy of every Teamster official in the country. When Carr came to work for the Alaska Teamsters in 1951, the union was struggling along with about 500 members and $600 in debts. By 1959, with the local by then a statewide organization and relatively independent of the international, it had shown modest growth to about 1,300 members and assets of $56,000.

The union's growth continued steadily for the next decade. Then, in the late 1960s, Carr was hit with personal troubles that threatened to end his grip on Local 959. In four federal indictments, covering six felony counts, Carr was charged with extortion, embezzlement, and making false statements in obtaining a government loan. One of the indictments alleged that he had threatened to close down a building materials firm "by cutting off the company's financing, by burning down the company property, and by taking whatever other steps he could to break the company." Although the indictments placed a cloud of suspicion over Carr, he was cleared in 1970 and 1971 on all six counts, without any of them reaching a jury. Four of the counts were dismissed on a directed verdict of acquittal by U.S. District Court Judge James A. von der Heydt. Two other counts were dropped by prosecutors because the government's key witness was too ill to testify.

In acquitting Carr of three of the counts, von der Heydt wrote:

> The government is not without any case at all. However, careful examination of the evidence . . . leads the court to the conclusion that proof as to these elements, though certain inferences can be gleaned therefrom, is not sufficient beyond a reasonable doubt to support a conviction.

Although it went unreported at the time of Carr's acquittal, the *Los Angeles Times* disclosed in July 1976 that Richard L. McVeigh, who was U.S. attorney for Alaska from 1964 to 1968, had been forced by the Justice Department to quit that post in 1968 for allegedly sabotaging the investigation of Carr. The *Times* reported that Justice Department officials said that McVeigh had leaked information concerning the probe to Carr's attorneys. The newspaper quoted on this point a number of present and former Justice Department officials, including Assistant Attorney General Henry Petersen. "We had to get him out," Petersen said. "He was either leaking reports or giving them information. We had to act." McVeigh's attorney, Edgar Paul Boyko (who, incidentally, was attorney general under Egan), acknowledged that McVeigh had shown a Teamster lawyer a five-page file on the investigation. But he added that prosecutors frequently opened files to potential defendants in white-collar criminal investigations. After leaving the U.S. attorney's post, McVeigh was elected to two terms in the state legislature and went into private law practice. Among his clients was the union he had allegedly helped while he was U.S. attorney. McVeigh served as a review attorney for Local 959's prepaid legal trust. In 1976, he was indicted on federal charges that he organized a gambling and prostitution ring to cash in on the trans-Alaska pipeline oil boom, but he was acquitted in early 1977. Several others indicted with McVeigh, including former top Egan aide Alexander Miller, also were acquitted.

In contrast to his free-wheeling image, Carr is something of a puritan. Very much like the teetotaling, nonsmoking Governor Hammond when it comes to "old-fashioned morality," Carr does not smoke and rarely drinks. Like Hammond, he is a diligent foe of marijuana smoking—but, unlike Hammond who signed into law the bill that decriminalized private marijuana smoking, Carr thinks the law is "terrible." He added: "We don't condone any type of dope in this union." Carr also imposes his rigid standards on others. Local 959's women employees are warned not to wear pants to the office; Teamster men are ordered to wear neckties when they appear in public on behalf of the union. In informal Alaska, that is an unusual burden. All Teamster employees are barred from drinking alcohol at lunch, and Carr also forbade any bar or liquor outlet at the Anchorage Teamster Mall. One lapse from old-fashioned values seems to be his blunt language, which is filled with expletives, especially when he is involved in collective bargaining.

The union leader also can trim his standards in order to deal with special problems. When we brought up discussions we had with some legislators who told us about marijuana being smoked—legally—at lobbyist Dischner's house during parties to entertain legislators, Carr responded: "He (Dischner) wouldn't be with me if that could be proven." Teamster public relations official Dean Berg then quickly cut into the interview to try to soften what his boss had said: "You have to realize that the lobbyist we're using, we're one of his clients. We don't have complete control over him individually, you know, morally or religiously or anything else. Now if he does something like that we would certainly say it's ill-advised and we wouldn't want it under the auspices of us." Carr then amended his earlier statement to say that he might not approve of certain things Dischner did, but "that's his moral standard."

Despite Carr's legal brush with federal authorities, the Alaska Teamsters have not equaled the notoriety of various Teamster organizations in the Lower-48, although hints of corruption have periodically surfaced. Instead, criticisms of the Alaska Teamsters have centered around the union's economic and political power.

Some of the criticisms Jess Carr finds downright enjoyable, such as those from management that collective bargaining with him is a one-sided process: Carr orders and management agrees, or else. In its Teamster series, the *Anchorage Daily News* quoted one observer of the Carr style as saying: "Hell, I'm not sure 'negotiate' is what you do with Jesse. It's more like playing Russian roulette with all the chambers full." One of the stories about Carr that makes the rounds in Alaska concerns the manner in which he comes into a negotiating session to receive a company's offer. After sitting and looking at the proposal for a minute, Carr wads it up, tosses it into the wastepaper basket, and kicks the basket across the room. Carr said the story is somewhat apocryphal, but that it does have some basis in fact. As he told an interviewer in mid-1976:

> Maybe I shouldn't say this because employers then get wise to your negotiating tricks. It's been a habit of mine over the years to say: "OK, here's your demands. Put it in the wastepaper basket. I don't want to talk about your demands. I don't want to talk about your contract. I want to talk about my demands." If you can get those employers talking about your demands, well, half the battle's won.

Once away from the bargaining table, however, Carr's views are identical to those of the oil companies and other super-growth forces regarding the development of Alaska. With an income of at least $90,000 ($75,000 from Local 959 and $15,000 as a member of the executive board of the international union[2]), a $55,000 condominium in Indian Wells (about twenty miles southeast of Palm Springs, California), a country club membership and occupancy of a lavish office, Carr has a style of life that compares favorably to that of the captains of industry. In fact, one can strongly infer from many of Carr's public pronouncements that he believes that what is good for big business in Alaska is generally good for the Alaska Teamsters. Typical of this was his statement of March 29, 1976, in which he labeled as "myopic and unconscionable" some legislators' proposals to increase taxes on oil companies, and the Hammond administration's plan to buy back leases the state had sold to oil companies in the ecologically important Kachemak Bay. Said Carr:

> I never thought I'd see the day when I would say "the poor oil companies," but that day has come. . . . The continued economic well-being of our state and all its citizens is dependent on a healthy or at least reasonable investment climate, which in turn provides critically needed employment. Further, it is unconscionable to single out a specific industry for tax penalty that is not consistent with other industrial tax formula. . . .
>
> The future of our state is being threatened. We must protect this future as we would our paycheck, for in the long run, they may be one and the same.[3]

[2] Carr was appointed by Teamster International President Frank Fitzsimmons as an international union trustee in early 1976. Historically, trustees—who review the union's books every six months—later move up to vice-president slots. The trustee post plum also illustrates Carr's close ties to Fitzsimmons.

[3] In declaring that increased oil taxes will cause oil companies to flee the state, Carr and the other super-growthers have set up a strawman. As Attorney General

While the more progressive labor leaders in the country regularly express concern for broader issues relating to social justice for working and poor people, Carr concentrates almost entirely on the well-being of Local 959. And he acknowledges that his local's success is due to straight old bread-and-butter economic issues. "You see, what has magically happened up here is, quite frankly, we've been so successful," Carr told us. "No place in the nation do union members get the kind of benefits that they get here at my pipeline. So, because of that, our organizers thought they had the easiest job of any organizers in the whole United States because we had more people coming knocking on the door saying, "Hey, how can I get aboard the wagon," than the other way around. And we have to be kind of judicious, too, because it doesn't make sense to get too many small segmented affiliations that we can't really service adequately."

Well, then is there a danger local 959 could get too big? "No." Does that mean you will organize the entire state?

> Well, that's my job, but you certainly have to use that with a little caution. Organize the whole state. What is that? You mean bankers? And lawyers and secretaries? . . . Well, that's my job, yeah. People are entitled to make a living. People are entitled to the best benefits they can receive. The old days are gone where you had to go beat each other over the head with a club to make a living, where they had armed guards pulled out to shoot pickets.

The secretary-treasurer scoffed at the notion that he has the muscle to shut down the state. Rather, he said, the record shows that Local 959 is not strike-happy and has not used its power to try to blackmail state and local governments or private employers: "I think you've got to look at our record. What happens? Do we run around shutting everything down? We've never had a strike in the construction industry. Never, never. In all the years I've been here, there have been three or four in the trucking industry and those were

---

Avrum M. Gross commented at a growth forum at the University of Alaska in Anchorage in October 1976:

"It's just ludicrous to say that additional taxes or increased royalties for the state will drive the oil companies right out of Alaska. It's our oil and we should get as much as we can for it. I once heard an oil company representative, in all seriousness, complain that Alaska's oil taxes were three times higher than Idaho's. My answer to him is, 'Why don't you just go to Idaho and look for oil?' The answer to that is obvious. The oil is here, not in Idaho. We have more oil than anywhere else in the United States. Those who say we'll drive out the oil companies, cost people their jobs, and bring economic collapse if we tax the oil companies even a penny more are just crying wolf."

isolated." But in private moments Carr has been less circumspect about his ambitions for Local 959. In 1976 he told officials of other Alaskan unions: "In three years, there is only going to be one union in this state."

It is precisely Carr's spirit of "new worlds to conquer" that has many Alaskans, including some who are pro-union, concerned. In a recent survey of the attitudes of 368 Anchorage voters toward the Alaska Teamsters, even those respondents who were *union members* thought, by a margin of two to one, that Local 959 was too powerful. Concern was heightened in late 1976 when it was disclosed that the Teamsters planned to try to organize state government workers.[4] One liberal Anchorage state legislator told us in November 1976 that some lawmakers had talked about introducing a bill providing that only bona fide public employee unions or associations could represent state and local government workers. In fact, the consumer-oriented Alaska Public Interest Research Group in 1977 got such a bill introduced in the state legislature. The measure, which died without even receiving a committee hearing, would have made it possible for existing state and local associations (such as the Alaska Public Employees Association) or for national public employee unions (such as the American Federation of Teachers, the National Education Association, and the American Federation of State, County, and Municipal Employees) to represent Alaska's state and local government workers—but not the Teamsters. Hammond took a similar position in calling for antitrust laws to be written that would apply to unions as well as to business. Such legislation, however, would probably conflict with federal statutes exempting labor unions from inclusion in antitrust laws. Nonetheless, AkPIRG's and Hammond's concern over the Teamsters' growth was understandable, since the Teamsters were continuing to march into territory usually occupied by other unions. In 1976, for example, the Teamsters organized Anchorage police and negotiated wages that were averaging $40,000 annually. In late November 1976, the Anchorage Municipal Employees Association, which represents 300 city workers, voted to affiliate with the Teamsters.

Yet, among the state's major politicians, only Hammond has been willing to tangle with Carr. Their feud goes back to the 1974

[4] Carr's vision even extended beyond the state's borders to a Pacific alliance. In June 1977 the secretary-treasurer publicly confirmed he was considering a merger between his 25,000-member union and three Hawaiian locals with 6,000 members. The merger might also include locals in Tahiti, Guam, and Micronesia, he said.

election, when the Teamsters vigorously opposed the Republican Hammond and worked for incumbent Democratic Governor William Egan, a growth advocate. Hammond's victory, although by a narrow 287-vote margin, was seen by many political observers as proof that the Teamsters did not yet have control of the state. After taking office, Hammond simultaneously attacked and needled Carr in various forums, sometimes in doggerel verse. For example:

> Just as Genghis had his Mongol hordes
> Bill Egan had his Teamsters
> Who thought they had the vote sewed up
> But proved out lousy seamsters
> But Jesse's troops had little chance
> Of tilting in the lists
> Against my hardy little band
> Of ardent alchemists

Carr, for his part, has charged the Hammond administration with being anti-development and anti-union and has called the governor a "son of a bitch." He has made it a top union priority to unseat Hammond in 1978, and is known to favor millionaire hotelman William Sheffield, a Democrat, and Anchorage Mayor George Sullivan, a Republican, in the governor's race. Typical was Carr's mid-1976 assessment of the governor's performance. The Hammond administration, charged Carr, "is throttling the future of Alaska, even as it throttles the growth of Alaska." Hammond's appointees were "representatives of those elements dedicated to making Alaska a moose, wolf, and polar bear preserve." In his interview with us, Carr expanded: "I like the guy personally. He's a personable guy, very articulate. But I think he's either got his head in the sand or the people around him have convinced him that the way for Alaska to progress is to regress. It's just not going to happen."

* * *

To truly appreciate the wealth of the Alaska Teamsters—and their concomitant economic leverage—requires that we return to a discussion of the pension funds. By mid-1976, at the height of the pipeline construction boom, more than $1 million, all from employers, was being deposited each week in Local 959's various trust accounts in the National Bank of Alaska. That figure is best understood when viewed as $2,000 per Alaska Teamster *per year*. In earlier years, the union invested 30 percent of its trust funds Outside. That policy was changed when the market failed to produce a rate of return the union felt was acceptable, and most trust funds in the 1970s were invested in Alaska, mainly in mortgages, real estate, and short-term certificates of deposits in banks within the state, which returned 9 to 9.5 percent. Incredibly, it has been estimated that as much as 10 percent of all capital investment in Alaska is Teamster money—most of it from the pension fund. Also, the pension trust of more than $100 million amounts to one-seventh of all savings deposits in Alaska banks.

But precisely how the Teamsters are investing the pension fund is not entirely known. While some of the uses of the pension trust have been made public, others have been hidden from public view. Documents we examined, on file with the U.S. Department of Labor, gave only a general, incomplete picture. For example, Local 959's report on its Employer Pension Trust Fund for 1975 (the latest year available during our research) showed that the fund owned $1,066,048 in common stock at the end of 1975. In addition, the report showed that $40,527,633 of the fund was invested in real estate loans and mortgages. This included $10,456,833 in the Teamsters Local 959 Alaska Building Corporation (ABC) for "building under construction" and $13,629,647 in Anchorage Community Hospital in the form of a promissory note, which gave the pension trust and its affiliates the right to name the majority of the hospital board of trustees. The new hospital, called the Alaska Hospital and Medical Center, is operated by the Anchorage Community Hospital. Teamster public affairs director Berg said the $23 million cost of the new hospital was "financed by trust funds of Local 959." Because of this, the new hospital is commonly referred to in Anchorage as the "Teamster Hospital." Interestingly, an IRS audit revealed that the cost of the Teamster hospital was 50 percent higher per square foot than a new equally modern addition to Providence Hospital, across town. The Teamsters also are planning another $12-million medical facility in Fairbanks.

Pension funds from the Teamsters and another union, Alaska Laborers Local 341, also were used to help millionaire hotelman Sheffield acquire the Royal Inn of Anchorage from its bankrupt parent corporation. Sheffield's acquisition of the hotel was financed by $1.4 million from the Alaska Teamsters Pension Trust, $800,000 from Local 341, and $2 million from Seattle First National Bank of Washington. Local 959's 1974 financial report to the U.S. Labor Department disclosed that the union owned $8,639,876 worth of buildings throughout Alaska, and $167,362 in land in four Alaskan cities. The union had also purchased an additional $1.8 million worth of land that year—$1,408,085 in Anchorage, and $403,633 in Fairbanks. The *Anchorage Daily News* in late 1975 estimated that the direct property holdings of the union totaled $33 million. By 1977, the figure exceeded $70 million.

The previously mentioned Alaska Building Corporation of Local 959 was another example of the Teamsters' growing economic strength in Alaska. *International Teamster*, the magazine of the international union, called the establishment of the building corporation one of the "new frontiers for unionism" that Carr's leadership had produced. It didn't exaggerate, for the ABC is unusual in that is is a for-profit corporation that is owned by the membership of Local 959. The corporation owns buildings in Anchorage, Fairbanks, Juneau, Kenai, and Valdez.

Given the impact of Teamster capital in Alaska, it is hardly surprising that Carr is a member of the board of directors of the National Bank of Alaska, the state's largest and dominant financial institution. Through this seat, and through the Alaska Teamsters' short-term certificates of deposit in other Alaska banks, Carr and Local 959 exert a strong influence on major decisions made by the state's financial community.

This situation is unprecedented. It is not unusual for unions with large sums of money to invest to have a significant economic impact on a community or state. But the Alaska Teamsters have gone one full measure beyond this. Local 959 is not only a part of the state's business establishment, it is an integral part of it. When you talk about big business in Alaska you must necessarily include the Teamsters. It is this state of affairs that has caused Alaska Attorney General Avrum Gross to express the almost heretical wish that the Teamsters invest "more of their money outside the state." And it's criticisms like Gross's and Hammond's that cause Carr to bristle:

> We are putting seventy to eighty million dollars in pension money in this state. What would the governor say if we invested it in Russia or somewhere else? Our money is available for long-term investments, for buildings and homes. We don't tell the banks who to loan money to. Alaska needs long-term capital. Dave Beck told me that long ago.

Carr and other Teamsters officials miss the point, Hammond told us. "I don't think Jess Carr is intent upon destroying Alaska," he said, but "any time any group has within it a substantial portion of the electorate, you have a potentially dangerous siutation." When you add to that the financial strength of an organization like Alaska's Teamsters, Hammond said, the result is "the vesting of arbitrary power." To illustrate the Teamsters' political muscle, Hammond likes to cite the so-called "Teamsters' Mall lease." Hammond's predecessor, William Egan, was very closely allied with the Teamsters—a number of his top administration officials became Teamster executives.[5] Under the Egan administration, the Teamsters were granted a lease to operate a nonprofit corporation in 18½ acres of choice state land in Anchorage for a tiny annual rent of $4,110. The lease was controversial not only because it involved a virtual giveaway of public land, but because the site was being used to house commercial profit-making enterprises, including a travel agency which listed the Teamster lobbyist and Carr friend, Dischner, as a partner. The lease was declared invalid by the Hammond administration and later renegotiated at an annual rate of $65,994—sixteen times greater than the original lease.

No real estate is more symbolic of the Teamsters' growth and power in Alaska than the Teamsters' Mall. Built at a cost of $7 million, the Mall houses Local 959's headquarters, as well as commercial facilities for the public, and the new "Teamsters' Hospital." It is under the roof of the mall that most of the Teamsters' members' cradle-to-grave benefits are provided. The Mall, in addition to the hospital, includes a health and welfare administration office; facilities to provide prescription, dental, optical, and surgical care; a credit union; and administrative offices for the pension fund and the other Teamster-employer trusts. If a Teamster or his family cannot get to the Anchorage Mall, Local 959 has six pilots and four "flying ambulances" to bring a person to the nearest medical facility—or, in emergency situations, to the new Anchorage hospital. But since they

[5] Commerce Commissioner Kenneth Kadow (Teamster Training Trust coordinator); Commerce Commissioner Emmitt Wilson (manager, Teamster credit union, and lobbyist); Labor Commissioner Lewis Dischner (Teamster lobbyist); Labor Commissioner B. Gil Johnson (prepaid legal attorney); Deputy Labor Commissioner James Witt (in-house lawyer); Deputy Labor Commissioner William Jermain (prepaid legal attorney); Deputy Labor Commissioner Leo Brown (Fairbanks business agent); Veterans Affairs Division Deputy Director Helen Irick (Teamster credit union officer); gubernatorial aide Wes Coyner (Teamster lobbyist); gubernatorial aide and Revenue Department administrator Jefferson Barry (business agent). In addition, some Hickel and Hammond administration officials also were hired by the Alaska Teamsters. Edgar Paul Boyko, attorney general under Governor Walter J. Hickel, served as a Teamster prepaid legal attorney; Tom Evans, deputy labor commissioner under Governor Hammond, became a Teamsters Training Trust employee.

were only used for this medical purpose an average of seven times a year, the leased planes—two Merlin turbo-Props and two Lear jets—also were used to carry Carr and other Teamster executives around the state and to the Lower-48. In fact, this appeared to be their primary purpose, and even some pro-Carr Teamsters criticized the boss's royal use of the "emergency" planes to ferry him to his California condominium. The criticism became especially harsh when the already formidable 40-cents-per-hour dues ($16 per 40-hour week) each Teamster paid to Local 959 was increased to 50 cents in 1976 so that Carr could lease two more planes. As of early 1977, of the remainder of the 50-cent dues, 15 cents went to a recreation fund, 15 cents to a strike fund, 7 cents to the credit union, and 3 cents to the local's building corporation. Among the uses to which the members' dues were applied was the purchase of eight season tickets—at a cost of about $2,500—to the Los Angeles Dodgers' home games, even though L.A. is 2,400 miles from Anchorage.

In addition to the Anchorage Mall, a $6.5 million mall, which also houses union offices and shops, was dedicated in Fairbanks in August 1976. Completed at the same site in 1977 was a $5-million-plus indoor recreational facility with tennis courts, handball courts, Olympic-sized swimming pool, etc. Construction of a similar, $7.5-million recreational facility for union members was also completed in Anchorage the same year.

In addition to the previously mentioned indictments against Carr and some allegations of illegal campaign contributions, other serious questions have been raised about the outside business activities of Teamster lobbyist Dischner. Because of his close friendship with Carr and his lobbying efforts for Local 959, Dischner is generally thought of by the public as first and foremost the Teamsters' man at the legislature. His private business activities, according to the *Anchorage Daily News*'s 1975 Teamsters series, vividly illustrate Dischner's ability to use connections in state government to get things he (or the Teamsters) want. The *Daily News* series raised questions about the propriety of three of Dischner's enterprises receiving state funds.

Much of Dischner's political influence dates to his early close relationship with former Governor Egan. Dischner was appointed by Egan as the state's first labor commissioner in 1959. During Egan's second term he served on the state Workmen's Compensation Board, but later resigned to avoid having to file a financial disclosure statement. In the 1960s, he served as Local 959's business agent before becoming the union's chief Juneau lobbyist. He also represents other lobbying clients, including Alaska Airlines, the North Slope Borough, Alaska International Air, and the Alaska Carriers Association. Dischner's success in getting favors from the legislature and the state government caused Hammond to accuse him of using "bulldozing tactics" and threats of political retaliation.

In addition to the other controversies surrounding him, Dischner once came up against criminal charges in connection with his activities. In early 1976, he pleaded guilty to a federal charge that he willfully failed to file a federal income tax return for 1972. He was fined $10,000 and required to pay taxes due for the period 1969 through 1972, plus a civil fraud penalty of 50 percent. In accepting the guilty plea and imposing the fine, U.S. District Court Judge James Fitzgerald dismissed three other counts alleging Dischner failed to file returns for 1969, 1970, and 1971.

In addition to lobbyist Dischner's tax troubles and Carr's tangle with federal prosecutors, Local 959 had legal problems of another sort with the Teamster-run North Star Terminal in Fairbanks, which was the central supply warehouse for the trans-Alaska oil pipeline. It was long suspected that drugs and other corrupt dealings emanated from there. The *Daily News* Pulitzer-winning series said that the Teamsters, rather than management personnel, ran the warehouse and that many of them had criminal histories, including the number one man, Fred (Freddy the Fix) Dominic Figone. Although the *News* quoted anonymous law enforcement officials and a "source close to the North Star operation" to the effect that there was considerable theft from the warehouse, the newspaper also wrote that "officials have revealed no evidence of theft from the facility." Other law enforcement people told us that they strongly suspected the warehouse was a center for distribution of drugs to pipeline camps, where drugs of all types were always plentiful.

Speculation about illegal activities at North Star increased substantially when two top Teamster union officials there disappeared in July 1976. The body of one of the officials, Jack (Red) Martin, the area-wide union steward at North Star, was found August 4. An autopsy revealed he died of multiple gunshot wounds to the head. Police sources said they expected that the other missing man, Harrold (Harry) Pettus, also had been slain. Pettus was the number two Teamster at North Star. The cases were still under investigation in early 1977.

Carr, in his interview with us, flatly stated that no illegal activities were occurring at North Star. As for the criminal backgrounds of some Teamster officials at North Star, he said:

> . . . one of them had been out of prison, what, twenty-nine years, never had a problem, and if society doesn't give a person a second chance you know something's wrong with us. Secondly, if any one of them is proven to be doing something like that [theft or fencing], well, we would help prosecute him. But no one has brought it to our attention and, in fact, Alyeska has said that's the most efficient warehouse on the line . . . We get sick and tired of listening to this over the last year or so. If they've got the proof, put them in the jailhouse. . . . Quit, talking about it. . . . Just go get them, prosecute them . . .

Another allegation leveled at Local 959 is that it has discriminated against Natives, who have, in the past, been barred from Teamster jobs which required no real qualifications other than a willingness to work, Native leaders charge. In addition, they add, the union has resisted proposals to initiate training programs to enable Natives to become eligible for jobs which the Teamsters said they were unqualified for.

As a former Teamster and a Native, Roy Huhndorf, president of Cook Inlet Region, Inc., one of the Native regional corporations, is not anti-union. But he noted to us that many Natives have felt the sting of Teamster discrimination and may not look kindly on future efforts by Local 959 to organize workers at Native-owned businesses. "I hesitate to say this," Huhndorf said, "but I foresee that a greater degree of confrontation will occur between the Teamsters Union and the Native-owned businesses. . . . The unions have not been friends of the Native people. . . . There's no great degree of love lost between them. It's hard to forget those types of injustices." Other Natives cited examples of what they considered to be continuing discriminatory practices by the Teamsters. One college-educated Native told us how, on the basis of a written test, he was told by Teamster officials that he was unqualified for a pipeline job. When he appealed that decision to a higher union official, he said, the official began going back over his paper; the official found several places where the test corrector had awarded too few points and his score was boosted up to a passing grade. "I'm convinced that the reason I passed was because I complained," the Native said. "My complaining about my score showed the Teamsters that I might file charges of discrimination against them. So they gave me a passing grade just so they wouldn't make more trouble for themselves. But it made me wonder how many other Natives there were who deserved to pass but who didn't go and complain."

After great resistance by the Teamsters—which resulted in a successful discrimination suit filed by Alaska Legal Services—Alaska Natives were eventually hired for the pipeline project in greater numbers than had been foreseen by state and federal agencies and even Native leaders. The Alaska Federation of Natives in late 1976 reported: "Coordinating its efforts with those of state, federal and local Native organizations, the AFN, Inc., Manpower Division was successful in locating jobs and training positions for well over 6,000 Alaska Natives during the two peak years of construction, 1975, 1976."

Discrimination against Natives is indicative of the Teamsters' attitude toward social issues in general. As James Love, director of AkPIRG, told us:

> The trouble is that the Teamsters in Alaska want socialism for their members and free enterprise for everyone else. . . . They're totally unconcerned with the plight of anyone but their members. The union is run autocratically so its members have no voice in the direction the union will go; the members' views are never solicited. Carr and the people who run the union have a very narrow view of things. . . . They're not tuned in to issues having to do with equality, justice, unequal distribution of wealth. They see their organization as a vehicle for increasing the dollar wealth of their members and aren't concerned with the rest of society . . .

It is this kind of philosophy that has many progressive, prounion Alaskans concerned. Still others, such as state Senator Chancy Croft (Democrat, Anchorage), are more sanguine, perhaps unjustifiably so. Croft, a former senate president, told us he can't see the Teamsters ever really running the state because Alaskans traditionally "don't want to be dominated by any large group," be it big unions or big business. "There's a natural resistance by Alaskans to that," he said. In any event, Croft added, when it comes to political influence the Teamsters are "the gang that couldn't shoot straight." Croft wasn't alone in his sanguinity. As mentioned earlier, Alaska's three members of Congress voiced similar sentiments that the Teamsters had little chance of dominating state politics and economics. Representative Young told us he felt Hammond's criticisms of Carr were "political" rather than philosophical in nature. Senator Gravel commented that the Teamsters "do one hell of a job for their members," that he could not fault the union for trying to win as many new members as possible, and that it was the right of Alaskans (and all Americans) to join whichever union they felt would best represent their interests. It should be noted that Gravel, Young, and Stevens have been as careful as mice at a convention of cats not to arouse the ire of Jess Carr and risk political retribution.

In any event, the Alaska Teamsters are indisputably the union that provides the biggest bang for the buck. It is not surprising, given Local 959's record, that many Alaskans are anxious to become Teamsters—and this is the crux of the problem that Alaskan politicians have so far successfully ignored. The more successful Local 959 is, the more workers join, the more money flows into its tills, the more economic power it wields, the more political clout it exerts, the more conservative and business-oriented it becomes. It is an expanding circle of power which in many ways parallels the evolution of a business monopoly—except that, as already noted, antitrust laws don't apply to the growth of a union, and the stakes involved in Alaska are nothing less than control of the state.

There is no easy solution. But at the very least, much closer scrutiny of Local 959 on the part of the state's press, and some gutsy criticism on the part of state leaders, are essential. Standing alone, the Teamsters' political and economic influence in Alaska would be impressive enough. In concert with the state's dominant industry (oil), the state's most widely read and influential newspaper (the *Anchorage Times*), and the state's business establishment, the Teamsters' power is nothing less than awesome, and very dangerous.

X

The Untold Minerals

WITH ATTENTION focused on Prudhoe Bay and the other potentially oil-rich areas of Alaska, scant public notice has been made of the other enormous mineral wealth that lies buried beneath the state's surface. Although it seems hard to believe, the potential value of Alaska's other minerals is scores, perhaps even hundreds, of times greater than that of the North Slope oil bonanza. As one oil company executive told us: "The state probably has fifty Prudhoe Bays just in coal deposits alone."

By all reliable accounts, he was not exaggerating. Geologists estimate that Alaska has half of the nation's uranium reserves; fantastically large copper deposits; perhaps the richest molybdenum find in the United States; and nickel deposits that may exceed those of any in the world. And coal. Lots of coal. According to a 1975 report by the Alaska Department of Natural Resources, at least 132.9 billion tons in "demonstrated and inferred" resources. Translated into its energy equivalent in barrels of oil, this would exceed 500 billion barrels—enough to take care of current U.S. requirements for the next 68 years. Compare this with the oil companies' conservative estimates of reserves of 9.6 billion barrels from Prudhoe Bay, and one can see why big business has its eye on more than just Alaska's oil.

But the 132.9 billion figure is probably too low. There is a strong likelihood, according to the same state report, that Alaska has a storehouse of another 1.9 *trillion* tons of coal—or the equivalent of 7.1 *trillion* barrels of oil. This would give Alaska about 63 percent of the nation's estimated coal reserves. A later 1975 state report upped the estimated potential coal reserves to almost 3 trillion tons. That second report said the Cook Inlet Basin in southern Alaska, by itself, could have coal reserves of 1.3 trillion tons—or more than a third of the nation's estimated supply.

With such staggering riches involved, Alaska's environment and way of life will face an ever-increasing number of challenges in coming years. In addition to major mining interests, the same oil companies which are tapping the state's Prudhoe Bay fields and seeking oil elsewhere in the state, are also hoping to set off a boom in other minerals. Big Oil has shown a particular interest in the state's uranium deposits because Alaska is believed to contain 47 percent (259 million pounds) of all United States uranium reserves. By controlling Alaska's uranium mining, the oil industry could tighten its grip on U.S. energy sources and use the Alaskan uranium to push for more intensive development of nuclear power plants.

Among the many major oil companies that either have filed claims or, according to the state's division of geological and geophysical surveys, are "interested in mining possibilities" [other than oil and natural gas] in Alaska, are: Amoco, Atlantic Richfield (Arco), Cities Service, Exxon, Mobil, Union, Phillips, British Petroleum, Standard Oil of California, Gulf, Shell, and Skelly—a veritable list of Who's Who in Big Oil. Also actively involved in the pursuit of Alaska's mineral holdings are other formidable firms, including Anaconda Company (purchased, subject to antitrust approval, by Arco in 1976), Kennecott Copper, Sunshine Mining, Noranda Mining (of Canada), Bethlehem Copper (of Canada), Chevron, Placer Amex, U.S. Borax, El Paso Natural Gas, Consolidated Edison, American Smelting and Refining, Bethlehem Steel, International Minerals and Chemical Corp., International Nickel Company of Canada, Ltd., Union Carbide, Urangesellschaft mbH & Co., Uranerz (Germany), Mitsubishi (Japan), Phelps Dodge, Westinghouse, and U.S. Steel. Among others.

Adding to the pressures for development of the state's mineral resources are the plans by many of the newly formed Native regional corporations. During a panel discussion we attended at the October 1976 convention of the Alaska Miners Association, several leaders of Native corporations made it clear they wanted mineral development on their lands—either through their own ventures, or through leases or sales to private firms. "Make us an offer," one Native leader told the convention.

Although the Native corporations' land selections of 44 million acres were still snarled in legal and bureaucratic difficulties in early 1977, Native corporation leaders from all areas of the state told us they expected to go into mineral exploration and development in a big way. Some corporations had already entered into agreements to search for minerals. The state government reported in 1975, for example, that during the previous year Phillips Petroleum had conducted surface geological and geophysical work in cooperation with the Bristol Bay Native Corporation in an effort to find copper near Perryville on the Alaska Peninsula in southern Alaska.

As we shall see later in the chapter, mining interests face special obstacles in trying to extract minerals from most federal and state government lands. As a result, these interests find Native-owned lands increasingly attractive for mining opportunities.[1] The *Alaska Native Management Report*, published by the Alaska Native Foundation, took note of this in late 1972, about nine months after enactment of the Native Claims Settlement Act:

> Alaska miners and mineral industry observers [believe] . . . that mining companies will be able to make far more advantageous agreements with Native corporations . . . owning vast tracts of prime mineral lands than they ever could have with state or federal ownership of the same lands. There's even the hope that eventually Native corporations might help finance exploration ventures on Native lands through joint-venture agreements with companies. This is good news for an industry that has always been hard-pressed to raise risk capital for new exploration. . . .

So far, oil and natural gas have received the greatest boost from the super-development cheerleaders in the state, but in coming years, the Boomers can be expected to step up their call for increased mining activity. The *Anchorage Times* already periodically chimes in with editorials lauding the Native corporations' interest in mineral development. Governor Hammond's commissioner of commerce until 1977, Tony Motley, was also pleased with the prospects. He happily predicted in an interview in the summer of 1976: "The next generation [after oil and natural gas] is hard-rock minerals."

In addition to coal and uranium, the state has quantities of some thirty other minerals, including copper, molybdenum, nickel, lead, zinc, gold, silver, tin, tungsten, fluorite, iron, mercury, gemstones, antimony, platinum-group metals, barite, zeolite, chromite, sand,

[1] Ironically, the Miners Association that is now wooing the Natives is the same organization that opposed a land claims settlement for the Natives. As George Moerlein, representing the Alaska Miners Association, told congressional hearings on the Native claims in 1968: "Gentlemen, I submit to you that neither the U.S., the state of Alaska, nor any of us here gathered as individuals owes the Natives one acre of ground or one cent of the taxpayers' money."

gravel, and stone.[2] This new realization that oil is not the only game in town, or even the biggest, has sent big and small companies scurrying all over the state in an effort to strike it rich. Virtually all areas of the state have some potentially rich mineral deposits, but in recent years significant private exploratory attention has focused on the environmentally critical Brooks Range of the Arctic North, the Alaska Range in the central area, and on the southeastern part of the state. Recently, the increasing value of many minerals in world markets has helped spur the exploration activity.

In addition to the private exploration in Alaska, state and federal government agencies have been actively involved in studies, surveys, mapping, and testing efforts to identify those areas of the state with the highest mineral potential. Federal studies of the entire North Slope after World War II provided important data later used by the oil companies that made possible the successful strikes at oil-rich Prudhoe Bay. Studies by the U.S. Geological Survey and the Alaska Division of Geological and Geophysical Surveys have also helped private industry decide which areas are worth exploring further for mineral potential. In addition to a number of joint federal-state projects, the government has contracted with private firms for more sophisticated testing, such a aeromagnetic surveys.

State and federal surveys which we studied and interviews we conducted with various mineral authorities, produced this rough picture of the state's known mineral potential:

- Arctic area: coal, oil, natural gas, phosphate, sulphur, gold, silver, uranium, nickel, antimony, copper.
- Seward Peninsula (northwest Alaska, just below the Arctic Circle): tin, iron, tungsten, lead, zinc, gold, silver, uranium.
- Alaska Range (central Alaska): molybdenum, lead, zinc, gold, silver, coal, mercury, copper, tin, antimony, uranium, nickel.
- Southeastern: nickel, copper, uranium, tungsten, molybdenum, chromite, gold, silver, coal, antimony, iron, barite, coal.
- Southwestern: coal, gold, mercury, platinum, uranium.
- Aleutians, Alaska Peninsula, Kodiak: coal, lead, zinc, sulphur, tungsten, iron, copper.

This list gives only a partial idea of mineral distribution because many valuable minerals such as uranium have been the subject of rela-

[2] Even diamonds were being searched for in the summer of 1975 in northwestern Alaska in the Kotzebue area. Claims had been staked in the area in 1972 by two individuals after geologic mapping and radiometric surveys were completed.

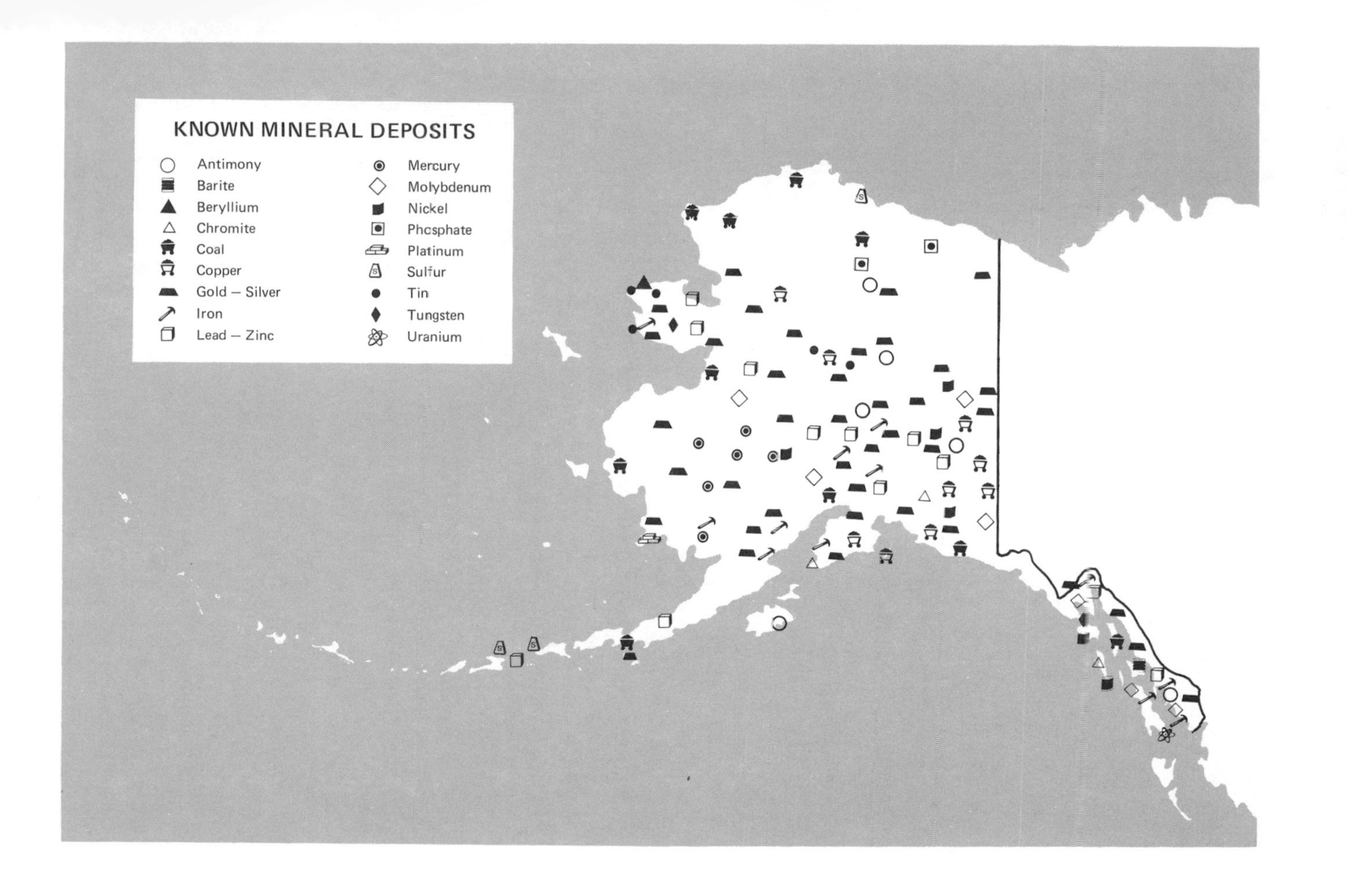

KNOWN MINERAL DEPOSITS
Antimony
Barite
Beryllium
Chromite
Coal
Copper
Gold – Silver
Iron
Lead – Zinc
Mercury
Molybdenum
Nickel
Phcsphate
Platinum
Sulfur
Tin
Tungsten
Uranium

tively little exploration, but are believed to be present over a wide area of the state.

All this mineral testing and exploration activity has sent chills up the spines of environmentalists and other Alaskans who fear the consequences of widespread mineral development in Bush areas. If the mineral developers have their way, new roads and transportation corridors would be established in areas which are still unspoiled sanctuaries for wildlife. The mining itself could pollute the water and, through open-pit mining, scar the land. (Open-pit mining is expected for most of the future possible mining activities.) The trans-Alaska pipeline would be only a tiny scar on the Alaskan wilderness by comparison.

Even before the North Slope oil boom focused attention on Alaska, geologists in state, federal, and private business offices believed that Alaska was mineral-laden. But relatively little exploration had been done, in large part due to an inhospitable climate and inaccessible terrain. Combined with labor costs far higher than in the Lower-48, tapping Alaska's hard-rock riches was little more than a miner's dream, even assuming no special costs for environmental precautions. As former Alaska House Speaker Mike Bradner noted to us, the initial heavy mineral development in the state is most likely to occur near the coast, rather than in the interior, "because you have a set of economic factors which means that every mile you come from the coast escalates your transportation costs tremendously, especially if you're in the world price market."

Production has also been deterred by the dearth of privately owned lands. In other states, mining has generally been undertaken on private lands owned by individuals because it was easier dealing with an individual than with government agencies. But there has been little opportunity for this in Alaska with government owning all but about one million of Alaska's 375 million acres until recently. Some 67.5 million acres of federal land were available to mineral entry in 1976 under federal mining law and existing federal policy; an additional 40 million acres of patented state lands also were open to the mining industry. But under the 1971 Native Claims Settlement Act, some 83 million acres of environmentally valuable "national interest" lands (often referred to as "(d) (2)" or "D-2" lands because of the section in which they are described in the act) were closed, at least temporarily, to mining claim location. (See Chapter XI). Most other federal land in the state was also closed to mining claim location, including most wildlife refuges, Mount McKinley

National Park, Katmai National Monument, the Kenai Moose Range, and military sites. Thus, with the Native land selections still largely incomplete, less than 30 percent of the land in Alaska was open to mining interests in 1976.

Beyond these immediate deterrents to mineral production in Alaska, other variables militated against overnight production of known mineral deposits. According to industry authorities, mining companies often plan production decades ahead as they seek the most favorable market conditions, costs, and methods of obtaining capital financing. While these variables may discourage mineral production for the moment, Hammond, who regularly downplays the extent of Alaska's hard-rock mineral wealth, has observed that "when the price is right, our minerals—coal, copper, gold, iron—will be exploited." As with most other major development issues, Hammond told us minerals should be extracted without state subsidies and only if they can be mined in an environmentally sound manner. And so, against mining interest pressures, Hammond has vigorously rejected any notion that the state establish "incentives" for hard-rock mining. In reference to the rich copper deposits in the mineral-laden Brooks Range, the governor said:

> Unless they can be developed without subsidization, they should be left in the ground until they can. For example, there's been ridiculous suggestions that we build a hundred-million-dollar road to tap a $30 million mineral deposit. Moreover, I think you should build the transportation means once you have determined it is needed, not build it and hope the needs are out there somewhere.

Mining interests respond that such statements by Hammond prove he is anti-mining. Wallace McGregor, president of the Northwest Mining Association, said in 1975 that Hammond had underestimated the value of the Brooks Range copper by a hundredfold. "To imply that the Brooks Range mineral deposits are worth $30 million is comparable to representing the $600 million Alaska state budget as $6 million," McGregor said.

Whatever the value of the Brooks Range copper, though, it is clear that the industry views it as one of the richest areas of Alaska. In mid-1975, two major mining companies, the Anaconda Company and Sunshine Mining Company, operating jointly, announced they had found a rich lode of copper just north of the Arctic Circle. The two companies disclosed that a drill hole on the 50,000-acre site about 300 miles northwest of Fairbanks had contained nearly 6.8 percent copper, an exceptionally promising yield. Two other drill holes produced 1 to 4 percent copper ore and a concentration of other precious metals, including lead, zinc, and silver. Irwin Underweiser, board chairman of Sunshine, which operates the nation's largest silver mine at Kellogg, Idaho, was impressed. "This is the most important project our company has been associated with in more than ten years," he said. And consulting geologists in Seattle commented that the finds indicated "a possible bonanza discovery."

The Anaconda-Sunshine discovery was in the so-called Ambler River Quadrangle which, with the adjacent Survey Pass Quadrangle, makes up what is known as the Brooks Range Copper Belt. Geologists estimated that the area may be more valuable than the heretofore top-producing United States copper areas of Bingham Canyon, Utah; Butte, Montana; and Bisbee, Arizona. By mid-1974, most geologists familiar with the area were estimating that copper and other minerals were present in an area 70 miles long and about 15 miles wide. Other geologists even have suggested that the copper belt extends across the entire midsection of Alaska right up to the Canadian border. Other major companies, including Bear Creek Mining and Noranda Mining Company (of Canada), also have explored heavily in the same area. Noranda was understood to have filed as many as 2,000 claims between the two quadrangles by mid-1975. Bethlehem Copper, another Canadian firm, engaged in exploratory operations in the area.[3]

Even before the Anaconda-Sunshine announcement in 1975, there had been an earlier copper find of apparently considerable proportions in the Brooks Range. The value of that discovery by the Kennecott Copper Corporation in the same Ambler River–Survey Pass area was never publicly disclosed by the company. But it was generally believed in mining circles that the company had found a deposit of at least 20 million tons of ore with a gross value as high as $2 billion. The *Anchorage Daily News* reported in mid-1975 that sources had told it that the Kennecott discovery had been assayed at 2 to 5 percent copper, 4 to 8 percent zinc, 2 percent lead, and 10 percent other metals. There also were trace amounts of gold and silver. Kennecott was not producing its Brooks Range claim by 1976, apparently because of costs for both transportation and meeting environmental stipulations.

[3] Canadian firms had become increasingly attracted to Alaska, not only because of proximity, but because of what they regarded as unfavorable taxing and mining policies in British Columbia province, which borders on Alaska.

According to industry officials, copper veins discovered by 1977 in the Brooks Range would be best removed by open-pit mining—a method which could be especially destructive in the Brooks Range's delicate tundra. Opening up large areas of the Brooks Range to mining interests would further disrupt wildlife and Native culture in a manner first begun with construction of the trans-Alaska pipeline and its Haul Road. Still, many minerals and lots of dollars are involved, and the major companies cannot be expected to back off just because of environmental concerns.

With the exception of the late nineteenth and early twentieth century Gold Rush, the rich Kennecott copper mine in the Copper River Valley, and the more recent oil production, Alaska has not been noted as a mineral-producing state. Between 1950 and 1970, for example, revenues from all mineral production in Alaska, including oil and natural gas, totaled only $1.56 billion. Of this, almost 63 percent came from oil and natural gas, 8 percent from coal, and 6.9 percent from gold. The remaining 22.1 percent was distributed in considerably smaller quantities among mercury, antimony, copper, lead, platinum, tin, uranium, silver, gemstones, sand and gravel, barite, and peat, for average annual production revenues of about $75 million for those twenty years. In more recent years, total oil and mineral production increased considerably. After topping $100 million a year for the first time in 1967, with $134.6 million, it climbed to $329 million in 1973, $434 million in 1974, and about $444 million in 1975. But, as in the earlier years, the bulk of this production was in oil and natural gas—85 percent in both 1974 and 1975—and most of that came from Cook Inlet, which is near Anchorage and thus easily accessible. And of the approximate $66 million from minerals other than oil and natural gas in 1975, about 60 percent came from sand and gravel, which is not usually considered "mining." This left less than $30 million from production of (in decreasing order of value): stone, coal, gold and silver, barite, platinum-group metals, antimony, mercury, gemstones, and tin.

Exploration activity in 1975 gives a good idea of where mining interests expect to strike it rich. In all, some $34 million was spent by private interests in 1975 for exploration, which was spread fairly evenly throughout the state. According to the state's *Mines and Geology Bulletin*, 46 percent of the exploration activity in 1976 occurred on federal lands; 39 percent on state lands; 8 percent on Native lands; and 7 percent on private lands. The bulletin noted that the percentage of activity on Native lands was expected to increase substantially, however, after the Native corporations had gained clear title to their land.

Mining interests have spent more than $100 million over the last thirty years in Alaska on exploration, according to industry publications. The $34 million expended on mineral exploration in 1975 alone represented a $28 million increase over 1974, when state officials estimated that the industry spent about $6 million for mineral exploration. The increase in exploration can be put in perspective by comparing the $6 million figure for the entire year of 1974 with the estimated $5.6 million spent for exploration in just the summer of 1976 in just one area of the state, southeastern Alaska. The number of new claims filed in the state also has stepped up considerably, from 5,920 in 1973 to 10,623 in 1974, and to about 11,500 in 1975.

The extent of the state's potential mineral wealth was underscored in early 1976 when the giant U.S. Borax Chemical Company disclosed that it had found molybdenum near Ketchikan in the Tongass National Forest in southeastern Alaska. (As a "multiple-use" area, the Tongass can be opened to mining as well as timber cutting and recreation uses.) The discovery led company officials to assert that the molybdenum potential in that area could make it "one of the major ranking ore bodies in the world." U.S. Borax officials said they envisioned a mine that would produce "several billions of dollars" worth of molybdenum over the next twenty-five to seventy-five years.

The U.S. Borax discovery, naturally enough, set off a new binge of exploration in southeastern Alaska. In August 1976, El Paso Natural Gas joined the molybdenum sweepstakes by filing sixty claims on land bordering the U.S. Borax discovery. Placer Amex also was lured to the area for claim-filing north of Ketchikan and exploration on nearby Revilla Island. Molybdenum, the cause of all this sudden turmoil, is highly prized as an alloying agent to impart hardness, strength, and corrosion resistance to steel, cast iron, and nonferrous metals. Industry representatives say that research has been undertaken to determine molybdenum's effectiveness as a catalyst for automobile emission controls and coal gasification and as a superalloy for industrial gas turbine engines and for aircraft.

To get at its molybdenum discovery, U.S. Borax said, would require construction of an access road into the area, known as Quartz Hill, near Ketchikan. In late 1976, an application to construct such a road was pending with the U.S. Forest Service. By mid-1976, U.S. Borax had prepared a draft environmental impact statement for the proposed road. The statement was immediately assailed by conservationists and commercial fishing interests, who argued that any such statement should address itself to the entire mining project envisioned by U.S. Borax—and not just the access road. The Tongass Conservation Society charged that the impact statement failed to provide in-depth analysis of long-term impact of the project on fish, wildlife, watershed and scenic values. The TCS expressed particular concern over possible damage to fish, saying that "it is TCS's understanding that [U.S. Borax] is currently investigating the possibility of a hydroelectric project on the Wilson River—a heavily used recreation area and king salmon spawning stream." Another danger to fish would come from the mining process which, company officials said, would release "a significant volume of effluent"—or "tailing wastes"—into nearby streams, which included the salmon-rich Wilson, Blossom, and Keta Rivers. The waste would include several types of chemicals, oils, and toxic metals. Robert Kendall, the U.S. Borax executive vice-president for operations, admitted in an August 1976 meeting with state officials, "Our failure to supply information on the total concept is because we don't have all the facts yet. It's unsatisfactory, but I don't know what to do about it."

U.S. Borax also had no readily available information concerning the impact the establishment of a full-scale molybdenum mining operation would have on the state's fiscal situation. During that same meeting with state officials, company officials said the mining operation probably would require construction of an entire new town at the head of Wilson Arm. The town would be needed to service the mine, which company officials said would employ as many as 1,000 persons during construction and about 500 after mining operations were begun. Hammond and other state officials said that in addition to serious environmental questions raised by construction of the mining operation and a town, they wondered about the fiscal impact on state government. Would state-financed services be required?

Company officials stressed that construction of the access road was an absolute necessity if the company was to be able to carry on the bulk sampling. And bulk sampling was needed to help the company decide whether to spend the $300 million necessary to develop the project. But beyond questions of profitability, financing for such a project would probably be impossible "unless and until we could assure lenders that we do have actual proven and existing access to the property and can operate with reasonable economy," said E. D. Lemon, manager of environmental affairs for U.S. Borax.

What the U.S. Borax proposal vividly illustrated was industry's desire to get at Alaska's mineral wealth as quickly as possible without fully considering the environmental, social, and fiscal costs—to create an inevitability about development. Alaska Attorney General Avrum Gross put the issue in perspective in October 1976 at a growth forum in Anchorage:

> Now we could have said to U.S. Borax, "Fine, come in. What tax benefits can we give you?" But I don't think many Alaskans would say that was very sound public policy. Instead we said, "Fine, come in. But you're not going to screw up the environment and you're going to pay your fair share."

Gross's reasoning runs counter to the "national interest" argument: Alaska, because it has most of the oil and mineral wealth in the United States, has an obligation to supply the rest of the country. That argument is certain to be cited increasingly by the *Anchorage Times* and other development advocates in the years to come, especially regarding a metal like uranium, which is needed to advance nuclear power.

In a massive 400-page 1976 report[4] designed to stir interest in Alaska's uranium potential, Gilbert R. Eakins of the state's Division of Geological and Geophysical Surveys noted that Alaska remains "relatively unexplored for uranium." But he added: "This picture can be expected to change, and perhaps rather quickly. The present energy crisis has resulted in several exploration companies undertaking uranium programs in the state. . . ." By the summer of 1976, uranium prices had shot up from $7 to $40 a pound, causing increased searches for uranium in Alaska. In southeastern Alaska alone in the summer of 1976, several energy companies were looking for uranium: Exxon, in the McLean Arm of Prince of Wales Island; Consolidated Edison, in Kendrick Bay; Domes Mines, Limited, in the Moira Sound area of Prince of Wales.

Despite the upswing in activity, the exploration for uranium in Alaska remained in a fairly preliminary stage by early 1977. Eakins noted a number of factors working against uranium exploration in Alaska, including a lack of geological information, the remoteness of most areas with uranium potential, and the accompanying high costs of operations; the presence of swamp (or muskeg) and permafrost

[4] *Investigation of Alaska's Uranium Potential*, Special Report 12, Division of Geological and Geophysical Surveys, College, Alaska.

over a large portion of the state; the inhospitable climate; and the lack of demand for additional uranium. However, as Eakins noted, this could change very quickly.

And if the federal Energy Research and Development Administration had its way, discovery and mining of uranium in Alaska would come sooner rather than later. As part of its effort to move the U.S. deeper into the ominous nuclear power age, ERDA was pushing uranium exploration in the state. In late March 1976, ERDA granted a $568,000 contract to the Texas Instrument Company of Dallas to use sophisticated equipment to cover wide areas of Alaska in a search for uranium. Later in the year an Anchorage-based firm, Watts, Griffis, and McQuat (WGM, Inc.), received a $98,000 contract from ERDA to conduct geological evaluations of the Cook Inlet and Susitna Basin areas, near Anchorage, to determine uranium potential.

While uranium is one major mineral of the future in Alaska, gold is *the* mineral identified with its past. Yet, even though the Gold Rush days are now a part of Alaska's colorful history, the state still is a treasure house of gold. In fact, substantial sums of the precious metal still are to be found in the old Gold Rush areas of the Yukon, Nome and Juneau. A look at the maps of known mineral deposits put out by the state Division of Geological and Geophysical Surveys indicates there is gold in virtually every major area of Alaska —from the Arctic North, to the interior of central Alaska, to within a few miles of Anchorage in south central Alaska, to southeastern Alaska. But long gone are the romantic days when an individual prospector could make his fortune with a pick and shovel or a pan. An investment of at least $150,000 in heavy equipment is needed today even for a small operation.

Even in locations where it is known that there are large quantities of gold, mining companies today often say it's not worth their while financially. For example, in the spring of 1975, eight firms which had expressed an interest in redeveloping the old Juneau goldfields concluded that the high cost of exploration and the declining price of gold at that time made renewed gold mining in the area unfeasible. A geologist from Anaconda, one of the firms that had expressed an interest in exploration and development proposals put forth jointly by the Juneau City and Borough and the Alaska Electric Light and Power Company, said: "There is no question that considerable gold still remains in the properties and that the price of gold today is much higher than it was when these mines shut down.

But so are costs very much higher. . . . It is not likely that the Juneau . . . [gold mines] could be put into production unless the price of gold remained well over $200 per ounce." At the time, the price of gold was running at about $165 an ounce. Other firms that had expressed interest in the Juneau gold were Homestake Mining and American Metal Climax, Inc. (AMAX).

Still, some old, established gold mines were operating profitably in Alaska. One such operation, the Chandalar Mine near Fairbanks, was being touted in late 1976 by some authorities as a possible high-grade mine in the near future. The mine had been operated after World War II by Frank Birch until his death in 1972. His heirs then took over but sold it to the Noranda Mining Company of Canada.

Even with uranium being promoted as one of Alaska's minerals of the future, and gold continuing to be important in Alaska's mining picture, it is coal which many supporters of mining interests say will be king in the very near future. Uranium exploration is still in its relatively early stages; but not coal. In the March 1975 report on Alaska coal (cited early in this chapter) prepared for the state Department of Natural Resources, Don L. McGee and Kristina M. O'Connor reported that there were at that time 132.9 billion tons of coal "which [are] considered economic with present mining technologies." It was this same report that said the state also had 1.9 trillion tons of "hypothetical coal resources." The report defined "hypothetical" as being "undiscovered coal that may reasonably be expected to exist in an area under known geological conditions." It added that "no consideration is given to the commercial extraction of this coal." Commenting on the state's coal potential, Dr. Ernest Wolff, director of the University of Alaska's Mineral Industry Research Laboratory, said: "Coal is going to have to get us through this period between oil and . . . [whatever] energy source . . . is going to last us for the next thousand years."

Alaska's coal is characterized generally by low sulphur content, which makes it environmentally desirable, and large tonnages, which help make it economically so. The two major producing coalfields in the state in this century are the Matanuska field north of Anchorage and the Nenana field south of Fairbanks. The Matnuska field produced some 7.5 million tons between 1916 and 1969. The Nenana field, still productive today, has produced some 16.5 million tons since it was opened in 1918. Annual production has run between 700,000 and 750,000 tons in this operation of Usibelli Coal Mine, Inc. All of the coal produced at Usibelli is used within the state. Thus, despite its enormous coal resources, Alaska wasn't even producing one percent of the 600 million tons of coal that are mined in the U.S. each year.

One of the most troublesome problems working against Alaskan coal and other mineral production is transportation. Mining company president Joe Usibelli said his mine could double its production but there was no practicable way of shipping the coal out of the state. He noted that the Japanese are extremely interested in Alaska's coal resources and that he could have sold coal to Japan as early as 1973 if there had been a way of getting the coal out of Alaska. "You don't handle coal like you do groceries," he said. Despite much speculation in 1975 that AMAX Carbon Products, Inc., a giant coal company and a subsidiary of American Metal Climax, was about to buy out the Usibelli operation, the deal fell through. The main reason for the failure was the absence of dock facilities to handle the coal. But transportation problems of these kinds can be remedied, and many coal experts predict that Alaska will be exporting coal—lots of it—within ten years.

In addition to the lack of transportation and the high labor costs working against Alaskan coal development, there are other key factors. For starters, the McGee-O'Connor report notes that: "At this time, 82 percent of the total coal potential land is not leaseable for coal development." This is due mainly to the fact that most of the best coal lands are included in federal reserves that are closed to mining activity at this time. The biggest impact from the federal land withdrawals occurs on the 23-million-acre Pet 4 Reserve—renamed "*National* Petroleum Reserve in Alaska" when the Interior Department assumed jurisdiction over it from the navy in mid-1977—which includes 44 percent of the total known coal potential land in Alaska, according to the state report. With some sympathetic friends in Washington, however, this hurdle could be cleared, too.

Writing in the October 1972 *Mining Engineering* publication, Cleland N. Conwell, mining engineer with the state Department of Natural Resources, said that the northern coalfield, of which NPR-4 is the major component, "contains the largest coal reserves in Alaska *and ranks with major coal deposits in the world.*" [Emphasis added.] Using figures that appear conservative compared to later estimates, Conwell said, "Of U.S. deposits, the known strippable reserves place this field as second in subbituminous coal, with reserves of 5 billion tons, and third in bituminous coal, with more than 2 billion tons."

Note that Conwell used the word "strippable." The bulk of the coal mining that has occurred in Alaska to date has been by strip-mining. Much of the other recoverable coal, if the mining companies have their way when the time comes to go after it, will also be strip-mined. As Conwell noted in *Transactions*, the publication of the Society of Mining Engineers:

> Coal mining in Alaska started in 1855 at Port Graham on the Alaskan Peninsula. This and other early-day mining was underground, but as the demand for coal increased and new equipment was developed, underground mining was gradually replaced by open-pit or strip-mining. By 1960, underground mining had ceased.

In case the implications of such a shift in mining methods are not clear, a bulletin of the Wilderness Society painted the proper picture of what strip-mining and coal transportation could do to Alaska's vulnerable environment:

> The vastness of the Alaskan landscape is misleading, for the membrane of life is stretched exceedingly thin. Seemingly indestructible mountains and massive glaciers contrast with the fragile arctic tundra where a tire track can last for generations, worsening with time. In a land of harsh climate and sparse vegetation, vast acreage is indispensable to the survival of wildlife populations. If critical habitat is destroyed, whole species can plunge rapidly to the brink of extinction and perhaps disappear forever. It has happened elsewhere, and it could happen in Alaska.

Such a description is useful here because some state officials, including Conwell, minimize the fears of environmentalists that strip-mining would be especially damaging to the permafrost-covered tundra of Alaska. Despite ample evidence of blighted and scarred land throughout many of the strip-mining states in the Lower-48, Conwell contends that strip-mining would be beneficial to Alaska's land and would enable it to be used for agriculture:

> The term "tender tundra" is a myth—a well-developed myth—but contrary to the fact. Any area that supports herbivores must have a plant base to supply food. In Alaska, herds of caribou migrate and live north of the Arctic Circle. If there is enough growth in the moss and lichens and arctic grass to support a caribou herd, the "tender tundra" can heal after it has been disturbed by mining. . . . Whether it is reclaimed by advancing the productivity from forest to agriculture or is allowed to remain a wildlife habitat,

Alaskan land will revegetate. Reseeding speeds reclamation, but left to nature, native species will reclaim the land whether it was disturbed by forest fires, roads, villages, or mining. In fact, it is impossible to find many of the old gold mining camps.

Conwell, in an interview with us in August 1976, made the same point—namely, that reclamation is easier in Alaska than in the Lower-48. While his contentions appall the environmentalists, they are most welcome to the mining interests.

Guy Martin, Alaska's commissioner of natural resources until early 1977, noted that the state has no law covering surface mining on private lands—which means that the state has "basically no controls" over any mining on the 44 million acres of land that will go to the Native corporations and the other one million acres that are in other private hands. On federal lands, Martin told us, the state "would have few tools to stop mineral development, but could frustrate it"—for example, by refusing permission to build roads across state lands. On state lands, Martin said, the state would have the ability to block undesirable mining through laws and procedures relating to air and water pollution and access to the site. Nonetheless, it is disturbing that the state has not yet adopted a surface mining law, as well as legislation to impose royalties and severance taxes on its hard-rock minerals.

As of early 1977, the state was entitled to no royalties or severance taxes from any hard-rock minerals extracted in the state. Hammond in 1975 and 1976 proposed legislation to establish a mining severance tax, which mining interests immediately opposed, characterizing it "a mineral royalty similar to that operating in British Columbia." Hammond said at the time that he saw a need to establish "an equitable mining tax structure in Alaska in an atmosphere of objectivity"—that is, before mineral production begins in a big way. The mining industry supporters argued that any severance tax would just drive up the costs of doing business in Alaska and lessen the chances of mineral development. Dr. Wolff, of the University of Alaska, said in mid-1976 that the proposed severance tax was another attempt to overregulate the mining industry. Wolff, who also operates a gold mine in the Yukon area, said that the public already was earning a fair return on nonrenewable resources in Alaska through corporate taxes, income taxes, and a mining license tax of 7 percent on any profits over $100,000.

Despite the threat that many mining activities pose to the state's environment, there were a few hopeful signs that environmental and social considerations would, in some cases, take precedence in the Last Wilderness. For example, in late 1976, with the D-2 wilderness lands question still unsettled, conservationists won a key victory in Congress when legislation was passed to provide some environmental protection against future mining exploration at Glacier Bay National Monument in southeastern Alaska. The bill—which also applied to five other units of the national park system, including Death Valley National Monument—barred future mining entries in the six park units and also set up provisions under which all mining activity in these areas could be halted. This protection was especially important at Glacier Bay because, according to state officials, a discovery there several years ago by Newmont Mining Company, "may prove to be the largest nickel deposits in the United States." Other authorities have gone even further to describe it as "probably the largest nickel deposit in the world."

While there is a great temptation to develop such a rich deposit, there is a major problem: it is buried deep beneath Brady Glacier in the area of Alaska that was described by former Senator Ernest Gruening as "a scenic wonderland" and by another writer as having "rugged glacier-clad mountains and steep-sided fjords . . . scenically and glaciologically . . . one of the most spectacular parts of Alaska." Conservationists, who have halted any mining of the nickel discovery through a lawsuit, argued that it is precisely such areas that should be protected from any and all mining and other developmental intrusions. With the nickel deposits located on the western rim of the monument area, development interests hoped that their argument that mining can proceed without detracting from the area's esthetic values will prevail. This skirmish is an important one, for it portends many similar ones. And there is little doubt that the pressure to develop Alaska's mammoth mineral resources will substantially—and quickly—escalate. As state official Eakins said in opening a speech to the Northwest Mining Association's annual convention in Spokane in December 1972: "As metal and energy shortages loom ominously before us, industry is seeking new sources of fuels and minerals in Alaska. . . . It is obvious that the country urgently needs to plan for the development of these resources." Can a "mineral crisis" be far off?

Mining and other development interests will, of course, continue to argue in the future as they have in the past that Alaska's wilderness is so incredibly huge that one mine, or dozens of mines scattered throughout it, would make scarcely a dent in all that vastness.

Yet, as one writer observed, that argument is "the rationale for the Alaska pipeline all over again." The impact of the pipeline, as we have seen, has been felt far beyond its 800-mile-long corridor. Would mining do less?

"Permafrost Brasilia," and Other Conflicts

"North to the Future"
—State Motto.

IMAGINE WHAT WOULD HAPPEN in most states if a politician proposed that the state capital be moved to some undeveloped site at a potential cost of up to $2,500 per resident! Such a foolish public official would be laughed out of office or, worse, impeached. In Alaska, precisely such a proposal has not only been made, but is close to fruition. And no one is laughing.

This lack of hilarity is probably the best testimony of all to the influence *Anchorage Times* publisher Bob Atwood holds over the future of the state of Alaska. The idea of relocating the state capital from isolated Juneau[1] in the southeast to a more central area—the capital move issue, as it has come to be called—was the brainchild of Atwood and has been one of his most cherished pet projects for almost two decades. Indeed, such an extraordinary issue would have to be "created"; it is certainly one of the most unusual controversies to confront the citizens of any state in recent years.

But selling the voters on his creation wasn't easy for Atwood. As we saw in Chapter III, since statehood was granted in 1959, the *Times* has carried scores of editorials and news stories explaining why the capital should be moved. Despite the barrage, voters in the earlier years of the capital move campaign decisively rejected statewide ballot initiatives in 1960 and 1962. Finally, in 1974 the proposal

[1] The capital of the Alaska Territory was moved from Sitka to Juneau in 1900.

was again put on the ballot through a successful petition drive,[2] and was approved by a 57 percent majority.

The ballot item carried a curious stipulation: that the new capital city could not be Anchorage or Fairbanks, or within thirty miles of either city. This provision was included because politicians and business people in the state's two largest cities were basically suspicious and fearful of each other's power and influence; both had lobbied hard to make sure that the other city wouldn't get the new capital. In a move to create maximum support for the relocation, supporters of the move eliminated Anchorage and Fairbanks as potential sites.

It was agreed that any new capital site would be in an undeveloped area, a compromise that would satisfy the Anchorage-Fairbanks rivalry and spur growth in the new capital city as well. No specific sites at all were listed on the 1974 ballot, however. And no cost estimates were available—for one thing, no one knew where the capital would be located. Citizens were thus voting for a concept—without blueprints, location, or price tag. If this seems like an unusual way to choose a new capital, it was.

After the 1974 vote approving the capital move, newly elected Governor Jay Hammond, a foe of the move, acceded to the "will" of the voters and appointed a site selection committee to propose and evaluate possible locations for the new capital. The committee came up with three alternatives, and its private consultants provided some cost estimates: Willow, about 35 air miles north of Anchorage—$2.445 billion;[3] Larson Lake, about 80 air miles north of Anchorage—$2.56 billion; and Mount Yenlo, about 70 miles northwest of Anchorage—$2.7 billion. It was then up to the legislature to pass legislation to bring the issue before the voters again.

In preparing the 1976 referendum bill on the three sites, some state legislators attempted to amend it so citizens could vote "none of the above." But that effort failed, in effect disenfranchising those voters who preferred to leave the capital in Juneau or who wanted to move it somewhere other than the three selected sites.

[2] Only 10,000 signatures of registered voters are needed to put a proposal on the ballot.

[3] The consultants said about one fifth of these estimated costs would be borne by the state, the rest by private developers. By early 1977, there still were no comprehensive studies on what the actual relocation costs would be, but off-the-cuff projections ran as high as $1 billion for the state government alone.

By a wide margin, the voters in 1976 selected Willow, which had been estimated to be the least expensive of the three ballot choices. The specified site is less than a mile east of the existing town of Willow (population 32 in 1970) and covers about 100 square miles of state-owned land. According to the site selection committee, the town could reach a population of 25,000 by 1990. The area's chief advantage is that it is within 90 minutes of Anchorage by car and is also near the Alaska Railroad lines, making it easily accessible to the almost half of the state's population that lives in the Anchorage area.

The Willow site thus meets the overriding criterion laid down by supporters of relocation: accessibility. They had argued that a site nearer the state's geographical and population center would be far superior to Juneau, which is isolated, sparsely settled, and inaccessible from most parts of the state except by plane.

Opponents of the move cited the extreme cost; warned that it would lead to further unwanted development in the bush; and noted that Juneau, with its mountains, forests, and fjords, offered the most beautiful capital site of any state in the country. Secondarily, Juneau residents argued that moving the capital would ruin the economy of their community of 17,000 in which state government is the main industry.

All this is not to suggest that Willow is without natural charm. *New Yorker* magazine writer John McPhee, writing on Alaska in 1976, noted that Anchorage "might be a sorry town, but it has the greatest out-of-town any town ever had." And so it is with out-of-town Willow, in a lovely setting at the southern end of the Talkeetna Mountain Range. Residents of the new capital would have views of the Matanuska Valley, Knik Arm, Knik Glacier of the Chugach Range, Cook Inlet, and spectacular Mount McKinley. This scares the environmentalists. Indeed, development interests were supporting a proposal to build a bridge for a road crossing at Knik Arm. The road would cut the 90-minute commuting time from Anchorage to Willow almost in half and would increase pressures for suburban sprawl between the two cities, and into the wilderness.

Even before the Willow site was selected by the voters, the private land that was available in the Matanuska-Susitna Valley[4] nearly doubled in price between 1975 and 1977 in anticipation of the move. Under the terms of the 1974 initiative, the prospective capital

[4] The Matanuska-Susitna Valley is Alaska's major agricultural area and has enormous untapped potential. Unfortunately, growth and development in that area will eat up potentially productive farmland.

sites had to be on state-owned land. And so while the boom in land prices wouldn't affect the cost of the capital land to the state government, it would boost the cost of the surrounding privately owned land. And Willow would become a very expensive place to live in, making the actual cost of the capital move much more than projected. In fact, many of the opponents of the move were hoping that despite the 1974 and 1976 votes the cost would eventually scuttle what Sitka state Senator Pete Meland called a "Permafrost Brasilia."[5]

With the 1976 vote, the issues left facing the state government on the capital move were how it was to be financed and what form it would take. The move could be paid for through revenues to the state from North Slope oil, which began flowing in mid-1977. Or voters could approve payment through a bond issue—which would give opponents the chance to mobilize opposition to defeat or delay the move, or prompt a massive rethinking of the issue. In fact, in April 1977 capital move opponents launched a petition drive seeking to get on the 1978 ballot an initiative requiring that Alaskans approve a bond issue for relocation of the capital before it can be moved. The *Fairbanks Daily News–Miner*, which supported the capital move in 1974 and then later soured on it, was among those suggesting a repeal effort. In an October 27, 1976 editorial, one week before voters selected the Willow site, the *News–Miner* wrote in an editorial ("The Capital Move Fiasco"):

> We can pick any one of the three sites on the ballot—each one is a loser—and we still won't be out of the capital move mess until we repeal the capital move initiative on the 1978 ballot. It's something to think about.

Bill Parker, a liberal Anchorage Democrat who opposed the capital move, was defeated in his bid for reelection to the state House of Representatives in 1976 largely because the *Anchorage Times* blasted him for his anti-move advocacy. Parker believed that the fiscal argument would eventually sink in and that voters would then demand that the capital be left in Juneau. "Right now," he told us just before the 1976 election, "people don't care about the cost of moving the state capital. They're really schizophrenic. Voters come up to me all the time and say 'cut spending, cut spending' and 'move the capital, move the capital,' all in the same breath. Some day

[5] A reference to Brazil's relocation of its capital from Rio de Janeiro to Brasilia, a new city carved out of that nation's remote central plateau.

they're going to wake up and see that the capital move isn't going to cut spending. And I guarantee that it will cost a lot more than that two-billion-dollar price tag they're putting on it now."

Hammond was among those who originally opposed moving the capital, but after the 1974 vote approving the move he began talking more about abiding by the voters' wishes than continuing to fight relocation. Still, as late as an April 1976 press conference, while saying he would fulfill the voters' mandate to move the capital, the governor stated it would make more sense to move it to Anchorage—with its many state offices, already a de facto second capital—or to someplace other than the three sites selected to go on the ballot. However, by the time we talked to Hammond later in the year, he seemed certain that the fight to stop the capital move was over, and that it would be shifted to the site selected by the voters in November.

Still, opponents of the move were hoping that the issue would somehow be put in rational perspective. Certainly, the procedures leading up to the 1976 referendum were not milestones in the democratic process. The most orderly procedure would have been for the legislature to study the issue, come up with cost estimates for alternative sites, and then submit the question to the voters. This process was short-circuited, though, and by 1977, Alaska's voters had yet to be given a true choice in the matter, namely: whether the capital should stay in Juneau, or be moved to Willow at a public cost of up to $1 billion, or about $2,500 per state resident.[6]

By early 1977, there was at least one straw in the wind indicating that Alaskans still preferred Juneau over any other site for their capital. A survey of 314 rural and urban residents were asked the open-ended question: "Where should the state capital be?" The survey was conducted by the Rowan Group, an Anchorage firm hired by the state government as part of the governor's Public Forum program to sample citizens' opinions on a variety of issies. Juneau received the nod of 41 percent of those polled, followed by Anchorage with 15 percent. Willow was favored by only one out of eight respondents (13 percent), Wasilla by one of fourteen (7 percent).[7] The others were undecided, or named other locations in the state.

[6] In none of the newspaper accounts or other discussions of the capital move that we found was the cost issue posed on a per capita basis—which might have put the issue in better perspective for many voters.

[7] Wasilla is just 15 air miles north of Anchorage, which apparently made it an attractive choice to many Anchorage area residents.

* * *

The capital move is not the only major development in Alaska little known to most Americans. "People in the Lower-48 don't know what's going on in Alaska," Robert Belous, a park planner with the National Park Service's Anchorage office, told a *New York Times* reporter in October 1976. "All they hear about is the pipeline. In fact, there's a big battle in the offing over what to do with the rest of the state. The whole country has something at stake in Alaska."

The "big battle" involved scores of millions of acres of land which, if Congress approved, would become national parks, monuments, wildlife ranges. These areas would be closed to development and preserved as wilderness or in the words of a January 18, 1977, editorial in the *Fairbanks News–Miner*, it would be "the final closing of the door, the final turn of the key on the futures of all Alaskans." The dispute over these so-called "national interest" lands was certain to be the most important environmental and land-use issue for Alaska in months and years to come. Indeed, the "national interest" lands battle was the most controversial topic in Alaska in early 1977, even though it had received scant attention in the Lower-48.

The crux of the debate was ownership of Alaska land, and the development rights that go with ownership. Until Alaska achieved statehood in 1959, the federal government owned almost all of the territory's 375 million acres. The statehood act ceded 102.5 million acres to the new state of Alaska, of which just 16 million had been patented by the state as of 1977—out of more than 70 million selected.[8] Less than 500,000 acres were privately owned in 1959; today it is still only one million acres, most of it acquired under the Federal Homestead Act[9] and near existing communities and road networks.

To appreciate fully the importance of the national interest lands dispute, some background is essential. The proportion of the statehood land grant of 102.5 million acres to the state's total land mass of 375 million acres was similar to percentages deeded by the federal

[8] Delays in selection and patenting of state lands were caused by Interior Secretary Udall's land freeze a decade ago, and then later by the state's having to alternate with the Native corporations in making land selections.

[9] The federal homesteading program, begun in Alaska in 1898, enabled people to gain title to land by living on it and farming it. The program was ended in 1974 in order to "keep people from killing themselves in the wilderness," according to the Bureau of Land Management, which administered the program. During the program's existence, some 5,000 people gained title to more than 500,000 acres in Alaska.

government to other western states in earlier decades.[10] But the procedure by which Alaska chose its acreage was quite different. In previous land grants to other western states, the federal government generally designated two to four sections of a 36-section township (6 miles square) for state ownership, and kept the remaining land for itself. This prearranged checkerboard pattern of state-federal land ownership made it difficult for states to effect comprehensive land use planning and control. In Alaska, however, the state "was granted a virtually unrestricted right to select its grant lands from anywhere within the 'vacant, unappropriated, and unreserved' federal lands in Alaska," according to a 1975 report by the Federal-State Land Use Planning Commission for Alaska (*Agenda for State Lands*). "*In no other instance*," the report added, "*has the federal government granted a state such an opportunity to use the power inherent in land ownership to plan and shape its own future*" [original emphasis]. Nowhere was this opportunity more generous than in the state's selection of oil-rich Prudhoe Bay. Had the state been required to follow federal land distribution patterns used in other western states, it would have had to share Prudhoe Bay with the federal government—thus substantially reducing the revenue it would receive from the area's oil.

Yet thousands more failed in homesteading attempts—some because of the climate, some because the land on which they settled was poor farming land. Despite the fact that the program put more than one-half million acres into private hands, many authorities regard it as a failure. Janet McCabe, land management planner for the Federal-State Land Use Planning Commission for Alaska, said the program imposed unnecessary hardships on settlers, often resulted in excessive environmental damage, and produced few true farmers.

From 1968 to 1973, a state government "open-to-entry" program granted some 3,400 five-acre tracts (17,000 acres) to individuals. The program was intended to open up wilderness recreation sites, rather than farmland, to individuals. The program was halted, however, because speculators were acquiring more than one tract by having others stake out individual sites for them. Since statehood in 1959, the state has transferred some 125,000 acres to private parties under various programs, and has leased another 325,000 acres. Most of the transferred land (57 percent) is in the Anchorage and Fairbanks area, with the bulk of the remainder near other existing communities.

[10] Alaska has fared much better than other western states (generally those states most recently admitted to the union) in terms of the percentage of land owned by the state government and private individuals. After the Statehood and Native Claims acts are fully implemented, the federal government will own 60 percent of Alaska's land area, while state and private interests (mainly the Native corporations) will own 40 percent. Three states have a greater percentage of their land mass owned by the federal government than will Alaska—Nevada with 86.6 percent, Utah with 66.1 percent, and Idaho with 63.7 percent. Four other states—California, Oregon, Arizona, and Wyoming—have between 42.8 and 52.6 percent of their lands under federal control.

Under the Statehood Act, Alaska had until 1984 to complete its land selections.[11] Boroughs and cities were given the right to select 10 percent of the "vacant, unappropriated, unreserved state land" within their boundaries, under state legislation passed in 1963 and amended in 1970. But because some small-population boroughs encompass wide areas, some inequities resulted. For example, the sparsely settled Matanuska-Susitna Borough selected 385,000 acres, the equivalent of 40 acres per borough resident, while the populous Greater Anchorage Borough's choice of 15,000 acres and the Fairbanks North Star Borough's choice of 69,000 acres represented the equivalent of about 0.1 acres per Anchorage resident, and about 1.2 acres per Fairbanks resident.

After statehood, the next major shift of land ownership in the state came with the 1971 Alaska Native Claims Settlement Act, which will eventually transfer 44 million acres of federally owned land to Native regional corporations. After the Statehood and Native Claims acts are fully implemented, presumably before 1985, ownership of Alaska land will break down as follows: federal government, 226 million acres (60 percent); the state (and its local governments), 104.5 million acres[12] 27 percent); the Natives, 44 million acres (12 percent); and private owners (excluding Natives), one million acres (less than one percent). Though it is difficult to predict what state programs may be created over the next few years to put more land into private hands, Hammond and various legislators have proposed bills to transfer small amounts of state lands to individuals desiring home sites.

Besides granting the 44 million acres to the Natives, the Native Claims Act contained another provision that will drastically affect land use in Alaska for decades to come and has already provoked considerable debate. It is the provision for "national interest" or "D-2" lands. Section 17 (d) (2) of the Native Claims Act directs the secretary of the interior to designate 80 million acres of Alaska's federally owned lands for national parks, wildlife refuges, national monuments, national forests, and wilderness scenic rivers. The act

[11] By 1976, just over 800,000 acres of the 102.5 million acres granted to the state had so far been selected by eleven boroughs and eight cities. But less than half of this amount had actually been secured through patents by the local governments. Although we were unable to obtain a precise figure, it appears that local governments are entitled to something less than one million acres from the state.

[12] The additional 2 million acres above the 102.5 million granted at statehood are contained in special federal grants for specific uses, including ones for mental health and university purposes totaling 1.1 million acres.

barred development on any of the 226 million acres of federally owned land until the 80 million acres were withdrawn.

Following the mandate of the Claims Act, Interior Secretary Rogers C. B. Morton in 1973 recommended that 83.3 million acres be set aside for permanent protection.[13] The proposal covers an area equal to the states of Maine, New Hampshire, Vermont, New York, Massachusetts, Connecticut, Rhode Island, and New Jersey combined. (The additional 3.3 million acres were designated for permanent protection by the interior secretary under his authority contained in another law.) Congress will make the final decision on which areas, if any, to protect. It could place the entire 83 million acres in wilderness categories, or it could designate less—or more. But if Congress is to designate any national interest lands, it must act on the secretary's recommendations by December 18, 1978. After that date, the lands designated by Morton will no longer be protected under the Claims Act, and could be opened up for leasing and development. And so the Native Claims Act didn't really settle the Alaska wilderness issue. Rather, it brought the issue to a head, and it touched off a fierce, if little publicized, battle between national and state environmental organizations and development interests and their allies in Congress.

A number of proposals, some of them introduced in previous sessions, were being considered by Congress in early 1977. Besides the original Interior Department bill covering 83.3 million acres, the environmentalists proposed protection for 116 million acres in bills introduced by Representative Morris K. Udall (Democrat, Arizona) and Senator Henry M. Jackson (Democrat, Washington).[14] At the other extreme were various Alaska politicians and the Boomers, who favored sufficient "flexibility" in any D-2 legislation so that no land would be permanently "locked up" from development. Then there were various hybrid schemes, including one by Senator Mike Gravel

[13] Morton's recommendation did not include some 45 million acres of federal land already permanently protected as national parks and monuments (about 7.5 million acres); forests (18 million acres); and wildlife refuges and ranges (19.8 million acres).

[14] Udall is chairman of the House Interior and Insular Affairs Committee, which will consider D-2 legislation. Jackson is chairman of the Senate Interior and Insular Affairs Committee. Both introduced their bills at the request of the Alaska Coalition, a group of national and Alaska-based environmental organizations including the Wilderness Society, Sierra Club, National Audubon Society, Friends of the Earth, Alaska Center for the Environment, Alaska Conservation Society, and six others.

to establish some type of co-managerial system by the state and federal governments so that comprehensive land use planning could be done for the entire state.

Such were the battle lines. Predictably, both the environmentalists' proposal for 116 million acres, and the Interior Department's initial bill[15] for 83.3 million acres, were roundly denounced by pro-development forces as "no-growth" in nature. Equally predictably, conservationists labeled Interior's proposal, despite its magnitude, inadequate to protect Alaska's wilderness. And many of them feared that the late 1978 deadline for making final D-2 selections would not be met by Congress and that the protection afforded federal lands under the Native Claims Act would not be extended. "We consider the D-2 lands fight to be of the highest priority," Jack Hession, Alaska representative of the Sierra Club, told us in late 1976. "We lost the fight over the pipeline, and since then have turned much of our attention to protecting the rest of the wilderness. We realize we cannot stop all development in Alaska, but we can slow down its rate and see to it that this nation's last great wilderness is protected."

The bill first proposed by conservationists in 1975 covered the same general areas as the Interior Department's 83.3-million-acre proposal, but substantially enlarged the size of the proposed wilderness areas. By environmentalists' standards, Interior's proposal provided some protection to the wilderness but also made generous concessions to development interests. Environmentalists cited Interior's proposal to create an 8.36-million-acre Gates of the Arctic National Park in the Brooks Range in northern Alaska. The area selected by Interior excluded huge portions of environmentally valuable land which were believed to contain rich deposits of minerals, particularly copper. In order to protect the proposed park's ecosystem, environmentalists recommended that the area covered be expanded to 12.2 million acres.

Another disagreement was Interior's proposed creation of four new national forests totaling 18.8 million acres—about one fourth of the D-2 land authorization. Environmentalists argued that this designation of federal lands as national forests did not provide adequate protection for the lands. Under the management of the develop-

[15] The Carter administration's Interior secretary, Cecil Andrus, said in response to questions during his confirmation hearings that he felt that the 1973 Interior proposal for 83.3 million acres "remain[s] a solid base for congressional deliberation" and that he was essentially adopting it as his position on the issue.

ment-oriented Forest Service of the Department of Agriculture, national forests are open to multiple uses—that is, logging, mining, and recreation, as well as protection of fish and wildlife. Environmentalists wanted no new federal land to be placed in national forests. Pro-development interests, on the other hand, preferred to have federal lands designated as national forests or placed under the Bureau of Land Management in those cases where they could not get land excluded from federal protection. The Wilderness Society pointed out in a late-1976 bulletin that even if development interests could not obtain such designations, "more than 200 million acres of other federal, state, and Native lands will still be available for resource development—more than two thirds of Alaska. . . ."

The environmentalists' central concern over the vital D-2 issue was this: in a nation as vast and as geographically diverse as the United States, could we not afford to set aside one major wilderness area to be untouched in perpetuity? Patrick L. Dobey, a top state government oil and mineral official, made the same point to us, with some passion:

> Now Alaska is our last wilderness. It is a beautiful place. It has values that in a very crowded world in the year 2000 and beyond would be invaluable. Now some people say, "Who would be able to afford to visit it?" My God, if they could just see pictures of it and believe it was still there that would be something, just knowing it was still there. And it also is delicate. . . . The question again is what would be the ultimate value of our last wilderness in a world that doesn't have one remaining? . . . I spent my whole life in oil and I still feel that I'll live long enough to see the end of the petroleum era. . . . I spent sixteen years with Mobil Oil Company. I quit the company to stay here just three years ago. . . . With every drop of blood I've got, I'm going to fight. There's no doubt about it, that we do have a choice here in Alaska. By God, we've gone to the end where there's no wilderness left, there's no frontiers left . . . and if we can't do it right this time . . .

Environmental groups did not include lands on the Pet-4 Reserve in their initial wilderness lands proposal in 1975 because the 23-million-acre area was not then eligible for inclusion. At the time, it was already protected from commercial development as a national defense reserve to meet the nation's emergency oil needs. However, new legislation transferred the reserve to the Interior Department on June 1, 1977, and Interior designated the Bureau of Land Management to oversee it. The Pet 4 legislation allowed for eventual oil, natural gas, and mineral development on the reserve, with congressional approval. The new legislation prompted conservation groups to include some portions of Pet 4 in their "national interest" lands proposal in 1977. These areas included the Teshekpuk Lake area, valuable for accommodating nesting and migratory waterfowl, and the Utukok Uplands area which serves as calving grounds for the caribou. As the Sierra Club's Hession put it:

Pet-4 contains nationally significant critical habitat for the Arctic caribou herd, for millions of migratory birds, and for the endangered peregrine and gyrfalcon.[16] Its production of wildlife is vital to the subsistence requirements of the Native residents of the Arctic Slope. It contains examples of Arctic landforms and habitats unique in the nation, and its archeological resources are internationally significant. It is the largest de facto wilderness in the nation.

The need to protect the area was echoed by a Bureau of Land Management paper that noted "the critical decline in the population of the western Arctic caribou herd" from 243,000 in 1971 to 70,000 in 1975 to 35,000 in 1976. Just as the slaughter and disappearance of the buffalo ended a way of life for the Plains Indians, the demise of the caribou could have the same result for the Arctic Slope Natives.

Many Natives who hunt, fish, and gather food expressed misgivings to one degree or another over the various D-2 proposals. Their concern was that the final D-2 decision would not make adequate provision for Native access to lands. They did not want to be excluded from the use of their traditional subsistence lands in the name of the environment. The Calista Native Corporation, in a position paper submitted to the 1975 Senate Interior and Insular Affairs Committee hearings on the D-2 issue, said that all the proposed bills were too restrictive and would hurt the Natives' subsistence cultures. The environmentalists' bill, the corporation said, "makes no distinction between sportsmen and subsistence users." Commenting on all the bills, Calista concluded:

The Natives of Alaska have lived in Alaska for hundreds of years. Subsistence is our way of life. We have not depleted the stocks. We have not endangered the flora and fauna. Rather we have maintained a balance between man and nature in the region. The bills which are presently proposed assume that we are no longer capable of maintaining this balance. There is no evidence that this is true. We therefore find this legislation not only a danger to our way of life, but an insult to our reputation for careful use of the land and its resources.

[16] The peregrine and gyrfalcon are birds of prey, members of the falcon family.

The controversy over the D-2 lands involved not only which areas and how many acres would be preserved as wilderness, but also who would administer Alaska's vast land resources. While the Interior and environmentalists' proposals emphasized federal management of the wilderness, many Alaskans—Boomers as well as moderates on the growth issue—favored various schemes that would give the state more control over federal lands. The Boomers, of course, supported as much leeway as possible for private enterprise to gain ownership of and access to the lands. Others—Hammond and Gravel, for example—favored different proposals for comanagement by the federal and state governments.

In 1975, Hammond proposed a plan, which he was later to compromise on, under which 36.6 million acres would be placed in the federal park, refuge, and forest systems. Another 62 million acres of federal land would be designated "Alaska resource lands," to be managed jointly by the federal and state governments. Hammond's proposal called for voluntary cooperative management on other federal and state-owned land, with private landowners also having the option to include their lands. The governor also wanted to establish an Alaska Land Commission, consisting of state and federal members, which would be a policy-making body with "broad cooperative authority over Alaska resource lands and designated federal and state lands." Exactly how this "voluntary" planning could be effected was not made clear; nor was it clear why private landowners would want to be part of such an arrangement. The governor argued that various other proposals, including those by environmentalists, "place all D-2 lands under exclusive control by federal agencies. I believe this is neither desirable nor necessary." Hammond said his proposal, "unlike the others, emphasizes what *can* be done upon the land rather than what can't. We want to avoid placing needless restrictions upon the land if it can be used without harm to the land itself or to the life it nurtures."

Gravel's proposal went somewhat farther than Hammond's original one. The senator wanted to create a permanent Federal and State Planning and Land Use Commission which would determine development policies for *all* land in the state. Gravel told us his proposal would "for the first time give a state some right to determine policy for federal lands, while also giving the federal government some authority over land it had ceded to the state." Some federal land could go into one of the "four systems"—national parks, forests, monuments, wildlife refuges—while the rest would be co-managed under what Gravel called "a fifth system." The land-use commission would have broad authority to determine "the highest and best use for all lands in the state, both public and private." In the event of disagreement, the Interior secretary could veto proposals for land use on federal lands, while the governor could veto proposals for development on state lands.

The other two members of Alaska's delegation in Congress were taking a somewhat more development-oriented approach. Representative Don Young, the most Boomer-minded of Alaska's congressional delegation, said in a February 1977 interview that he favored "a moderate approach" to the D-2 issue as opposed to the "lock-up", freeze-them-out approach" of the environmental coalition. "What the environmentalists have done," said Young, "is to choose all the lands that would be available for use as mining, forest, and agricultural lands, and all the natural seaports" for their D-2 proposal. In addition, the environmentalists' proposal would "surround all state and Native lands with parks and refuge lands," thereby limiting their development as well. Young denounced the 116-million-acre proposal in the bills introduced by Udall and Jackson as "the greatest crime ever committed against American society because it prevents us from getting the resources that are necessary to the survival of the American society. We have thirty-one known minerals in Alaska. To take that away from the American people in the guise of saving for the future puts us totally at the mercy of the exporting countries. I don't want that as an Alaskan; I don't want that as an American." The Udall-Jackson bills, he said, would "lock up" an area larger than the entire state of California.

Senator Ted Stevens said that he viewed himself as a conservationist and that, as a former assistant secretary of the Interior, he had in 1960 pushed for the creation of the 8.9-million-acre Arctic National Wildlife Range in Alaska. But, he told us in February 1977, the environmentalists' D-2 proposal caused "the pendulum to swing too hard" in the other direction. The result would be to deny to the people of the nation resources they need by withdrawing "a substantial overwhelming percentage" of land on which these resources are located.

By the spring of 1977 Stevens, Young, and Hammond had agreed to support legislation which would designate 25 million acres as federal wilderness areas and put another 55 million acres under multiple-use management, under guidelines issued by a special joint federal-state planning commission. Multiple use, of course, would permit development of oil and other minerals. For Hammond, this marked a retreat from his earlier position on D-2 lands. Gravel decided not to go along with the Hammond-Young-Stevens bill, and continued to push his own proposal.

In some cases, environmental groups and the Interior Department differed over the extent of protection that should be given to a particular area under the D-2 provision. For example, under Interior's proposal, the Wrangell and Saint Elias mountains in southeastern Alaska would themselves be included in the national park system, but the wooded lowlands would become part of the multi-use national forest system. The problem with this, conservationists argued, was that these lowlands are among the richest in wildlife in Alaska; wildlife and their habitat would be threatened by future mining and logging operations. The conservation organizations favored putting both the mountains and lowlands into an 18.1 million-acre national park—which would make it the nation's largest national park, more than eight times the size of Yellowstone.

In fact, many environmetal groups already referred to the area as the Wrangell-Kluane *International* Park because Canada had established a 6.8 million-acre Kluane National Park and Game Sanctuary in its part of the region just across the border. And Canadian officials had expressed an interest in setting aside an even larger area in connection with any national park that might be established on the U.S. side. The key value of the binational area was that it contained the greatest concentration of peaks higher than 14,500 feet in North America, topped by 18,008-foot Mount Elias in Alaska and 19,850-foot Mount Logan (only 470 feet smaller than Mount McKinley)[17] on the Canadian side. The mountains also include the most extensive glacial system in the U.S. and provide some of the most awe-inspiring scenery in the world.

The conservationists' 116-million-acre proposal was designed to protect entire ecosystems and critical habitat for all manner of wildlife, sea mammals, fish, and fowl. For those readers who are interested, here is a breakdown of the proposal by geographical area and protected species:

- Arctic and subarctic (northwest and north central Alaska): Gates of the Arctic National Park, 12.2 million acres; Noatak River National Ecological Reserve, 7 million acres; Kobuk Valley National Monument, 1.9 million acres; Selawik National Wildlife Range, 2.1 million acres. Together with

[17] The tallest North American mountain.

the previously-mentioned areas of Pet-4, some 30 million acres of adjacent areas in the Arctic, and their abundant wildlife, glaciers, sand dunes, nesting and migratory waterfowl, would be protected.

• The arctic interior ecosystem (arctic and subarctic in northeast Alaska, adjacent to Canada): Arctic National Wildlife Range, an addition of 5.6 million acres to the 9-million acre wildlife refuge established in 1960; Yukon Flats National Wildlife Range, 12.3 million acres; Yukon-Charley Rivers National Park, 2 million acres. The inclusion of these areas would protect the calving and migrating patterns of the Porcupine and Arctic herds of caribou in the Arctic Wildlife Range; protect salmon and more than two million ducks in what the Sierra Club terms "one of the single most productive waterfowl habitats on earth" in the Yukon Flats area (as many as 15 percent of all canvasbacks in North America are born in the Yukon Flats area); afford protection for three fourths of Alaska's migratory waterfowl, some 200 species of birds, and numerous species of mammals, and a rich variety of flora and fauna in the Yukon-Charley Rivers area.

• South central and southeast Alaska: The previously mentioned Wrangell-Saint Elias National Park, 18.1 million acres; Kenai Fjords National Monument, 300,000 acres. The Kenai proposal would protect the Harding Ice Field, seals, sea lions, sea otters, whales, bears, moose, and bald eagles.

• The Alaska Range–Aleutian chain (south central Alaska, Alaska Peninsula): Mount McKinley National Park additions, 4.2 million acres (to go along with the existing 1.9 million acre park); Lake Clark National Park, 5.8 million acres; Lake Iliamna National Wildlife Range, 1.6 million acres; Katmai National Park, to be created from the existing 2.8 million acre Katmai National Monument, plus another newly designated 2.8 million acres; Aniakchak Caldera National Monument, 700,000 acres; Alaska Peninsula National Brown Bear Range, 4.9 million acres. The Mount McKinley additions are vital, according to the environmentalists, because the current park boundaries do not cover more than half the mountain, including its most spectacular glaciers. Important ranges for wolves, moose, caribou, and bears are not included in the present park. The Lake Clark park would include glaciers, volcanoes, a spectacular coastline, waterfalls, streams, lakes, and wild rivers, as well as trumpeter swans, wolves, eagles, brown and black bears, Bristol Bay salmon, rainbow trout, and the Mulchatna caribou herd. The inclusion of Lake Iliamna would protect migratory birds, rainbow trout and the world's largest population of red salmon, as well as North America's only colony of freshwater seals and the migrating area for Beluga whales in Bristol Bay and upstream. Consider also that in October, the entire world population of emperor geese migrates to the Bristol Bay region, which would be included in the Iliamna wildlife range. The Katmai inclusion would protect some spectacular scenery and essential habitat for such endangered creatures as the Alaskan brown bears, osprey, and red salmon. The Anianchak inclusion would provide protection for the caldera

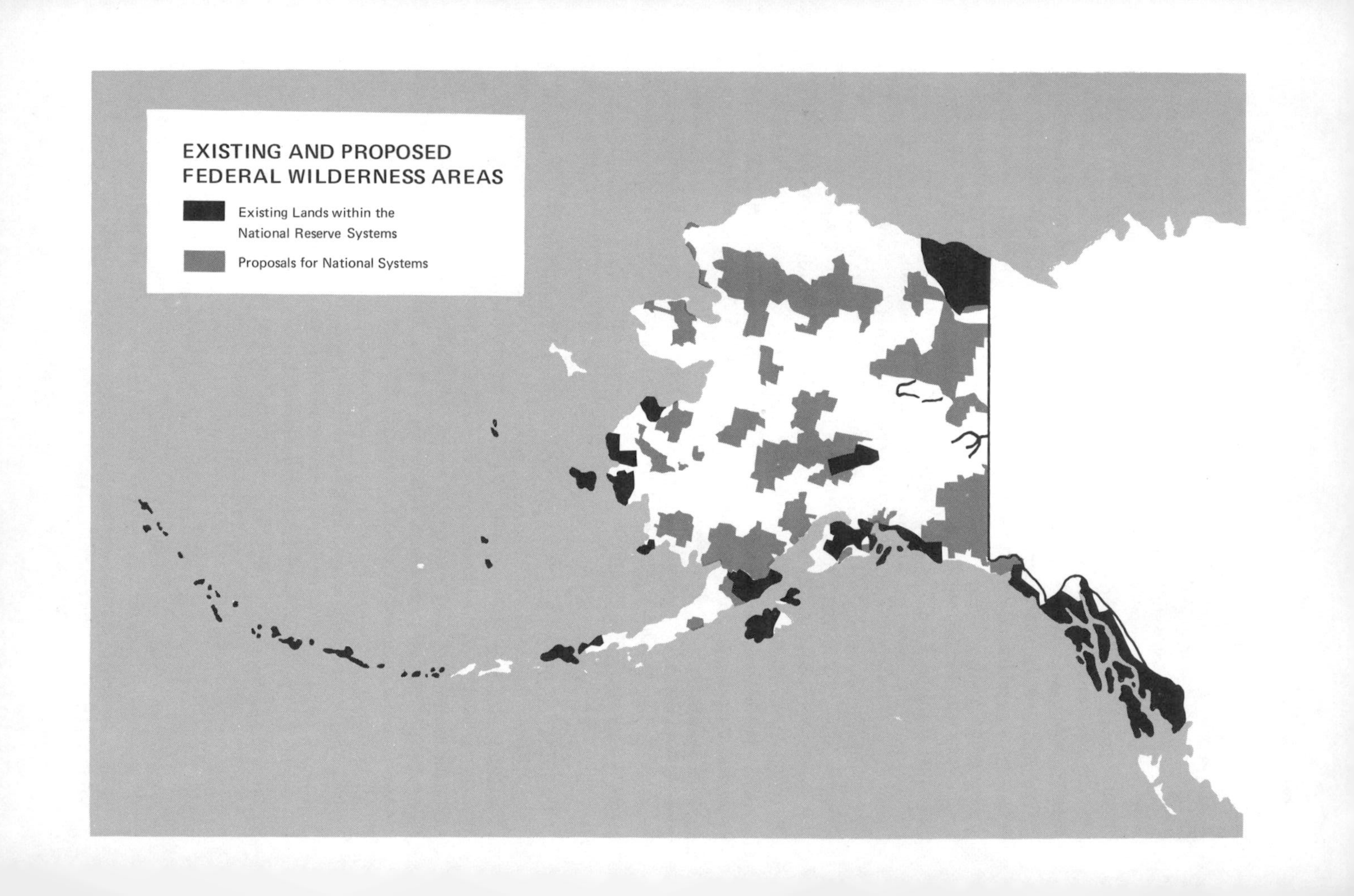

EXISTING AND PROPOSED
FEDERAL WILDERNESS AREAS
Existing Lands within the
National Reserve Systems
Proposals for National Systems

of an extinct volcano that covers thirty square miles. (A caldera is a large, basinlike depression resulting from the explosion or collapse of the center of a volcano.) The Alaska Peninsula addition would ensure essential habitat for the giant brown bear.

• Western and central Alaska: Togiak National Wildlife Range, 3 million acres; Yukon Delta National Wildlife Range, 5.4 million acres; Koyukuk National Wildlife Range, 8.2 million acres; Coastal National Wildlife Refuge, 500,000 acres. These proposed inclusions would, among other things, protect the second most productive waterfowl habitat in North America (Yukon Delta), where two million ducks, geese and swan and countless shorebirds breed; protect other migrating birds (in the Togiak, Yukon and Koyukuk wildlife ranges), and safeguard marine birds and the rookeries of marine mammals in the Coastal Refuge.

• Northwest Alaska: Chukchi-Imuruk National Ecological Reserve, 4 million acres; Cape Krusenstern, 350,000 acres. According to Edgar Wayburn, chairman of the Sierra Club Alaska Task Force, the Chukchi-Imuruk land, on the Seward Peninsula, "is rich in human history, offering abundant clues to ancient human migration patterns from Asia," as well as providing important habitat for migratory birds. Said Wayburn:

> The shoreline in this region is a nearly continuous strip of prehistoric and more recent Eskimo sites. In the northern portion of the [proposed] reserve, there are remnants of unique ash explosions that have completely preserved ancient ecosystems. In the southern portion of the unit, lava flows have encased an ancient tundra world. Scientists will be able to study both the human record and the corresponding natural record of the area from prehistoric times to the present, thus offering a chance to reconstruct a remarkably complete account of man's relationship to the land. The Cape Krusenstern area also could be expected to provide information concerning early inhabitants there.

In addition to the proposals already listed, the environmental groups recommended that thirty-three rivers be classified as wild and scenic rivers, compared to twenty recommended by the Interior Department.

* * *

Closely related to the D-2 lands issue were proposals to establish transportation or energy corridors in the state. By early 1977 a variety of proposals had already been advanced by development interests which hoped that multitudes of roads, pipelines, etc., would be constructed across federally reserved lands, so that mineral wealth from Alaska's interior could be brought out as soon as possible. In 1975, the federal Bureau of Land Management issued a report entitled *Multimodal Transportation and Utility Corridor Systems in Alaska*, and an accompanying map, frequently referred to as the "spaghetti map." Interior Secretary Rogers C. B. Morton, in contrast to the BLM, proposed a single north-south corridor with an east-west connector. The BLM report called for reservation of specific corridors to transport resources—rather than relying on customary eminent domain procedures for acquiring rights-of-way. The spaghetti map is a confusing jumble of thin lines. In fact, it is almost indecipherable: slurries, railroads, roads, oil and natural gas pipelines crisscrossing the state, north to south, east to west, and seemingly around in circles at some points. Several of the proposed corridors resemble a noose around the neck of the dwindling caribou herds, which are especially sensitive to development that deflects them from their customary breeding and migrating patterns.

The desire by the development interests for a corridor system was bluntly stated during an August 1975 visit to Alaska by Dr. Thomas Falkie, director of the U.S. Bureau of Mines. Said Falkie: "There will be a corridor system if we have anything to say about it." Needless to say, the BLM report, and variations thereof, repeatedly drew sharp attacks from environmentalists who saw the proliferation of the energy corridors as leading inevitably to development of potentially mineral-rich—but environmentally sensitive—lands in the interior. Where mineral development is not severely detrimental to the environment, the conservationists argued, air transportation could be used to get the minerals out. The environmentalists pointed to a 1974 study by the University of Alaska's Mineral Industry Research Laboratory which concluded that air transportation of ore concentrates could compete successfully with rail transport.

In addition to energy corridor proposals, there are a number of proposals to build roads into areas of the state currently accessible only by air, and in some cases, by ship. But many of the states's political leaders to whom we talked seemed not to have given much thought to the future of transportation in Alaska. One exception was Hammond, who established a nine-member Alaska Transportation Planning Council in late 1976 as a means of soliciting public views on Alaska's transportation policy. The governor noted that transportation decisions in the past had been made without any "public input or consideration of the effect of each project on all transportation needs." Often, he said, construction decisions were made before the public was even aware that a road or transportation system was being contemplated someplace in the state. He also recommended to the legislature that a state Department of Transportation be established.[18] Until the new department

[18] The danger with this proposal is that, like other government agencies, the Transportation Department would have a vested bureaucratic interest in expanding its domain and could become an advocate for numerous transportation schemes.

was created, Hammond said, the Transportation Planning Council could be used as the vehicle for obtaining public sentiment on transportation issues.

* * *

The need for some kind of coherent state transportation policy was best pointed up by the continuing controversy over the North Slope Haul Road, built by Alyeska in 1974. Alyeska was required under an agreement with the state to construct the road, at a cost of $250 million, to meet secondary highway standards so that it could be used for general transportation purposes after pipeline construction was completed.

The Haul Road, 360 miles long, extends from the Yukon River north of Fairbanks to Prudhoe Bay. It is the state's only ground connection (with the exception of the abortive Hickel Highway discussed later) to the area north of the Arctic Circle. Since its completion, it has been limited to uses connected with pipeline construction, maintenance and supplies. Under terms of Alyeska's agreement with the state, the road was to be turned over to state ownership when the pipeline was completed. This left the Hammond administration with a dilemma: who would be allowed to use the road after pipeline construction, and for what purposes?

Hammond had already made an interim decision in September 1976 to keep the road closed to the public. For the time being, use would be restricted through a permit system, "to resident miners and owner-users for the development of the Arctic oil field," he said. Hammond also said he would look into an interim method for financing maintenance of the road so that users would "bear the costs of opening and maintaining the road during this period. There's no justification for asking all the taxpayers of the state to pick up a subsidy of several million dollars to provide for the benefit of but a few." He added that a final decision on opening the road to the public would be deferred until after further study and "until the peak industrial demands for the road have subsided."

The Haul Road issue was of great importance—both substantively and symbolically—to the contending Boomer and environmental forces in the state. As Doug McConnell of the Alaska Public Forum put it during a broadcast of the "Alaskan Advocates" television program on September 26, 1976:

> The future use of the North Slope Haul Road is an important key to what the future of Northern Alaska and, hence, the entire state will be.

Hammond, in announcing his interim decision to keep the Haul Road open to existing industrial uses, put the importance of the road in a more political perspective:

> To completely open the road now would remove all options for the future because once opened, we would likely never be able to modify that access. . . . If during our interim period it's clear the public wants to drive on the Haul Road to the Arctic Ocean, then the public must make clear they are willing to pay for the increased costs to cover maintenance, police, recreation, lodging, and cleanup costs. To add to the immense subsidy for transportation already borne by the state can only increase the growth of bureaucracy and budget.

With the Hammond administration trying to straddle a middle ground and to buy some time, other interested parties continued to battle over the Haul Road. Those who favored opening the Haul Road to virtually all traffic argued not only that the road was needed to get at resources vital to the state's and the nation's futures, but that those who opposed opening the road were an elite group of snobs who wanted to deny others the incredible privilege of viewing the Arctic. As Anchorage attorney Allen McGrath said:

> We oppose those members of the community who would restrict the Arctic experience solely to a group of people who have the wealth and sufficient leisure in order to be able to afford the access, the expensive access, the only accesses [airplanes, ships] that are available today.

Support for opening the Haul Road came from not only the usual group of super-growthers, including the *Anchorage Times*, but from the Alaska Carriers Association, the trucking industry lobbying and trade organization. Larry Venable, director of the association, said that the Haul Road would be needed for at least ten to fifteen years after the completion of the pipeline. To close it down, he predicted, would have a serious adverse economic impact on the state.

The road, through its links to the Alaska Highway (Alcan), would mean a direct road connection from the Lower-48 to the Alaskan Arctic. And opponents of the Haul Road argued that its opening would: result in additional undesirable mining activity; put more pressure on dwindling wildlife populations through legal and illegal hunting, noise, and increased human presence; cause serious terrain damage from off-road vehicles; lead to pressure for spur roads to aid mining and other development activities; and result in commercial activity—motels, restaurants, gas stations, etc.

Alaskan conservationists were of varying opinions concerning the road. Some favored closing it altogether, while others thought it could be kept open to existing industrial uses. From a financial standpoint, closing the road altogether presented problems to the state. A little history explains why.

The road was built in 1974 after the state was granted a road right-of-way across federal lands by the Department of the Interior. Alyeska had planned only to build a construction road, but the state required that the road be built 28 feet wide with a crushed gravel surface—that is, to meet the state's secondary highway standards. Until its construction, usable state roads ran only as far north as the Yukon River. Alyeska spent $258 million for the road and for its part of the cost of a bridge across the Yukon. The Federal Highway Administration, at the state's request, contributed $27 million for Haul Road construction—of which $24 million went for the bridge. It was the opinion of state officials that, if the state closed down the road, it would have to pay back the money advanced by the Federal Highway Administration, and Alyeska itself might be entitled to certain damages.

Yet the issue of what to do with the Haul Road was far from clear-cut. Anchorage attorney Hugh Fleischer, an activist in consumer and environmental causes, was one of those who believed the road should be shut down entirely regardless of the one-time cost to the state of paying back federal funds. Said Fleischer: "If the state had to pay back every cent of money that had been expended on this road, we would be in far better economic shape than having to maintain the outrageous costly road for the foreseeable future." There was evidence to support Fleischer's claims. According to estimates prepared by the Hammond administration, the cost of maintaining, improving, and policing the road in its first year under state control, with access to the entire public, would be $27.6 million. The second year the cost would drop off to about $11 million, and presumably would stay at about that level in future years.

Before leaving the discussion of roads, an earlier comic-tragic effort to plunge a road into the Arctic bears noting. In late 1968, after the Prudhoe Bay oil discovery, Governor Walter J. Hickel won approval for a winter road to be built from north of Fairbanks to the North Slope as a sop to the trucking industry, which was upset that the airlines were making a killing by flying supplies to the oil fields. But construction of the road did not go well. Instead of insulating the permafrost by piling snow on it, the state Department of Highways used bulldozers and gouged out large chunks of the tundra covering the frozen soil beneath. This removed the protective layer that kept the permafrost from thawing. So when spring came, the road thawed and what had been officially dedicated as the Walter J. Hickel Highway turned, ingloriously, into the Walter J. Hickel Canal. After expensive efforts to reroute it failed, the little-used road was closed. The whole fiasco was an acute embarrassment to Hickel, who by 1969 was secretary of the Interior and was trying to make his mark as a conservationist; and it proved, if nothing else, the delicate nature of Alaska's terrain. Even Alaskans, who should know better, are sometimes surprised by the realities of their unusual environment.

* * *

Wheat fields waving in the sun. Unusually nutritious grain. Harvests among the best in the nation. Sound like Kansas? Improbable as it may seem, the description could be of Alaska. Of all the development issues in Alaska today, none is more surprising—or promising—than agriculture.

Alaska today is not exactly a major farm state,[19] but there are a number of indications that its potential is substantial. The U.S. Soil Conservation Service has estimated that there are about 16 million acres of potential farmland in Alaska—an area equal to the farm acreage in Ohio, Indiana, or Wisconsin, and one thousand times the current acreage in production in the state—plus 108 million acres that could be used as range for livestock grazing.[20] Senator Stevens has estimated that these 16 million acres could produce $1.5 billion worth of grain annually—enough to make Alaska one of the major grain-producing states in the nation. According to U.S. Department of Agriculture officials, wheat and barley—already grown in small quantities in Alaska—are among the grains that could be produced in abundance in the state. Based on 1974 figures, North Dakota was the top state in cash value of crop in both categories with $1.4 billion in wheat, and $209 million in barley. If Stevens's $1.5 billion projection is accurate, Alaska would trail only North Dakota in those two

[19] The state's largest cash crops, according to 1975 figures, are milk, $2,817,000; hay, $2,782,000; potatoes, $1,434,000; silage, $532,000; eggs, $417,000; beef and veal, $410,000; barley, $287,000; and lettuce, $252,000. In addition, cabbage, carrots, and other vegetables are produced, as well as some pork, poultry, meat, and wool.

[20] Some pro–mineral development state officials contend that future reclaimed strip-mined land could add 25 million usable agricultural acres.

major crops. In addition, state-sponsored tests conducted on a 40-acre wheat and barley crop grown in the Fairbanks area in 1976 showed that the barley had *double* the protein content of the best Lower-48 grain. Wheat raised on the same site had between 40 and 60 percent more protein than the *highest quality* Kansas wheat.

Stevens gave his estimate of the potential value of Alaskan grain crops during testimony at congressional hearings on various D-2 land proposals in late 1975. A strong advocate of development of Alaska's natural resources, the senator complained that the Interior Department's D-2 proposal, as well as those of environmentalists, "incorporate fifty percent of the tillable land and would cripple the state's agricultural potential." Although Stevens was more concerned about access to federal lands for mineral and other development, his point was well taken that Congress should consider Alaska's agricultural potential in weighing the various D-2 proposals. Not only could such a renewable economic resource greatly benefit the state's long-range well-being, but Alaska could help meet the growing world demand for food.

Governor Hammond understands that the future of his state rests not primarily with non-renewable resources—oil, natural gas, minerals, etc.—but with renewable resources such as fishing, agriculture, and timber, and with relatively "clean" industries such as tourism. Hammond told us:

> The most critical goal is to strengthen our renewable resource industries—such as fishing and timber—for the day when the nonrenewable resources run out. We're already moving in that direction . . . [with] fisheries rehabilitation and enhancement. . . . We are also establishing a loan program to create nonprofit hatcheries. We are going to be involved shortly in exploring the possibility of stepped-up agricultural development. Apparently, there is a strong potential for growing certain types of grain in the interior. Using fertilizer produced from some of our natural gas, this kind of farming could have a significant economic capability.

Most of the people we talked to in Alaska, sensing a sort of inevitability about exploitation of the state's resources, had very little to say about agricultural possibilities in the state. Even the governor was only vaguely familiar with the state's agricultural possibilities. This was not too surprising in light of the state's limited involvement in farming at present. In the most recent full-scale agricultural census in 1969, Alaska had 1,604,211 acres classed as farmland, including some 72,000 acres in large grazing leases. But only one percent of that land—some 17,000 acres—was actually being used for crop production. The 322 farms in the state averaged about 470 acres, with average income per farm in 1974 at $17,713; total farm production was only $9,298,000 in 1975.

The Matanuska Valley produced almost 80 percent of the total commercial crops, with dairy farming, including feed crops for cows, as the primary agricultural activity. But with a 120-day growing season that includes as many as nineteen hours of sunlight daily, warm temperatures and moderate rainfall, the Matanuska Valley offered a prime opportunity for increased agricultural production. However, with the population growth fanning out from Anchorage, more and more valuable agricultural land appeared likely to be turned over to residential, commerical, and industrial uses. Already, state officials told us, increasing amounts of Matanuska Valley land had been taken over for non-agricultural purposes. In fact, in recent years as the capital relocation moved closer to reality, the amount of Matanuska land in cultivation actually declined.

An area with even greater agricultural potential in Alaska was the Tanana Valley, near Fairbanks, which accounted for about 15 to 20 percent of the crops produced in the state. The Tanana Valley—with just ninety frost-free days—has a shorter growing season than the Matanuska Valley, and its lower precipitation levels means that more irrigation is needed for some crops than in the Matanuska. But its advantages include warm temperatures during the growing season, plus the presence of large tracts of reasonably flat land with easily cleared brush.

Other areas of the state with some agricultural production include the Kenai Peninsula, south of Anchorage, which had minor production in beef, potatoes, and hay; Kodiak Island, which produced more beef than any other area in the state (one official of the Koniag Native corporation told us that Koniag might eventually consider investing in increasing beef production on the island); and Umnak and Unalaska Islands, which grazed about 12,000 sheep for wool.

One encouraging sign was that, although there had been little emphasis on agriculture by state officials and opinion makers, production and the value of crops had risen in the state in recent years. Production value went from less than $4.6 million in 1969 to $9.3 million in 1975.[21] Some optimistic Alaskans saw much greater po-

[21] In typical Alaskan fashion, some of the vegetables attain gargantuan proportions, partly because of the extremely long summer daylight hours. Turnips as heavy as 30 pounds, for example, and cabbages of up to 70 pounds, have been produced.

tential for agricultural development in the state. James Ellis, of the Alaska Workers Alliance, writing in the October 25, 1976, issue of the *Northern Observer*, a consumer-oriented Anchorage community newspaper (which has since folded), noted that the Siberians, in overcoming a harsh climate similar to Alaska's, had not only become self-sufficient in food production, but were exporting more food than they were importing. Alaska, which imported 95 percent of its food, could do the same, Ellis said. He proposed making the state's agricultural land "separately zoned to keep it from land speculators and parking-lot style development. Taxes must be reformed to give the small farm a decent chance in a system that at present heavily favors agribusiness." He further suggested that investment revenue from the Permanent Fund (the repository of at least 25 percent of the eventual revenues the state will get from North Slope oil and other mineral development) be used to help each region set up "agricultural people's resource cooperatives . . . to help make Alaska an independent food producer."

But time was getting short. *The Alaskan Economy*, a 1976 report of the state's Department of Commerce and Economic Development, noted that field crops and vegetables "require large, relatively flat ground that can be farmed in contiguous blocks for maximum efficiency. Unfortunately, this type of land also tends to be that which is most desired for urban expansion. . . ." The formulation of a long overdue state agricultural policy was helped along in 1976 with a resolution passed by the state legislature. It established a task force to determine future agricultural policy and programs. In his State of the State message on January 11, 1977, Hammond reported that "a special team has examined the potential of expanded agriculture" and would submit a final report later in the year. And in early 1977, the state announced it planned to clear a test plot of 300 to 600 acres near Fairbanks to study the potential for barley production in that area. If successful, the state would dedicate up to 50,000 acres of land for barley growing.

* * *

Earlier, we noted that Hammond favored development of other renewable resource industries—such as forest products. But development of forest products was by no means as uncontroversial as agricultural development. Some fierce environmental battles have been waged in Alaska over clear-cutting of forests and pollution from a pulp mill in the southeastern part of the state. These battles cast doubt on the job the U.S. Forest Service and other federal agencies were doing in protecting Alaska's wild places.

A look at some basic statistics and information underscores the importance of the timber industry to Alaska and also puts some of the environmental issues in perspective. Alaska has 16 percent of the nation's total forest land—as much as in Washington, Oregon, Montana, and California combined—although it is generally of lower quality. Of the total of 119 million acres of forests in the interior and in coastal areas—primarily in southeast Alaska—about 28 million acres—less than one fourth—are classified as commercial, that is, as land capable of producing annually at least 20 cubic feet per acre of usable wood. In the interior, the main trees are white spruce, paper birch, quaking aspen, and balsam poplar. The best stands of trees in the interior are found mainly on the slopes and valleys of the larger rivers and their main tributaries—the Yukon, Kuskokwim, Tanana, Copper, and Susitna—and in the western half of the Kenai Peninsula. Because of a number of factors—primarily climate, cost, and transportation—development of the state's interior forest resources has been slow.

The overwhelming majority of the state's timber operations to date have been in southeastern Alaska in the Tongass National Forest. Of the 11 million acres of forest land in that area, about half are of commercial value—and 92 percent of these commercial trees are in the Tongass. More than one third of the national forest is commercial timber, representing 77 percent of all the saw-timber in Alaska, 70 percent of the nation's supply of Sitka spruce, and 40 percent of its western hemlock saw-timber. Average volumes per acre for saw-timber stands in southeast Alaska compare favorably to similar stands in forest-rich Oregon and Washington.

Despite frequent warnings by industry that more timber must be harvested to meet growing needs in the United States, Alaska has in recent years been exporting between 80 and 95 percent of its forest products—almost all of it to Japan. All of the pulp produced in southeast Alaska was being sent out of the state, with about 40 to 45 percent going to domestic markets in the Lower-48 states, and the rest to Japan. The Forest Service defended these extensive exports in a draft guide to the Tongass National Forest:

> The selling of timber to foreign countries is recognized as part of the world market in all goods and, as such, is contributing indirectly to the national supply situation. There is the possibility that Japan would purchase timber from Canada if the United States did not supply Japan with timber—thus causing United States consumers to lose favorably priced wood now being imported from Canada.

The forest products industry—which accounts for about 3,500 jobs and $63 million in wages annually—ranks third in Alaska in wholesale product value behind petroleum and fisheries.[22] After the total valuation of all timber harvested in Alaska reached more than $6.2 million in 1974, however, the industry went into a slump. In 1975, the total valuation of timber harvested in the state was down to $5.1 million[23] and the volume of timber declined. And, as the state's Department of Commerce and Economic Development noted, "The volume harvested in 1975 was less than the volume harvested in each of the preceding ten years." The main reason for this decline, the department said, was the "reduction in the level of economic activity in Japan and the United States during 1975 and late 1974. As the level of general economic activity declined and as final product producers attempted to reduce their inventories of wood pulp and lumber, the demand for Alaskan forest products declined." But in 1976, although no figures were available, production and value of timber increased significantly over 1975, state officials said.

The future timber situation in Alaska was unclear in early 1977, as the state government and the Native corporations were still in the process of selecting the lands granted under the Statehood and Native Claims Settlement acts. Many expect the Native corporations to be a major force in future forest operations in Alaska, especially the Sealaska Corporation, which is entitled to select 200,000 acres from Tongass National Forest lands. Peter M. Huberth, general manager of Sealaska's Forest Products Division, a concern created in August 1976, told us that his division would "provide the major cash flow and profit opportunities for the corporation."

In southeastern Alaska, conservation groups have vehemently attacked the U.S. Forest Service's management of the Tongass National Forest. Forest Service policies, the conservationists alleged, resulted in inadequate protection of fish and wildlife and interfered with legitimate recreational uses. Alan M. Stein, a Port Protection commercial fisherman, charged that the Forest Service had "allowed logging to damage many hundreds of miles of fish streams in southeastern Alaska alone," resulting in destruction of a conserva-

[22] These figures include logging, sawmill, and pulp mill operations.

[23] The $6.2 million and $5.1 million for 1974 and 1975 respectively reflect only the value of the timber harvest, and do not include other facets of the state's forest products industry. Total value of the wood products industry in Alaska in 1974 was $222.8 million.

tively estimated 500 miles of salmon stream, with consequent loss of 63,000 adult fish and some $630,000 to fishermen. Said Stein:

> The fishermen are sick and tired of being restrained from catching the fish only to find that when the fish try to spawn they are blocked by improperly placed culverts or trees in the stream; and if they do spawn, the eggs freeze, fry[24] suffocate, or changed stream conditions eliminate insect food for the young. Even though water-quality violations continue to occur and could be eliminated or drastically reduced through buffer-strip construction, the Forest Service continues to exercise its discretion in creating them and continues to permit clear-cutting timber off banks of fish streams.

Clear-cutting has been one of the biggest environmental controversies in Alaska in recent years. The roots of the conflict date back to 1965, when the Forest Service announced it was planning to sell 8.75 billion board feet in the Tongass National Forest in the largest timber sale ever in the history of the Forest Service. The Forest Service estimated that the average cut per year would be more than 6,750 acres—over 10 square miles—and would be accomplished by clear-cutting.

Clear-cutting is a method abhorred by environmentalists because it involves removing all trees larger than an inch or two in diameter from a specific area. The process removes valuable habitat for wildlife and results in ugly scars on the landscape. The Forest Service defends it as being beneficial to "scientific forestry." Clear-cutting advocates contend that it aids growth of tree species that need sunlight and also exposes mineral soil to sunlight, which thereby, in the words of a Forest Service brochure, "improves conditions for seed germination and rapid early growth of young trees."

The Forest Service's 1965 timber sale proposal also required that the purchaser of the timber construct and equip a sawmill in or near the site that could handle at least 175 million board feet annually. The successful bidder on the contract, signed September 12, 1968, was U.S. Plywood–Champion International Papers, Inc. But even before the contract was signed, Plywood-Champion had been negotiating with the Japanese—and on February 18, 1969, it agreed to sell much of the timber it would remove from Tongass to the Kanzaki Paper Manufacturing Company of Japan. The renewable contract called for the entire processed timber output to go to Japan for the first fifteen years. The Forest Service, despite the size and potential impact of the operation—part of the harvesting was to be on

[24] Baby fish.

Admiralty Island in a totally virginal forest—treated the proposal as just another sale.

In September 1970, a federal lawsuit seeking to block the harvesting of the timber and the use of the pulp mill was filed by the Sierra Club and the Sitka Conservation Society. The plaintiffs cited potential environmental and wildlife damage, among other things. The suit disclosed that the Forest Service, in offering timber for sale on Admiralty Island, knew little of soil conditions there. In its own Admiralty Island plan of 1964, the Forest Service wrote that "little or no work has been done to study or classify the soils on Admiralty." Likewise, the Forest Service's own 1965 multiple-use plan contained virtually no information about wildlife, saying: "The limited amount of wildlife data available is based on professional opinions and token field work. This is a deterrent to an accurate inventory of the resource. . . ."

Thus, on matters of environmental impact, soil conditions and protection of wildlife, the Forest Service was relying on admittedly insufficient data—in fact, practically no data at all. In addition, Gordon Robinson, a veteran forester and consultant to the Sierra Club, went out in 1970 to study the area proposed for cutting and determined that the Forest Service had sold more trees than existed in certain parts of the forest. A Plywood-Champion study for the Yakutat part of the timber sale showed that Robinson was correct: the contract said that Plywood-Champion, over a 50-year period, would get between 2.5 and 2.75 billion board feet of timber for the Yakatat area; yet the study showed that only 1.8 billion board feet in the Yakatat part of the sale could be harvested. Finally, Plywood-Champion's own study team from the School of Forestry and Conservation at the University of California at Berkeley reported that clear-cutting would harm wildlife habitat and the recreational and esthetic value of the Hood Bay area, one of the areas from which timber was to be taken. The team suggested that the Plywood-Champion plan be cut back considerably to limit clear-cutting, and to extend the cutting period from 50 to more than 100 years, thereby limiting the amount of timber taken at any one time. The company never accepted its own consultants' report.

Meanwhile, the lawsuit tied up Plywood-Champion and no timber was cut. The environmental groups lost in the lower courts, then won a limited remand for a new trial. But the lower court judge never ordered the new trial. The appeals court had ordered the new trial on the issue of whether the timber sale violated the multiple-use act for national forests—that is, whether the extent of the sale precluded use of the forest for anything but timber cutting. In 1976, after a delay of eight years and what it said were changed market conditions that made the Tongass timber deal no longer look so attractive, Plywood-Champion canceled its plans for the pulp mill complex at Berner's Bay, and was in turn released from its timber contract with the U.S. Forest Service.

Meanwhile, a series of landmark federal court decisions held that an 1897 statute banned clear-cutting in national forests. In late 1976 Congress passed, and President Ford signed into law, the Forest Management Act of 1976. The new law permitted clear-cutting in national forests, with certain restrictions, such as allowing it only in areas where it could blend with the terrain. Also it specified the minimum ages at which trees could be cut, and required that all trees taken in clear-cutting be marked as "mature" before cutting. Although some environmentalists said the bill was an acceptable compromise, others maintained the new measure offered little protection for wildlife.

Warren (Skip) Matthews, an Anchorage lawyer who represented one of the environmental groups in the Tongass suit, told us in late 1976 that as the result of environmentalists' efforts to tie up the Tongass operation, he doubted that the Forest Service would ever again attempt such a large-scale sale. In fact, the Forest Service announced in mid-1976 that there would be no new timber sales in Tongass for at least two years, until a land-use plan for the forest was completed. John McGuire, head of the Forest Service, said that he was sure future sales would be made, including ones in the same area as the Plywood-Champion sale, but that he was also certain that the sales would be much smaller in scope, would cover probably no more than a ten-year period and that there would be much sharper control over the size and shape of clear-cutting operations.

Another major environmental issue fought in southeastern Alaska in recent years was over the efforts by the federal Environmental Protection Agency to get Alaska's two pulp mill operations to comply with waste water treatment requirements of federal law. Alaska Lumber and Pulp in Sitka, a Japanese-owned company that has operated in the state since the early 1950s, said it would be able to comply with the secondary waste treatment requirement. However, the Ketchikan Pulp Company announced in early 1976 that it could not afford to install the $30 million worth of water treatment equipment that EPA was requiring and would have to cease operating in mid-1977. KPC operated a pulp mill and four sawmills under a fifty-year contract with the U.S. Forest Service on 800,000 acres of land in the Tongass National Forest. As of 1977, the contract, which allows KPC to cut 4.9 billion board feet of timber, had twenty-seven more years to run.

State officials and Ketchikan area residents were extremely concerned that the closing would eliminate 1,232 jobs—about 600 at the pulp mill and the rest in logging operations and tugboat, towing and marine cargo operations—which would be 19 percent of all the jobs in the area. Total payroll lost in the first year of closing would have been about $27 million, according to the Hammond administration. KPC, at the time of the announced closure, was jointly owned by Louisiana-Pacific Corporation and FMC Corporation, a major conglomerate. In late 1976, Louisiana-Pacific agreed to buy out FMC's share of ownership for $40 million. It also was announced that an estimated $80 million would be spent to transform the operation from a pulp to a paper mill. The changeover would cut pollution by one third, company officials said, and they hoped this would satisfy EPA requirements. Environmentalists had charged that KPC's water discharge permit was too lenient in allowing all kinds of poisonous wastes to be discharged into Ward Cove, degrading the waters and harming marine life.

The controversies over logging and mill operations in southeastern Alaska point up the dangers involved in unchecked use of the forests in the state. One issue which cuts across all the development questions, including timber, is subsistence. Dozens of Native villages are located in or near commercial timber areas, and careless practices can result in harm to their hunting, fishing, and trapping way of life. Reckless use of the forests also can make them useless for recreational activities.

There are yet other development issues in Alaska that could be discussed at length. We have said nothing, for example, of the controversy over proposals to permit the U.S. Army Corps of Engineers to build hydroelectric power projects in the Upper Susitna Basin. Environmentalists and some Natives fear that the project could harm downstream salmon fisheries and also disrupt the Nelchina caribou's herd's migration patterns, eliminate its habitat and increase hunting pressures. They also fear that it would affect large areas of moose winter habitat and would seriously reduce the grizzly bear range in central Alaska.

As is evident by now, the development issues come thick and

fast in Alaska. There is much that could be developed and much that must be protected. But few of the issues match the proposals for crash oil exploration and development of Alaska's outer continental shelf. As we shall see in the next chapter, perhaps no other development scheme in Alaska has quite the potential for disaster.

XII

Troubled Waters

When the earth's oil is all burned up, people will have to develop a substitute for oil to keep the machines running. Question is, can we supply the human body with a substitute for protein? Will the oil taste good down to the last drop, Uncle Sam?

—Pete Isleib, Cordova fisherman, on dangers to the fishing industry of plans for outer continental shelf oil development in the Gulf of Alaska.

Talking about resource development, what are we developing OCS for? What are we doing in the highest-risk area in the world—we're crashing ahead with an OCS program to put more oil into surplus. It just doesn't make sense.

—Sterling Gallagher, Alaska's Commissioner of Revenue.

It scares the shit out of us, in all honesty.

—Tom Casey, manager, United Fishermen's Marketing Association, Kodiak Island.

WHAT IS AT STAKE in the exploration of Alaska's outer continental shelf are reserves that have been estimated at up to 60 billion barrels of oil—about six times higher than oil company estimates for the fantastic Prudhoe Bay discovery. And the exploration could yield as much as 344 trillion cubic feet of gas—enough to meet U.S. consumption for more than fifteen years. Alaska is crucial to the oil industry's hunger for more profits because it contains more than 60 percent of the United States' entire outer continental shelf and holds approximately the same percentage of the nation's undiscovered offshore oil, according to estimates by the U.S. Geological Survey. (The outer contintental shelf is defined as that part of the continent submerged under relatively shallow waters. State-owned OCS areas extend for three miles offshore; federal OCS lands lie beyond the three-mile limit.) One controversial federal OCS lease sale—Northeastern Gulf of Alaska—was held in 1976; one more federal lease sale in Alaska was scheduled for late 1977, five for 1979, and three for 1980.

But what is also at stake in the development of Alaska's OCS program is the fishing industry, long a mainstay of the Alaskan economy and of increasing importance to the United States and the world. About 8 percent of total annual U.S. commercial catches are made off Alaska, and these fish are worth a slightly larger percentage of the total annual value of all U.S. commercial catches. This harvest by U.S. fishermen off Alaska represents only a small percentage, though, of the entire fishing activity in Alaskan waters. Foreign fishing fleets, particularly the Japanese and the Russians, have caught more than 4 billion pounds of fish annually from Alaskan waters, compared to the 500 million pounds caught by the U.S. in the same waters.

Pacific salmon continues to be the most important fish caught in Alaskan waters. Alaskan fishing grounds provide 30 percent of the worldwide harvest of Pacific salmon, and about 90 percent of the U.S. harvest. In addition to these commercial enterprises, some one million salmon are caught annually for subsistence use. But this cornucopia is not limitless; overfishing and poor fisheries' management have seriously depleted salmon stocks, leading some Alaska fishermen to fear that OCS oil production would be a near fatal blow.

The crash development of the United States outer continental shelf was inspired by the famed "energy crisis" of 1973–74, best remembered for its alleged shortage of domestic fuel oil supplies and long lines at gasoline stations. The OCS crash program assumed a new national urgency when the Middle East OPEC (Organization of Petroleum Exporting Countries) nations imposed a six-month oil embargo on the United States beginning in October 1973.

On April 18, 1973, six months before the embargo but with some gasoline and natural gas shortages already being reported throughout the nation, President Nixon sent Congress an energy message asserting that the U.S. has "the capacity and the resources to meet our energy needs if only we take the proper steps—and take them now. . . ." Noting that the United States, with just 6 percent of the world's population, was consuming almost one third of all the energy and having to import petroleum to meet its needs, Nixon advocated an energy program of national self-sufficiency that, among other things, would step up reliance on nuclear power, deregulate wellhead natural gas prices, continue tax breaks for energy exploration, expand development of coal resources—and greatly accelerate the OCS program.

Two months later, in a June 29, 1973, speech, Nixon disclosed that the Council on Environmental Quality, a presidential advisory panel, had begun a study of "the environmental impact of drilling on the Atlantic outer continental shelf and in the Gulf of Alaska," which would be completed by the spring of 1974. Faced with the oil embargo by Middle East nations, Nixon, on November 25, 1973, announced his "Project Independence 1980," which he defined as "a series of plans and goals set to insure that by the end of this decade Americans will not have to rely on any source of energy beyond our own." This policy was adopted by Nixon's successor, Gerald Ford, whose only major modification was delaying the target date for energy "independence" five years to 1985. The race for oil on Alaska's outer continental shelf and elsewhere continued, even though, as Anthony Sampson pointed out in his book *The Seven Sisters: The Great Oil Companies and the World They Shaped:* "By the end of the year [1973] Project Independence was a joke, and self-sufficiency by 1980 inconceivable; by the end of 1974 the United States was more dependent than ever on Arab oil."

As promised, the Council on Environmental Quality in April 1974 released its assessment of the environmental impact that development would have on Alaska's outer continental shelf. It was not a report to cheer environmentalists. The study pointed out that the Gulf of Alaska had the highest environmental risk of all the undeveloped OCS areas being considered for federal leasing. The Gulf's underwater seismic activity is "as violent as any place in the world," the CEQ said. It added, among other things, that in the eastern Gulf of Alaska area the "probabilities for a spill coming ashore are no lower than 40 percent in winter and exceed 95 percent in summer. . . . Major earthquakes of Richter 7 magnitude are common. Tsunamis also are frequent and would create damage at fixed-berth tanker sites." Tsunamis are unusually large sea waves produced by an earthquake or undersea volcanic eruption.

The Gulf of Alaska rests on the "ring of fire," a geological belt of constant volcanic and seismic activity that encircles the entire Pacific Ocean. Between 1899 and 1974, Alaska itself experienced nine earthquakes equaling or exceeding a Richter scale[1] reading of 7. The OCS leasing sites lie in "an area susceptible to earthquakes with magnitude of 6 to 8.8 where major structural damage could occur," according to geologists. In addition, geologists warn that the gulf is susceptible every twenty to twenty-five years to earthquakes topping a magnitude of 8—meaning the next one should occur between 1984 and 1989, during an expected peak period of gulf oil activity. The CEQ also said the gulf has more frequent storms than anyplace else in the Northern Hemisphere: "Gale force winds occur year around, gusts of 60 knots or greater occur during the winter season, and wave heights frequently exceed 20 feet in the months from September through April."

Despite such warnings, the Ford administration plunged ahead. On November 13, 1974, U.S. Interior Secretary Rogers C. B. Morton announced the "tentative" OCS leasing schedule for the entire nation through 1978. Nine sale areas were designated for leasing off Alaska between August 1975 and December 1978. The areas were Lower Cook Inlet, northeastern Gulf of Alaska, Bering Sea (Saint George Basin), Gulf of Alaska (Kodiak Basin), Beaufort Sea, Outer Bristol Bay Basin, Bering Sea (Norton Basin), Gulf of Alaska (Aleutian Basin), and Chukchi Sea. Some of the leasing areas proposed at that time were later deferred, but all were veiwed as eventual OCS development areas.

Hearings on a preliminary environmental impact statement for all proposed OCS lease areas were held in Anchorage; Trenton, New Jersey; and Beverly Hills, California, in early 1975. The environmentalists' warnings of potential disaster for OCS development in Alaskan waters received surprisingly strong support from the U.S. Environmental Protection Agency. EPA, in a letter to the Bureau of Land Management, which administered the lease sales, said that the draft environmental impact statement was "inadequate."

> The impact statement fails to evaluate or justify the necessity for this size offering, and the need to simultaneously enter Atlantic and Alaskan virgin

[1] A device for measuring the amount of energy released by earthquakes. The measurement scale is logarithmic—that is, a magnitude 8 earthquake is 10 times stronger than a magnitude 7 earthquake. The Alaska earthquake of 1964, which killed 115 persons and caused $750 million in property damage, reached a magnitude of 8.4 to 8.6.

areas. Nor is any consideration given to data derived from Project Independence studies which seem to clearly refute the expediency of this size offering . . .

Some of these areas, especially the Gulf of Alaska, contain unique and vulnerable natural resources combined with significant natural hazards that would make precipitous development highly undesirable from an environmental standpoint. [The plan] takes no cognizance of this assessment and further disregards the recommendations of the CEQ study . . . . [Emphasis added.]

The EPA letter also stated that "leasing in Alaskan waters should not be considered at this time and that substantial technical and biological research is required." Significantly, EPA warned that an "immoderate acceleration policy will be economically and environmentally costly," adding that, "production by 1985 in the Gulf of Alaska can be surplus to the nation's needs and should, at a minimum, be preserved for future years."

In the final environmental impact statement, the U.S. Coast Guard admitted that adequate technology to cope with oil spills in the Gulf of Alaska did not exist. But the Interior Department, hell-bent on carrying out the administration's policy, responded this way: "We agree that present technology is not capable of handling spills in the extreme environmental conditions present in the Gulf. . . . Technology, however, is advancing rapidly and *could* enhance cleanup capability in the Gulf." [Emphasis added.]

Calling it an unacceptable risk, the EPA rejected the final environmental impact statement for the Gulf of Alaska on December 18, 1975. EPA then turned the matter over to the President's Council on Environmental Quality for a more thorough review. On January 23, 1976, the CEQ informed Interior Secretary Thomas S. Kleppe that the one-million-acre lease sale should be delayed until results from biological and oceanographic studies in the Gulf of Alaska were completed, until geological hazards had been studied for another season, and until Alaskan villages adjacent to the leasing areas could prepare for the shocks that OCS would bring to their culture, commercial life, and public services. The CEQ also wrote that if it was found not to be in the "national interest" to delay the entire lease offering, the sale of the entire 189 tracts should be limited to 27 tracts near Icy Bay which "cover an area which appears to be highly promising in oil and gas potential and relatively low in vulnerability to environmental damage." EPA had estimated that these 27 tracts alone contained 30 percent of the total oil in the entire proposed Gulf lease area.

The Alaskan state government was pushing to have the Gulf of Alaska sale delayed. As Governor Hammond told us, given the great environmental risks involved in the Gulf of Alaska, "simple logic dictated that it should be placed at the bottom of the priority list, not at the top." One Gulf Native community, Yakutat, already had been severely affected after becoming a prospective onshore OCS service area—even though no leases had yet been sold in the Gulf.

In hearings on the California OCS program, Representative Alphonzo Bell (Republican, California), who favored legislation giving Congress a veto over offshore leasing, charged:

> You should know that there is a general belief in Los Angeles that these hearings are meaningless; that the decision to lease has already been made in Washington; and that no amount of testimony, scientific or otherwise, will reverse that verdict.

Alaska officials also felt that once the leasing decision was made, no amount of contrary evidence was to be considered by federal officials.

They were right. Brushing off the warnings, Interior Secretary Kleppe announced on March 12, 1976, that the OCS oil and gas sale covering 189 tracts and one million acres in the northern Gulf of Alaska would be held April 13 in Anchorage. Hammond immediately announced that the state was filing suit in U.S. District Court in Washington, D.C., in an effort to invalidate the sale. In the summer of 1976, a federal judge rejected the state's argument; he found the leases valid even though the government had ignored environmental dangers posed by the Gulf's hazardous waters.[2] The first exploratory drilling under the new leases began near Yakutat September 1, 1976, with a multicompany effort involving Shell Oil, Atlantic Richfield, Texas Eastern Exploration Company, and Offshore Oil Development Company of Texas.

In the bidding, the first ever for Alaska's federally owned outer continental shelf, there were a total of 244 bids from more than 70 companies for 81 of the 189 tracts offered for sale. The sum of the high bids for each tract was $571.8 million. Atlantic Richfield and Shell (teaming up with Texas Eastern and Offshore Oil) made the highest offers, submitting successful bids totaling more than $250 million.

[2] The case was still under appeal in early 1977.

The draft environmental impact statement for the northern Gulf of Alaska released by the Interior Department in June 1975 generally minimized the detrimental repercussions OCS development would cause in the Gulf. Still, even in its understated form, the prognosis was frightening enough. The statement said, for example, that oil exploration itself could result in annual spillage of 11,873 barrels, plus another 32,000 spilled barrels from tankers carrying oil from the Gulf. Oil pollution near major spawning streams or within salmon migration paths could wipe out certain salmon runs, and oil contamination would kill birds in the Gulf. Despite any efforts to lessen the impact on wildlife, "General gas and oil activity in coastal areas would result in chronic levels of disturbance and pollution which would be disruptive to fish and wildlife populations."

In addition, the statement said five major coastal communities would be substantially affected by the onshore impact of offshore oil activities. It was calculated conservatively that Gulf of Alaska oil development would add 11,487 people to coastal communities at its peak, with 9,074 more people moving into Anchorage, already burgeoning from the trans-Alaska oil pipeline boom. OCS development, according to the statement, would sustain the boom in Valdez, the terminal port for the oil pipeline; would increase living costs and congestion in Cordova, and produce shortages of housing, schools, water, and sewage facilities; would cause Seward, used as a summer playground for south central Alaska residents, to "largely disappear" as a small, quiet community under "high development conditions." In an understatement which astounded city and state officials, the report claimed Yakutat would gain only 115 residents when OCS in the Gulf reached its peak in 1984. The statement also blithely predicted that the traditional Native way of life would not be threatened by such an increase.

One former Interior Department employee, who worked on OCS environmental impact statements in Anchorage, said that the statements were prepared on a crash basis on orders from department officials in Washington. At the time of our interview with this employee, in October 1976, she said that the environmental impact statement (EIS) then being prepared for the Kodiak area of the Gulf of Alaska was being written by "half of the Los Angeles" OCS office staff assigned on temporary duty to Alaska. She said that people working on the statements started out with the idea of doing a good job but, because of unreasonable time pressures and refusal by the department to allow special studies of areas that would be affected, the impact statements were inadequate. "It's a sad story of the wearing down of high ideals," she commented. The former employee charged that OCS environmental impact statements have often amounted to little more than rewrites of environmental impact statements for other areas. One such statement, for a Gulf of Mexico OCS leasing area, was prepared by an employee "who took an old EIS, Xeroxed it, and just went through it and edited it and changed the names."

She also alleged that many environmental impact statements, especially those prepared for Alaska, rely on outdated information, inaccurate census figures, and other faulty data. A University of Alaska anthropology professor, Dr. Kerry Feldman, who worked on the cultural impact sections of the Gulf of Alaska OCS lease proposal, told us in October 1976 that the impact statements could not possibly assess the cultural impact OCS would bring because no on-site investigations of any coastal communities were conducted.

In March 1976, Feldman had filed an affidavit supporting the state of Alaska's effort to block OCS lease sales in the Gulf of Alaska. Feldman, head of the University's Division of Behavioral Sciences, said in the affidavit that his final report was distorted and that many of his conclusions were changed or omitted by Interior Department officials to soften his criticism of the impact of proposed OCS leasing. He charged that the Bureau of Land Management's Outer Continental Shelf office in Anchorage had made "several significant editorial changes" which "resulted in an EIS containing a description of social-cultural impacts that were (a) less severe than I anticipated in my original report and (b) made to appear more ambiguous than was my considered professional opinion."

One of the most serious alleged distortions of Feldman's findings involved the previously mentioned population projections for the small Tlingit Indian town of Yakutat. If OCS went into that community in a big way, Feldman had concluded that there could be as many as 4,000 people in the town by 1985, a 900 percent increase over ten years, based on a report by the President's Council on Environmental Quality. But he said that Donald Henninger, of the Bureau of Land Management's OCS office in Anchorage, insisted that he use the number developed by that office—a population gain of 115 persons (a 29 percent increase) by 1985. Henninger, in response to Feldman's allegations, acknowledged that some of Feldman's findings and recommendations were deleted. "It was not his job to estimate population impact from the sale," Henninger said. "Some of his statements were subjective, political opinion." Besides, Henninger added, "Kerry was hired as a temporary employee. Therefore, he has no inherent right to assume that what he writes will go forward as he writes it. He's subject to the same amount of review" as anyone else who submitted studies for inclusion in the impact statement.

The reality of Yakutat's situation is clearly closer to Feldman's portrayal than the environmental impact statement's. Yakutat residents found that the oil companies had almost overwhelmed their simple fishing village way of life through plans that were set in motion long before the OCS lease sale for the gulf was even held.

Byron Mallott is one of the Native leaders in Yakutat. His family has always exercised considerable influence in the town, which listed a population of 190 in 1970 and about 400 by late 1976. Mallott himself was a former mayor; his father was mayor for twelve years; his brother-in-law was the mayor when we interviewed Mallott in October 1976; his sister was chairperson of the local planning and zoning commission and also a school board member. Mallott was state commissioner of community and regional affairs in the 1970 to 1974 administration of Democratic Governor William Egan. After Egan was defeated in his reelection bid, Mallott went back to Yakutat to run his own policy and program development consulting business. In early 1977, he became president of the Alaska Federation of Natives. With the announcement in October 1974 that the northeast gulf would be the first OCS lease sale area in Alaska, Mallott said, "Yakutat instantly voiced its concern. . . . The city's concern was heightened by the fact that the oil companies had already purchased (from owners of a defunct salmon cannery) all available property that could be used for oil service-related activity. We were presented with a fait accompli."

Working with the state, the community tried to delay the OCS lease sale through the courts. That effort failed when a federal judge refused to block the sale, but the town moved ahead, with the state as its ally, on other fronts. In January 1975, the community began developing its first planning and zoning program. A town commission soon re-zoned the land already purchased by the oil companies to non-industrial uses, thereby preventing its use for OCS-connected activities. In that way, Mallott said, the town took control of the onshore support area which OCS would need. Because of its close cooperation with the community, the state government agreed not to turn over any of its waterfront property to the oil companies without the town's approval. "Of course, the state administration or the city administration could change and decide that we do want growth and lots of it," Mallot said, "No one at any time is ever in complete control, but we feel we are doing as well as possible. We hope our approach can be an example to other communities."

In preparing for the impact of OCS on Yakutat, Mallott obtained a $15,000 grant from the Alaska Federation of Natives to survey Yakutat residents' opinions regarding the coming of OCS. He explained:

> Yakutat is essentially a fishing economy. It's been involved in seasonal salmon-fishing for almost its entire existence. The economy can be characterized as being almost perennially depressed. Welfare is the normal mode of living for quite a number of local residents. So, as you might expect, some conflicting attitudes showed in our study. The results showed people, of course, were concerned about OCS. A large majority felt they wanted to maintain Yakutat as a small town. The people were concerned about the maintenance of natural resources needed for subsistence that could be negatively impacted by population growth. But they were also concerned about unemployment, and wanted the employment opportunities OCS could offer.

Interestingly, Mallott said, residents generally showed "no real concern about the technological aspects of OCS—the oil rigs, oil spills. It really became a population growth issue. People showed strong, healthy skepticism and feared what would happen if Yakutat's growth were to triple."

Mallott tried to steer a cautious course on the OCS issue. He didn't like the OCS program much, but realized that since it appeared inevitable, the community should have as much control over it as possible to minimize its impact and maximize its economic benefits. For example, what onshore facilities are developed, Yakutat leaders told the oil companies, must be owned and operated by the residents and concentrated in a location away from the center of town. The oil companies, as of early 1977, had agreed to all the Natives' terms, prompting Mallott to boast: "They need Yakutat, but we don't need them."

"Basically I share what the local people feel," Mallott said. "I'd like Yakutat to remain a small town. I don't want the Native people submerged, wiped out by insensitive development." Still, despite the town's and the state's best efforts, the speculative boom had already hurt Yakutat. After the accelerated OCS schedule was announced in late 1974, property values increased more than 100 percent in two years. The town, in preparing for the OCS impact, had to increase its budget from less than $100,000 a year to about $500,000 for various services, including street maintenance and police and fire protection, and raised its property tax rate almost threefold.

There was, however, a brighter side. In Mallott's words, "The employment picture has changed pretty significantly." Some thirty persons, all local residents, had been hired by the autumn of 1976 for construction of the OCS service bases, thus reducing many of the local residents' dependence on welfare. In addition, the village Native corporation leased an old Distant Early Warning (DEW) system base from the Air Force, which it converted into housing for transient oil workers.

On Kodiak, the Native regional corporation, Koniag, Inc., has introduced another wrinkle into OCS's onshore impact: dissension among Natives. Native fishermen on Kodiak Island have charged that, in its headlong dash to get its onshore share of the OCS oil dollar, Koniag ignored the detrimental impact offshore oil exploration could have on commercial and subsistence fishing and the village life-style. These conflicts between for-profit Native corporations and Natives who want to preserve their traditional way of life will no doubt intensify in coastal communities throughout Alaska as OCS development spreads.

The federal government, under Presidents Nixon and Ford, had shown little concern for residents affected by OCS impact and it also had been unconcerned—or positively reckless—in its attitude toward the vast fishing resources of the Gulf of Alaska. In our visits to Kodiak Island we found the fishermen there in a virtual state of rage over what OCS development would do to some of the richest fishing grounds in the world. Tom Casey, manager of the United Fishermen's Marketing Association, a group of 450 king crab and salmon fishermen on Kodiak, told us:

> It's ironic that the Americans now turn their attention to the oceans as an alternative food supply while simultaneously we rush ahead with this oil development that can cancel out any future gain from the very fertile and shallow continental shelf waters of Alaska. It particularly enrages us that the Japanese, who have so destroyed many of Alaska's fisheries in the last fifteen years, may very well become the benefactors of OCS oil development. I can't convey to you how outraged it makes me without lighting a fire someplace.

And, from an economic standpoint, even minor oil spills would be enough to cripple the commercial fishing interests, according to Casey:

It's very grave. The development of oil offshore from Kodiak can bring the fishing industry to a screeching halt. The marketing of our shellfish and salmon is very sensitive to rumor of any imperfection in the product. . . . Can you imagine how susceptible our shellfish will become . . . when people know that we're producing shellfish and salmon from an area that's potentially contaminated by oil spills? . . . It scares the shit out of us, in all honesty. It keeps me awake at night and I don't know what to do except to publicize the risk involved. What are we going to do now, go out there and pump that oil out of the ground and endanger the fisheries to send it to Japan? Or are we going to act a little more wisely and delay the development until we have technology that's foolproof? All they have to do is dump a little oil out there two or three times and the people in Seattle that buy our product are going to tell us to go to hell when we compete for market prices with crab produced in noncontaminated areas. What are we going to do for labor if, in fact, there is a large oil development around Kodiak? There's no way we can pay ten dollars an hour to people who process our seafood.[3]

In his office in Kodiak, Edward Naughton pointed to a map showing a group of numbered tracts off Kodiak where OCS exploration was planned. And then he pointed to key shrimp, salmon, and crab areas—which overlapped with the OCS lease tracts. Naughton, a respected member of the state House of Representatives when we interviewed him in late 1976, also heads the Shrimp Trawlers Association, an organization which represents Kodiak's shrimp fishermen. Naughton recounted many possible hazards that OCS posed to the fisheries. Besides the problem of snagging shrimp nets on underwater pipelines, and the possibility of major spills, minor spills would likely occur which could interfere with the reproduction process of crab and salmon.

Now the thing that concerns us is that if you add just minute amounts of crude oil to water in which you find Tanner crab, for instance, it completely louses up their communication system, and the female can be ready to copulate and the male won't get the signal because of this oil in the water, or just the reverse.

Marine biologist John L. Culliney raised similar concerns in his 1976 book, *The Forest of the Sea: Life and Death on the Continental Shelf*. Culliney wrote that OCS development in the Gulf of Alaska

[3] Seafood processing workers were getting about $4.50 an hour.

. . . raises the possibility of disruption of salmon runs because of chemical interference with the fishes' olfactory homing mechanism. In experiments at the NMFS [National Marine Fisheries Service] laboratory at Auke Bay, salmon fry reacted to and even tried to avoid as little as 1.6 [parts per million] of Prudhoe Bay crude oil in water. Big fish returning to spawn could be just as sensitive. . . . A large oil spill or simple, widespread, low-level contamination, hanging in the water across the continental shelf, conceivably could block thousands of fish from reaching their home rivers. Even if the navigational disruption is only temporary, effects on the delicate timing of egg production and spawning could reduce the reproductive effectiveness of runs in streams throughout southern Alaska.

The Interior Department's final environmental impact statement for the Gulf of Alaska made the same point.

At various hearings on OCS, the oil industry minimized the likelihood of destructive oil spills. Some supporters of OCS development even suggested that spills of large quantities of oil may be harmless to fish and wildlife. Author Culliney and Noel Mostert, author of the tanker classic, *Supership*, both stress that little is known about the effects of oil pollution on the marine environment, but what is known is pretty frightening. In the May 1975 *Audubon* magazine, Mostert wrote:

We still know practically nothing about [oil's] long-term effects upon plankton and phytoplankton, the basic life in the sea upon which all other life directly or indirectly depends because of their critical place in the marine cycles. . . . Crude oil is one of the most complicated natural chemical mixtures on earth. It poisons, smothers, burns, coats, taints. Among many consequences, it can start carcinogenic processes in sea animals, affect reproduction, and cause imbalance in the cycles of plant life. It affects respiratory organs and clogs the filtering mechanisms of fish; it affects the balance, mobility, and resistance of seabirds, when it doesn't simply choke or suffocate them to death. . . . Oil at very low concentrations may cause no deaths but may affect whole marine populations and communities because of different tolerances to it; sensitive species may eventually decline while resistant ones flourish, thus upsetting a delicate balance.

Mostert goes on to detail numerous other examples of what happened to marine life in the wake of other major oil spills over the last two decades. It is not a cheery picture, or one that would lighten the worries of Alaska's fishermen. For example, when the *Tampico Maru* spilled 60,000 gallons of diesel oil at Baja California, Mexico, in 1957, "the spill caused almost total biological devastation immediately. Life was 90 percent restored after three or four years, but certain species were still somewhat changed twelve years later." In 1968, following a spill of 83,000 gallons of crude oil by the *Ocean Eagle* in San Juan harbor, Puerto Rico, "many subtidal and intertidal organisms were killed or damaged by oil and emulsifier, including mollusks, crustaceans, and algae. Ten species of fish were found dead or in a state of stress; fish smother or die in shock," Mostert wrote.

Culliney, writing specifically of the Gulf of Alaska's marine life, said:

> That oil and seabirds do not mix is known to everyone, but this modern law of nature has so far received little attention in the North Pacific. Among the most susceptible birds are densely flocking migrants, especially eiders and other sea ducks. Hundreds of thousands of birds from the Gulf of Alaska to Puget Sound will at various times of the year be in the potential drift path of oil from tanker accidents or blowouts. Even the Alaskan offshore birds, the solitary soarers which include the magnificent spring and summer visitors, the blackfooted and Laysan albatrosses, all close relatives, have unusually low body temperatures and presumably low metabolic rates, which means they could be affected severely by even a light oiling. Losing only a small proportion of insulating protection, they might succumb to hypothermia or irreversible chilling, while a bird with a higher metabolic rate would survive. The Gulf of Alaska, with its fearsome storms and frequent earthquakes, *is quite possibly the worst place on earth so far slated for large-scale petroleum production.* [Emphasis added.]

Given these kinds of examples, it is no wonder that the Alaskan fishing industry especially fears the development of offshore oil and the use of tankers to transport the oil through some of the world's most hazardous waters. Fishermen are especially concerned because their staple catch, salmon, already has seriously declined in Alaskan waters in recent decades.

Statewide salmon harvests hit their all-time high in 1936 with 126 million fish caught. This dropped steadily until 1959 when the catch was 25 million. Poor federal management practices before statehood, which led to overfishing, helped deplete the supply. Particularly controversial in pre-statehood days was the use of fish traps by fishing interests based on the Lower-48. The traps, made illegal immediately after statehood, were so efficient that they picked up huge quantities of salmong going to and from breeding grounds, thus interfering with normal reproduction cycles.

After statehood was achieved and the state assumed control of its fisheries in 1960, the salmon catches increased considerably during the 1960s, to more than 50 million salmon per year. Then, the catches began to decline again, according to Alaskan fishermen, because of overfishing by foreign fleets, particularly the Japanese. At any rate, the U.S. salmon harvest in Alaskan waters fell from 47.5 million in 1971 to 32 million in 1972, then dropped even further in 1973 and 1974 to 22 million both years. In 1975, catches were up somewhat, to 26 million; then they jumped to 41.7 million in 1976, the best season since 1971 but considerably below the 1965–70 levels of about 68 million salmon. Southeastern Alaska, the hardest hit by salmon overfishing, continued to experience the worst shortages of any salmon area of the state.

Despite the overall upswing, state officials were not overly optimistic that the salmon fisheries were on their way to the levels of the 1930s—or even the 1960s. Carl Rosier, director of the state's Division of Commercial Fisheries, told reporters in late 1976: "It's a little difficult to say we are on the road to recovery . . . [based on] the catch figures."

In an effort to keep salmon stocks from being further depleted, the state enacted a "limited entry" law in 1973 to limit the number of fishermen permitted in the Alaska salmon fisheries at the 1972 level. The rationale for the law was that between 1961 and 1973, the number of people harvesting the dwindling stocks had more than doubled. Some 9,040 salmon fishing permits were issued under the new legislation, with 78 percent of those going to Alaska residents. The complicated, controversial measure was supported by some conservation-minded people, but attacked by others of like mind. Some argued, for example, that while the law limited the number of fishermen, it didn't limit their catch, and the catch was the relevant factor in restoring the salmon fisheries. Defenders of limited entry claimed that the law was the only thing preventing a new onslaught of fishermen from the Washington State area, where a court decision had severely limited the number of salmon commercial fishermen could catch in waters off that state. That extremely controversial 1973 federal court decision granted Indian tribes 50 percent of the annual salmon harvest in Washington under an old treaty. Their previous share of the catch had been about 5 percent. This left some 5,200 non-Indian commercial fishing boats in that state suddenly cut off from almost half of their traditional salmon harvest.

An effort to repeal Alaska's limited entry law was put on the ballot in 1976, but the voters chose to retain the program. And limited entry had probably been of some minimal help in the attempt to replenish the state's fisheries. However, it was clear that different strategies were still needed to improve the fish supply. Edward Naughton, the Kodiak shrimp fishing representative quoted earlier and an opponent of limited entry, suggested one:

> The real need is for proper enforcement of the existing conservation regulations. With or without limited entry, we need sufficient enforcement to insure propagation of future salmon stocks. The real problem is the wide geographic distribution of spawning streams and the need for larger protection forces. . . .
>
> But there are other reasons for depressed fish stocks than just too many boats and fishermen robbing the creeks. Lack of proper water temperature in spawning beds, low water volumes, shifts in currents, fluctuating predator populations,. etc., all affect fish populations.

Another strategy, strongly backed by some state officials, was upgrading state hatchery operations. A big step in that direction occurred in 1976 when voters approved a $29.2 million bond issue for hatchery and rearing facilities for five Alaskan species of Pacific salmon. And the Fishery Conservation and Management Act of 1976, which imposed U.S. jurisdiction over fisheries to 200 miles from its shores, gave the U.S. the leverage to try to reach a satisfactory agreement with Japan over that nation's harvest of salmon and other fish in the high seas off Alaska. Under the law, fishery management plans and catch limits were devised for various areas of the country and types of fishing, including the Japanese high seas salmon catches off Alaska. The draft environmental impact statement for the plan, prepared by the National Marine Fisheries Service, noted that until World War II, salmon fishing in North America was confined to coastal areas and rivers of Canada and the United States. But this soon changed:

> Over the past twenty-five years many millions of salmon of North American origin, mainly from rivers in western Alaska, have been intercepted by Japanese fishing vessels. The interceptions have impacted severely on the onshore salmon fisheries of western Alaska, and there is a need for more effective control of Japan's high seas salmon fisheries.

According to the draft environmental impact statement, high seas salmon fishing is "biologically wasteful" because it "reduces productivity by harvesting immature fish" which, if not caught in their immature state, would grow and reproduce, thereby increasing the salmon supply. In addition, the statement noted that the Japanese use of nylon gill nets—illegal for U.S. fishermen—on the high seas results in "one fish killed (and lost) for every [immature] fish landed," and one fish dead for every three mature fish landed.

Besides salmon, Alaska's fisheries are noted for king crab, snow (Tanner) crab, shrimp, and halibut. Overall shellfish catches by Alaskan fishermen increased substantially since the advent of statehood, rising from 42.1 million pounds in 1960 to about 260 million pounds in 1974, although dropping off slightly to 245 million pounds in 1975. Catches of Alaska's renowned king crab, however, sharply declined. The catch plummeted from a high of 159.2 million pounds in 1967 to a low of 52.2 million pounds in 1970. After slight improvements in 1971 and 1972, the catch dropped back to 55.8 million pounds in 1973, then increased the next three years to 76.8 million pounds, 95.4 million pounds, and about 100.1 million pounds. Mid-1976 figures showed that the catch at that point for king crab was 70 percent higher than for the previous year at the same point, while shellfish catches overall were almost double what they were the previous year. State economists attributed the overall increase to "strengthening prices."

In addition to these better known fish and shellfish, Alaskan waters are also rich in what are known as bottomfish or groundfish. However, the U.S. makes little use of these potentially valuable resources, leaving them to be taken instead by foreign fleets, particularly those of Japan and the Soviet Union. In 1975, mainly Japanese and Soviet fleets harvested an estimated 4.3 billion pounds of bottomfish—pollock, Pacific Ocean perch, and herring—off Alaska in the Gulf of Alaska and Bering Sea. Economists in Alaska estimate these bottomfish are worh $300 million to $400 million a year to fishermen.

The problem with the bottomfish for the American market is that, although they are just as nutritious and tasty as many "brand-name" fish, they are generally unknown to the U.S. consumer. According to statistics compiled by the U.S. General Accounting Office, more than one third of the fish products bought by U.S. consumers are canned tuna and shrimp. Canned salmon and fish sticks—the latter manufactured from frozen blocks of fillets, primarily cod—made up about 20 percent of U.S. fish consumption. Despite a rising U.S. demand for fish, the U.S. industry has not kept up, and the nation has imported more and more fish over the years. The biggest catches of edible fish by U.S. fishermen came in 1950 when 3.3 billion pounds were landed. The catch of edible fish declined steadily in the 1950s, and has leveled off between 2.3 billion and 2.6 billion pounds in the 1960s and 1970s.

While the U.S. catch has declined and then stabilized, other fishing nations have increased their activity. The world catch increased from 73 billion pounds in 1958 to 145 billion pounds by 1972. After being the second most active fishing nation behind Japan for years, the U.S. had dropped to sixth place by the early 1970s, with a catch amounting to just 4 percent of the world's total catch. At the same time, the U.S. was the world's largest importer of fish products, running a fish balance-of-payment deficit of more than one billion dollars annually for the last decade. Imports reached a high of $1.58 billion in 1973, then declined somewhat in the next two years to $1.5 billion and $1.36 billion in 1974 and 1975, according to U.S. Commerce Department figures.

Bottomfish have attracted little interest from U.S. industry. According to the Alaska Department of Commerce and Economic Development, "groundfish production has not been undertaken because of economic risk in the face of competition with good quality, low-cost imports from Japan, Iceland, Denmark, Canada, and Norway." Also, according to a May 1975 General Accounting Office report on bottomfish, "The fundamental technological research necessary to improve existing products or place new products on the market is generally beyond the financial means of individual members of the industry." From the standpoint of the American consumer, however, the increased availability of domestic pollock would appear to be advantageous. Already, the United States imports over 100 million pounds of pollock annually. The National Marine Fisheries Service estimates that U.S. fishermen could catch 3.6 billion pounds of Alaskan pollock annually if other nations' fleets were restricted in their pollock catches. The magnitude of this figure can be put into proper perspective by noting that it is 1.3 billion pounds greater than the *entire* 1973 U.S. catch of edible fish.

Recognizing that the U.S. is not in a position to exploit Alaska's bottomfish at this time, the regulations promulgated by the National Marine Fisheries Service under the new 200-mile-limit law permitted continued heavy levels of bottomfishing by foreign nations. However, one of the chief purposes of the law is to develop U.S. capabilities of so-called "under-utilized" fisheries, particularly the bottomfisheries around Alaska. The Alaska Department of Commerce and Economic Development has begun a program to provide limited financial subsidies to encourage production of Alaska's bottomfish.

The state legislature in 1976 appropriated $300,000 to support bottomfish development, and the state administration also was applying to the federal government for money for technical assistance in developing the industry.

This discussion of Alaska's fisheries seeks to underscore one point: that Alaskan fish are a resource that has helped supply a sizable percentage of the world's fish products; and it has far greater potential for the future if proper management techniques can be brought to bear on it. Seen in this light, the rush to develop the oil on Alaska's outer continental shelf fishing areas of southern Alaska (Gulf of Alaska) and western Alaska (the Bering Sea) appears all the more ominous and difficult to justify. As Kodiak's Tom Casey put it in late 1976:

> This is the first year in the past three that the Russians grew enough to eat [without importing]. The Americans have had problems with floods and droughts in the last three years in the production of corn, wheat . . . The fishery resources of the world's oceans may well supplement the world diet, if the climate continues to become colder as it has in these latitudes lately. And yet so little attention is paid to the preservation of these resources.

If OCS development poses a special threat to the fishing industry in sub-Arctic waters off Alaska, consider the possible consequences of OCS drilling in the Arctic North: under-ice wells spouting oil for an entire winter; dangers in using pipelines in treacherous ice-filled waters to carry the OCS oil ashore; ice flows carrying spilled oil into both the North Pacific and the North Atlantic from the Beaufort, Chukchi, and Bering Seas; birds, animals, sea life killed. Dr. Gunter Weller, a professor of geophysics at the University of Alaska in Fairbanks, gave some chilling examples of what could happen during the course of OCS exploration in Arctic waters. Weller, when we interviewed him in the summer of 1976, was under contract to the Arctic Project Office of the U.S. National Oceanic and Atmospheric Administration (NOAA), serving as project manager for an OCS environmental assessment program in the Beaufort Sea. Said Weller:

> If you drill from a drill rig from a ship, and since you have only a very short season in which the whole Beaufort Sea is ice-free—about two months, three months at the most—and at the end of that season you hit a well, a blowout, you can't hope to drill a relief well before the ice comes in. You have to leave the area with your ship, and the possibility exists that for the whole winter that well will spout oil into the environment.

In his book, marine biologist Culliney detailed the impact of such blowouts in Arctic waters:

> If this [blowout] occurred in late summer or fall, shortly before the freeze-up, Canadian experts point out that the well could run wild for nine or ten months. Stopping a blowout on the open shelf of the Beaufort Sea is now considered impossible. The usual technique is to drill another hole by the first and force great amounts of heavy drilling mud down to plug the area around the underground openings, thus holding back the reservoir pressure. But the drilling equipment on the open shelf cannot be left in place during the winter, since it would be swept away by the shifting ice. An average well, running out of control for nearly a year, would spew nearly 90,000 cubic meters of crude[4] into dark, frigid waters . . . spread in a thin layer over hundreds to thousands of square kilometers.

Weller told us that the danger of oil spills on ice would diminish "if you drill from a gravel island or a fixed structure." But, he added, "that technology doesn't exist today. In deep water you have to drill from a ship, so only in the very near-shore areas can you hope to dig a relief well in a hurry [in the event of a blowout]. In the deeper waters, you have to drill from a ship and there the prospect of a big blowout, or the possibility of big pollution, is really quite fantastic."

In drilling that has been authorized in Canada off its shores in the Beaufort Sea, the Canadian government has mandated a very short season for exploration and has required the posting of a $50 million oil spill cleanup bond. The bond may prove to be a moot requirement, Weller said, because "I don't think there's any effective technology that allows you to mop up oil on ice. No effective technology at all."

When oil spills do occur in Arctic waters, their potential for destroying fish, animals, birds, and sea mammals is great. This, in turn, would prove greatly harmful to the subsistence life-style of the North Slope Eskimo communities. According to documents published by the Arctic Project Office, such destruction of marine and wildlife could be spread over wide areas because of the tricky nature of sea ice:

> Generally, in ice-covered waters the oil is transported by the ice which is driven primarily by the wind, often in the opposite direction to ocean currents. . . . An under-ice well blowout scenario must consider ice trajectories throughout the Arctic Ocean and the possibility of the ice carrying the oil both into the North Pacific and North Atlantic.

[4] About 23.5 million gallons.

Oil spills, according to the Artic Project Office, could severely harm sea birds, which it describes as "highly vulnerable to oil pollution. Direct effects include loss of insulating characteristics of feathers, loss of ability to swim or fly, ingestion of oil as a result of feeding or preening, and failure of oil-coated eggs to hatch." Marine mammals (beluga and bowhead[5] whales, ringed seals, bearded seals, walrus) and polar bears also could be seriously harmed by an oil spill. The Arctic Project Office stated:

> One critical aspect of the ice-dominated environment that may tremendously magnify the potential impact of oil on the mammals is the limited amount of open water that is present in or about the edge of the pack ice. The small open areas are vital to the ice-associated mammals for movement, breathing, and feeding and such areas may hold oil concentration for long periods of time. Contamination of fur in polar bears and of the respiratory passages and digestive tracts in all the mammals, would probably be an inevitable result of such an exposure.

All of these horror stories are of special concern to the Inupiat Eskimo people of the North Slope, who have lived for thousands of years by hunting, fishing, and trapping.

Eben Hopson is mayor of the North Slope Borough, which is a huge mass of land, the largest local government area in the U.S., making up more than one seventh of the state's land area. It stretches across the top of Alaska, and has a population of only about 4,500. Hopson is regarded as something of a visionary by many Natives. In addition to having been prominent in the Alaska Native land claims fight, he also is a leader in an effort to create a "Circumpolar Inupiat Assembly," which would bind together all of the Arctic Eskimo peoples—in Alaska, Canada, Greenland, and eventually, the Soviet Union. His views often place him at odds with some other Native leaders on the North Slope and throughout the state who are willing to warmly embrace oil developments. Hopson sees the Arctic being overrun by "the politics of oil" if the OCS program is not slowed down or delayed:

> The North Slope Borough has twelve hundred miles of municipal coastline to worry about and protect from harm that could come from unproven and under-developed OCS drilling and extraction technology. The problem seems to be that there is a serious technology gap between what the oil industry wants to do in the Beaufort Sea, and what the industry can now do

[5] Bowhead whales are among several endangered species in the area that could be affected by OCS development.

safely and responsibly. The Beaufort Sea is not safe for oil industrial experimentation. For until we Inupiat are satisfied that the oil industry possesses the means to develop the Arctic shelf oil and gas reserves safely, responsibly and economically, we will continue to challenge the plans of the oil industry offshore in the Arctic.

It should be noted again that, even in dealing with spills in less tricky, non-Arctic waters, the technology is woefully inadequate. The 1976 draft environmental impact statement for OCS exploration in the warmer Lower Cook Inlet in southern Alaska, made the following assessment of existing oil spill containment and cleanup technology:

Presently no known method of containment or cleanup is effective in turbulent seas where wave heights exceed eight feet. Mechanical cleanup devices are generally limited to calm waters. . . . Straw, manufactured fibers, and absorbent clays are spread on a slick, with the oil, and collected. Straw is the most cost-effective absorbent, as it holds five times its weight in oil and costs $25 to $50 per ton. However, spreading and collecting the absorbents as well as disposing of the oil-contaminated materials pose serious logistical problems. The use of dispersants as well as burning and sinking agents in U.S. coastal waters is strictly limited by the National Contingency Plan because of their potentially toxic effects on marine organisms.

This statement alone should have been enough to sink OCS plans in virtually all Alaskan waters, for the time being at least. We have already mentioned the frequency of storms in the Gulf of Alaska. But this impact statement shows that even on "average" days in the Gulf of Alaska, oil spill containment would be close to impossible.

On August 12, 1976, state officials were treated to an oil spill cleanup demonstration project by Union Oil Company in Kenai. The demonstration, the state reported, "represents the most recent oil spill technology currently existing" and it took place in relatively calm Cook Inlet where state-owned offshore oil has been produced by the oil companies for a number of years. The system, operating from aboard the *Recovery*, a converted purse seine vessel, used a skimmer for collecting the oil and 1,000 feet of boom for containing the collected oil. According to a publication of the Alaska Coastal Management Program of the governor's office, the system was totally inadequate.

Commander Nichols feels that in any kind of current there is no way that the oil can be contained around the platform or drilling rig since the current will push the containment boom and tear it up. He feels the system will work at 1.5 knots. This containment efficiency appears to be totally inadequate as the mean maximum speed of Cook Inlet tidal currents is 3.8 knots and often exceeds 6.5 knots.

The state publication commented that viewing officials had reached the following conclusions:

- The system will only work in nonstorm conditions.
- It will only contain small spills, and would need to be standing nearby to do that.
- Good try by Union, but demonstration only shows that a much greater and larger effort will need to be made to contain a large spill.

Fears of oil spills in Alaskan waters increased as the date for the opening of the trans-Alaska pipeline drew near in 1977. These fears were exacerbated by the well-publicized spate of oil tanker accidents in U.S. waters in late 1976 and early 1977, and by the North Sea oil well blowout which sent 20,000 tons of crude spewing into the waters off Norway in April 1977. With the Prudhoe Bay oil and most future petroleum from OCS and other Alaska sources expected to be transported to markets by tankers, the horrible record of six Liberian-registered tankers involved in accidents in U.S. waters between December 15, 1976, and January 4, 1977, was especially chilling to many Alaskans:

- December 15—The *Argo Merchant* ran aground off Nantucket Island, Massachusetts, leading to a 7.6-million-gallon oil spill called the worst ever on the U.S. Atlantic Coast.
- December 17—The *Sansinena* exploded in Los Angeles harbor, killing nine persons and injuring more than fifty.
- December 24—The *Oswego Peace* spilled 2,000 gallons of oil in Connecticut's Thames River.
- December 27—The *Olympic Games* ran aground in the Delaware River near Marcus Hook, Pennsylvania, spilling 133,500 gallons of oil.
- December 29—The *Daphne* ran aground in Puerto Rico's Guauanilla Bay, but was refloated without a spill.
- January 4—The *Universe Leader* ran aground in the Delaware River, off Salem, New Jersey, about twenty miles downriver from where the *Olympic Games* ran aground eight days earlier. No oil was reported spilled.

In addition to the Liberian-registered ships, the *Grand Zenith*, a Panamanian-registered ship carrying 8.2 million gallons of oil, was reported missing in early January 1977 somewhere in the North

Atlantic, off the New England Coast, and was believed to have sunk.

The seeming rash of tanker accidents was not really a rash at all. It was just that the press had been paying little attention to what had been going on in the tanker world. Scarcely a week went by, industry figures show, that there wasn't a tanker accident somewhere in the world. As it turned out, 1976 was a record year for tanker oil spills and tanker destruction, with figures for the first nine months of the year alone surpassing those for any previous full year. The Tanker Advisory Center, a New York–based industry organization, reported in early 1977 that thirteen tankers, with a capacity of 940,000 dead-weight tons, were declared a total loss in the first nine months of 1976. This exceeded the previous full year's high of 815,000 dead-weight tons lost, set in 1975. Tankers in the first nine months of 1976 spilled 198,277 tons of oil into the world's waters, exceeding the previous record for a full twelve months. (The all-time single most disastrous tanker oil spill occurred in 1967 when the Liberian tanker *Torrey Canyon* ran aground off the Scilly Isles and spilled its entire 123,000-ton cargo in the English Channel and on the beaches of the British and French coasts.)

The National Academy of Sciences estimates that some 6.1 million metric tons of oil from various sources, including 2.1 million metric tons from tankers, finds its way into the world's seas anyally. *Supership* author Mostert has written that this is undoubtedly a conservative estimate. With more and bigger tankers operating in world waters every year the chances of more—and worse—accidents and spills[6] occurring are enhanced.

The well-publicized tanker incidents of late 1976 and early 1977 were not very cheering to many Alaskan fishermen and environmentalists. It is this kind of spectacle of tankers running amok in the warmer, less hazardous waters of the Lower-48 that leads to the Alaska fishermen's nightmares.

The makeup of the tanker fleet that was secheduled to take the Prudhoe Bay oil from the Alaskan port of Valdez to West Coast markets also had many fishermen, environmentalists and state officials worried. State Pipeline Coordinator Charles Champion told a U.S. Senate Commerce Committee hearing in early January 1977 that the U.S. flag tankers that will carry the Prudhoe Bay oil to

[6] To say nothing of possible future risk of a liquid natural gas explosion at sea if the El Paso proposal for bringing Prudhoe Bay gas to market is selected.

market "don't meet the minimum safety standards." Champion, representing Governor Hammond, urged the adoption of nine new federal safety measures as safeguards against major oil spills. "Do we need an environmental disaster to accomplish what we need to accomplish?" Champion asked the committee. Among Champion's recommendations for new safety measures were ones to require that:

• All tankers have segregated ballasts—separate tanks for oil and ballast water. Tankers without segregated ballast routinely discharge a mixture of oil and water during cleaning operations. Water pollution caused by such discharges may account for as much as 90 percent of all oil pollution in the world's waters, many scientists say, making such deliberate spills more significant overall than the headline-grabbing tanker disasters.

• All tankers be fitted with double bottoms or double hulls. A Coast Guard study has indicated that double bottoms would prevent 87 percent of oil pollution when ships are grounded.

• All ships be equipped with long-range navigational equipment to tie into a sophisticated U.S. Coast Guard system called Loran-C, which covers the entire U.S. and Canadian West Coast.

• Gas inerting systems be installed on all tankers to deal with the possibility of an explosion, such as occurred in Long Beach, California in December 1976, killing eleven persons.

• There be at least two marine radar systems, including some form of collision avoidance system, on all tankers.

• The ships achieve more maneuverability, either through installation of special equipment called lateral thrusters or through the use of tugboats.

Champion charged that former Interior Secretary Rogers C. B. Morton had reneged on a promise he made to Congress in 1972—one year before the pipeline authorization bill was passed—to increase safety measures for tankers operating in Alaskan waters. (Morton had testified before Congress's Joint Economic Committee that the Alaska tankers would be required to have segregated ballast systems, incorporating a double bottom.) Of the 36 tankers designated by the oil industry to carry the Prudhoe Bay oil, only 10 had either double hulls or double bottoms, and only 16 had segregated ballast tanks. Regulations promulgated by the U.S. Coast Guard in early 1976 required all new tankers to have segregated ballasts; however, 20 of the ships in the Alaska fleet were not covered by these regulations. Seventeen of the tankers also lacked gas inerting systems, and 21 had no collision avoidance systems.

The concern over the inadequacy of the tankers' safety systems was heightened by the narrow channel from Prince William Sound to Valdez, the presence of frequent storms, high waves, winds, and fog along the tanker routes, and the great potential for earthquakes in the Prince William Sound area.

Champion told the Senate Commerce Committee that the safety standards he was proposing would add only one fourth of a cent a gallon to the cost of gasoline at the pump, a small price to pay to lessen the danger of irrevocable environmental damage. He said new regulations were needed because of Coast Guard refusal to set stricter standards for U.S. and foreign vessels. The governors of Alaska, Washington, and Oregon had asked the Coast Guard to set stiffer standards for U.S. ships engaged strictly in domestic trade, such as those carrying Prudhoe Bay oil, but the Coast Guard said it had no authority to differentiate between foreign and U.S. vessels. A group of environmental organizations, which sued the U.S. Transportation Department in 1976 to get it to require the Coast Guard to impose stricter tanker regulations, called the Coast Guard "woefully timid and ineffectual."

One other not-so-cheering thought: foreign tankers are much less safe than U.S. tankers. And if some Alaskan oil is eventually shipped to Japan, it can be sent in foreign tankers. The Jones Act, discussed more fully in the next chapter, requires that shipments only from one U.S. port to another (and not from a U.S. port to a foreign port) be carried in U.S.–made ships flying U.S. flags. It costs considerably more to ship products in U.S., rather than foreign tankers, mostly because of higher labor costs.

In the event of a spill of Alaskan oil, the Interior Department has proposed a limited liability system. On January 19, 1977, the department published proposed regulations which would set up a $100 million oil spill liability fund for tankers transporting oil from Valdez to the domestic markets. The fund, called the Trans-Alaska Pipeline Liability Fund, would be built up by a five-cents-per-gallon assessment on the owner of the oil at the time it is loaded on a tanker at Valdez. The owner and operator of the vessel involved in an accident would be liable for the first $14 million of claims allowed, with the fund paying the balance of further claims up to $100 million. Claims of more than $100 million would be handled through court suits. As proposed, the fund would be dominated by the industry, and there would be no public, or environmental, representatives. Each oil company owner of the pipeline and a representative of the secretary of the interior would administer the fund.

The state also planned to announce later in 1977 its own proposal to create a liability fund of $30 million to cover spills in state waters. Instead of a per-barrel fee on oil, the state fund would accumulate the monies from owners of oil tankers and oil terminals based on assessments of their risk. Thus, for example, tankers with safety features, such as double bottoms, would pay lower premiums than those with single bottoms.

Oil spills, of course, can not only destroy fishing grounds but kill wildlife and ruin beaches, as the Santa Barbara channel blowout in 1969 showed. Although it is not widely recalled, the Santa Barbara horrors indirectly resulted in a reprieve for Alaska's offshore areas. In early 1969, the Interior Department had issued a call for nominations for areas to be leased in the northern Gulf of Alaska. Twenty-six companies proposed approximately 4.6 million acres for leasing. The sale was tentatively scheduled for mid-1969 but was canceled after protests throughout the United States over the Santa Barbara affair and over the dangers posed by outer continental shelf development.

In August 1976 Guy Martin, then the state commissioner of natural resources, wrote federal Interior Secretary Thomas S. Kleppe, asking for a delay in the federal OCS leasing timetable for Alaska. Martin wanted more time for studies of areas where environmental damage could be severe, or where risks could be great. For example, under the state's proposal, no date would be set for leasing in the pack ice area of the Beaufort Sea, or in the Bristol Bay and Saint George basins of the Bering Sea. Other areas of the Beaufort Sea would be the last leased in April 1981.

The Hammond administration cited a host of problems which it said made the delayed schedule necessary:

- Coastal communities laboring under great time pressures needed more time to plan for OCS.
- Onshore support activities for OCS already had exacted a high per capita cost from Alaskans.
- The lack of West Coast oil refinery capacity could mean that oil from Alaska's OCS would merely add to the oil glut expected on the West Coast when the oil began to flow through the trans-Alaska pipeline.
- More complete environmental information of all types was

needed to make objective, rational decisions on the safest offshore areas to lease.

• There were doubts about technological capability of drilling and oil spill cleanups, particularly in icebound waters.

• OCS threatened damage to fisheries.

No dates were proposed by the state for the Saint George or Bristol Bay basins, Hammond said, because the state saw a considerable need for more research to insure protection of the fisheries in those areas. No date was suggested for the pack ice area of the Beaufort Sea because that hinged on improved technology for drilling and cleaning up oil spills in pack ice. Because the Beaufort Sea lies directly north of the vast quantities of oil already discovered on land at Prudhoe Bay, the industry strongly suspects substantial offshore oil wealth there and sees it as one of the biggest prizes in the Alaska OCS hunt.

In the waning days of the Ford administration, the Interior Department delayed the leasing timetable, but Martin said the schedule was still more fast-paced than Alaska desired. In the proposed revision offered by the state, the Hammond administration reluctantly acceded, in the spirit of compromise, to federal plans to hold a lease sale in early 1977 for the Lower Cook Inlet in south central Alaska. To many environmentalists and fishermen, Hammond's decision not to fight the Lower Cook Inlet leases ran counter to his own earlier commitment to protect the ecologically valuable Kachemak Bay, adjacent to the Lower Cook Inlet.

It is useful to examine the Kachemak Bay controversy as it relates to OCS, because it is an unusual oil story. Kachemak Bay is regarded as commercially one of the most productive shrimp and crab breeding grounds in the world. The North Pacific Fisheries Association reported that the highest harvest per acre (200 pounds) is gathered each year from this bay. In addition, commercial fishermen in the bay annually catch some 5.2 million pounds of shrimp, 2.1 million pounds of king crab, and several thousand pounds each of salmon, herring, and dungeness crab. In 1974, the commercial fishery harvest there totaled $11.2 million. In addition, the bay's environs are inhabited by millions of birds, sea otters, seals, stellar sea lions, whales, and such endangered species as the peregrine falcon and the gray whale.

The value of Kachemak Bay was recognized by the Alaska State Legislature when it passed a law in 1974 making the bay a "critical habitat" area. The legislature, in passing the law, noted the bay's valuable fishing resources and the fact that it serves as the breeding grounds for three species of crab and five species of shrimp. But in late 1973, shortly before that legislation was passed, the administration of Governor Egan leased for oil exploration 98,000 acres of offshore state lands in Cook Inlet and Kachemak Bay for $25 million. Public hearings on the sale did not come until *after* the sale. In November 1974, angry fishermen and other residents of Homer and Seldovia formed the Kachemak Bay Defense Fund and filed suit, asking the court to declare the sale illegal on the grounds that the state had ignored the law requiring public notice of such sales. Initially, the suit was thrown out of court on the ground that it had not been filed soon enough after the sale. But in July 1976, the state Supreme Court ruled that the dismissal of the case by the lower court was in error, and ordered a new trial. Two of the court's five justices in a minority opinion said that the sale was clearly illegal and that no new trial should even be needed.

In 1976, while the suit was pending and before the Supreme Court decision, Hammond asked the state legislature for authority to buy back the Kachemak Bay leases—or take them back by eminent domain condemnation proceedings, if necessary. The proposal, needless to say, set off a storm of protest from the pro-development forces, who charged that the state was reneging on a deal and was showing that it couldn't keep its word in transactions with business interests. Especially vehement were the *Anchorage Times* and Teamster boss Jesse Carr, both of whom charged that Hammond's action further demonstrated how the governor planned to stifle and strangle growth in the state. Hammond, in his 1976 State of the State address, defended his action, saying the request was necessary because the citizenry had not been consulted in advance about oil development occurring in this rich, productive bay, which also served as "the recreational backyard of our largest urban center (Anchorage)." The legislature passed the measure, allowing Hammond to negotiate with the oil companies on a buy-back price and, if that failed, to reacquire the leases through condemnation proceedings in which the courts would ultimately determine a fair price for the land. Though many legislators complained that Hammond did little to lobby for passage of the bill, the governor still put himself on the line in support of a highly volatile proposal. Much of the credit for passage was given to then senate president Chancy Croft (Democrat, Anchorage), a gutsy and effective liberal, who rounded up the necessary votes. Spurring passage was an extraordinarily timely oil spill that occurred in Kachemak Bay just before the vote when the drilling rig *George Ferris* became stuck in the bay's mud and had to be blasted free with explosive charges. In early January 1977, the governor announced that the state had reached a buy-back agreement with the major Kachemak Bay leaseholder, Standard Oil of California. The agreed-upon payment to the company was $21.1 million—which included the $16.6 million price originally paid to the state, plus rentals for the leases paid over three years, interest on the rentals, and exploration work already performed. Similar agreements were reached later in the year with two of the other three oil companies holding Kachemak Bay leases.

Many environmentalists and fishing interests were thus puzzled by Hammond's support for the lease buy-back and his administration's later acquiescence to the federal OCS lease sale for Lower Cook Inlet. In his administration's revised OCS lease sale proposal to the federal government in August 1976, Hammond said the state would agree to the Lower Cook Inlet sale and would sell its own leases on state offshore land in the Beaufort Sea—if the Interior Department would indefinitely delay scheduled federal lease sales in the Bering Sea, Bristol Bay, and the pack ice areas of the Beaufort Sea. Jack Hession, of the Sierra Club's Anchorage office, said that Hammond's trade-off made no sense from either a practical or an environmental standpoint:

> The estimated 200 miles of offshore pipeline in Cook Inlet will be the largest single source of oil spills next to tankers, according to the draft environmental impact statement. And yet, the statement fails to adequately define the impact of the pipelines. The fact that the pipeline routes are not even identified yet leaves the impact statement unquestionably deficient. The statement has not demonstrated the proposed lease sale to be justified either environmentally or economically. . . . The statement provides convincing evidence that there will be massive oil pollution, destruction of human cultural values and possible human health hazards. The fishing industry will be harmed through inflationary economic adjustments, fishing gear destruction and fisheries contamination. Oil spills will sometimes go uncontrolled since there is no adequate spill control mechanism.

Given this background, Hession said, Hammond's proposal to reschedule lease sale dates was a toothless compromise for environmentalists and fishermen. And from a practical standpoint, OCS development on federal lands in the Lower Cook Inlet could result in the oil companies' also draining off oil on the state's offshore lands in the inlet. Hammond opposed oil operations on state lands in Kachemak Bay, yet paradoxically, by not staunchly opposing federal OCS lease sales in Lower Cook Inlet, allowed the oil industry to "establish its first beachhead on Kachemak Bay," Hession maintained.

After the Interior Department moved in late 1976 to schedule the Lower Cook Inlet OCS lease sale for 1977, a number of organizations representing Natives, environmentalists, and fishermen filed suit in U.S. District Court in the District of Columbia in an effort to block the sale. The primary plaintiff, the Native-owned English Bay Village Corporation, stated in court papers:

> The people of English Bay have traditionally lived by subsistence hunting and fishing in the waters on the shores of Lower Cook Inlet in complete harmony with their environment. In analyzing the consequence of the development of OCS oil in Lower Cook Inlet, . . . resulting offshore and onshore impacts of development of an oil and gas field, with a life expectancy of twenty-five years, will destory the subsistence life-style, culture, and heritage of the people of English Bay. . . .

The suit, although unsettled as of early 1977, apparently had some effect, because the Interior Department announced on January 18, 1977, that thirty-two blocks originally slated for leasing had been removed from consideration—including areas near English Bay and two other shore communities, Port Graham and Seldovia. On February 7, 1977, the Interior Department, by then under control of the Carter administration, postponed the Cook Inlet sale, saying it would study the matter further and make a decision later on whether to hold the sale at all. In May, Interior Secretary Cecil Andrus announced that the Cook Inlet sale would be held five months later. At the same time, he also rescheduled the Kodiak area sale from late 1977 to 1979, and the joint federal-state Beaufort Sea sale from 1978 to 1979.

One state official, Robert LeResche,[7] who was director of the Division of Policy Development and Planning in the governor's office, summed up the OCS-versus-fishing dilemma when we interviewed him in late 1976: "If you take people away from these [traditional] industries, fine, it's their choice, they're getting rich. But twenty years from now—or six years, if they don't find anything—then zap, they [oil companies] are gone and what do you have left? You don't have a fishing industry left. And that's what's scary."

[7] LeResche was named by Hammond in early 1977 to succeed Guy Martin as state natural resources commissioner.

XIII

The Japanese Connection

When the bitter winter of 1976–77 was at its coldest, and shortages of natural gas supplies were hitting many areas of the country, Americans were surprised to learn from news accounts that all gas being produced in and shipped out of Alaska at the time was going to Japan. Under a fifteen-year contract with the Phillips Petroleum Company and Marathon Oil Company, the Japanese were receiving all of the 51 billion cubic feet of gas in liquid form exported every year from the Phillips-operated gas liquefication plant at Nikisi in south central Alaska.

While the reports of this arrangement may have been news to most Americans, they weren't to Alaskans, who were aware of the intimate economic bonds between the state and Japan. The Japanese, in fact, were by 1977 well on their way to becoming one of the major economic forces in the state. It was conservatively estimated that Japanese corporations already had invested $300 million in Alaska, primarily in such key state industries as fishing and timber. And that figure was certain to increase because Alaska had much of what Japan needed—oil, gas, fish, timber, and hard-rock minerals. And even though Japan and other nations were forbidden by federal law from obtaining any of the Prudhoe Bay oil, several Japanese corporations had invested in the search for oil, as well as for coal and minerals, in other areas of Alaska. In short, as a nation that must import almost all of its energy resources, Japan lusted after Alaska's oil like a fox after a plump chicken.

A brief listing of the Japanese corporate giants with investments in Alaska shows the great hope Japan has for securing some of Alaska's vast wealth. Investors include Teikoku Oil, Japan's largest oil firm; Taiyo Gyogyo Kabushiki, Japan's largest seafood company; Iwakura-Gumi, Japan's largest lumber company; Mitsubishi Corporation, the world's largest trading company.[1] The presence of these huge foreign companies has produced no major controversy in Alaska, perhaps because the state has a long history of Outside domination. Little has been written in the state's press about the Japanese influence, and most Alaskans, while well aware of the Japanese connection, were only vaguely aware of the specific activities of the Japanese firms.

To some promoters of Alaska's development, in fact, the Japanese presence was welcome, for finding markets for the state's products was crucial to Alaska's future economic growth. And for a variety of reasons, they saw Japan, rather than the Lower-48, as Alaska's best trading partner. Yet some Alaskans resented the influx of Japanese corporations. The state's fishermen in particular felt their livelihoods threatened by "monopolistic" practices on the part of the Japanese-controlled fish processing industry in the state. Other fishermen, however, saw Japanese control of the processing industry as neither better nor worse than the Seattle interests' control of the state's processing industry for decades before the Japanese began buying them out.

And there were benefits accruing from the Japanese links. For one thing, Japanese investment in Alaska strengthens the tie of friendship between the U.S. and Japan. The United States, after all, has invested in numerous other countries, so it is difficult to object on nationalistic grounds to Japanese investment in the U.S. Also, Japanese investment creates jobs in Alaska and helps the state's economy.

Still, there were a number of potential and existing problems related to foreign investment in Alaska, including:

- Tax avoidance. Through complex accounting methods, large foreign corporations could shift their profits to operations outside of

[1] Although the Japanese have a much greater stake in Alaska than do other countries, they are far from being the only nation interested in the state's newfound wealth. The British, for their part, are well represented in Alaska by British Petroleum, which through its merger agreement with Sohio owns the major share of the proven Prudhoe Bay oil reserves. In addition, the British-American Tobacco Co., Ltd., based in the United Kingdom, was listed in state reports as owning two floating fish processing plants operating in Alaska under the name Vita Food Products, Inc. And, as noted in an earlier chapter, a number of Canadian and West German companies were actively engaged in the search for the state's vast mineral resources. Also, in February 1977, it was reported that Saudi Arabia was holding preliminary discussions with the Native-owned Koniag, Inc., about possible Saudi backing for a Koniag bid on Alaska's offshore oil leases.

Alaska, thereby avoiding state and possibly federal corporate income taxes.

• Increased development. Foreign demand for Alaska's resources would accelerate development beyond current domestic demand, thus raising additional environmental concerns and depleting resources the U.S. might itself need in the future. Alaska could become a virtual resource colony of Japan.

• Potential foreign political influence in the state. Foreign corporations in Alaska could win influence through campaign contributions and well-financed lobbying efforts.

• Secrecy. It is difficult enough under ordinary circumstances for federal and state governments to break through U.S. corporate secrecy; it is even more difficult with foreign-based corporations because their overseas records are less accessible and because many use multiple sets of books.

• Monopoly. Japanese corporations operate overseas as virtual extensions of their government. Thus, the normal problems of regulating a monopoly are increased.[2]

Alaska was particularly vulnerable to foreign corporations' influence in 1977. Indeed, the circumstances could not have been less propitious: a state with great mineral wealth, an enormous land mass, a tiny population, and a small government—an irresistible combination for ambitious multinational corporations. As we saw in Chapters VII and VIII, the state was virtually overwhelmed by the pipeline and failed, for various reasons, to give it anything close to the economic and environmental scrutiny it deserved. In future years, as plans for a natural gas pipeline and various other development schemes fly thick and fast, the state is going to find it increasingly difficult to maintain effective controls over major projects. In trying to monitor Japanese and other foreign corporations, the state will find itself confronted with added problems: how to obtain adequate data from, and legal leverage over, enormous foreign-based multinational corporations which act as virtual arms of their government. As of 1977, Alaska officials did not even know the extent of Japanese in-

[2] In their book, *Global Reach: The Power of the Multinational Corporations*, authors Richard J. Barnet and Ronald E. Müller noted these ties between Japanese government and business: "The partnership of government and big business has reached new heights in Japan. The great trading corporations and official ministries are so intertwined that only a sophisticated legal mind can discern where one leaves off and the other begins. Indeed, U.S. business literature employs the code term 'Japan, Inc.' to describe the complex competition from the East."

vestment in the state. Alaska state officials candidly admitted to us that what figures and reports did exist on the subject were incomplete.

Although Japanese corporations were diversifying their investments in Alaska, their greatest impact on the Alaskan economy was clearly in fishery and forest products. The exact amount of Japanese influence was hard to measure because of the lack of comprehensive state or federal studies on the issue. But a rough picture of the situation emerges from those studies that do exist, and from interviews with state officials and business representatives.

In the state's fishing industry, the Japanese were a major force in seafood processing. In fact, some fishing industry representatives told us they believed the Japanese had monopolistic control in the field. One state official, Robert Palmer, special projects coordinator for the governor's Fisheries Council, said the Japanese have a near monopoly, if not an actual one. One state study in 1974 by the Department of Economic Development said that the Japanese controlled at least 20 percent—as much as $70 million worth—of all of Alaska's seafood production. Yet various state officials and fishing industry representatives told us that the study was incomplete and considerably understated the extent of Japanese influence. Representative Don Young put the figure substantially higher. "I believe 90 percent of the canneries are controlled by Japanese money," Young told us.[3] Despite the inadequacy of the studies, it was clear that the Japanese dominated the fish processing industry in certain areas of Alaska, such as Kodiak Island, and were an important force in the industry elsewhere in the state.

One limited study in 1975, after the state Department of Economic Development study, was conducted by the National Marine Fisheries Service. It showed that:

- In 1975, of twenty-six firms in the U.S. fishing industry that were reported to have foreign capital invested in them, twenty-two were in Alaska. All but one of these foreign firms were Japanese. The other was British.
- The largest single Japanese investment in Alaska's fishing industry was in Whitney-Fidalgo Seafoods, Inc., which had a number of seafood processing plants, buying stations, and offices in Alaska

[3] Of all Alaskan officials we interviewed, Young expressed the sharpest criticism of the growing Japanese investment in the state. U.S. citizens had "taken their dollars and bought Japanese Toyotas, Datsuns, etc." and now the Japanese were using those dollars to get Alaska's resources, he said.

(and Washington State), including ones in Anchorage, Ketchikan, Kodiak, Naknek, Petersburg, Port Graham, and Uyak. The company was 98 percent owned by the Kyokuyo Hogei Company of Japan, which had an estimated $11 million investment in the operation. Whitney-Fidalgo alone reportedly produced some 15 percent of all the salmon canned annually in Alaska, as well as other fish products.

• In addition to Kyokuyo, other apparent large investors in Alaska's fishing industry were: Marubeni-Iida, which owned 100 percent of three companies, and had shares ranging from 25 to 50 percent in five others; Taiyo Gyogyo, which owned one company and a 70 percent share in another; and Nichiro Gyogo, which owned 30 percent of one company and, along with Mitsubishi, 50 percent of another.

A third study was made by the U.S. Embassy in Japan in 1975; it too was admittedly incomplete. A look at Kodiak Island's processors gives some idea of just how incomplete the three studies we have mentioned were.

None of the studies listed any more than seven processors on Kodiak Island as having Japanese investment. Yet, Edward Naughton, who heads the Shrimp Trawlers Association on Kodiak, told us that "only two of Kodiak's sixteen processors are not Japanese-dominated," or heavily influenced by Japanese investors. By this, he meant that fourteen of the sixteen processors had at least 25 percent Japanese ownership, or had received loans from Japanese firms or had allowed the Japanese to control their marketing. So, he said, the Japanese dominated Alaska's processing operations, either indirectly or directly. "The Japanese sat down and divided up the state and decided who was going to have what."

We asked Naughton if this was any worse than the days when Seattle fishing interests dominated Alaska. "No, it really isn't any more dangerous," he replied. It's really "a problem of nationalism. In Alaska, we're constantly fighting the problem of being colonized. And to me, it doesn't make too much difference if the head of the colonial firm is in Seattle or Tokyo."[4]

But Naughton's point was that a monopoly situation in Alaska fish processing was harmful, no matter who controlled it, and that it was important to Alaska fishermen that this control be broken. "I've

[4] Naughton first noted that Japan had bought out so many fishing industry firms in Seattle "that when you say 'Seattle' today, you really mean Tokyo."

approached the Russians about buying raw shrimp from our fishermen," Naughton said. "You've got to find a way to break the more or less monopoly the Japanese have on the seafood industry here. One way to do this is to get other countries involved."

Tom Casey, the manager of the United Fishermen's Marketing Association, also complained that there was "predominant ownership of processing plants by the Japanese. We believe the Japanese exert a heavy influence on the price structure." Gubernatorial aide Palmer said he hoped that American-controlled firms would move more heavily into the fish processing industry and reduce the opportunity for Japanese monopoly control. Some Native firms appeared to be moving in that direction.

With the passage of the U.S. 200-mile-limit law, and with prospects of a new international law of the sea agreement and a U.S.–Japanese treaty, the amount of fish the Japanese are allowed to take from Alaskan waters would decrease substantially. The 1977 quota under the 200-mile-limit law was 11 percent below Japan's 1976 catch in U.S. waters.[5] This permissible foreign catch could decrease further if Alaskan fishermen moved into the bottom-fisheries, which they had left to the almost exclusive use of the Japanese, the Russians, and a few other nations.

Because any new law of the sea agreement among the world's fishing nations might severely curtail Japanese fishing operations all over the world, it became imperative for the Japanese to seek investments in fishing companies located in the U.S. and other nations. In this manner, the Japanese could insure themselves a substantial supply of fish from outside their own waters to meet the growing demand for seafood at home. The *Japanese Economic Journal* reported on May 14, 1974, that the major Japanese fishing companies were actively forming joint ventures all over the world in order to secure a measure of influence over other nations' fishing grounds. Eventually, the *Journal* reported, imports from these joint ventures would

[5] In early 1977, the Japanese asked the U.S. State Department to reduce the fees proposed to be charged to Japanese fishing in Alaskan waters. Japan said that its fishermen would have to pay more than $10 million annually, and that this rate should be reduced by two thirds. The fees, plus reduced catch quotas, would drive some Japanese fishing operations out of business and force others to cut back sharply, a Japanese government representative said. This would, in turn, create widespread unemployment in the Japanese fishing industry and increase prices for fish, which the Japanese depend upon for 51 percent of their annual protein. "It is the problem of every household in Japan," said Kunio Yonezawa, head of the Japanese negotiating team in U.S.–Japanese fishing treaty discussions.

account for almost one half the total production of Japan's major fishing companies. So what was happening in Alaska is not some dark economic conspiracy by the Japanese, but rather an effort on their part to buy themselves some security for their future seafood needs. Nonetheless, it did not mitigate the need for the state of Alaska and the U.S. government to prevent foreign interests from controlling vital domestic fish resources.

While little was known about Japanese investment in the Alaskan fishing industry, even less was known about the quantity of Alaskan fish exported to Japan. According to 1973 figures, only about $6.6 million in seafood products were exported *directly* from Alaska to Japan that year. That figure was laughable; most of the seafood exported from Alaska went to Japan by way of the Seattle Customs District or custom districts other than Alaska's and thereby lost its identity of origin in the process.

This shuffling around of Alaskan seafood benefits the Japanese financially. "They own the processing plants and the distribution systems right on down the line," Naughton said. The Japanese "harvest and process the fish here in Alaska . . . or sometimes they fish it, cook it and freeze it here, then send it for processing to Washington State," which has no processing tax. Thus, the Japanese use the system so that they "don't let their profits show until they want to, in order to avoid taxes." On certain deals, such as Japanese sales to some Latin American countries, the Japanese firms end up paying no taxes at all to any government. In his capacity as chairman of the Alaska House Budget and Audit Committee, Naughton said that he was told by an official in 1972 that Taiyo Fisheries[6], Japan's largest seafood company, "had never paid a dime of [income] taxes in Alaska and had taken out millions of dollars of products." This was a prime

[6] According to the 1974 and 1975 studies of the Alaskan fisheries mentioned previously, Taiyo had a 90 percent share ($315,000) in B & B Fisheries, Inc., of Kodiak, and a 100 percent share ($550,000) of Western Alaska Enterprises, Inc., both based in Seattle. The Western Alaska firm also was incorporated to do business in Alaska in 1963. Western Alaska Enterprises does not itself operate processing facilities in Alaska. Instead, it manages the production of salmon roe and other products throughout Alaska. B & B Fisheries on Kodiak was a joint venture established in 1967 by Taiyo and a Kodiak processor. Between 1965 and 1971, Taiyo also was involved in a joint venture—Pacific Alaska Fisheris, Inc.—with Peter Pan Seafoods of Seattle. The joint venture was active in the salmon and shrimp canning business in Bristol Bay and on the Alaska Peninsula. In 1975, the Bristol Bay Native Corporation purchased Peter Pan Seafoods for $8 million, acquiring all of its capital stock.

example of how Alaskans were being denied their fair share of the profits of some foreign corporations operating in their state, he said.

Stock ownership in a company is not the only way in which the Japanese exercise their influence over the Alaska fishing industry. The August 1974 study of Japanese investment by the state's Department of Economic Development noted that because fishing in Alaska "is a very seasonal and unstable business, large amounts of operating capital are required during the summer months." And many Japanese firms were only too willing to supply "short-term advances of operating capital for the purpose of obtaining purchase options on future production," the report said. The report went on to note several possible dangers posed by increased Japanese investment in the fishing industry:

> With sufficient involvement Japanese interests may directly or indirectly be able to exert a political influence on policies for fisheries management and regulation. Another concern is that less processing of fish and shellfish may be accomplished in Alaska, leaving more customary work to be done in Japan by lower-cost labor, thus reducing the actual level of the industry to Alaskans. Along this line, it is possible that a vertically integrated Japanese firm could operate in Alaska on a break-even basis and take profits in Japan, thus escaping both state and federal taxes.

Sterling Gallagher, the state's commissioner of revenue, was among those who were disturbed over the influence of Japanese corporations on Alaska's fisheries and other industries. "I'm basically a radical on the subject," Gallagher told us in a late 1976 interview. "We've been ripped off by alien corporations so long I'm sick and tired of it." Gallagher was irritated at how the Japanese sell fish taken from Alaskan waters at extremely low prices to their processing facilities in Washington, and then ship them on to Japan—without paying a processing tax. Also, because they show little or no profit from the sales to their Washington processing plants, they end up paying little or no taxes in Alaska. In an effort to end this apparently legal tax avoidance, the state devised a new "total picture" tax formula to try to get at the foreign-based companies doing business in Alaska, Gallagher said. The state determines what percentage of its business a firm does in Alaska, how much property the firm owns in Alaska relative to its worldwide holdings, and what proportion of its worldwide payroll is in Alaska. If the answers to these three questions were, for example, 3 percent, 30 percent, and 6 percent, respectively, the state would add these together, divide by three and estimate that 13 percent of the corporation's worldwide activities were in Alaska. The state would then apply its tax to 13 percent of the firm's total earnings.

One of the problems to date with adequately taxing foreign firms' operations within the U.S., according to one well-placed source, is that the Internal Revenue Service hasn't had the teams of economists necessary to ferret out the tax liabilities of corporate giants whose operations extend across national boundaries. And, he added, "you can't compute a tax liability if you don't have the information." In addition, the source said, "The State Department has bargained away going after these companies." As a prime example, the source disclosed that one U.S.–based subsidiary of a Japanese firm, the Alaska Lumber and Pulp Company (ALP), had been operating—very profitably, he claimed—in the state since 1953 but "had not paid a cent of income tax, state or federal" as of late 1976. According to an internal memo we obtained that was prepared by the lawyers for ALP on January 11, 1977, the Internal Revenue Service as of early 1977 was contending that ALP owed $4 million in U.S. income taxes for 1968–70. If the IRS prevailed it could then seek an additional $13 million for subsequent years through 1977.

ALP, according to the memo, claimed that it "operated at a loss until recently." At issue with the IRS was a complicated accounting device in which ALP issued some notes to help finance construction of a dissolving pulp mill at Sitka. The notes were issued to what at the time was ALP's parent company, Alaska Pulp Co., Ltd. (APC), a Japanese corporation. Because of financial problems, the memo said, ALP was unable to repay principal and interest on the notes according to the original schedule, and had to renegotiate the repayment schedule. The principal financing had come through the Export-Import Bank of Japan. The IRS contended that the notes actually did not represent indebtedness, under the U.S. tax law definition, but rather were a form of equity investment by ALP's parent company and, therefore, were not deductible for U.S. tax purposes. In its memo, ALP claimed that the IRS "has seized upon narrow technical arguments to recharacterize the nature of these transactions" involving the notes—and had chosen to do so "nearly twenty years after the fact" of their issuance.

ALP was important for more than just the tax problem it presented to the U.S. and the state: it also was a mainstay of the Alaska economy. As of early 1977, it owned one of the only two pulp mills in Alaska (in Sitka); the other, Ketchikan Pulp, although at one time owned partly by the Japanese, was American-owned. According to Jack Shepherd in his book, *The Forest Killers: The Destruction of the American Wilderness*, the ALP firm was "entirely financed with Japanese funds solicited from 15 chemical-fiber manufacturing companies, 21 trading companies and 13 pulp-and-paper companies. The firm contracted with the Forest Service in January 1956 for 5.25 billion board feet of timber to be cut over a 50-year period from Baranof and Chichagof Islands, the part of the Tongass surrounding Sitka."

Because 70 to 75 percent of Alaska's timber production is exported to Japan, any cutbacks in the harvest are keenly felt by the Japanese. As we saw in the controversial 1968 deal (Chapter XI) in which U.S. Plywood–Champion International received the contract—later cancelled—to cut 8.75 billion board feet of timber from the Tongass over a fifty-year period, the chief beneficiary of this largest sale in the Forest Service's history would have been Japan. Because the Japanese are such an important customer for Alaskan wood, any cutback in Japanese demand hurts the state's industry. As a 1976 report by Alaska's Department of Commerce and Economic Development noted:

> Between 1974 and 1975, the volume and value of all the wood harvested from lands in Alaska declined by 26 percent and 34 percent respectively. The volume harvested in 1975 was less than the volume harvested in each of the preceding ten years. . . . As the level of general economic activity [in Japan and the U.S.] declined and as final product producers attempted to reduce their inventories of wood pulp and lumber, the demand for Alaska forest products declined.

The clear message is that Alaska's timber and forest products industries, while relying to a certain degree upon the movements of the U.S. economy, are even more dependent on economic conditions in Japan. Giant timber sales in Alaska have a history of ending up in that country. After Ketchikan Pulp received a fifty-year contract in 1951 to cut 8.25 billion board feet of timber, it turned right around and sold the timber to Japan. Even in 1969, when the National Timber Supply Act was passed by Congress in order to meet what industry and federal government officials said was a timber shortage, almost 70 percent of the wood products from the Tongass were exported, mainly to Japan.

Since ALP was founded in 1953, Japanese investment in Alaska's forest products industry grew to more than $150 million by 1976. As with the fishing industry, Japanese corporations have exerted additional influence by advancing unknown sums of money as credit or working capital to logging contractors and domestic sawmills in Alaska. ALP was by far the biggest Japanese investor in the Alaskan forest products industry. A 1974 state estimate placed ALP's investment at $125.6 million, of which $102.6 million was in its pulp mill at Sitka, $20 million in the Wrangell Lumber Company, and $3 million in Alaska Wood Products, purchased in October 1968. ALP had also invested about $1 million in a housing subsidiary and a store for its employees in Sitka.

The parent Alaska Pulp Company of Japan also had moved into Alaska's seafood industry, and owns Harbor Seafoods in Wrangell. In addition, ALP maintained lobbyists at the Alaska State Legislature, apparently the only Japanese-controlled corporation in the timber and seafood industries to do so. During the 1976 session, the corporation's expenditures for lobbyists' services totaled $5,271. The only other known foreign-controlled company operating in Alaska that was listed as employing lobbyists was British Petroleum, which spent an impressive $45,242 on lobbyists' service and expenses in 1976.

The Japanese have also invested to a more limited degree—an estimated $12.4 million through 1974—in petroleum and mineral exploration in Alaska. A Japanese corporation, North Oil, Inc., invested $1.2 million in oil exploration on the North Slope before Congress passed the trans-Alaska pipeline legislation which banned shipment of Prudhoe Bay oil to foreign countries. Under the law banning the oil shipments abroad, there was one loophole; the president could, with congressional approval, make a determination that it was in the national interest to allow oil to be exported. As we saw in earlier chapters, some of the Prudhoe Bay oil companies were lobbying in 1976 and 1977 to try to divert to Japan some of the expected glut of oil on the West Coast after the pipeline began operating in mid-1977. In addition, according to state figures, Japanese firms had about $10 million invested in 1974 in petrochemicals, primarily in the gas fields of Cook Inlet and the Kenai Peninsula. Japanese investment in these areas was primarily in long-term contracts for liquefied natural gas and urea. As mentioned in the beginning of this chapter, the Japanese were receiving all of the natural gas from Cook Inlet–Kenai Peninsula, which by 1977 was the only area of Alaska producing natural gas for shipment outside the state. Under the contract with Japan, the Phillips and Marathon oil companies provide the 51 billion cubic feet of liquefied gas every year at a delivered price of $1.95 per 1,000 cubic feet. By comparison, during the height of the cold 1976–77 winter, U.S. pipeline companies were paying about $2.15 per 1,000 cubic feet in the nation's biggest market, the Texas Gulf Coast.

In addition to oil, natural gas and timber, the Japanese were eyeing Alaska's many other natural resources. By 1976, Japanese firms had expended more than $1.5 million in mining feasibility studies for coal, iron, magnetite, and fluorite. Although it was difficult to predict what Japan's future in mining in Alaska would be, one likely development, according to some state officials, was for Japanese corporations to enter into mineral exploration ventures with the Native regional corporations. As early as 1973, in fact, at least two of the corporations—Doyon, Ltd., and the Arctic Slope Regional Corporation—had already begun exploring the possibilities of such a mutual venture with four Japanese firms. Former state Commissioner of Economic Development Frank Murkowski said at the time that the chances of Japanese-Alaska Native cooperation in mineral exploration were quite high because "Japan needs resources and the Natives will eventually have control of resources." John Sackett of Doyon added: "People tend to believe that Alaska will just look to American firms for development. That is not our intention. We want to find the best possibilities for our future."

The prospect of Native-Japanese ties raises the possibility that the Native firms might sell some of their land to the Japanese. Some Natives even speculated nervously to us that the Japanese might acquire stock in Native corporations when Native members become legally free to sell it in 1991. Even if the Japanese firms do not become working partners with the Native corporations, however, it appeared likely that the Japanese would be among the Native groups' most important customers.

Tourism may become yet another significant form of Japanese expansion into Alaska. State officials suggested in the early 1970s that the Japanese might come into Alaska and develop recreational facilities and tourist services, as they had done in Hawaii and Guam. One Japanese corporation, the Koskusai Trading Company, even considered developing a ski resort in the Chugach Mountains, but withdrew its plans because of inadequate snow conditions at the site. According to the 1974 report of the state Department of Economic

Development, "Other Japanese companies have, at various times, investigated the possibility of purchasing almost every large hotel property in the Anchorage area."

By 1975 the Japanese had established in Alaska a number of tourist-related businesses which employed about 250 state residents. Alaska travel was promoted in Japan with the theme that it is a land of beauty, recreation, and clean air—in contrast to Japan, where environmental problems are legion and recreational land scarce. In 1973, when 12,000 Japanese tourists flocked to Alaska in record numbers, Japan Air Lines initiated service between Tokyo and Anchorage and also started a subsidiary firm, International In-Flight Catering, at the Anchorage airport. The facility, housed in a new $1.4 million building, turned out some 1,500 meals a day.

* * *

The close business ties between Japan and Alaska were underscored some years ago when Japan established a consulate in Anchorage. The state of Alaska for its part has maintained an office in Tokyo which serves as a contact point between Japanese businessmen and Alaskans. Interestingly, Alaskan imports from Japan would have been virtually nonexistent in recent years were it not for the construction of the trans-Alaska oil pipeline. The $100 million contract for steel pipe for the pipeline initially was won by three Japanese companies in 1969 when it was discovered that no American company made the 48-inch diameter pipe that was needed. By early 1976, Alaska's imports from Japan had declined from 50 percent of all foreign imports in the early 1970s to 42 percent, again most of the imports being steel products and pipe. On the other hand, since 1970 Japan annually has imported goods valued at between 72 and 87 percent of all goods exported from Alaska—more than $200 million worth in 1975.[7] The imbalance, of course, is due mainly to the fact that Japan needs the resources that Alaska has in abundance.

There were other factors which contributed to the close ties between Japan and Alaska. First, Anchorage is considerably closer geographically to Japan than is any other U.S. mainland port. The distance by ship from Anchorage to Tokyo, for example, is 3,900 miles, compared to 5,200 miles between Seattle and Tokyo. A second reason was Japan's removal of strict controls on its investment

[7] In the six-year period 1970–75, Alaska's imports from abroad totaled just under $800 million, with roughly $400 million coming from Japan. Foreign exports from Alaska in the same period totaled almost $1.1 billion, with more than $800 million worth going to Japan.

abroad, which were imposed at the end of World War II. The gradual lifting of the restrictions, completed in 1971, greatly encouraged Japanese investment abroad, which has far outstripped America's in recent years. As we have seen, a not insignificant portion of that investment has been in Alaska. Third, Alaska found it more profitable to trade with Japan than with the Lower-48 states because of the Merchant Marine Act of 1920. Known as the Jones Act, the law requires that all maritime cargo shipped between American ports be carried in American-made ships. By exporting to Japan, Alaska can send goods far less expensively on cheaper foreign ships than it can by sending the same goods on a U.S. ship to a U.S. port—even though the U.S. port might be much closer. As the Alaska Department of Commerce and Economic Development put it: "Higher shipbuilding costs in the United States and higher American wages have created a significant cost disparity between American and foreign shipping costs." State Revenue Commissioner Gallagher told us that the Jones Act adds about one third to the cost of goods shipped between Alaska and other Lower-48 ports. "If there's anything that kills Alaska and Hawaii, it's the Jones Act," Gallagher added. Alaska is in a slightly better position than Hawaii when it comes to importing goods because it at least has a highway link to the Lower-48 states. A state Department of Economic Development publication summed up the case for Alaska-to-Japan exports this way:

> [The Jones Act] alone makes Japanese investment in, and consequent export of, Alaska resources in foreign, primarily Japanese, ships more economically advantageous [to Alaska]. An additional factor is that the Japanese consistently outbid competitors for resource materials.

With corporations from Japan, and other nations, certain to become more of a factor in Alaska's economy in the years to come, it is essential for the state and federal governments to monitor more closely the activities of the foreign corporations. This should be done not out of any xenophobia, but rather to help insure that foreign firms pay their share of taxes and that decisions that affect the fate of Alaska's resources and wilderness be made by Alaskans and other Americans, not by foreign governments and multinational corporations.

As President Eisenhower once observed, "capital is a curious thing, with perhaps no nationality. It flows where it is served best." And as Thomas Jefferson noted: "Merchants have no country of their own. Wherever they may be they have no ties with the soil. All they are interested in is the source of their profits." Although spoken almost two centuries ago, Jefferson's thought is worth recalling in Alaska today; it is an axiom which guides not only the Japanese but all those engaged in Alaska's Second Gold Rush.

Sources

Listed below are many of the sources we used for this book. We have not listed all of the hundreds of newspaper articles which we drew upon; instead, we have listed major articles which provided substantial information or a special insight into an issue. Many of the scores of interviews we conducted in preparation for this book are noted in the text of the chapters. In addition, there were dozens of persons interviewed whose names appear nowhere in the text but who, nonetheless, provided valuable information.

I. Call of the Semi-Wild

STATISTICS ON STATE SIZE

U.S. Census Bureau, 1970 census, updated by interview, January 1977.

Facts About Alaska: The Alaskan Almanac (Anchorage: Alaska Northwest Publishing Company, 1976), pp. 57–66.

CHANGE IN ALASKA

Wallace Turner, "Alaska 15 Years After Statehood," *New York Times*, July 7, 1974.

Bil Gilbert, "The Devaluation of Alaska," *Audubon*, May 1975.

Ron Rau, "The Taming of Alaska," *National Wildlife*, October–November 1976, pp. 18–23.

Michael Rogers, "The Dark Side of the Earth," *Rolling Stone*, May 22, 1975.

Joseph Judge, "Alaska: Rising Northern Star," *National Geographic*, June 1975.

NATIVES

Alaska Native Claims Settlement Act, Public Law 92-203, December 18, 1971, and amendments to the act, January 2, 1976.

POVERTY

Among other studies that deal with this issue are a series of reports by Robert R. Nathan Associates under the general title, *2(c) Report: Federal Programs and Alaska Natives.* The reports discussing this issue are the "Introduction and Summary," "Task I—An Analysis of the Natives'

Well-Being," and "Task II—Federal Programs for Alaska Natives' Benefit." Prepared for U.S. Department of the Interior (Washington, D.C.: U.S. Government Printing Office, 1975).

SEPARATISM

Mary Clay Berry, *The Alaska Pipeline* (Bloomington: Indiana University Press, 1975), pp. 81–82.

TELEPHONE RATES

Long-distance rates obtained from Chesapeake and Potomac Telephone Company, Washington, D.C., March 1977.

CHAUVINISM: REACTION TO STORIES ON ALASKA CRIME

Mike Goodman and William Endicott, "Alaska Today—Runaway Crime and Union Violence," *Los Angeles Times*, November 18, 1975.

FEDERAL LAND HOLDINGS

"Westerners Chafed by U.S. Land Holdings" (Associated Press), *New York Times*, March 13, 1977.

NEWCOMERS

Bryan Hodgson, "The Pipeline: Alaska's Troubled Colossus," *National Geographic*, November 1976.

HOMESTEADING

Janet McCabe (Federal-State Land Use Planning Commission for Alaska), "History of Land Disposal under the Alaska Division of Lands," speech to the Division of Lands Ad Hoc Committee on State Land Practices and Procedures, September 8, 1976.

DEVELOPMENT

"Hickel Claims Imagination Can Tap World's Resources," *Anchorage Times*, October 22, 1976. Hickel quote.

LOBBYING

"Report on Lobbying—1976 Alaska State Legislature," Alaska Public Interest Research Group, October 2, 1976.

WORK FORCE AND BUSINESS STATISTICS

The Alaskan Economy: Mid-Year Performance Report 1976, State of Alaska Department of Commerce and Economic Development, 1976.

Bill Wilson, "Unemployment at 11 Percent," *Anchorage Times*, January 26, 1977.

Alaska Blue Book 1975, Alaska Department of Education, Division of State Libraries, 1975.

AIR TRAVEL

Air fares were provided to us by Alaska Air Lines; Wien Air Alaska; United, and American airlines.

"Poor Safety Record," *Anchorage Times* editorial, October 20, 1976.

SATELLITE HEALTH CARE

Heather E. Hudson and Edwin B. Parker, "Medical Communication in Alaska by Satellite," *New England Journal of Medicine*, December 20, 1973.

II. Call of the Wild

HISTORY

Ernest Gruening, *The State of Alaska* (New York: Random House, 1968).

Berry, *Alaska Pipeline* (previously cited).

Olivia Vlahos, *New World Beginnings: Indian Cultures in the Americas* (Greenwich, Connecticut: Fawcett, 1972).

William Brandon, *The American Heritage Book of Indians* (New York: Dell, 1968).

Lael Morgan, *And the Land Provides* (Garden City, N.Y.: Doubleday, 1974).

Robert D. Arnold, *Alaska Native Land Claims* (Anchorage: Alaska Native Foundation, 1976).

Claus-M. Naske, *An Interpretative History of Alaskan Statehood*, (Anchorage: Alaska Northwest Publishing Company, 1969).

Robert R. Nathan Associates, Inc., *2(c) Report: Federal Programs and Alaska Natives*, "Introduction and Summary" (previously cited).

III. Citizen Atwood

"OIL AND THE PIPELINE" SECTION

Headlines cited come from *Anchorage Times*'s "Oil and the Pipeline" sections of August 28, 1976, and October 23, 1976.

ATWOOD BIOGRAPHY, PERSONAL FINANCIAL WORTH

Jim Scott, "Robert B. Atwood: Anchorage Times," *Editor and Publisher*, October 20, 1974.

John Greely, "Bob Atwood: His Life and Times," *Alaska Advocate*, January 6, 1977; also, same issue, "What Is Bob Atwood Worth?" and "Swanson River Saga."

TIMES EMPLOYEES' TRIPS AT OIL COMPANY EXPENSE

Howard Weaver, "The Alaska Information Game," *Alaska Advocate*, January 6, 1977.

TIMES OPPOSITION TO NATIVE CLAIMS

Berry, *Alaska Pipeline*, pp. 70–75.

1956 ELECTION

John Greely, "Bob Atwood: His Life and *Times*," *Alaska Advocate*, January 6, 1977; Gruening, *The State of Alaska*, pp. 499–501, and footnote, p. 631.

JOINT OPERATING AGREEMENT

In addition to numerous interviews, information concerning the joint operating agreement and the *Daily News*'s financial problems came from perusal of a copy of the agreement itself; from the previously cited *Editorial and Publisher* article on Atwood; and from numerous news articles in the *Anchorage Times* and *Daily News*, other Alaska newspapers such as the *All-Alaska Weekly* in Fairbanks and the now defunct *Northern Observer* in Anchorage, as well as many "Outside" papers, such as the *Washington Post* (Flip Todd, "Liberal Paper May Fold," January 3, 1977); the *Wall Street Journal* (Mike Dougan, "Anchorage Daily News Files Suit to Break Joint Operating Accord With Rival Paper," Feburary 14, 1977); and the *New York Times* ("Hopes for Anchorage Paper Rise After Appeal to Avoid Bankruptcy," November 24, 1976).

DAILY NEWS HISTORY

Howard Weaver, "Champagne and Tears," *Alaska Advocate*, January 6, 1977.

IV. The Bush-Rat Governor

Quotes from Governor Hammond's speeches are taken, for the most part, from texts published by the governor's press information office. Much biographical information on Hammond also was furnished by the governor's press office.

BIOGRAPHY

"Plane Dives Off Marina," *Syracuse* (N.Y.) *Herald-Journal*, July 8, 1946.

"Vet Pilot of Wrecked Plane Tries Again," *Syracuse Herald-Journal*, July 30, 1946.

James A. White, "Scotia School Star of 1940 Nears Alaska Polls Victory," *Union Star–Knickerbocker News* (Albany, New York), November 12, 1974.

Richard Saltonstall Jr., "The New Man in Juneau," *Living Wilderness*, winter 1974–75.

VIEWS, PHILOSOPHY

"Interview with Alaska Governor Jay Hammond," *U.S. News and World Report*, June 10, 1976.

"The Today Show," NBC Television Network, interview of Governor Hammond by Jim Hartz, July 16, 1975.

"A Talk with Gov. Hammond on Wolves, Oil Taxes, and Easements," *Fairbanks Daily News-Miner*, February 23, 1976.

Jay Hammond, "Alaska—a Forum for the Future," *First Monday*, Republican National Committee, Volume 5, Number 8.

Jay Hammond, "Who Shall Control Alaska's Land?," *Journal of Soil and Water Conservation*, May–June 1976.

Jay Hammond, "What Lies Ahead for Alaska?," *Northwest* (magazine of *Portland Sunday Oregonian*), February 22, 1976.

"Governor's Appointees Show Environment History," *Anchorage Daily News*, January 28, 1975.

Saltonstall, "New Man in Juneau" (previously cited).

V. The Greening of the Natives

CORPORATIONS' BUSINESS ACTIVITIES

"Regional Corporations: Looking at More Than Just the Profits," *Alaska Industry*, July 1976.

A. Richard Immel, "Native Corporations Are Changing Alaska, Providing Vital Capital," *Wall Street Journal*, November 29, 1976.

Rosemary Shinohara, "Native Corporations Looking Ahead," *Anchorage Daily News*, November 8, 1976.

Virginia McKinney, "Native Regional Firms Slowing Pace of Investment," *Alaska Industry*, July 1976.

Morgan Parker, "Native Corporations: Still On The Move," *Anchorage Times*, November 14, 1976.

Peter Gruenstein, "Alaska's Natives, Inc.," *Progressive*, March 1977.

KONIAG, INC.

Koniag, Inc., Annual Reports, 1974 and 1975.

Harry Carter quote came from seminar, attended by authors, on outer continental shelf oil development during the October 1976 convention of the Alaska Federation of Natives in Anchorage.

NATIVES' SUBSISTENCE, CULTURE, TRADITION AND HISTORY

Arnold, *Alaska Native Land Claims* (previously cited).

Yupiktak Bista (nonprofit Native organization in western Alaska), *Does One Way of Life Have to Die So Another Can Live?* report, 1974.

Gruening, *State of Alaska*.

Edward Moffat Weyer Jr., *The Eskimos: Their Environment and Folkways* (New Haven: Yale University Press, 1932).

Brandon, *American Heritage Book of Indians* (previously cited).

Alaska: The Land and the People, by Evelyn I. Butler and George A. Dale (New York: Viking, 1957.

James W. Vanstone, *Point Hope: An Eskimo Village in Transition*, (Seattle: University of Washington Press, 1962).

Merele Colby, Federal Writers Project, *A Guide to Alaska: Last American Frontier* (New York: Macmillan, 1939).

NATIVES' EDUCATION

Sam Kito, "Give 'Yes' Vote To Rural Education," *Anchorage Times* column, October 31, 1976.

Jeanne Abbott, "Hootch Settlement Approved As 'Fair,' " *Anchorage Daily News*, October 28, 1976.

E. Dean Coon, Anne E. Just, and Jerry N. Waddell, *School Finance in Alaska*, (Fairbanks; Center for Northern Educational Research, University of Alaska, 1976).

LEGAL WRANGLES OVER CLAIMS ACT

Berry, *Alaska Pipeline*, Senator Lee Metcalf quoted, p. 9.

Douglas E. Kneeland, "Alaska Natives' Pact: Reality Intrudes," *New York Times*, August 16, 1975.

Transcript of testimony of Roy Huhndorf, president, Cook Inlet Region, Inc., before the U.S. Senate Committee on Interior and Insular Affairs, June 10, 1976.

Monroe E. Price, *Region-Village Relations under the Alaska Native Claims Settlement Act*, reprinted as a booklet by the Alaska Native Foundation, Anchorage, 1976, from the *UCLA-Alaska Law Review*, Fall 1975 and Spring 1976 issues.

Local Easements in Alaska, pamphlet, U.S. Department of the Interior, Bureau of Land Management, Alaska, undated.

Rosemary Shinohara, "Trespass Case Has First Hearing," *Anchorage Daily News*, November 4, 1976.

COOK INLET REGION, INC.

Cook Inlet Region, Inc., Annual Reports, 1974 and 1975.

BERING STRAITS NATIVE CORPORATION

"Group Charges Illegal Political Contributions," *Anchorage Daily News* December 17, 1976.

"Jamie Love Tackles Native Corporation," *Tundra Times*, December 22, 1976.

Copy of letter from James Love, director, Alaska Public Interest Research Group (AkPIRG), to Alaska U.S. Attorney G. Kent Edwards, asking probe of campaign contributions.

"Antitrust Action on Mobile Home Sales," and "Bering Straits Native Corporation Campaign Contributions," AkPIRG newsletter, January 11, 1977.

THE ALEUT CORPORATION

Aleut Corporation Annual Report, 1975.

BRISTOL BAY

"Westward Hotel Sale in the Works," *Anchorage Daily News*, August 13, 1976.

CHUGACH

Chugach Natives, Inc., Annual Report, 1976.

SEALASKA CORPORATION

Sealaska Corporation Annual Report, 1974, 1975, 1976.

People and Progress, periodic report to stockholders, January–July 1976, October–December 1975, April–June 1975, January–March 1975, October–December 1974.

"Sealaska Faction Vies for Control," *Anchorage Daily News*, November 8, 1976.

NANA REGIONAL CORPORATION, INC.

NANA Regional Corporation, Inc. Annual Report, 1974.

Virginia McKinney, "NANA Regional Corporation: Small, Conservative, Profitable," *Alaska Industry*, August 1976.

Rosemary Shinohara, "NANA—On the Move," *Anchorage Daily News*, October 19, 1976.

DOYON, LTD.

Doyon, Ltd., Annual Report, 1975.

Peter J. Schuyten, "A Novel Corporation Takes Charge in Alaska's Wilderness," *Fortune*, October 1975.

CORPORATIONS' PROFITABILITY

Dean F. Olson and Nickolas Jackson, "Comparative Financial Analysis of ANCSA Regional Corporations 1975," *Alaska Native Management Report*, November 1, 1976.

NATIVE LEGISLATORS BECOMING MORE CONSERVATIVE

Copy of testimony by North Slope Mayor Eben Hopson before the Canadian Berger Commission hearings on Mackenzie Valley pipeline inquiry, September 21, 1976.

"Rich Natives: They Will Run Alaska," editorial, *Anchorage Times*, May 11, 1975.

DISSIDENT STOCKHOLDERS

"Sealaska Faction Vies for Control," *Anchorage Daily News*, November 8, 1976.

MENOMINEE SETTLEMENT

Yupiktak Bista, *Does One Way of Life Have to Die* (previously cited), p. 35.

GENERAL ARTICLES

Eric Treisman, "The Last Treaty," *Harper's*, January 1975.
Donn Liston, "Native Corporations: A Blessing and a Curse," *Anchorage Daily News*, May 21, 1975.
Alaska Federation of Natives Annual Reports, 1975 and 1976.

VI. Pipe Dream

HOW MUCH OIL IN ALASKA?

"For Anchorage, Oil Pipeline Is Only Tip of Iceberg," *Advertising Age*, December 13, 1976.
Bob Porterfield, "How Much Oil Is There in Alaska?" *Anchorage Daily News*, June 30, 1975.
"Energy and Mineral Resources of Alaska and the Impact of Federal Land Policies on Their Availability: Oil and Gas," Alaska Open File Report 50, State of Alaska, Department of Natural Resources, Division of Geological and Geophysical Surveys, June 1974.
Mary Clay Berry, "After Ecology, Monopoly," *Nation*, November 5, 1973.
May B. Skelton (Associated Press), "Kleppe Cites Oil Demands, Says Options are Limited," *Anchorage Times*, October 25, 1976.

HISTORY OF BATTLE LEADING UP TO PIPELINE CONSTRUCTION

Berry, *Alaska Pipeline* (previously cited).
Transcripts of U.S. Interior Department hearings on the environmental impact statement for the trans-Alaska pipeline, Washington, D.C., and Anchorage, February 1971. Quotes in this chapter from the Anchorage hearing, February 24, 1971, Volume 1: Edgar Wayburn, pp. 279–87; Lowell Thomas, Jr., pp. 120–22; Tom Fink, pp. 149–50.
New York Times, April 19, 1973, excerpts from President Nixon's April 18 energy message to Congress.
Various Alyeska and oil company publications, including: April 1976 Alyeska news memo, "Chronology of Major Events Relating to the Trans-Alaska Pipeline"; undated Alyeska news memo, "Pipeline Facts," listing various oil companies' share of the pipeline, other data about size, capacity, etc., of the pipeline; Alyeska pamphlet, "Questions and Answers," January 1976.

HIGH COST OF PRUDHOE BAY OIL AND PIPELINE CONSTRUCTION

Thomas O'Toole, "Alaska Pipeline Firms Seek Oil Prices Higher Than Current Import Costs," *Washington Post*, March 10, 1977.
Roberta Hornig, "Alaska Pipeline Costs Soar to $9 Billion; ICC Doing an Audit," *Washington Star*, October 9, 1976.
Edward L. Patton's quote from transcript of U.S. Interior Department pipeline environmental impact statement hearing, Anchorage, February 24, 1971, Volume 1, pp. 172–85.
Bryan Hodgson, "The Pipeline: Alaska's Troubled Colossus," *National Geographic*, November 1976.

CANADIAN ALTERNATIVE FOR OIL PIPELINE; PREDICTIONS OF WEST COAST OIL GLUT

O. K. Gilbreth quote from transcript of U.S. Interior Department environmental impact statement hearing, Anchorage, February 24, 1971, Volume 1, pp. 94–99.

Charles J. Cicchetti, *Alaskan Oil: Alternative Routes and Markets* (Washington, D.C.: Resources for the Future, Inc., 1972) distributed by Johns Hopkins University Press, Baltimore.

Thomas Brown, "That Unstoppable Pipeline," *New York Times Magazine*, October 14, 1973.

Berry, "After Ecology, Monopoly."

"Hearings on a Northern Pipeline," *Canada Today/D'Aujourd'hui*, November 1976.

Robert Sherrill, "The Trans-Alaska Pipeline: Unsafe At Any Width," *Nation*, June 11, 1973.

RENEWED EFFORT TO SEND PRUDHOE OIL TO JAPAN

"The Pipeline Tangle," *Environmental Defense Fund Letter*, November/December 1976.

Wallace Turner, "Industry Expected to Press Plan to Export Alaskan Oil to Japan," *New York Times*, November 28, 1976.

"Questions Mount over Alaska Oil Destination," *Wilderness Report*, October 1976.

Sally W. Jones, "Alaska's Crude—No Room at the Refinery," *Anchorage Daily News*, November 15, 1975.

"A Kink in the Pipeline," *Newsweek*, September 27, 1976.

Roberta Hornig, "Carter May Reverse Ford Policy, Let Japan Buy Oil from Alaska," *Washington Star*, April 9, 1977.

VII. Pipeline: The Untold Story

PIPELINE THEFT

Peter Gruenstein, "Waste: The Real Problem With the Alaska Pipeline," *Washington Monthly*, January 1977.

Mike Goodman and William Endicott, "Alaska Today—Runaway Crime And Union Violence," *Los Angeles Times*, November 18, 1975. Includes quotes from Edward Patton and Mel Personnett.

Richard A. Fineberg, "The Pipeline Watch: Domesticating a Dinosaur," *All-Alaska Weekly*, May 23, 1975. Quotes letters from Frank Moolin to Bechtel Corporation.

ESCALATING PIPELINE COSTS AND INEFFICIENT MANAGEMENT

Roberta Hornig, "Errors Blamed for Pipeline Costa," *Washington Star*, September 11, 1976.

Charles J. Cicchetti, "The Wrong Route," *Environment*, June 1973. Discusses BP-Sohio desire to get pipeline operating as soon as possible; also says that Canadian route is superior to Alaska route for pipeline.

Berry, *Alaska Pipeline*, p. 123. How BP-Sohio interests clashed with Exxon's.

Anthony Sampson, *The Seven Sisters: The Great Oil Companies and the World They Shaped* (New York: Viking, 1975; paperback edition by Bantam, 1976), pp. 212–14. Clash between BP-Sohio and Exxon.

Michael Tanzer (Tanzer Economic Associates, Inc.), "Alaska's Prudhoe Bay Oil: Profitability and Taxation Potential," a report to the Alaska legislature, January 9, 1976, reprinted in the Alaska Senate Journal Supplement, Number 14, June 29, 1976. Shows oil companies' potential profits from Prudhoe Bay.

Alyeska, undated, untitled memo prepared for authors, giving estimated cost figures that were made at various points in the planning for, and construction of, the pipeline. Also explanations of many of the increased estimates.

Alyeska press release Number 496, January 23, 1976, giving latest cost estimate for pipeline at $7 billion, up from $6.38 billion of previous June.

Alyeska press release Number 609, June 30, 1976, giving latest estimate for pipeline of $7.7 billion, up from $7 billion five months earlier.

Henry R. Lieberman, "Five-Year Fight on Alaska Pipeline Made It Better and More Costly," *New York Times*, May 26, 1974.

Robert Lindsey, "Alaska Pipeline 42% Done Despite Delays," *New York Times*, October 4, 1975.

Sally W. Jones and Rosemary Shinohara, series of articles in *Anchorage Daily News:* "Pipeline Cost Pinches Owners," July 13, 1976; "Questions of Quality on the Line," July 9, 1976; "River Crossings Jack Up Line Costs," July 10, 1976; "Sohio Oil Profits Go to BP," July 14, 1976.

"Arco's President Defends North Slope Oil Development," *Alaska on Alaska*, October 25, 1976. Thornton Bradshaw quote on pipeline construction efficiency.

STATE PROBE OF PIPELINE COST OVERRUNS

Annual Reports, 1974 and 1975, State of Alaska, Office of the Pipeline Coordinator, Charles A. Champion, state pipeline coordinator. Reports present a number of allegations of waste, inefficiency and environmentally damaging procedures during pipeline construction.

Rosemary Shinohara, series of articles in *Anchorage Daily News:* "Line Tariff Battle Simmers," July 15, 1976; "Probe Begins on Line Costs," November 23, 1976; "Pipeline Prober Sees 'Challenge,' " December 15, 1976; "State Probes Line Repairs," December 22, 1976.

Wallace Turner, "Fight Is in Prospect over Pipeline Tariff," *New York Times*, December 12, 1976.

ENVIRONMENTAL PROBLEMS WITH PIPELINE CONSTRUCTION

G. M. Zemansky, board member, Fairbanks Environmental Center, "Noncompliance with Provisions of the Federal Right-of-Way Agreement and General Technical Stipulations," August 12, 1976.

Thomas M. Brown, "That Unstoppable Pipeline," *New York Times Magazine*, October 14, 1973.

G. M. Zemansky, "Environmental Noncompliance and the Public Interest," paper presented August 4, 1976, at the Twenty-seventh Alaska Science Conference, University of Alaska, Fairbanks.

U.S. House Interstate Commerce Committee's Energy and Power Subcommittee, staff report to Representative John D. Dingell (Democrat, Michigan), September 8, 1976. Tells of environmental problems, falsification of weld records, mismanagement on the pipeline.

THE WELDS CONTROVERSY

Richard A. Fineberg, "The Pipeline Watch: Champion's Project Assessment Emphasizes Economic Priorities," *All-Alaska Weekly*, April 11, 1975.

"Fakes May Total 132," Fairbanks Daily News-Miner, November 13, 1975.

Rosemary Shinohara and Sally W. Jones, "Welds the Hottest Hassle on the Line," *Anchorage Daily News*, July 17, 1976.

Betty Mills, "Interior Official Raps Panel's Pipeline Report," *Anchorage Times*, October 22, 1976.

Edward Cowan, "House Staff Raises New Questions about Welds on Alaska Pipeline," *New York Times*, December 12, 1976.

Roberta Hornig, "Pipeline Firm Wants Consumer to Pay Repair Bill," *Washington Star*, October 8, 1976.

"Surveillance Report on Status of Pipeline Welding and X-ray Work," State of Alaska, Pipeline Coordinator's Office, March 19, 1976.

U.S. House Interstate Commerce Committee's Energy and Power Subcommittee, staff report (previously cited).

U.S. Department of Transportation fact-finding team, headed by Deputy Transportation Secretary John W. Barnum, "Report to Energy Resources Council of the July 11–14, 1976 Trans-Alaska Pipeline System Fact-finding Mission."

OIL SPILLS DURING CONSTRUCTION; POTENTIAL LEAKS

Richard A. Fineberg, "The Sound of One Eye Winking," *Alaska Advocate*, February 10, 1977.

Mary Jean Haley, "Oil from Alaska: Just a Pipeline Dream?" *Rolling Stone*, December 2, 1976.

Richard A. Fineberg, " 'Small' Leaks May Escape Pipeline Warnings," *Fairbanks Daily News-Miner*, January 23, 1976.

FEDERAL PIPELINE MONITORING AND CONFLICT-OF-INTEREST CHARGES

Jack Anderson, "Pipeline Watchdog Rollins Took Favors from Contractor," syndicated column, *Anchorage Daily News*, December 23, 1976.

Betty Mills, "Rollins Inquiry Begins," *Anchorage Times*, December 27, 1976.

ENVIRONMENTALISTS' FAILURE TO MONITOR PIPELINE ADEQUATELY

"More Humbling Moments," *The Anchorage Times* (Oil and the Pipeline Supplement), August 28, 1976.

Zemansky, "Noncompliance with Provisions of Federal Right-of-Way Agreement" (previously cited).

PIPELINE IMPACT

Joseph Judge, "Alaska: Rising Northern Star," *National Geographic*, June 1975.

Michael Rogers, "The Dark Side of the Earth," *Rolling Stone*, May 22, 1975.

Bil Gilbert, "The Devaluation of Alaska" (previously cited).

Winthrop Griffith, "Blood, Toil, Tears, and Oil: How Boomtown Greed Is Changing Alaska," *New York Times Magazine*, July 27, 1975.

IMPACT ON FAIRBANKS

"Quality of Life," editorial, *All-Alaska Weekly*, July 11, 1975 (reprinted from May 10, 1974 issue).

"Pipeline Impact Information Center Reports," and "Special Reports," published approximately monthly, by the Fairbanks North Star Borough Pipeline Impact Information Center. Special reports have dealt with "Minority Hire and Alaska Hire on the Pipeline"; "Senior Citizens: The Effects of Pipeline Construction on Older Persons Living in Fairbanks"; and "Questions and Answers About the Cost of Living in Fairbanks." Typical issues carry articles on the impact of pipeline construction on food stamps, traffic volume, churches, airports, food prices, rental housing, etc.

Andy Williams, "Life and Breath in Fairbanks," *Alaska Advocate*, Feburary 3, 1977.

IMPACT ON VALDEZ

Michael Baring-Gould and Marsha Bennett (Department of Sociology, University of Alaska, Anchorage), "Social Impact of the Trans-Alaska Pipeline Construction in Valdez, Alaska,

1974–1975," testimony based on state funded study, prepared for the Canadian Mackenzie Valley Pipeline Inquiry, 1976.

Linda Leask, "Valdez Today Is Okay," *Alaska*, September 1976.

IMPACT ON ANIMALS

Jim Rearden, "Alaska," *National Geographic*, December 1974.

OIL COMPANY INFLUENCE PERMEATING THE STATE

"More Humbling Moments," *Anchorage Times*, August 28, 1976 (Peg Tiletson quotes).

Rau, "The Taming of Alaska" (previously cited).

David Engels (attorney, president of the Alaska Public Interest Research Group Lobby), "The 'Common Sense' Campaigns," *Anchorage Daily News*, October 28, 1976 ("Alaska Forum" column).

VIII. Son of Pipe Dream

NATURAL GAS PIPELINE: THE THREE PROPOSALS

Stuart Perry, " 'Gassing Up' For Plunder in the Tundra," *Environmental Action*, November 18, 1974.

James G. Deane, "Viewpoint," *Living Wilderness*, April–June 1976.

Ernst W. Mueller, "Alaskan Oil—the Energy Crisis and the Environment," *Arctic Bulletin*, Volume 1, Number 5, 1976.

William Borders, "Five-Billion Gas-Pipe Clearance Asked," *New York Times*, March 22, 1974.

Richard Corrigan, "The Pipeline Battle, Chapter 2," *Washington Post*, April 7, 1974.

U.S. Department of the Interior, "Alaska Natural Gas Transportation System: Alternatives," final environmental impact statement, March 1976.

PROCEDURAL LEGISLATION FOR GAS PIPELINE

"Congress Passes Measures of Significance to Alaskans," *Anchorage Times*, October 23, 1976.

Lewis Brigham, "FPC Chairman Has Reservations about Alaskan Natural Gas Act," *Journal of Commerce*, October 13, 1976.

Federal Power Commission (news release), "Alaskan Natural Gas Fact Sheet," February 1, 1977.

LEGAL CHALLENGES TO GAS PIPELINE CURTAILED

Brec Cooke, representing the Wilderness Society, testimony before the House Commerce Committee's Subcommittee on Energy and Power, hearings on Alaska natural gas transportation systems, August 6, 1976.

STATE SALES CONTRACTS FOR PIPELINE ROYALTY GAS

Susan Andrews, "Legislature Begins Royalty Gas Hearings," *Anchorage Times*, January 25, 1977.

P. L. Dobey and K. M. O'Connor (Division of Geological and Geophysical Surveys), and O. K. Gilbreth, J. C. Miller and H. H. Hamilton (Division of Oil and Gas), "Projected Alaskan Royalty Gas Production and Its Relationship to Projected Natural Gas Demand," report by the Alaska State Department of Natural Resources, April 1976.

LOBBYING FOR ALL-ALASKA ROUTE

"OMAR Supports El Paso Proposal as Quicker and Cheaper Gas Line," *Arctic Sun*, November 1976.

Governor Hammond, speech to OMAR gas pipeline seminar, Anchorage, September 11, 1976.

TEAMSTER SUPPORT FOR ALL-ALASKA ROUTE

Bill Wilson, "Union Supports Gas Line," *Anchorage Times*, August 7, 1976.

Jesse L. Carr (Teamsters), "Alaska Line Is Critically Needed," *Arctic Sun*, November 1976.

ENVIRONMENTALISTS' OBJECTIONS TO ARCTIC GAS PROPOSAL

Wilderness Society, Sierra Club, National Audubon Society, and Alaska Conservation Society, statement submitted to Federal Power Commission proceedings on a Prudhoe Bay natural gas line, 1976.

Perry, "Plunder in the Tundra" (previously cited).

Deane, "Viewpoint" (previously cited).

Cooke testimony August 6, 1976 (previously cited).

JUDGE LITT'S DECISION

Federal Power Commission news release, "FPC Judge Recommends Approval Of Arctic Gas's $8.5 Billion Alaskan Gas Project," February 1, 1977.

"Alaska to Fight Judge's Gas Decision," *Washington Star*, Feburary 2, 1976.

"FPC Staff Urges Canadian Route for Alaskan Gas," *Wall Street Journal*, December 8, 1976.

"Piping Home the Gas," editorial, *New York Times*, Feburary 27, 1977.

COMPANIES' VIEWS OF FEDERAL BAILOUT OF PRUDHOE GAS LINE

Copies of letters dated August 13, 1976, from Representative John D. Dingell (Democrat, Michigan), chairman of the U.S. House Interstate and Foreign Commerce Committee's Subcommittee on Energy and Power, to officials of El Paso, Arctic, and Northwest. Copies of letters to Dingell from John C. Bennett, vice-president of El Paso, August 23, 1976; John G. McMillian, chairman and chief executive officer, Northwest; and William W. Brackett, vice-chairman, Arctic Gas, undated, but received by Dingell on August 24, 1976.

NAVAL PETROLEUM RESERVE NUMBER 4, DESCRIPTION

Stewart French and John C. Reed, *Boundaries and Status of Naval Petroleum Reserve Number 4*, pamphlet, for Arctic Institute of North America, Fairbanks, revised and expanded September 1971.

Public Law 94–258, Ninety-fourth Congress, April 5, 1976, "National Petroleum Reserve in Alaska," bill transferring authority over NPR-4 from the Navy to the Interior Department, and changing the name to National Petroleum Reserve in Alaska as of June 1, 1977.

Department of the Interior, Bureau of Land Management, proposed rules for BLM administration of NPR-4, September 13, 1976.

OIL, GAS POTENTIAL OF PET 4

"The Exploration, Development and Production of Naval Petroleum Reserve Number 4," report prepared for the Federal Energy Administration by Resource Planning Associates, Inc., Cambridge, Massachusetts, July 19, 1976.

Bruce Ingersoll, "Key to the Oil Crisis May Lie under Pet 4," *Anchorage Daily News* (reprinted from *Chicago Sun-Times*), December 21, 1974.

"The Exploration, Development, and Production of Naval Petroleum Reserve Number 4," report prepared by Federal Energy Administration, Strategic Petroleum Reserve Office, Office of Oil and Gas, for the U.S. House and Senate Committees on Interior and Insular Affairs, August 1976.

MOSS, STEVENSON QUOTES ON OIL RESERVES

Representative John E. Moss (Democrat, California), testimony before the House Interior and Insular Affairs Committee's Subcommittee on Public Lands, hearings on oil and gas development on public lands, December 18, 1973.

George L. Baker, "The Navy's Oil: Up For Grabs," *Nation*, April 13, 1974 (Senator Stevenson quote).

TEAPOT DOME SCANDAL

Frederick Lewis Allen, *Only Yesterday* (1931; reprint ed. New York: Bantam, 1959), pp. 96–112.

Carl Solberg, *Oil Power: The Rise and Imminent Fall of an American Empire* (New York: Mentor, 1976), pp. 83–107.

Engler, *The Politics of Oil*, (Chicago: University of Chicago Press, 1961), pp. 83–84.

QUOTES FROM DANIELS, VINSON, MOSS

Josephus Daniels and Carl Vinson both quoted in Engler's *The Politics of Oil*, pp. 83 and 85, respectively.

Representative Moss, testimony December 18, 1973 (previously cited).

EFFORTS TO REMOVE RESERVES FROM NAVY CONTROL

Mark Panitch, "Interior, Navy Clash on Pet 4 Exploration," *Anchorage Daily News*, March 31, 1975.

Bruce Ingersoll, "The Fight over Oil Reserves," *Anchorage Daily News* (reprinted from *Chicago Sun-Times*), December 21, 1974.

CLEMENTS'S TASK GROUP ON PET 4

Eliot Marshall, "Oil Underground: The Navy and the Poachers," *New Republic*, February 23, 1974.

Baker, "The Navy's Oil" (previously cited).

IMPACT OF PET 4 DEVELOPMENT

"Pet 4 Impact a Minimum," *Anchorage Times*, March 7, 1977.

Richard A. Fineberg, "Pet 4 Oil Looms: Barrow Fears Culture-Choking Growth," *Anchorage Daily News* (reprinted from *Fairbanks Daily News-Miner*), March 3, 1976.

ENVIRONMENTALLY SENSITIVE AREAS OF PET 4

Jack Hession, Alaska representative, Sierra Club, statement at U.S. Bureau of Land Management hearing on proposed regulations for management of Pet 4, Anchorage, October 29, 1976.

Undated, untitled Bureau of Land Management map and memo describing environmental value of Teshekpuk and Utukok areas of Pet 4.

PUBLIC VERSUS PRIVATE DEVELOPMENT OF PET 4

Susan Andrews, "Horton: Industry Will Tap Pet 4," *Anchorage Times*, August 12, 1976.
Resource Planning Associates, report on Pet 4, July 19, 1976 (previously cited).
"$400 Million Cost to Explore Pet 4," *Anchorage Daily News*, November 24, 1975.

REPORTS RECOMMENDING OIL TAX INCREASES

Jerome M. Zeifman and Kenneth S. Ainsworth, "The Taxation of the Petroleum Industry Under Alaska's Corporate Income Tax," a report prepared for the Alaska Legislature and the Alaska Department of Revenue, January 1977. Zeifman is associate professor of law, Santa Clara (California) University School of Law; Ainsworth is a professor of economics and chairperson of the Department of Economics, Allegheny College, Meadville, Pennsylvania.

Alaska State Department of Revenue, "Alaska's Oil and Gas Tax Structure: A Study With Recommendations for Improvement," February 1977.

Tanzer, report to Alaska legislature January 9, 1976, on Prudhoe Bay Oil (previously cited).

PERMANENT FUND

Andy Williams, "Delegates Disagree on Permanent Fund," *Anchorage Daily News*, October 19, 1976.

Susan Andrews, "Lawmakers Would Shape Permanent Fund," *Anchorage Times*, October 24, 1976.

Peter Gruenstein, "Alaska's Plight—Too Much Money," *Washington Post*, December 19, 1976.

"State of Alaska Official Election Pamphlet," general election, November 2, 1976, published by lieutenant governor's office. Ballot Proposition Number 2 (Permanent Fund) summary, plus statement of arguments for and against, pp. 76–77.

ALASKA, INC.

John Greely, "The Great Juneau Oil Dollar Giveaway," *Alaska Advocate*, January 20, 1977.

Joe Josephson, "Major Concerns About Alaska, Inc.," *Anchorage Times* column, February 6, 1977.

"Hammond's Money Plan Draws Yawns, Yays, Nays," *Anchorage Times*, January 12, 1977.

Paul Nussbaum, "Bill May Share Oil Wealth," *Anchorage Daily News*, December 23, 1976.

OIL TAX LEGISLATION, CONSULTANTS' REPORTS

"Legislative Consultant Says Prudhoe Taxes Can Go to 80%" and "Are High Oil Industry Tax Rates Unfair?" *Fairbanks Daily News-Miner*, January 22, 1976.

"Oil Report Says Decade May Bring $10 Billion," *Anchorage Times*, November 1, 1976.

Rosemary Shinohara, "Billion Lost on Oil, Gas?" *Anchorage Daily* News, February 17, 1977. (Norgaard on lost oil revenues because of ineffective state leasing policy).

Zeifman-Ainsworth, report to Alaska legislature January 1977 on taxation of petroleum industry (previously cited).

Alaska State Department of Revenue, "Alaska's Oil and Gas Structure," February 1977 (previously cited).

Tanzer, report on Prudhoe Bay oil (previously cited).

GREATER GOVERNMENT ROLE IN OIL DEVELOPMENT

Fink quote from public forum we attended at the University of Alaska, Anchorage, October 30, 1976.

OIL COMPANIES VERSUS NORTH SLOPE BOROUGH ON TAXATION

Kay Brown, "The North Slope Borough: An Arctic Struggle," *Anchorage Times*, October 17, 1976.

IX. Boss Carr

ALASKA TEAMSTER MEMBERSHIP, JOBS

"Teamster Local 959, a Polished Jewel in the New Frontier," "Anchorage and Fairbanks Are Hubs of Teamster Activity," and "Teamsters Are Part of the New Frontier . . . Alaska," *International Teamster*, September 1976.

"Do The Teamsters Own Alaska?," Volume 8, Number 24, "60 Minutes," CBS Television, June 6, 1976.

Howard Weaver and Bob Porterfield, "Teamsters: How Much Power?," *Anchorage Daily News*, December 4, 1975.

PENSION, OTHER TRUST FUNDS

Jim Babb, series of articles in the *Anchorage Daily News*, "Trusts: $ 1 Million Each Week!" December 4, 1975: "Trusts: Where the Money Goes," December 5, 1975; "Pension, Planes May Grow Larger," December 19, 1975.

TEAMSTER POLITICAL POWER, CONTRIBUTIONS

Howard Weaver and Bob Porterfield, series of articles in the *Anchorage Daily News*, "Teamsters: How Much Power?," December 4, 1975; "The Teamster Lobbyist: A Man With Connections," December 11, 1975; "How Teamster Lobbyist Builds His Own Empire," December 12, 1975.

Craig Smith, "Teamsters: In Politics a Force to be Reckoned With," *Fairbanks Daily News-Miner*, October 25, 1975.

CARR BIOGRAPHY

Howard Weaver and Bob Porterfield, "Jesse Carr, The Empire Builder: A Study in Power," *Anchorage Daily News*, December 5, 1975.

Tom Nicholson and Peter S. Greenberg, "The Strongman Of Alaska," *Newsweek*, September 27, 1976.

Mike Goodman and William Endicott, "Alaska Today—Runaway Crime and Union Violence," *Los Angeles Times*, November 18, 1975.

CARR'S BARGAINING TACTICS

Howard Weaver and Bob Porterfield, "Bargaining: 'They Tell You What To Do'," *Anchorage Daily News*, December 15, 1975.

CARR AND OIL TAXES

"Carr Blasts Oil Tax Proposals," Alaska Teamster press release, March 29, 1976.

TEAMSTERS AND PUBLIC EMPLOYEES

"Workers Go Teamsters (City Force Will Join Local 959)," *Anchorage Times*, November 23, 1976.

"Consumer Group Studies Union," *Alaska Journal of Commerce*, Feburary 21, 1977.

"State Jobs Target of Local 959," *Anchorage Daily News*, August 3, 1976.

HAMMOND VERSUS CARR

"Teamsters' Carr Outlines State's Ills," statement by Jesse Carr printed in full, *Fairbanks Daily News-Miner*, August 3, 1976.

"View From Behind the Governor's Desk," statement by Governor Hammond, December 29, 1975.

PENSION FUND

Jim Babb, series of articles in *Anchorage Daily News:* "Trusts: $1 Million Each Week!" December 4, 1975; "Trusts: Where the Money Goes," December 5, 1975; "Who Run the Union Trusts," September 14, 1976.

International Teamster, September 1976 (articles previously cited).

Bob Porterfield, "Labor Union Funds Used in Hotel Buy," *Anchorage Daily News*, March 10, 1976.

CBS "60 Minutes," June 6, 1976 (previously cited).

Teamster General Counsel John W. Real responding to *Los Angeles Times* articles critical of Local 959, Teamster news release, November 19, 1975.

TEAMSTER MALL

"Union Wealth Shown in New Construction," *Fairbanks Daily News-Miner*, October 25, 1975.

Howard Weaver and Bob Porterfield, "Teamsters: How Much Power?," *Anchorage Daily News*, December 4, 1975.

International Teamster, articles previously cited.

EGAN ADMINISTRATION OFFICIALS WHO GOT TEAMSTER JOBS

"How the Empire Is Built," *Anchorage Daily News*, December 4, 1975.

TEAMSTER DUES

Jim Babb, "Pension, Planes May Grow Larger," *Anchorage Daily News*, December 19, 1975.

LEWIS M. DISCHNER AND THE TEAMSTERS

Howard Weaver and Bob Porterfield, series of articles in *Anchorage Daily News:* "The Teamster Lobbyist: A Man with Connections," December 11, 1975; "How Teamster Lobbyist Builds His Own Empire," December 12, 1975.

Bob Porterfield, "Dischner Fined for Tax Evasion," *Anchorage Daily News*, March 13, 1976.

Alaska Public Interest Research Group, "Report on Lobbying—1976 Alaska State Legislature," October 27, 1976.

NORTH STAR TERMINAL

Howard Weaver and Bob Porterfield, "Union Fiefdom Rules Fairbanks Warehouse," *Anchorage Daily News*, December 18, 1975.

Howard Weaver, articles in *Anchorage Daily News*, "Two Teamsters Are Feared Dead," August 3, 1976; "Missing Teamster Murdered, Police Say," August 5, 1976.

X. *The Untold Minerals*

COAL RESOURCES

Don L. McGee and Kristina M. O'Connor, "Mineral Resources of Alaska and the Impact of Federal Land Policies on Their Availability: Coal," Alaska Open File Report 51, published by Alaska State Department of Natural Resources, Division of Geological and Geophysical Surveys, Energy Resources Section, March 1975. Also Open File Report 74 on Cook Inlet Basin, same two authors, July 1975.

Bob Porterfield, "Inlet Coal Reserves May Be One Trillion Tons," *Anchorage Daily News*, July 18, 1975.

Ted Bartimus (*Associated Press*), "Alaska Is Loaded With Coal, But Shipping It Is a Problem," *Washington Post*, September 15, 1976.

Cleland N. Conwell, "Alaskan Coal May Prove a Big Plus in Future Exports Picture," *Mining Engineering*, October 1972.

URANIUM RESOURCES

Gilbert R. Eakins and Robert B. Forbes, "Investigation of Alaska's Uranium Potential," Special Report 12, published by Alaska State Department of Natural Resources, Division of Geological and Geophysical Surveys, 1976.

Gilbert R. Eakins, "Uranium Investigations in Southeastern Alaska," Geologic Report 44, published by Alaska State Department of Natural Resources, Division of Geological and Geophysical Surveys, 1975.

Gilbert R. Eakins, "Uranium in Alaska," Geological Report 38, published by Alaska State Department of Natural Resources, Division of Mines and Geology, May 1969.

"Claims Are Jumping," *Alaska Miner*, October 1976.

"Texas Firm to Fly Radiometric and Magnetic Survey in Alaska for ERDA's National Uranium Resource Evaluation Program" (reprint of U.S. Energy Research and Development Administration [ERDA] press release, March 30, 1976), *Mines and Geology Bulletin*, May 1976.

"ERDA to Conduct Copper River Basin Uranium Study" (reprinted from ERDA press release, July 22, 1976), *Mines and Geology Bulletin*, September 1976.

"State Has No Tax on Hard Minerals," *Anchorage Daily News*, June 28, 1975.

OIL COMPANIES EXPLORING FOR MINERALS

Alaska State Department of Natural Resources, Division of Geological and Geophysical Surveys, "Companies Interested in Alaskan Mining Possibilities," Information Circular Number 17, March 4, 1974.

"Claims Are Jumping," *Alaska Miner*, October 1976.

MINERS AND NATIVE CLAIMS

Berry, *Alaska Pipeline*, p. 57, Moerlein quote.

Judy Brady, "Native Land Ownership to Aid Mining Interests?" in *Alaska Native Management Report*, published by Alaska Native Foundation, as reprinted in the *Anchorage Daily News*, October 9, 1972.

MINERAL RESOURCES IN GENERAL IN ALASKA

Alaska State Department of Natural Resources, Division of Geological and Geophysical Surveys, Annual Reports, 1969, 1971, 1972, and 1973; and Biennial Report, 1974–75 (published February 13, 1976).

State of Alaska Department of Commerce and Economic Development, "The Alaskan Economy: Mid-Year Performance Report," 1976.

"Land and Minerals Data" for Alaska from "Alaska Forest Data," compiled March 1976 by the Division of Information and Education of the Regional Office, U.S. Forest Service, U.S. Department of Agriculture (USDA), Juneau, Alaska.

Bob Porterfield, "How Valuable Is Mining to Our Economy?" *Anchorage Daily News*, August 9, 1975.

Cleland N. Conwell, "Hard-Rock Mining in Alaska: Some Operations Since 1938," *Western Miner*, July 1976.

State Department of Natural Resources, Division of Geological and Geophysical Surveys, "Proper Claim Staking in Alaska," Information Circular Number 1, revised August 6, 1976.

Gilbert R. Eakins, "Mineral Exploration in Alaska in 1972," speech to the Northwest Mining Association's Seventy-eighth Annual Convention, Spokane, Washington, December 1, 1972.

"Mines, Government Make Uneasy Pair," *Anchorage Daily News*, July 26, 1976.

Bob Porterfield, "Miners See Gold in State's Metals," *Anchorage Daily News*, October 30, 1976.

MINING ON FEDERAL LANDS

"Northwest Mining Association Aids Mining Laws in Alaska," *Mines and Geology Bulletin*, March 1976 (excerpts reprinted from *Western Miner*, January 1976).

COPPER RESOURCES

"Hammond Antimining, Says Group," *Anchorage Daily News*, September 30, 1975.

Bob Porterfield, two-part series of articles in *Anchorage Daily News:* "Copper: The Latest Stampede in Alaska," June 14, 1975; "Brooks Range Copper: Alaska's Next Boom?" June 16, 1975.

MOLYBDENUM RESOURCES

Richard Foley, "U.S. Borax Road Plan Draws Initial Criticism," *Anchorage Daily News*, June 2, 1976.

Paul Nussbaum, "Japan Market Key for 'Moly' Mine," *Anchorage Daily News*, December 28, 1976.

"U.S. Borax Confirms Promising Find of Molybdenum," *Mines and Geology Bulletin*, May 1976 (reprinted from *Alaska Business Newsletter*, March 19, 1976).

GOLD RESOURCES

"The Gleam of Gold Draws Hope Miners" (Newhouse News Service), *Anchorage Daily News*, August 16, 1975.

"Companies Decide Juneau Gold Mining Not Feasible," *Alaska on Alaska*, November 24, 1975.

RECLAIMING STRIP-MINED LAND

Cleland N. Conwell, "Reclaiming Mined Lands in Alaska," *Transactions*, publication of the Society of Mining Engineers, March 1976.

NICKEL RESOURCES

A. Cameron Edmonson, "State Hopes to Avoid Fight Over Glacier Bay Nickel," *Anchorage Daily News*, June 19, 1972.

"Mining Protection Won For Glacier Bay," *Wilderness Report*, October 1976.

XI. "Permafrost Brasilia," and Other Conflicts

CAPITAL MOVE

"Capital Choice Is Willow," *Anchorage Daily News*, November 3, 1976.

Suzan Nightingale, "Land Speculation Grows in Valley," *Anchorage Daily News*, August 11, 1976.

"Survey Says Alaskans Prefer Capital at Juneau," *Ketchikan Daily News*, January 15, 1977.

"Plans to Shift Alaskan Capital Stir Some Fear," *New York Times*, November 7, 1976.

John McPhee, "A Reporter At Large: What They Were Hunting For," *New Yorker*, September 27, 1976, and October 4, 1976.

"Capital Move Fiasco," editorial, *Fairbanks Daily News-Miner*, October 27, 1976.

Leonard Lane, "Alaska Moves Its Capital. The Site Selection Process: An Engineering Viewpoint," *Northern Engineer*, Summer–Fall 1975.

Pat Wilson, " 'Save Talkeetna' Group Growing," *Susitna Valley Chronicle*, October 12, 1976.

"Voters To Select Capital Site," special eight-page tabloid, *Anchorage Times*, October 19, 1976.

Carl Sampson, "We Want the Capital, Willow Committee Says," *Anchorage Times*, October 25, 1976.

Governor Hammond, press conference, April 9, 1976.

"Alaska's Land—1975," annual report of the Federal-State Land Use Planning Commission for Alaska, 1976.

D-2 WILDERNESS LANDS

"Alaska's Land—1975," (previously cited).

Boyce Rensberger, "Protection of Alaska's Wilderness New Priority of Conservationists," *New York Times*, October 31, 1976.

Max C. Brewer, "A Look at Alaskan Land Concerns," *Fairbanks Daily News-Miner*, August 24, 1976.

Peggy Wayburn and Edgar Wayburn, "Great Stakes in the Great Land: Alaska Lands for Public Good," Sierra Club pamphlet, undated.

"Alaska: Imperiled Heritage," brochure by the Alaska Coalition, Washington, D.C., undated.

"Alaska National Interest Lands," transcript of hearings before the U.S. Senate Committee on Interior and Insular Affairs, Ninety-fourth Congress, First Session, on S. 1687, S. 1688, and S. 2676, November 21, 1975, and December 11, 1975. Published by U.S. Government Printing Office, Washington, D.C., 1976. Witnesses included Senator Mike Gravel (Democrat, Alaska), pp. 169–72 and 227–34; Dr. Edgar Wayburn, chairman, Sierra Club Alaska Task Force, representing the Alaska Coalition, pp. 191–225; Dr. Robert Weeden, director, Division of Policy Development and Planning, State of Alaska, representing Governor Hammond, pp. 172–91; Nathaniel Reed, assistant U.S. Interior secretary for fish, wildlife, and parks, pp. 240–55; Senator Ted Stevens (Republican, Alaska), pp. 228–32; Representative Don Young (Republican, Alaska), pp. 234–37; position paper by Calista Native Corporation on subsistence use of D-2 lands, pp. 237–40.

"Dear Colleague" letter, sent to members of Congress by Representative Don Young (Republican, Alaska), January 25, 1977.

"New Year's Plans," editorial, *Fairbanks Daily News-Miner*, January 18, 1977.

"Udall Submits Land Proposal," *Anchorage Times*, January 19, 1977.

Betty Mills, "Senate Gets Park Plan: Jackson Submits Bill for Conservationists," *Anchorage Times*, January 31, 1977.

"Eleventh Hour in the Great Land," *Wilderness Report*, October 1976.

GENERAL LAND USE

"Agenda for State Lands," published by the Joint Federal-State Land Use Planning Commission for Alaska, December 1975 (homesteading and open-to-entry programs).

"Westerners Chafed by U.S. Land Holdings," Associated Press, *New York Times*, March 13, 1977.

TRANSPORTATION AND ENERGY CORRIDORS

Jack Hession, "Sierra Club Statement on Proposed Transportation Corridors in Alaska," to the Joint Federal-State Land Use Planning Commission for Alaska, May 9, 1974.

Gilbert, "Devaluation of Alaska" (previously cited).

HAUL ROAD

Kay Brown, "The Haul Road: Hardening the Battle Lines," *Anchorage Times*, August 15, 1976.

Andy Williams, "Fate of Haul Road Debated," *Anchorage Daily News*, August 14, 1976.

Mark G. Hickok, for the Alaska chapter of the Sierra Club, statement before the state of Alaska Growth Policy Council and the state Division of Policy Development and Planning, August 12, 1976.

Governor Hammond, "North Slope Haul Road Policy Statement and Background," September 1976.

"Should the North Slope Haul Road Eventually Be Open to Everyone as Part of the Alaska Highway System?" televised program, "The Alaskan Advocates," sponsored by the Alaska Public Forum of the Alaska state governor's office, taped September 18, 1976 and broadcast throughout Alaska beginning September 26, 1976.

HICKEL HIGHWAY

Berry *Alaska Pipeline*, pp. 95–97.

Rogers, "Dark Side of the Earth" (previously cited).

AGRICULTURE

"Agricultural Potential Said High for Alaska," *Alaska on Alaska, October* 11, 1976.

Senator Stevens's comment in testimony on "Alaska National Interest Lands," before U.S. Senate Interior and Insular Affairs Committee, December 11, 1975, hearing transcript, p. 229.

Facts about Alaska: The Alaska Almanac (previously cited). Agricultural Statistics, p. 3.

Alaska Blue Book 1975, published by Alaska State Department of Education, Division of Libraries, 1976. Agricultural statistics, p. 170.

The Alaskan Economy, Mid-Year Performance Report 1976, prepared by Division of Economic Enterprise, Alaska State Department of Commerce and Economic Development, 1976. Agricultural statistics, pp. 28–29.

FOREST PRODUCTS

Draft Guide: Tongass National Forest, USDA Forest Service, 1976.

O. Keith Hutchison and Vernon J. LaBau, "The Forest Ecosystem of Southeast Alaska, Number 9: Timber Inventory, Harvesting, Marketing, and Trends," USDA Forest Service General Technical Report PNW-34, 1975.

"Alaska's Forest Resources," U.S. Forest Service Resource Bulletin PNW-19, 1967, reprinted 1968.

"Alaska's Interior Forest," reprinted by U.S. Department of Agriculture, from the *Journal of Forestry*, June 1976, pp. 333–41.

Timber harvest statistics, from "Alaska Forest Data," March 1976, compiled by the Division of Information and Education of the Regional Office, USDA Forest Service, Juneau, Alaska.

"Proposed New National Forest in Alaska," unnumbered pamphlet, USDA Forest Service.

Forest products statistics, "Alaska's Economy in 1976: Midyear Review and Outlook," booklet published by the economics department, National Bank of Alaska. "The Alaskan Economy. Mid Year Performance Report 1976," booklet published by the Division of Economic Enterprise, Alaska State Department of Commerce and Economic Development, pp. 14, 15, 17. *Alaska Blue Book 1975 (previously cited), p.* 172.

CRITICISM OF FOREST SERVICE

"The Timber Barons Are After the Tongass," *Living Wilderness*, July–September 1975, pp. 22–23.

Jack Calvin, "Saws at Sitka: A Citizen Protests," pp. 37–38, and Alan M. Stein, "Logs Versus Fish in Southeast Alaska," pp. 38–40, *Living Wilderness*, April–June 1976.

CLEAR-CUTTING

R. T. Myren, "Clear-cutting Destroys Critical Wildlife Habitat," *Northern Light*, September 17, 1974.

"Clear-cutting in Coastal Alaska? Why?" undated pamphlet, USDA Forest Service, Alaska Region.

Harry Atkins (Associated Press), "Clear-cut Bill—Both Sides Accept," *Anchorage Daily News*, October 28, 1976.

"Silviculture Is Growing Trees," pamphlet, USDA Forest Service, June 1975.

"Forests Are for People," editorial, *Anchorage Times*, January 9, 1976 (on clear-cutting decision).

Edward A. Whitesell, Alaska chapter, Sierra Club, statement at U.S. Senate Agriculture Committee hearings on Southeast Alaska Forest Practices, August 18 and 21, 1976.

TONGASS TIMBER SALE TO PLYWOOD-CHAMPION FOR JAPANESE USE

Jack Shepherd, *The Forest Killers: The Destruction of the American Wilderness* (New York: Weybright and Talley, 1975).

Bill Wilson, "Motley: State's Economy Now Free of Boom, Bust," *Anchorage Times*, October 24, 1976.

PULP COMPANY POLLUTION PROBLEMS

Dixie M. Baade, "Ketchikan Pulp Delays as Pollutants Poison Bay," *Northern Light*, September 17, 1974.

Governor Hammond, testimony before Environmental Protection Agency hearing on Ketchikan Pulp, in Ketchikan, May 11, 1976.

"Firms Agree on Sale of Ketchikan Pulp," (Associated Press), *Anchorage Times*, October 21, 1976.

POWER PROJECTS, UPPER SUSITNA BASIN

Brec Cooke, representing the Wilderness Society, testimony before the Water Resources Subcommittee of the U.S. Senate Public Works Committee, August 5, 1976.

XII. Troubled Waters

INTRODUCTION

Pete Isleib, " 'Project Independence' Dream or Nightmare?" *Alaskan Fishery*, February 1976.

GULF OF ALASKA HAZARDS

John G. Mitchell, "The Selling of the Shelf," *Audubon*, May 1975.

Isleib, "Project Independence" (previously cited).

Bob Porterfield, "Gulf Quakes—a Major OCS Question," *Anchorage Daily News*, November 28, 1975.

Larry Makinson, "Earthquake: Oil Drilling a Hazard?" *Anchorage Daily News*, February 12, 1977.

GULF LEASE SALE AND AFTERMATH

Sally W. Jones, articles in *Anchorage Daily News:* "Oil Companies Nominate OCS Acres," February 12, 1976; and "Another Gamble on Alaska's Oil," April 10, 1976.

"Texaco Applies to Drill in Gulf," *Anchorage Times*, October 19, 1976.

Governor Hammond, copy of testimony, furnished by his office, at U.S. Interior Department outer continental shelf hearings, Yakutat, August 5, 1975.

ONSHORE IMPACT OF GULF OCS PROGRAM

Rosemary Shinohara, "Major Impact Seen on Gulf Communities," *Anchorage Daily News*, June 28, 1975.

Susan Andrews, "Exxon Puts Drilling Base in Seward," *Anchorage Times*, October 30, 1976.

"Companies, Natives Agree on Yakutat Oil Base Lease," *Anchorage Times*, January 24, 1977.

DISTORTIONS IN ENVIRONMENTAL IMPACT STATEMENTS

Mark Panitch, "Professor Claims Gulf Data Distorted," *Anchorage Daily News*, March 12, 1976.

YAKUTAT RESPONSE TO OIL COMPANY PRESSURE

In addition to our interviews, other quotes from Byron Mallott and other Yakutat residents came from: Bob Porterfield, "Yakutat: A Community Divided by Offshore Oil," *Anchorage Daily News*, August 25, 1975; G. Michael Harmon, Associated Press, "Yakutat Tells Big Oil, 'We Don't Need You,' " *Anchorage Times*, January 30, 1977.

KODIAK LEASE SALE

Copies of letters, dated October 18, 1976, to Kodiak Borough Mayor Robert Craig and Koniag, Inc., President Jack Wick from Guy Martin, Alaska state commissioner of natural resources, concerning onshore facilities for OCS programs.

Karl Armstrong, "OCS Impact Center Established," *Kadiak Times*, May 20, 1976.

Frank R. O'Connor and Patrick L. Dobey, "An Analysis of Future Petroleum Development on the Alaskan Outer Continental Shelf, Kodiak Area," a study for the Alaska State Department of Community and Regional Affairs by the State Department of Natural Resources, June 1976.

EFFECTS OF OIL POLLUTION ON FISH

Noel Mostert, *Supership* (New York: Knopf, 1974); also adaptation, "The Age of the Oilberg," for *Audubon*, May 1975.

John L. Culliney, *The Forest of the Sea: Life and Death on the Continental Shelf* (Sierra Club, 1976).

Mitchell, "Selling of the Shelf" (previously cited).

Isleib, "Project Independence" (previously cited).

SALMON STATISTICS

Alaska Catch and Production Commercial Fisheries Statistics, statistical leaflets 23, 25, 26, and 27, for years 1971, 1972, 1973, 1974, compiled by the statistics department of the Alaska state Department of Fish and Game.

Environmental Impact Statement: Preliminary Fishery Management Plan, High Seas Salmon Fisheries of Japan, U.S. Department of Commerce, National Oceanic and Atmospheric Administration, National Marine Fisheries Service. Draft statement September 1976; final statement January 1977.

Environmental Impact Statement: Preliminary Fishery Management Plan, Troll Salmon Fishery of the Pacific Coast, U.S. Department of Commerce, National Oceanic and Atmospheric Administration, National Marine Fisheries Service. Draft September 1976.

Michael Harmon (Associated Press), " '76 Salmon Run Best Since '71," *Anchorage Daily News*, October 23, 1976.

LIMITED ENTRY

"Limited Entry," editorial, *Southeast Alaska Empire*, August 23, 1976.

"Fishing War Erupts on Washington Coast" (Associated Press), *Anchorage Times*, October 19, 1976.

Helen Gillette, articles in *Anchorage Times* October 28, 1976: "Limited Entry Issue Is Charged with Emotion," and "Opinions Range Widely In Native Workshop."

Rosemary Shinohara, "Limited Entry Law Ballot Battle Fiercest," *Anchorage Daily News*, November 1, 1976.

"Why Limited Entry?," pamphlet published by Committee to Save Alaska's Salmon, 1976.

CRAB, SHELLFISH STATISTICS

Environmental Impact Statement: Preliminary Fishery Management Plan, King and Tanner Crabs of the Eastern Bering Sea, U.S. Department of Commerce, National Oceanic and Atmospheric Administration, National Marine Fisheries Service. Draft statement September 1976; final statement January 1977.

Environmental Impact Statement: Preliminary Fishery Management Plan, Shrimp of the Eastern Bering Sea and Gulf of Alaska, U.S. Department of Commerce, National Oceanic and Atmospheric Administration, National Marine Fisheries Service. Draft statement September 1976; final statement December 1976.

ALASKA BOTTOMFISH

Environmental Impact Statement: Preliminary Fishery Management Plan, Trawl Fishery of the Gulf of Alaska, U.S. Department of Commerce, National Oceanic and Atmospheric Administration, National Marine Fisheries Service. Draft statement September 1976; final statement January 1977.

Environmental Impact Statement: Preliminary Fishery Management Plan, Trawl and Herring Gillnet Fishery of the Bering Sea and Aleutian Islands, U.S. Department of Commerce, National

Oceanic and Atmospheric Administration, National Marine Fisheries Service. Draft statement September 1976; final statement January 1977.

Report to the Congress: U.S. Fishing Industry Can Be Strengthened by Developing Underutilized Fish Resources, investigation by the U.S. General Accounting Office on how the U.S. Department of Commerce, National Oceanic and Atmospheric Administration, National Marine Fisheries Service "can strengthen the U.S. fishing industry by developing new fisheries from underutilized fish resources." U.S. Government Printing Office, Washington, D.C., May 30, 1975.

Nancy Freeman, "New England Fish Company: 'Excited About Potential of Alaska Bottomfish,' " *Kadiak Times*, October 28, 1976.

"Alaska Groundfish Development," *Alaska Region Monthly Narrative Report*, U.S. Department of Commerce, National Ocean and Atmospheric Administration, National Marine Fisheries Service, April 1976.

"Alaska Coastal Zone Management Program Plan Formulation, Defining Alaska's Coastal Zone, Biophysical Definition," progress report by Alaska Department of Fish and Game, Marine-Coastal Habitat Management, OCS-CZM staff, Anchorage, October 19, 1976.

The Alaskan Economy: Mid-Year Performance Report, Alaska State Department of Commerce and Economic Development, Division of Economic Enterprise, 1976.

200-MILE LIMIT LAW

"Draft Foreign Fishing Regulations" (of U.S. Department of Commerce, National Oceanic and Atmospheric Administration), *Federal Register*, December 23, 1976.

"Fisheries Council Jurisdiction—from Mexico to Alaska," (Associated Press), *Anchorage Daily News*, October 19, 1976.

Governor Hammond, "United States–Japanese Fisheries Negotiations," text of speech, August 20, 1976.

FISHERIES' CONSERVATION

Salmon Enchancement in Alaska: An Economic Rationale, unnumbered pamphlet, Alaska Fisheries Council of the Alaska governor's office, March 1976.

Logging and Fish Habitat, booklet published jointly by USDA Forest Service and Alaska Department of Fish and Game, Alaska Department of Natural Resources, revised 1976.

EFFECTS OF OIL IN ARCTIC WATERS

"Arctic Project Bulletin Number 10," National Oceanic and Atmospheric Administration, Outer Continental Shelf Energy Program, Arctic Project Office, University of Alaska, Fairbanks, June 1, 1976.

Gunter Weller, "Outer Continental Shelf Environmental Assessment Program in the Beaufort Sea" (prepared for Arctic Project Office, National Oceanic and Atmospheric Administration, University of Alaska, Fairbanks), 1976.

"Drilling in the Beaufort Sea," *Canada Today/D'Aujourd'hui*, Canadian Embassy, Washington, D.C., Volume 8, Number 1, 1977 (excerpted from interview with Dr. R. W. Stewart, of Environment Canada, in *Contact*, October–November 1976).

Culliney, *Forest of the Sea* (previously cited).

TANKER ACCIDENTS AND LACK OF OIL SPILL CLEANUP TECHNOLOGY

Environmental Impact Statement: Lower Cook Inlet. Draft, in three volumes. Prepared by Alaska Outer Continental Shelf Office, Bureau of Land Management, U.S. Interior Department, July 1976.

"Cook Inlet Oil Spill Demonstration," *Alaska Current-ly*, monthly newsletter of Alaska Coastal Management Program, Alaska governor's office, October 1976.

"Oil Spill Perils Curb Richest Fishing Area" *Des Moines Register*, December 22, 1976 (about the spill from the *Argo Merchant*).

John Kifner, "Tanker Loss Record Set Last Year," *New York Times*, January 9, 1977.

"The Great Alaska Earthquake, March 27, 1964," Miscellaneous Paper Number 1, State of Alaska, Department of Natural Resources, Division of Geological and Geophysical Surveys, May 19, 1964.

Mostert, *Supership* (previously cited).

Betty Mills, "Champion Urges Tanker Measures," *Anchorage Times*, January 12, 1977.

Susan Andrews, "State To Create Spill Fund," *Anchorage Times*, January 25, 1977.

Rosemary Shinohara, three-part series of articles in *Anchorage Daily News:* "Tankers—the Next Oil Line," January, 28, 1977, "TAPS Fleet Shapes Up," January 29, 1977; "Safety Features Check Human Error," January 31, 1977.

"Oil Tanker Liability Fund Rules Published," *Journal of Commerce*, January 25, 1977.

STATE SEEKS OCS SCHEDULING DELAY

Copy of letter from Alaska Natural Resources Commissioner Guy Martin to U.S. Interior Secretary Thomas S. Kleppe, August 4, 1976.

"Oil and Gas Leases: Lease Sale Revision," *Alaska Current-ly*, October 1976.

KACHEMAK BAY CONTROVERSY AND LOWER COOK INLET LEASE SALE

Untitled press release on Cook Inlet lease sale schedule, U.S. Interior Department, Bureau of Land Management, Outer Continental Shelf Office, January 18, 1977.

"Kachemak—'A Bay We Can Never Surrender,' " *Alaskan Fishery*, February 1976.

"Kachemak Bay—A Case History," *Coastal Challenge* (newsletter), state of Alaska Coastal Zone Management Program, June 1976.

Appellants' brief to Alaska Supreme Court, case Number 2551, *Moore, et al.* v. *State of Alaska, et al.*, regarding Kachemak Bay lease sale.

Rodger Painter (Associated Press), "Response Favorable on Kachemak Proposal," *Anchorage Daily News*, January 14, 1976.

Jim Babb, "Bay Decision Splits Court, Area Residents," *Anchorage Daily News*, July 10, 1976.

Andy Williams, "Ferris Floats Free in Blast," *Anchorage Daily News*, June 24, 1976.

Elaine Warren, articles in *Anchorage Daily News:* "Protest Over Oil in Homer," May 19, 1974; and "It's Oil vs. Fish in Kachemak Bay," May 26, 1974.

Frank Tupper (Kachemak Bay Defense Fund) "Distortions About Kachemak's Mood," *Anchorage Daily News*, February 28, 1976.

Sally W. Jones, "No Agreement Emerges in Cook Inlet Hearings," *Anchorage Daily News*, August 25, 1976.

Rosemary Shinohara, "Oil and Culture Clash in English Bay," *Anchorage Daily News*, August 26, 1976.

"Fish vs. Oil," "Kachemak Issue," "English Bay," editorials, *Anchorage Daily News*, May 21, 1974, April 26, 1975, and August 28, 1976, respectively.

Susan Andrews, "Oilman, Fisherman Take Sides," *Anchorage Times*, June 16, 1975.

Kay Brown, "Can Homer Survive, or Will Paradise Be Lost?" *Anchorage Times*, May 30, 1976.

"State Buys Back Leases," *Anchorage Times*, January 8, 1977.

Copy of suit, *English Bay Village Corporation, et al.* v. *U.S. Interior Secretary, et al.*, U.S. District Court, District of Columbia, January 1977.

Copy of comments on draft environmental impact statement for Lower Cook Inlet by the Alaska chapter of the Sierra Club, August 1976.

GENERAL OCS INFORMATION

"Outer Continental Shelf: Information . . . Facts . . . Figures . . . ," pamphlet published by U.S. Interior Department, Alaska Outer Continental Shelf Office, Anchorage, 1976.

"Costs Slow Drilling In Gulf of Mexico," *Anchorage Times*, October 31, 1976.

"Prospective Basins Included in Alaska OCS Sale Plans," *Oil and Gas Journal*, June 7, 1976 (schedule of Alaska OCS lease sales).

Patrick L. Dobey, "The Fundamentals of OCS Impact Planning," paper presented to the Seventeenth Alaska Science Conference, August 5, 1976.

State Senate President Chancy Croft (Democrat, Anchorage) and State House Rules Committee Chairperson Bill Parker (Democrat, Anchorage), "Legislature on Environment," *Northern Light*, July 15, 1976.

XIII. The Japanese Connection

ALASKA NATURAL GAS GOES TO JAPAN

Stephen M. Aug, "Alaska Gas Rush Is On: Supply Going to Japan Could Save Us Money," *Washington Star*, January 29, 1977.

Alaska State Department of Revenue, "Alaska's Oil and Gas Tax Structure" (previously cited), pages I-16 and I-17.

JAPANESE INVESTMENT: AMOUNTS, COMPANIES

"Japanese Investment in Alaska," booklet, State of Alaska Department of Commerce and Economic Development, Division of Economic Enterprise, August 1974.

"Foreign Direct Investment in the United States," U.S. Department of Commerce, National Oceanic and Atmospheric Administration, National Marine Fisheries Service, October 1975, as excerpted in special newsletter, "Alaska Sea News: Fishing Report 1975," by Representative Don Young (Republican, Alaska).

"Capital Investment by Japanese Firms in Alaska Seafood Industry," report compiled by the American Embassy, Tokyo, March 1975.

JAPANESE BUSINESS, GOVERNMENT TIES

Richard J. Barnet and Ronald E. Müller, *Global Reach: The Power of the Multinational Corporations* (New York: Simon & Schuster, Touchstone paperback, 1976), p. 39.

JAPANESE IMPACT ON ALASKA FISH PROCESSING

Previously cited foreign investment studies by Alaska State Department of Commerce and Economic Development; by U.S. Department of Commerce, National Oceanic and Atmospheric Administration, National Marine Fisheries Service; and by American Embassy, Tokyo.

200-MILE LIMIT LAW: IMPACT ON JAPAN

"Japan Given Fishing Quota For U.S. Waters" (Associated Press), *New York Times*, February 19, 1977.

Wendy Cooper, "U.S. Japan Pact Doesn't Settle All Issues," *Journal of Commerce*, February 15, 1977.

ALASKA LUMBER AND PULP COMPANY, INC.'S TAX LIABILITY

Raymond W. Haman and Kenyon P. Kellogg, Alaska Lumber and Pulp Company attorneys, internal memorandum, January 11, 1977.

JAPANESE AND ALASKA FOREST PRODUCTS

Shepherd, *The Forest Killers* (previously cited).

Alaska State Department of Commerce and Economic Development, "The Alaskan Economy: Mid-Year Performance Report 1976" (previously cited).

JAPANESE RELATIONS WITH ALASKA NATIVE CORPORATIONS

Howard Weaver, "Native Corps. Eye Japanese Development," *Anchorage Daily News*, February 23, 1973.

"Natives To Discuss Fishing With Japan," *Anchorage Times*, November 13, 1974.

JAPANESE INTEREST IN TOURISM IN ALASKA

Andrew H. Malcolm, "Japanese Like the Climate (for Investment) in Alaska," *New York Times*, March 13, 1975.

ALASKAN IMPORTS FROM JAPAN

Berry, *Alaska Pipeline*, p. 104.

Index

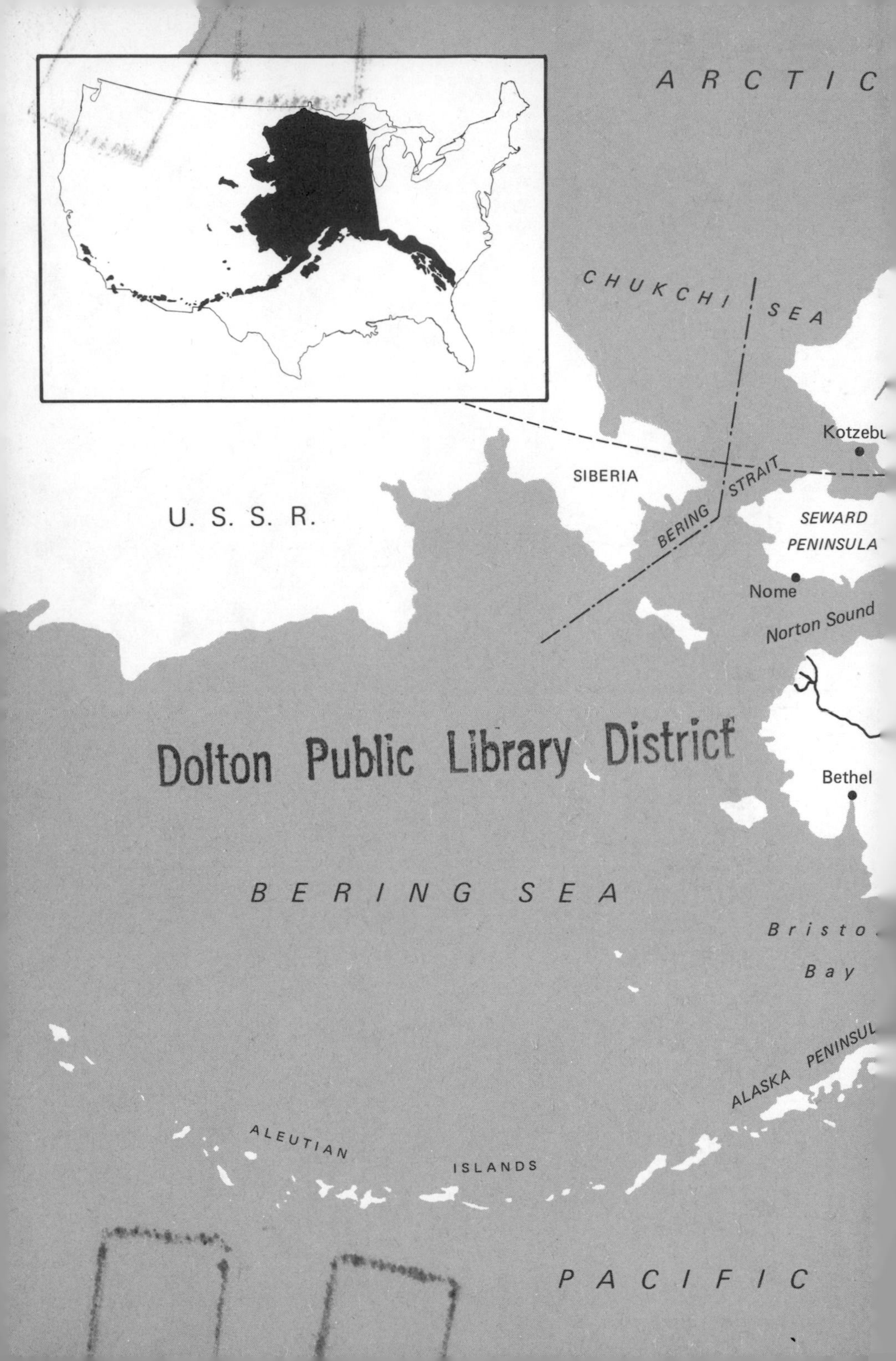
ARCTIC
CHUKCHI SEA
Kotzebu
SIBERIA
U. S. S. R.
BERING STRAIT
SEWARD PENINSULA
Nome
Norton Sound
Bethel
BERING SEA
Bristo
Bay
ALASKA PENINSUL
ALEUTIAN ISLANDS
PACIFIC